Writers on the Air

Donna Seaman

Writers on the Air

Conversations about Books

pdb   PAUL DRY BOOKS *Philadelphia 2005*

First Paul Dry Books Edition, 2005

Paul Dry Books, Inc.
Philadelphia, Pennsylvania
www.pauldrybooks.com

Text type: New Caledonia
Display type: Ellington
Composed by P. M. Gordon Associates
Designed by Adrianne Onderdonk Dudden

1 3 5 7 9 8 6 4 2
Printed in the United States of America

Library of Congress Cataloging-in-Publication Data

Seaman, Donna.
Writers on the air : conversations about books / Donna Seaman —
1st Paul Dry Books ed.
p.   cm.
Includes a collection of interviews.
Includes bibliographical references.
ISBN 1-58988-021-8 (alk. paper)
1. Authors, American—20th century—Interviews. 2. American literature—
20th century—History and criticism—Theory, etc. 3. Books and reading—
English-speaking countries. 4. Authorship. I. Title.

PS225.S43 2005
810.9'005—dc22
2005003146

ISBN 1-58988-021-8

*For Craig Kois
dear friend and radio guru*

CONTENTS

PART FOUR: RELATED READINGS

CREATING SANCTUARY, FEELING EXULTED

We sit across from each other at a plain table in a windowless room, microphones before us, bottles of water, books, notes, and pens at hand. We're about to record an edition of *Open Books,* an hour-long radio program. The writer and I have been talking, getting comfortable with each other as I describe the show and explain how we'll proceed. As always, I have the jitters. We fall silent, and suddenly it feels as though we're in a bathysphere, out of reach of the clamoring world. I look up at the control room window and wait for my producer, director, and friend, Craig Kois, to give me the signal to start. The music comes up; it's "Body and Soul." I chose the 1939 Coleman Hawkins recording as my theme song for its vibrancy and knowingness, and for its title. Written by Johnny Green in 1930, "Body and Soul" embraces the duality of existence—the union of the earthy and the spiritual, the sensuous and the ethereal, the real and the desired. For me, literature revolves on this axis.

The music fades; I lean in to the mike: "Hello, this is Donna Seaman welcoming you to *Open Books,* a show about outstanding books, remarkable writers, and the fine art of reading." *Open Books* airs on WLUW, a community radio station located on the campus of Loyola University Chicago, and operated under the auspices of WBEZ, Chicago's National Public Radio station. It's a modest operation, yet stellar writers honor us with their presence.

Most of the interviews in *Writers on the Air* took place in a small, somewhat shabby studio down a poorly lit hallway and far away from most of the radio station's operations. The studio door was usually closed and locked, the discrete sign easily missed, and very few Loyola people even knew of its existence—which could be a problem when an author arrived in the lobby before I did and asked for directions. But the studio's inconspicuousness made it a refuge, and though Room 207 was anything but state-of-the-art in terms of technology, it was all that a writer and reader could desire as a place for exchanging ideas and enthusiasms. Many of my guests called it a sanctuary.

In a brief essay titled "My Faith as a Writer," Joyce Carol Oates writes, "I believe art is the highest expression of the human spirit." I agree, and I believe that literature, in particular, enhances our perceptions and deepens our understanding of life. I treasure the solace of literature, its capacity to illuminate what is unique about an individual and what is universally human. Stories can transcend barriers—of place, generation, class, race, faith—and create gateways to understanding humankind's endlessly inventive responses to life's challenges and conundrums. Stories preserve lost worlds, express our sense of the sacred, and trace the grand web of life on earth. Literature describes more exquisitely than any other art form what it feels like to be alive, how the mind shifts through memories, emotions, thoughts, and sensations. It can entice us into contemplating diverse traditions and divergent viewpoints. It awakens empathy and fosters a sense of connection with others.

In the hope of transformation and pleasure, I'm forever falling into the arms of books. I cherish the intimacy that the act of reading demands. You curl up in quiet solitude, or sit within your own zone of concentration among fellow coffee drinkers or commuters, running your eyes over print so that by a wondrous alchemy of mind (to borrow from Diane Ackerman) entire worlds blossom in your imagination. Readers often spend more time communing with a writer than with people of their acquaintance. Consequently they feel profoundly connected to these disembodied voices. Radio is an intimate medium, too. The first form of electronic mass communication, it remains for many a great favorite by virtue of its directness and its appeal to the imagination. The best of spoken-word radio has a stimulating effect on the brain similar to reading; it creates a sense of connection between speaker and listener the way a book does between writer and reader. Books are an essential aspect of our collective consciousness and a key element in public discourse—contrary to routinely dire predictions of their demise—and I believe that literature and writers belong on the airwaves.

As an associate editor at *Booklist,* a review magazine published in Chicago by the American Library Association, I have the privilege of participating in the published conversation about books. This dialogue between readers and writers has been going on ever since literature began. Established in 1905, today *Booklist* continues to perform its mission to help librarians select books for their collections—albeit on a larger scale, as required by the spectacular changes a century of technological innovations has brought to publishing and librarianship. Each year we publish thousands of concise, evaluative (and, we hope, entertaining) reviews of books we consider worthy of a place on library shelves, and in the minds and hearts of readers.

An ardent reader, I found my place in the world at *Booklist.* Craig Kois, an advocate for documentary and spoken-word radio, found his at the helm of WLUW. One day I surprised myself by saying to Craig, "You need a book show." "I thought you'd never ask," he replied. "Now what have I done?" I asked myself.

I had no journalism background or media experience, so at first I did what I knew best: reading and writing about books. I wrote scripts and read them aloud, re-recording as necessary, and suffering from stage fright even though Craig was my only witness. Nevertheless, when publishers and authors began to ask if we were interested in having writers appear on *Open Books,* I realized that, in spite of my trepidation about conducting interviews on the air, speaking with writers was the way to go. One of the more maddening aspects of my work as a reviewer and critic is the knowledge that so very many wonderful books are published without fanfare, accorded scant critical attention, and allowed to slip out of view before readers have had the chance even to consider reading them. My heart sinks when, on telling a book-loving friend about a brilliant and prolific living writer whose work I revere, my friend says she's never heard of him. My mission is to bring as many literary writers to the attention of as many readers as possible, so I welcome as many guests on *Open Books* as I can. I'm grateful for the forum WLUW provides, and for the generous support of the Illinois Arts Council.

Yet in spite of my convictions, I'm assailed by self-doubt before each interview, and I half hope for a cancellation, a power outage —anything to keep me out of the studio. As the conversation gains momentum, however, an adrenaline rush inevitably replaces anxiety. A rapport is established. We're having fun. The writers I've enjoyed speaking with are compelling on the page and engaging in person. During our conversations, writers often mention how painstakingly they rewrite their work, how many drafts a novel goes through, how writing is about rewriting. Yet in person, each speaks fluently and animatedly about subtle and complex matters. Time after time, I've sat on the edge of my seat, riveted by a writer's revelations of all the hard work and out-of-the blue inspiration that goes into the writing. These conversations can be extremely moving. Writers and I have fought back tears, determined not to derail the conversation. I've laughed so hard I've lost track of what we were talking about. And I've been so stunned or chagrined by what a writer has to say, I've been left speechless.

Open Books depends on my guests' presence of mind and eloquence. I don't have the resources necessary for producing the sort of carefully edited interviews heard on NPR. My conversations with writers are broadcast in their original form. Consequently, I write out pages of notes and questions in preparation for each interview, hoping to structure a narrative arc so that each discussion has a story line and builds toward some sort of resolution. This approach makes for a focused give-and-take. I often feel as though the writer and I are walking toward each other on a tightrope. At the hour's close, we are elated.

Though radio is ephemeral, what writers have to say on *Open Books* merits more sustained attention. I wanted to preserve these exchanges in print so that they will be available to more people than WLUW can reach, and in a more permanent form. Each conversation is, in effect, a snapshot of a writer's life. Anyone interested in how and why books are written will find these interviews intriguing. I have edited each conversation to conform to print conventions and for ease of reading. My aim is to make each writer's spoken voice present on the page.

I'm grateful to everyone who has appeared on *Open Books;* I wish I could have included more conversations in *Writers on the Air,* but there were simply more interesting interviews than one book could contain. So in this collection I have selected interviews with prose writers, both fiction and non-fiction, that make for lively reading on the printed page.

In the conversations with fiction writers and writers of creative nonfiction that are collected here, we talk about how human beings use stories to make sense of the blur of daily existence, forge a self, and shape a life. I've also included discussions about how literature not only elucidates the often-perverse ways of humankind, but also our place in nature. I like fiction rich in metaphor, fiction that grapples with the complexities of relationships, fiction that imagines the consequences of inheritance, history and social mores, fiction laced with philosophy and questions of faith, and concerned with rampant technologies and environmental necessities, morality and spirituality, war and exile, art and remembrance, prejudice and compassion. Fiction full of wonder and terror, love and humor, folly and discovery.

Creative nonfiction reports on the same universe using the same literary devices as fiction, but without inventing characters, place, or predicaments. It, too, brims with metaphor, is spiked with irony and taut with drama, but in creative nonfiction the writer is unmasked and free to overtly express his or her opinion over the course of telling a true-life story. A versatile genre at once journalistic and lyrical, creative nonfiction covers a wealth of intriguing subjects. It includes works of natural history and meditations on the state of the environment, thus constituting, in my view, one of the most dynamic and important literary forms being practiced in our global times. Hence my conversations with creative nonfiction writers who write with concern about the earth as well as about the human condition.

In both nature and culture, diversity is the key to survival and vitality. Today's readers enjoy access to a spectacular number and variety of books, yet because so few of them are discussed in mainstream media, many readers don't know where to begin in choosing books to read for pleasure. Many readers read only one genre, limiting themselves to mysteries, for example, because that's what they're used to, and missing out on the clarity and intensity of creative nonfiction. Other readers never immerse themselves in fiction and have no concept of the vast spectrum of styles and themes found in short stories and novels. I hope this collection will pique your curiosity, and inspire you to experiment by reading a writer or genre new to you. To encourage further exploration, I've put together a Related Readings section in which I present a set of unapologetically idiosyncratic lists of books that I believe will continue the conversations begun in works by the writers featured here. Some of the lists are impressionistic, others are thematic or based on something as straightforward as a writer's own list of favorite books. Each list recommends books that possess the qualities I look for in literature: beautiful writing, lucid thinking, close observation, flights of imagination, risk-taking, moral inquiry, compassion, catharsis, wit, and wonder. I read to learn and to be moved. In *Where Shall Wisdom Be Found?* the critic Harold Bloom writes, "The mind always returns to its needs for beauty, truth, and insight." Bloom also lists the essential elements he looks for in literature, criteria to guide us all: "aesthetic splendor, intellectual power, wisdom."

Recently Loyola University launched an ambitious renovation project, and Room 207 is no more. We now record *Open Books* in a small, cluttered room in view (and earshot) of the bustle of the radio station. Though we are sorry to have lost our hidden haven, we've discovered that the feeling of sanctuary our writers experience does not require a particular room. Our guests sense the shelter created when minds meet and imaginations are kindled, the symbiotic relationship between writer and reader that brings books to life. These encounters are exhilarating for me, and I hope that you, too, find refuge in these conversations, as well as pleasure and enlightenment.

PART ONE: Fiction

SECTION ONE: FIRST-TIME NOVELISTS

Reading first novels is a gamble, especially for a book reviewer. One approaches each debut novel in the hope that it will be exceptional, and the fear that it will be a waste of time. So when a first novel proves to be out-of-the-ordinary, one feels relief, followed by the thrill of discovery, the pleasure of witnessing the emergence of a new voice, and the hope that one's positive review will help secure the writer a place on the literary map. The popularity of graduate writing programs—the source of most of today's published work—means that the majority of first novelists began by writing short stories. It is interesting to see how and how well they make the transition from a short form that can be held in the mind in its entirety (like a song), to the more expansive, complex, and symphonic scale of a novel. Though many produce admirable works, often their first novels cause barely a stir, and book and author soon vanish from sight.

Of course, a first novel may be quickly forgotten, such as *With Shuddering Fall* (1964), yet the author, in this case, Joyce Carol Oates, may go on to become a critically acclaimed and best-selling fiction writer. Conversely, a select few first novels take the world by storm, but fail to pave the way for future works. Harper Lee's *To Kill a Mockingbird* (1960), for instance, caused a sensation and continues to attract new readers, but she never wrote another novel. Joseph Heller's *Catch-22* (1961) towers over his later works. In another variation on the promise of a first novel, Marilynne Robinson's *Housekeeping* was a tremendous hit in 1980; her second novel, the exquisite (and well-worth waiting for) *Gilead,* didn't appear until 2004.

There is no telling what sort of writing life awaits the first-time novelists showcased in this section, but their debuts definitely fall into the big-splash category. Dennis Bock explores the legacy of Hiroshima in the highly regarded *The Ash Garden.* The literary world was stunned when Julia Glass's first novel, *Three Junes,* a many-faceted family drama that considers the ravages of AIDS, won the National Book Award. Edward P. Jones dramatizes the lives of black slave-owners in *The Known World,* an artistic inquiry into an overlooked aspect of our past that garnered the Pulitzer Prize, the National Book Critics Circle Award, and *Booklist*'s Top of the List.

It's fun to speak with first-time novelists because the process of bringing a novel into the world is fresh and exciting to them, so that, just as their readers are discovering a new writer, the new writer is discovering a great deal about their readers. You can read interviews with other outstanding debut novelists who appeared on *Open Books* in other chapters in *Writers on the Air:* Kate Moses, Alex Shakar, Aleksandar Hemon, and Lynda Barry. Every one of these first-time novelists is on my "writers to watch" list.

Dennis Bock

Born in Belleville on the north shore of Lake Ontario in 1964, Dennis Bock grew up in Oakville, Ontario, west of Toronto. The first book he remembers being stunned by, and the first to make him think about writing, was *Gulliver's Travels*. Bock wanted to be a marine biologist, but when he attended the University of Western Ontario, he studied English and philosophy. His first story was published in *Canadian Fiction* in 1992. Bock's first book, *Olympia*, is a set of seven linked short stories that illuminate strange and pivotal moments in the lives of several generations of a German immigrant family who found refuge in Canada. Their reminiscences of Germany and World War II, and musings over their New World experiences, are interwoven with imaginary outtakes from *The Olympiad*, Leni Riefenstahl's infamous film about the 1936 Berlin Olympics.

In his first novel, *The Ash Garden*, Bock turns to the war's Pacific front, specifically the dropping of the atomic bomb on Hiroshima and its tragic aftermath. As in his first book, Bock deftly puts into play innovative and arresting narrative strategies that combine literary and cinematic approaches to storytelling and documentation.

The power of Bock's work resides in his evocative language, his keen sense that deep sorrow and bitter irony are often aligned, and most important, his ability to make personal, even intimate, the profound and unpredictable consequences of momentous events. Bock has received grants from the Canada Council, the Ontario Arts Council, and the Toronto Arts Council, and he has been a writer-in-residence at Yaddo in New York, the Banff Centre of the Arts, and the Fundación Valparaiso in Spain.

Dennis Bock appeared on *Open Books* in late 2003.

DONNA SEAMAN: In both your short story collection, *Olympia,* and your novel, *The Ash Garden,* you consider the aftermath of World War II. What draws you to this subject?

DENNIS BOCK: Probably the fact that I'm the son of two German immigrants who, after coming to Canada and raising a family, told us their stories of the war. They were both very young children during the war, but, of course, they still have memories, and they passed those on to us. I think when my imagination started to form as a young boy, it started to coalesce around certain images that my parents shared with me, specifically my mother, whose war experience, in my memory, was very vivid and very difficult. And these images stayed with me.

DS: Did your parents' stories have something to do with your becoming a writer?

BOCK: Maybe. I don't like to think too hard about what drives me to write, but probably there's something to that. As a young kid, you close your eyes and you go somewhere. When I did that, I would go into this black-and-white world, trying to imagine my mother as a six-year-old child in a basement during an air raid. Not a very pleasant thing to do as a young boy, but it was formative, I think. I don't have a traumatized past or anything like that. I think I was just taught, unconsciously, by my parents, to be able to enter into other people's experience, through storytelling.

DS: There are hundreds of World War II novels, but I think the percentage of those novels that are about Hiroshima is minute. I'm grateful that you've written about the dropping of the atomic bomb; it's a reality, and a legacy, that we have a difficult time thinking about. I wonder what gave you the courage to proceed.

BOCK: Ah, the courage to proceed. Well, I'm not a very courageous person. I just put my head down and worked as hard as I could for as long as I could, and I ended up with this book. The reason I started with the central idea of the bomb is because it seemed to me to be a wonderful and horrible example of our technological brilliance. But at the same time, there was the question of how to apply that brilliance, that marvelous technology that was discovered and harnessed in 1945; and of course it was applied very tragically rather than in a positive way. So it stands in my imagination, and in the world, as a very troubling metaphor for what we're capable of doing.

DS: Do you have any idea why so few novelists have written about Hiroshima?

BOCK: No, and I didn't look for any fictional treatments of Hiroshima because I wanted to find my own voice. I didn't want to read some other writer's interpretation of what it must have been like. I consulted lots of documents and photo essays and historical data straight-up with as little interpretation as possible so that I could filter it in the way that enabled my novel to grow naturally. I'm very sponge-like. When I read novels I admire, I try to learn as much as I can, my ear picks up the language and I use as much as I can from the great books that I read. And so for fear of finding a really fabulous book on the bomb, I thought I better not look at all because I might end up inadvertently sounding like that novel.

DS: One of the main characters in *The Ash Garden,* Anton Böll, is a German scientist who ended up working at Los Alamos. He left Germany by choice, and much of the book is about his mix of pride over the scientific achievements involved in the making of the bomb, and the horror of its being used to kill and maim so many people. He is so complex a character that you managed to make me—a person adamantly opposed to nuclear weapons—sympathetic towards him and his moral quandary.

BOCK: Anton is very aware of people like you in the world. And he is very careful with the people who confront him, but in a cynical way, because he knows that the debate over whether the bomb was used justifiably or not will go on forever. He's a very ambitious and very intelligent man, and I think that he's smarter than he is ethically aware. Meaning, he can be manipulative, and talk himself out of difficult situations, such as when he crosses paths with Emiko, another central character, a woman who happened to live through the bombing.

DS: Yes, you put them on a slow but sure trajectory towards each other. Emiko is six years old, playing outside in Hiroshima when she sees the plane drop the bomb. She's grievously injured, but she survives. And you cut back and forth between her life, Anton's life, and the story of Anton's wife, Sophie, who, Austrian and half-Jewish, was sent away before the war was under full swing. Each facet of the relationships among these three characters is significant. For instance, Anton's marriage to Sophie, his love for her, is the essence of his goodness.

BOCK: Right. Although Anton is a profoundly amoral character—he's not immoral but he is amoral—he is waiting for some spark of life, something that will help him understand in a more human way how he has spent his time, what he has done. While he is the amoral center of the book, his wife is the moral, or ethical, center. As such, she provides him with a sort of ballast that, were he without it, he would have very few redeeming qualities. Sophie is also the person who facilitates the connection between Anton and Emiko.

DS: Sophie also seems to carry his guilt in her body. She suffers from lupus, which is manifest in stigmata-like markings that echo Emiko's scars and serve as a very powerful metaphor for culpability and empathy. Emiko is a fascinating character, too, and her predicament is incredibly revealing. For instance, she's brought to the United States as a teenager, one among a select group, for reconstructive surgery. Are the bizarre experiences that follow based on historical events?

BOCK: Yes, unhappily that did happen in 1955. Twenty-five Japanese girls were brought to the United States for reconstructive surgery. I just stumbled across this event during my year or so at the public library. I couldn't believe it when I discovered that this actually happened. I was between a rock and a hard place. A novelist's first obligation is to get his principle characters into the same room so that they can have their confrontation, and I had these two characters fairly well established in my manuscript, but I had no idea how to bring them together. Everything that occurred to me seemed wildly fabricated. It just didn't sound right. And then I came across this real episode. Not only were twenty-five Japanese girls invited to New York for reconstructive surgery, two of the girls later appeared on a television program called *This Is Your Life* as emblems of American benevolence. That they'd been invited to enjoy free facial reconstructive surgery was a wonderful humanitarian effort on the part of the doctors, but their efforts were manipulated for propaganda purposes.

DS: Discussion of the bomb has been increasingly detached over the years. It's so important to bring it back to a personal level.

BOCK: I wanted to start with two potentially stock characters: the evil German scientist and the long-suffering Japanese victim. But of course those people don't exist in the real world. And I took it as an artistic challenge to make these people as lifelike, as flesh-and-blood, as possible—which is even more interesting and difficult given the subject matter, because we've been taught to look at certain issues in a very simplistic, black-and-white way, especially during wartime or war hysteria, much like we're going through now. I think it's the job of good literature to try to break down the propaganda as much as possible, to insist that there are many more shades of gray than simply black and white. And the better the book, the better the antidote is against the propaganda that we're subjected to.

DS: Yes, that's why I read fiction. Works of the imagination allow us a more emotional and psychological perspective. Nuclear weapons have utterly changed life on earth, have put all of life in jeopardy in a way nothing else has before, and people are skittish about it. But people will read fiction; their love of story will carry them past their reluctance to face tragic facts.

And you do many things in the book to balance the grimness. You show how suffering can be alleviated by generous and creative acts, and you envision unexpected pairings. The very image of an ash garden, for instance, is a union of death and life, an eerily beautiful image of Hiroshima after the bomb.

BOCK: Yes, and the ash garden is also an ironic take on the garden of Eden. I'm very excited about the connections and parallels that are found in fiction, and which are more than the function of mere coincidence. It seems to me that these parallels between characters and their situations—Sophie's garden full of topiary figures contrasted to the ash garden, or her lupus scarring and the scarring suffered by Emiko—are homage to the magic realist books that I really loved reading about ten years ago. Wonderful books by Gabriel García Márquez, for example, where something very remarkable and magical happens in a very mundane and unremarkable context and draws no comment. It just happens, and life proceeds. In the same way, I see connections like that in my book, connections and parallels that are just a little more unusual than they should be. Just slightly magical. I'm very excited to see magic in everyday experiences.

DS: Do you feel that your novel will be read differently in the wake of September 11 and the war in Iraq?

BOCK: I don't know if it will be read differently, but I would argue that it is more relevant now, because it mines events that are ongoing. When I started writing this book in 1997, any discussion of the atomic bomb was purely academic. The bomb seemed almost like an historical curiosity. But no longer, sadly. Now, I would say that this novel reminds us that nuclear war is a threat, that it's not merely an academic or hypothetical question. It's a real situation that has to be dealt with on the international stage. This book is a reminder that when a war ends, it doesn't stop. People continue to live with all sorts of consequences.

Julia Glass

Julia Glass's first book, the novel *Three Junes,* won the National Book Award. But as startling and resounding an achievement as that is, Glass had already received a National Endowment for the Arts Literature fellowship, a New York Foundation for the Arts fellowship, the Tobias Wolff Award, three Nelson Algren Fiction Awards, and the Pirate's Alley Faulkner Society Medal: not bad for a writer who majored in art at Yale, worked as a copyeditor at *Cosmopolitan,* then supported herself as a freelance editor and writer specializing in corporate materials and magazine articles about pets and parenting.

But Glass has not had it as easy as this string of triumphs might suggest. Born in 1956, she has survived two bouts with breast cancer and endured the trauma and grief of her younger sister's suicide. Writing has been a source of strength, and Glass is warm, funny, animated, and wonderfully open and articulate. The mother of two sons, she is given to wearing brilliantly colored clothing, a visual expression of her resolve, positive outlook, and vibrant creativity. Glass has been a fellow at the Radcliffe Institute for Advanced Study, and after living in New York for many years, now makes her home outside Boston.

Julia Glass came to the studio in May 2003.

DONNA SEAMAN: You've won three Nelson Algren Awards for your short stories, and your first novel, *Three Junes,* was awarded the National Book Award. That's quite a feat. How much writing did you do before you started winning prizes?

JULIA GLASS: I was a painter before I was a writer. I majored in art in college, and I went to New York to support myself as a struggling artist by using my language skills. I have to say I had an incredible education in English, in reading and writing both, in high school and through college. I was an avid reader, and I was supporting myself by being a copyeditor. My funniest job was when I spent two years as a full-time copyeditor for *Cosmopolitan* magazine. From ten to five every day I was diligently correcting dangling modifiers in stories about how to be multi-orgasmic, or what it's like to get liposuction. Then I would go home and paint. But I got this overpowering urge to start writing fiction, and I started writing stories even though I felt guilty about not painting. The stories that I was writing were very long, and when I look back at them, I describe them as pregnant women who refused to understand that it's time to buy maternity clothes. In other words, I think I was always a novelist trying to burst out.

So I would submit these stories to various magazines and journals, and I got nice letters from editors, but they would say, "This is very long." And I'm sure the stories had other flaws, too. I mean, I didn't go to an M.F.A. program, and I was working in isolation as far as my writing was concerned. My first published story was called "My Sister's Scar," and in 1993 I submitted it to the Nelson Algren Awards, which is a wonderful literary award sponsored by the *Chicago Tribune.* They present one big award and three runners-up. I never got the big one, but they fly you out to Chicago and you win one thousand dollars, which was a huge amount in those days for a short story, and you attend this chichi banquet. I will never forget it. They held the event in the Chicago Cultural Center in an astonishing room which used to be the main room of the library. It glitters with green and gold mosaics and Tiffany glass. I remember walking in with my boyfriend, in my party dress, and on all the chairs around all the tables they had put the supplement that they publish with the winning stories. I picked it up off the chair and I opened it and I saw my story there, and nothing will compare with the feeling of seeing my first fiction in print.

DS: I'm intrigued with your art background because you're an exceptionally visual writer. You also seem to have a deep respect for creative vocations. Many of the characters in *Three Junes* are devoted to their callings, whether it's cooking or flower arranging or dog breeding or painting. Were you aware of putting a cast of creative people together?

GLASS: There's a saying about being an actor: that you can only be an actor if that's the only thing in the world that you want to be. Well, I've come to the conclusion that the opposite may be true for being a fiction writer. I think a good fiction writer is somebody who wishes they could be everything in the world. And creating characters with different vocations and avocations is a way of trying on different things that you might like to do. I would love to be a chef; I would love to have a bookstore; I wish I were still a painter; I would love to be a graphic designer. And there are still many more unexplored professions. I would like to be a microbiologist, for instance, and there's one in my next book. So I think there's a lot of daydreaming and role-playing that goes on for a fiction writer.

As far as my painting and its role in the book, once this book was really going well and I realized that this is what I really wanted to be doing in my creative life, I felt a little angry at myself for having spent so long being a painter. But when I hear people talk about the book and when I read from it at readings, I can hear and see exactly how my painter's eye has influenced my writing. And if I have a literary vice, it's the way I fall into description to a point where I'm sure the reader is going, "Okay, get on with the action." And, obviously, I've chosen some settings that are ripe for visual description: Greece, Scotland, and Long Island. These are also places I wish I could be rather than sitting at my kitchen table with a little computer.

DS: Frustration over one's life, one's failure to realize artistic dreams and to find meaning in life—these are key themes in the novel. In the first of the book's three sections, Paul McCloud, owner and publisher of a Scottish newspaper, recalls his disappointment over his war service. You write, "The war had not made him into what he had hoped it would. It had not given him the dark pitiless eyes of an artist." Later, a painter named Fern is thinking about a photographer she knows, Tony, who is just that sort of "piti-less" person. He's somewhat ruthless and orders his life without worrying about what other people think or need. She finds this dif-ficult to do.

GLASS: Yes, the issues of the creative life, and the longing of the creative life.

DS: And the cost of a creative life. All that one has to sacrifice.

GLASS: That's true I suppose. Although I'm not a lonely person, the creative life is lonely. Writing is lonely work in a way, though your characters do keep you company. You know, I didn't con-sciously think how much I had invested in these characters as cre-ative people. And although the book is almost completely autobio-graphical, I also surprised myself by making so much of it up. There is a lot in common between me and Fern, but I think a first novel always bears the mark of the self of the writer in a stronger way than most later novels do. And when I look at my novel now, I think that all three of the major characters share the same creative angst that I have had.

DS: Before I read your novel, I thought the title might refer to three women named June, but instead it refers to the month of June.

GLASS: Right, it's not a book about three women. My publisher worried about that, but we never came up with another title. The novel takes place over ten years in the month of June: June of 1989, June of 1995, and June of 1999. And the three characters are Paul McCloud, the Scottish newspaperman; his grown son, Fenno, a gay expatriate bookseller in Greenwich Village, in New York, where I live; and Fern, an artist.

DS: Your novel is a triptych, and there are a lot of "threes." Fenno is the oldest of three brothers, and the dynamics among them are fascinating.

GLASS: I am fascinated by the relationships among grown siblings, their relationships with their parents, and their warring visions of their childhoods. They say that every child in a given family has a different childhood. And that's something I wanted to explore.

DS: You raise many "big" questions, and trace the cycle of life over and over again, questioning assumptions about inheritance, about family and responsibility, about unconventional relationships, and about how loss changes us. You work on a large scale, but you render it in detail. Tony, the photographer, has one of my favorite lines in the book. In talking about what his "job" as a photographer, as an artist, is, he says, ". . . to take the very, very small and make it large. Make it get some attention. Give stature to the details. Where the devil lurks, you know?" I feel as though this is your credo, too, as a novelist.

GLASS: I guess that's true. I didn't think about it, but I guess I have given stature to the details, sometimes more stature than some readers can bear. I actually had an encounter with a woman in a book club who really disliked my book. She had a lot of very strong things to say about it, but she said one thing that struck me: "You know, there is too much in this book. There are topics in this book like infertility or losing a parent that should be in a whole novel by themselves. They shouldn't all be in one novel together." I didn't quite know how to respond, but I said, "I don't think the subject of a book has to be in proportion to the size of the book." I've read some masterful short stories. Look at Alice Munro: she can write a short story about an entire life. It's astonishing. But then there is a wonderful novel by John Casey called *The Half-life of Happiness,* a five-hundred-page novel about the demise of a marriage. I read that book in the middle of writing *Three Junes,* and it was very freeing for me because I was worrying that I was writing too long a book—that it wasn't really a saga, so did I really need all these pages? But in Casey's novel there's a grandeur to the attention that he gives marital love. And I was very admiring of that because I think we do live in an age in which if you're writing about a certain topic, if you're writing about domestic subjects, you're expected to turn in a book that's below a certain length. Only if you're writing about war or if you're writing a truly multi-generational novel, or if you're Don DeLillo, can you turn out tomes.

DS: I was struck by the breath of your "grand" attention, and by the psychological subtleties and evolution you trace as your characters change. Your approach reminded me of nineteenth-century novels, especially those by Thomas Hardy and George Eliot.

GLASS: Two of my all-time favorites. I've only recently realized that a lot of the fiction writers I admire most are northern writers. I'm not saying I don't like any southern writers, but I feel the greatest kinship with writers like Alice Munro and Jim Harrison, whom I worship, and certainly Thomas Hardy and all these writers whose characters live in the wilds of Michigan or on the damp moors. I think I'm drawn to northern writing because it expresses the belief that you never really leave behind the land that you're from. That's a very old-fashioned notion, especially in a country where people move willy-nilly, but I believe it. I do believe that the land of one's nativity is a part of us forever, our geographical nativity as it were.

DS: You write with great passion about place, capturing all the sensuous details that make a place, or a home, so uniquely precious. You also construct many variations on marriage and family and I was struck by how many compelling animals you portray. In fact, Fenno and his brothers suspected that their mother, Maureen, preferred her collies to them.

GLASS: One of the things I did to support my painting was to write about animals. I even fell into writing a pets column for *Glamour* magazine. How did I do this? I grew up in a house where animals were almost more important than people. There is an element of my own mother in Maureen. My mother is very gifted with dogs and actually quite proud of it. She was even a master of fox hounds, but they never killed the fox. This was in Massachusetts where it's all artificial. My mother would have died if they had killed a fox. But there were horses and hounds and four cats, and my sister always had some wounded squirrel or bird in a shoebox. I liked the animals fine, but I was more of an observer, and then I ended up in the city.

I didn't think that animals were going to be that big a part of my life again, but then I became involved in the late 1980s with a volunteer organization that helped people with AIDS take care of their pets so they didn't have to give them up because of the expense, or because they weren't able to care for them. My specific job was to find temporary homes for dogs whose owners suddenly had to go into the hospital. And it meant that I had a lot of direct connect with men with AIDS because the community we were helping consisted mostly of gay men in the West Village. In those days the side effects of the drugs were as bad as the effects of the disease. And most of these men knew they were just buying time. This made a deep impression on me, and that's part of what I wanted to capture in *Three Junes.*

When I started working on my second novel, I thought, "There won't be any important animals in here." Then all of a sudden there is this English bulldog. Then there is a character who rescues abandoned puppies and kittens.

DS: The animals in *Three Junes* are just as authentic as the people, and they have intrinsic roles. They're not just gimmicks. The novel feels mapped out, so cohesive. I wonder how aware you were ahead of time of all the elements and of how they would interconnect.

GLASS: I did not write this book from an outline. In fact, the first part grew all on its own as a novella titled *Collies,* which won an award. After I finished *Collies,* I knew that I wanted to turn it into a novel, but I wasn't quite sure how. That's when the voice of Fenno, the oldest son, began to seize me, and I just began writing through his voice. I really didn't know where I was going. And about two-thirds of the way through Fenno's part of the book, I thought, "Now where am I going? How am I going to end this book?" I had written 250 pages or so, and I knew I wanted to bring Fern back. I thought, "Okay, this is what I'm going to do," and I started to write part three as I was finishing part two, which was probably a smart thing because it forced me to finish part two, otherwise I think I'd still be writing Fenno's story.

But for me the key to the details is endless revision. I'm sure no writer really knows how many times they reread their own writing. I just revise and revise and revise. This is where a computer is really helpful. I went into writing on a computer kicking and screaming. I'm a wannabe Luddite. I didn't have a cell phone. I didn't have a microwave oven. I didn't have a CD player. But I realized how great the "search" feature is. And how useful it was to keep a timeline in the computer so I could keep track of when every character was born, and when they might have graduated from college, so I could figure out things like, "Were they wearing bellbottoms then?"

DS: Yet writing a novel is really difficult to do no matter what tools you use. And just think about the writers of the past who wrote in longhand and what they accomplished.

GLASS: I'll tell you an interesting story. I was fortunate enough to do a reading with Sue Miller. And after our reading, a reader asked the question that someone always asks, "Will you talk about your writing process, and do you write on a computer or in longhand?" I said, "I write on a computer," and Sue Miller said, "I write in longhand." She explained, "I always do the original writing in longhand, and then I type it into the computer." I was curious to know why. It turns out that she learned of a study that was done about the effect a computer has on your writing, and two findings made her realize that she didn't want to write on a computer. The study showed that writing on a computer enlarges your vocabulary and makes your sentence structures more complex. I thought, "What's so bad about that?" But she said, "I didn't want that to happen to my writing." This has made me think about Fenno's part of the book, in which there are a lot of big words, and about how when I was reading to a high-school audience, I realized, "They don't know these words." And then I thought, "Gosh, is this just because I'm writing on a computer and not because of my innate word-smithery?"

DS: Allow me to put in a good word, so to speak, for a rich vocabulary and for multisyllabic words. I believe that our working vocabulary is shrinking, and that its diminishment is a terrible loss, just like the loss of all the plant and animal species that are going extinct.

GLASS: That's an interesting analogy.

DS: Languages are living entities that evolved out of specific places and experiences. Language is how we understand life, so when I read literature, I hope to find language in all its splendor. Like painters, who mix many colors and shades, writers use vocabulary to create nuance, and to reflect the complexity of life.

GLASS: And when you dip into the classics, for lack of a better word, that's what you find. Even when I was a painter and I would read Eliot's *Daniel Deronda,* I would think, "That's it. There is nothing, no work of art, greater on this earth than a truly fine novel." And I see the dictionary as a mine that you go down into. Sometimes I'll use a word, then I'll think, "I use that word a lot, what does it really mean?" So I go look it up, and what inevitably happens is that its definition will include a synonym, and I'll look up that word. And then as I look it up, I'll pass words that look fascinating to me, or words I haven't used in a while, and I'll stop and think, "Say, I haven't used, oh, let's say *sultry,* for a long time." We all have words we gravitate towards. Interestingly, I've noticed that I gravitate towards words with *v*'s, such as *vivid* and *verb,* and *extravagant.* Especially words with two *v*'s. I actually was in the shower the other day and found myself playing this game, trying to come up with words with two *v*'s that I use quite a lot, and I thought of around ten. So that tells you something about me.

We all have habits as writers, and it's really helpful to go on tour and read your work aloud. I would hear habits that I would not have noticed otherwise. That's an important part of writing, to literally listen to it.

DS: I love to read literature out loud. One thing that art does is to slow us down a little bit, and induce us to linger over things like words, to savor them and think more deeply about their meaning and their sound. I argued earlier for a lush vocabulary. I would also advocate for lovely, long, and lucid complex sentences. Your syntax is beautifully varied and sustained.

GLASS: Well, there are people who have complained about my convoluted syntax in the second part of *Three Junes*. A couple of people have complained about the way I use parentheses. I used parentheses often; that's the way I talk. I'm always heading off on some side road and going "oops," and veering back onto the topic at hand.

DS: That seems utterly natural and quite pleasurable to those of us who share your sensibility. There is another great line in your book that applies to this. I really like your character Marjorie, a woman Paul meets on his tour in the first part of the novel. She's terrific not only because she's smart and funny, but also because she understands that she's annoying and not altogether appealing, and that doesn't hold her back one bit. At any rate, they're having a discussion about Homer, and she says, "Good art is never flabby."

GLASS: I was used to short stories, and found in writing my first novel that it's a very different experience to live with characters for a long time. You might start out thinking, "This is an obnoxious character, or this is a villainous character, or this is a saintly character," but if you live with a character for three hundred pages, it's just like developing a relationship in life. The people you start out idolizing inevitably reveal their flaws, and those who irritate you, you might gradually find endearing. But you also ask yourself, "Am I really grown up?" You do feel like a child with imaginary friends. And it's interesting that, as I'm working on my second novel, I have higher consciousness of being a novelist with a capital *N*. So some of the things that I did unconsciously before, I now find myself more aware of, and that's not always a good thing.

DS: Because *Three Junes* is a first novel, its choice as winner of the National Book Award came as a surprise to many of us. And most likely to you, too.

GLASS: Yes. It was a surprise to me. The foundation calls to tell you that you're a finalist. I was frantically folding the laundry because my kids were about to come home, and I hear a message on the answering machine saying, "Julia Glass, please call me. This is very important. This is Neil Baldwin with the National Book Foundation," and I didn't even know what the National Book Foundation was. So I called and he says, "It is my great pleasure to tell you that your book is a finalist." And I start asking him questions, and then I actually said, "Please tell me this isn't a crank call." And during the six weeks that you spend being a finalist I was thinking, "Oh, I just wish it could go on longer because it feels so wonderful just to be here, just to be a finalist." When you find out you're a finalist, you find out who the judges are, and many are writers I admire, but not writers I thought I had a lot in common with. I didn't know any of the judges, or have any connection with any of them. So I thought, "That's great, but these judges will not pick my book." But they did, and I felt that they really loved it. So winning the National Book Award has been a very complex thing for me. Frankly, nothing has sabotaged my fiction writing more than winning this award. My poor second novel is like a neglected child, and I feel like I'm waving from a distance saying, "I'll be there soon." And I felt like Cinderella. I really did. Even my publisher was shocked.

DS: By choosing a new writer for such a prestigious award, I believe that the judges restored many readers' faith in the process, and in the belief that quality work rises. I can also imagine that it must be a bit distracting to be so in demand, to be asked to put yourself out there as a personality rather than to be able to stay home and be an artist.

GLASS: But I would be dishonest if I said that it was an inconvenience or trial. I need to say that it is extraordinary. And I have been asked a lot of favors. I have already blurbed four novels by writers starting out like me because I was deeply touched by the three writers who wrote endorsements for my book: Richard Russo, Michael Cunningham, and John Casey—all of whom I admire, none of whom I knew—very busy, very important writers who take the time and make the effort to help out emerging writers. It makes a tremendous difference.

And the other thing I want to say about winning the major award is that when you win it for your third or sixth novel—let's say you're Richard Russo winning the Pulitzer Prize for *Empire Falls*—it's like being crowned. But when you win a big prize for your first novel, it's like getting a really huge hug, a big embrace, and it's being told to go forward. It's the greatest encouragement and love that you can get from the literary community, and now I have to prove that I was worthy of it by continuing to write. And that, I have to say, is a lot of pressure to feel while you're writing a second novel.

DS: Ah, but it's never easy. Do you have a working title?

GLASS: Yes, it's called *A Piece of Cake*.

Edward P. Jones

Edward P. Jones, born in 1950, attended the College of the Holy Cross, holds an M.F.A. from the University of Virginia, and lives in Arlington, Virginia. Jones worked for Tax Analysts, a business publisher, for many years, writing fiction whenever possible. His first book was an incandescent short story collection titled *Lost in the City*, and its fourteen perceptive and forthright tales illuminate hidden facets of African American inner city life in Washington, D.C., during the1960s and 1970s. *Lost in the City* received resounding praise and support: it was short-listed for the National Book Award, and Jones received the PEN/Hemingway Award and a Lannan Foundation Grant.

In his first novel, *The Known World*, Jones goes back in time and considers a little-known episode of American history, the existence of black slave-owners. Set in Virginia, this haunting book revolves around Henry Townsend, a former slave, a bootmaker, and now a slave-owning farmer. His parents worked hard to purchase the family's freedom, but rather than join them in leaving slavery behind, Henry chooses his former owner as a mentor. This puts William Robbins, who is white, in a quandary, given the vicious racism of his world. Not only is he sincerely fond and proud of his black protégé, he is also secretly in love with a black woman. Jones constructs a cloverleaf-like narrative that circles from the present to the past to the future and back again. Within this elaborate structure, he renders the inner lives of his characters with great subtlety, contrasting their longings and intentions with the brutality and paradoxes of their world.

The Known World electrified the reading community, winning *Booklist*'s Top of the List award, the National Book Critics Circle Award, and the Pulitzer Prize. Jones's next book is a collection of short stories titled *All Aunt Hagar's Children.* Jones has taught at the University of Virginia, Princeton University, George Mason University, and the University of Maryland, and he is the recipient of a MacArthur Fellowship. I spoke with Edward P. Jones in early 2004.

DONNA SEAMAN: Were you concerned about the impact of your portrayal of black slave-owners?

EDWARD P. JONES: No, I wasn't. I learned that there were black slave-owners when I was in college. Although I had no intention at that time of writing a novel, I do feel that the fact that those people existed gave me a license to do the novel. If there had been no black slave-owners in America ever, then I don't think I would have written a novel about that era. But it's a fact and there's nothing you can do about it.

DS: Your novel shows us that in spite of our desire to make things simple, or black and white, if you will, they aren't. There's nothing clear-cut in the world you revisit and re-imagine, and many of your characters defy categorization because they're of mixed heritage, or involved in relationships with people of other races or other backgrounds.

JONES: I'm trying to remember if I had all those people in my mind. I guess I did. Because I sat down and started writing after thinking the novel through for about ten years. The only writing I did over those years was about twelve pages, everything else was in my head. I wrote six pages of the first chapter, and six pages of the final chapter. Once I sat down to write the book, it took me only about two and a half months for the first draft.

DS: Where did these characters come from? Did you do a great deal of reading and research?

JONES: No. As a matter of fact, I had a lot of books I planned on reading but I never got around to them. Over those ten years, I just kept putting it off, and in the meantime, of course, I was creating the novel in my head. So finally I decided, well, I know enough about how that world looked back then, so I'm just going to go on that. I'm just going to use my imagination. Forget the research.

DS: At the beginning of the novel, one feels as though one might be reading a traditional historical novel because it seems as though there's lots of research backing it up and that you're giving us facts.

JONES: Yes, like the census. But all that is made up. I mention three people in the book who wrote histories of Manchester County. Of course, they couldn't write histories of a fictional place. And the names of those three people are names of friends of mine.

DS: Your narrative is densely layered and complex. Your omniscient point-of-view takes us back and forth in time within a single sentence. I wonder how you came to use that voice and that perspective.

JONES: The shifting around in time happened perhaps because I was writing more than 150 years after everything happened. I felt that as I looked back over all that time, and as I'm writing about a person, I should give the reader some idea of what happened to that person down the line. If I was writing about 1855 Virginia in, say, 1861, I wouldn't have been able to do that.

DS: You create a palpable tension between the novel's richly textured language and its incredible emotional restraint. That is to say, the narrative is remarkably understated given the acts of horrific brutality and the profound grief you describe. Was this a conscious choice?

JONES: Yes, it was because I didn't want to inject any more emotion into the situation. The events are particularly horrendous, so I wanted simply to report. The reader will bring his or her own feelings to it.

DS: Do you think it's important for us to try to understand how people felt in the past, to get a sense of the emotional dimension of their times, rather than to simply chronicle the circumstances of their lives?

JONES: I think the feelings were important to me, to put those forth. My sense has always been that people do things for a reason, and I need to explain why people do the things they do and how they got into those situations.

DS: Is this part of what inspires you to write fiction, the ability to reveal people's minds?

JONES: I think so, but actually it's a real messy business. For instance, one of the reasons I have a lot of people carving stuff in the novel is because I would rather have been some sort of woodcarver than a writer. If you have a piece of wood in your hand and you're carving a horse, for example, you can tell if the legs are too long or too short, or whatever; you can tell everything just by having it in your hand. But in a novel, you have all these pages and you can't see it all at one time. You can only hope that what you're building makes sense.

DS: Do you see a connection between the moral dilemmas that you create in your short stories, which are more contemporary, and the situations you've depicted in this novel of the mid-nineteenth century?

JONES: No. I think they are separate. I don't know what happened to my mind that I decided to write a novel about 1855 Virginia rather than something about 1950 or 1960 Washington. Maybe I'll get around to that.

DS: *The Known World* has been exceptionally well received. It's been critically acclaimed, and it's increasingly popular with readers. Has this affected you as a writer?

JONES: No, I'm still the same person. I do feel as if I've gotten some recognition. I noticed on the *New Yorker* issue on the newsstands, in which I have a short story, there's a sticker that gives my name, as if people will know who I am. So it was really something to see that. I have a name now.

DS: When you teach, do you encourage your writing students to think big, to grapple with serious questions, or do you let them find their own way?

JONES: I don't have any kind of agenda. I just deal with the work that they produce. I comment on their characters and plot and everything else. I figure writers should come to their material on their own.

DS: The way you describe the writing of your novel makes me think your approach to writing is intuitive.

JONES: Yes, it should seem like that. I remember something Toni Morrison said, "The prose should not sweat." In *The Known World* that's the result of thinking about it for ten years. Because I lived with it so long, it feels as if it's been worked and worked and worked. And actually it has been, because after the first draft, I went over it many, many times.

DS: What writers would you recommend to your readers?

JONES: Gabriel García Márquez. I like Faulkner. James Joyce's *Dubliners* was my inspiration when I sat down to write *Lost in the City*. Chekhov. But the problem with naming people is that I'll inevitably forget someone.

DS: Do you feel that you're part of a community of writers?

JONES: I'm not a social person. I do know some writers, but it's not like I hang out with them.

DS: How do you feel about being identified as an African American writer? And what do you think when you enter a bookstore and see books by African American writers in their own separate place?

JONES: I don't mind too much. I guess I haven't been doing it long enough to feel offended by that. For me, it's just nice to be in a bookstore at all. There are a lot of people out there who can't get their work published.

DS: I know some writers feel a sense of responsibility toward their community, whether it's defined by religion, race, or ethnicity. Do you feel that you have any form of connection, or mission, or obligation?

JONES: No, I don't. I feel that the only thing I have an obligation to do is tell the truth. And if some people come out looking not so nice, there's nothing I can do about that. If that's where the truth leads me, that's what I put down.

DS: I often feel the truth told in fiction is of a deeper caliber than the facts related in nonfiction.

JONES: Yes, I think that's true. I think that in stories and novels you can get to a certain truth that you can't get in any other way.

DS: One truth I think you've captured so beautifully and authentically in your novel is what I've taken to calling the "in the blink of an eye" phenomenon.

JONES: Ah, the first story in my new collection will be called "In the Blink of God's Eye."

DS: I believe that this is an aspect of life, its precariousness, its persistent and unexpected changeability, that literature gets at better than any other art form. On the subject of art, are you influenced by other art forms? Music, perhaps?

JONES: I would say about 90 percent of the book was written while I was listening to a tape I made of Judy Collins singing "That's No Way to Say Goodbye." I taped it ten times. And then I taped the opening credits for a Paul Newman movie, *The Life and Times of Judge Roy Bean*. I taped it over and over again, too, on the same tape. Both of these pieces of music are sort of melancholy, and I find that I write best with that kind of music playing.

DS: This must be a way for you to enter that other realm, the realm of the imagination.

JONES: Yes, it is. It puts me in a certain mood. You know, when you're writing, you're essentially doing what God did in those six days, you're creating a world. Writing is hard. I came up with dozens of characters, and you have to put them forth fully and as realistically as you possibly can.

DS: What were you doing during those ten years while you were working this novel out in your mind?

JONES: I was working for Tax Analysts. They put out several magazines on taxes and insurance. I collected articles, op-eds, and editorials on those issues and summarized them. I'd been doing that since 1983. I had five weeks of vacation in 2001 around Christmas time, and I said, "Well, it's time for me to start writing." I made that decision after I decided not to do any research. Two weeks into that vacation, they called me and said my job of nineteen years was gone. It hurt.

DS: It's interesting that your "front" mind was dealing with something that wasn't emotional or too consuming. This left your deeper mind free to conjure up an alternative world. I admire writers who work in the real world. I know the academy is terrific, and that teaching in M.F.A. writing programs is rewarding, but I think that that life becomes insular and that it can limit someone's range.

JONES: You're right.

DS: Do you believe that fiction helps us become more compassionate?

JONES: I do. It may depend on the person, but I do think that I have a better sense of the world and I feel better about people because of books that I've read. And I don't think I would have gotten that without having read fiction and literature.

This interview previously appeared in a slightly altered form in Booklist.

SECTION TWO: FICTIONAL LICENSE: NOVELS ABOUT REAL PEOPLE

Fictional characters are almost always based on actual human beings. Most writers go to great lengths to conceal the real-life inspirations for their inventions, but there are those who take the opposite approach. This breed of writer becomes so involved, even obsessed, with a celebrated real-life figure, an empress, for example, or a painter, that they decide to fictionalize the life of a famous, often famously enigmatic, individual. This form of portraiture has its pitfalls. Some novelists veer into hagiography, romanticizing their subjects to the point of superficiality. Other novelists rely too heavily on the facts, and churn out dutiful tales that have neither the magic of fiction nor the authority of biography. Novels about real-life geniuses often suffer from a lack of imagination and psychological verity and, consequently, reach no further than a pallid costume drama. But the more gifted of the biographically inspired novelists are able to transmute fact into story by discerning (or creating) the essence of the person portrayed, the wonder of his or her triumphs over adversity, and the significance of his or her accomplishments. By internalizing the story, writing lyrical and sensuous prose, and imagining their subject's inner life, these novelists go beyond the province of biography.

Such writers are often drawn to powerful people, especially individuals who changed the world in spite of humble or downright oppressive origins, prejudice, violence, illness, or other obstacles. Novelists fascinated by the role of the individual in history also revel in the tactile details of daily existence as they bring a past era vividly to life. I discovered over the course of our conversations that each of the writers in this section enjoyed doing research as much as writing, and indeed, each took great pains to describe everything from the clothes their real-life hero wears to the food he or she eats and the places he or she calls home. Ultimately, however, it is the novelists' empathy, their attunement to emotions and the mystery of fate, that result in the creation of art.

I was fortunate to speak with novelists who wrote literary novels about very different types of historical figures and about diverse lands. Madison Smartt Bell steeped himself so deeply in the culture and history of Haiti, and in every facet of the improbable life of the Haitian revolutionary Toussaint Louverture, he ended up writing a set of three monumental novels. Australian novelist Peter Carey delved into the checkered past of his homeland in order to imagine the inner life of Ned Kelly, a controversial folk hero. Chinese American writer Anchee Min, a novelist with a marked interest in extraordinarily tough and resourceful women, portrays in dazzling detail not only the demanding, often harrowing life of Empress Orchid, but also the final years of Beijing's Forbidden City. Writers are also drawn to the lives of writers who have gone before them, hence Kate Moses's novel about poet Sylvia Plath, and all the novels about writers, and painters, listed in the Related Readings at the end of this book.

Madison Smartt Bell

Born in 1957, Madison Smartt Bell, the son of a lawyer and an accomplished equestrienne, grew up on a farm in Williamson County, Tennessee, where he indulged his precocious love for books. He left the South to attend Princeton University, then lived in New York City, the setting for his early novels. Bell found a mentor in Southern writer George Garrett, with whom he studied at Hollins College, earning an M.F.A. in creative writing. Thanks to Garrett's support, Bell published his first novel, *The Washington Square Ensemble,* in 1983 when he was twenty-five years old. A jazzy, multivoiced thriller about a diverse group of philosophical drug dealers, it is the first in a string of novels in which Bell uses a noirish plot and tone to camouflage what is, in fact, a tale about the spiritual quests undertaken by streetwise men who long for peace in a violent world. Bell is also profoundly concerned with race relations, and both spirituality and race emerge as pivotal themes in his twelve novels and two short story collections.

Early on, Bell recognized the crucial role that misfits, renegades, and outsiders play in society, whether they are criminals, artists, seers, or revolutionaries. Consequently, his characters include an apocalyptic-minded artist who joins a terrorist cell in *Waiting for the End of the World,* a Vietnam vet, wounded both physically and psychically, who has just returned home to Tennessee in *Soldier's Joy,* an insomniac American hypnotist and ex-junkie, living in London and steeped in the teachings of hermetic Gnosticism in *Doctor Sleep,* and a hubristic if well-intentioned inner city Tae Kwon Do teacher in *Ten Indians.* After a string of tales in which violent, live-for-the-moment characters wreak havoc in crime sprees infused with metaphysical implications, Bell strikes a more reflective and redemptive note in *Anything Goes,* in which a young musician comes to terms with his unusual heritage and finds his voice as a songwriter.

One figure, however, towers over Bell's work: the Haitian leader and visionary Toussaint Louverture, who orchestrated the Haitian Revolution after it began in 1791 with a bloody slave uprising. Bell became so immersed in the story of Toussaint, and in the rich history of the only nation founded by black slaves who liberated themselves, he ended up writing an epic trilogy comprised of *All Souls' Rising, Master of the Crossroads,* and *The Stone That the Builder Refused.* Each novel is intensively researched and a significant work in its own right.

Versatile and virtuoso, Bell writes quickly and precisely and rarely revises. He possesses a vivid sense of place on both intimate and panoramic scales, a gift for group dynamics, and the uncanny ability to synthesize historical information and religious teachings into dramatic, masterfully structured plots. He seems to channel the voices of his persona non grata characters—individuals castigated by virtue of the color of their skin, their spiritual beliefs, artistic obsessions, outlaw ways, or poverty—as though they were speaking through him in the way that Haitian Vodou worshippers are possessed by the gods.

We spoke just after *Master of the Crossroads* was published in 2000. At the end of the interview, Bell says that he hopes to finish the final novel in the Haitian trilogy in time for it to come out in 2004, Haiti's bicentennial. He succeeded: *The Stone That the Builder Refused* was released in November of that year.

DONNA SEAMAN: You've explored our perceptions of race and the ravages of racism in nearly all your novels and stories. Many white writers ignore the subject of race altogether. What sensitized you? Why have you written about relationships between blacks and whites?

MADISON SMARTT BELL: I come from the South. I grew up on a farm where black people lived and worked, so I've lived with black people, and I was partially raised by black people. I don't think in my first several books I was really engaging the subject of race as a social problem, but I did have black characters, often important black characters, in the early books I wrote. It just came naturally to me, yet somehow it seemed in the eyes of readers and reviewers to be a political statement, and unusual. And because of my name, which could be a black name, I was sometimes expected to be black by readers who didn't know me, so I began to get a little more interested in the subject.

DS: Do you consider yourself a Southern writer?

BELL: Yes, I do. The majority of my work has not been about the South, but I think it's all conditioned by the fact that I come from the South, from that culture, and because I grew up on a working farm, which would have been a fairly usual experience for somebody a generation before me. Also, the first serious reading I did was Southern literature, and I was fairly well steeped in that by the time I started to write my own books.

DS: You write about the land, primarily about Tennessee and particularly in *Soldier's Joy*, with such passion, the reader gets a profound feeling for the country which seems to well up right through your characters' feet.

BELL: Yes, although I wrote a lot about other settings before I felt like taking that up. *Soldier's Joy*, my fifth book, was the first novel that really began with a political idea about race and race relations, particularly in the South. As I started working on it, it seemed as though David Duke might have had some success in forming the Klan into a legitimate political party, or at least that's how they were trying to present it. So I thought that some white Southerner should argue with that idea a little bit.

DS: The novel's hero, Laidlaw, is a Vietnam vet, and he and his neighbors are experiencing a spiritual hangover from the Vietnam War.

BELL: In a way you could say that *Soldier's Joy* is my first attempt to write a historical novel. I was slightly too young for Vietnam, so I had no direct experience of it. It's not overtly discussed very much in the book, but the war does condition Laidlaw's personality.

DS: That book was on my mind a great deal when I was reading your Haitian novels. They seem related. What brought you to Haiti?

BELL: I'd already been interested in the religion of Haiti, and then I became interested in Toussaint Louverture. He was a black man born in slavery in Saint-Domingue, which later became Haiti. He was about fifty years old when the French Revolution destabilized French colonial society. In that atmosphere, a slave revolt broke out on a very large scale, and it was basically Toussaint Louverture who turned it from a rebellion into a real revolution that resulted, finally, in the independence of Haiti. I saw that there was a novel to be written about the career of Toussaint Louverture, which had not been done in English.

DS: It is an amazing story. And you've done a tremendous amount of research for these novels.

BELL: Oh, I'm still doing it.

DS: They are so rich in detail. You cover everything: from the clothes different types of people wear to a bizarre document that specifies an elaborate spectrum of sixty skin colors.

BELL: I found out later on from a friend of mine who teaches in the University of Chicago anthropology department, Michel-Rolph Trouillot, that, in his view, the author of that book that contains the sixty-four different shades of color classification was operating under the influence of Benjamin Franklin, but he was a fugitive colonist, a property holder from Saint-Domingue, and he ended up finishing his three-volume work on the colony in Philadelphia, where he was in exile. And I guess he did become a member of Franklin's circle and sort of had this mania for classification, which was going on generally in French and English intellectual circles at that time. So, it's a little artificial. Nevertheless, it's such an extraordinary thing that I'm still fascinated by it, and it's reprinted as an appendix to *Master of the Crossroads.*

DS: Even if it's an exaggeration, it still comes out of a certain sensibility, and the groups you describe on the island are definitely color-coded, and all sorts of class and power structures are associated with color.

BELL: One of the interesting things that's different about the French slavery system versus the English slavery system is that the French acknowledge a third race, a mixed-blood race, and that's where the classification sprang from. Whereas, in the English system, which became the American system, down to 1/16th you were considered to be black; after that, you were white. But really, at 1/8th you can't tell anymore.

DS: You mentioned earlier that you were attracted, before you started traveling to Haiti, to Vodou. I would say that not only are you a Southern writer, but that you're also a religious writer. There are spiritual quests in almost all of your books, and you write often about various practices used to contact the other world, the hidden world.

BELL: There has been a mystical or a visionary thread in all my work. Even in my first novel, I was beginning to write a little bit about African religions syncretic with Christianity, especially Catholicism. I read a lot, and I was writing about Santeria at a time when there was very little research available, but there was lots and lots about Haitian Vodou, which anthropologists really like because it is so pure. I was fascinated with the idea that the spirits would actually appear and you could talk to them and so forth, that the gods were manifest in the bodies of the believers.

DS: Did the American intervention in Haiti inspire your interest in the country's politics?

BELL: I have no ambition to become a commentator on present-day Haitian politics, but it was the intervention that made it possible for me to go there. I was actually planning to go in 1991 right before Aristide was deposed. I had written the first hundred pages of *All Souls' Rising*. I had a leave from my job, and I was going to go down to Haiti to start doing field work, and then it really didn't seem possible to do that. I'd never been there before, so I gave up, at that point, and I sat home and wrote the book on the basis of research alone. I was able finally, only because of the intervention, to get down there and take a quick look around the country before *All Souls' Rising* came out. It was frustrating at the time to be in that situation, but in the end, I think it was somewhat to my advantage that it worked out that way because when I returned to Haiti to do research for *Master of the Crossroads*, I had *All Souls' Rising* to show to people to kind of prove that I was serious and already knew something about the country. And I think people were much more willing to talk to me and help me because of that.

DS: You present a tremendous cast of characters caught up in a great swirl of incredibly violent activity, and you write from many points of view, but one man, the good French doctor, Antoine Hébert, emerges as the reader's guide and touchstone.

BELL: Originally, he was paired with the primary black fictional protagonist, a runaway slave, or a maroon as they were called, named Riau. The two men actually became friends across the course of the whole story; they served as dual protagonists in a way. But when *All Souls' Rising* was getting ready to be published, the editors felt that the white character should be emphasized more so that the reader could fasten a little bit more easily on a single person. Hébert is the person who has most in common with the typical reader, regardless of race, because he's an outsider. He has recently arrived there, he doesn't know what's happening, he has to learn as he goes along.

DS: The doctor becomes a guide on many levels, sensuous, emotional, and intellectual, and he's fascinated by Toussaint and his strategies, and is attuned to everyone he meets. He also bridges color distinctions by falling in love with a woman of mixed race.

BELL: There is a romantic story that runs through all three novels. Hébert hooks up with a woman who is from a very distinct level of society, that of high-class prostitutes, and he and she end up having a child and, to put it very anachronistically, a committed relationship. That becomes one of his motives for survival, and that love carries him through the whole thing. Standard practice was to simply maintain women like that. Sometimes such relationships were quite long-lasting, but you couldn't marry a woman of that social class. Under the colonial system, before the rebellion and the revolution had begun, you lost your status as a white person if you did. So the issue of whether Hébert and Nanon are going to get married becomes a key question.

DS: It is very dramatic; there are other significant love stories, many of them triangular in their complexities. These subplots are like microcosms for the revolution, which becomes so complicated as Toussaint creates turmoil, distrust, and hostility among the Spanish, the English, and the French. One can read these novels as military dramas, or as tales of love during times of war and radical change. Were you aware of setting up this macrocosm-microcosm structure?

BELL: I think so. The romantic subplots have the usual attraction of romantic subplots, but at the same time, children are produced by these relationships, and it's the future of these children that becomes a subterranean force because the background of the entire event had to do with the three races trying to completely destroy the other two.

DS: So much action in such a small place.

BELL: I don't even talk about quite half of it. Basically, what I've done in all three books is restrict myself to dramatizing events that happen in the northern part of Haiti, and there were a lot of other things going on. For such a small place in such a short period of time, the complexity is really overwhelming.

DS: *Soldier's Joy* and *Doctor Sleep* are also big novels with lots of characters, but you also excel at writing taut, noirish tales about just a few desperate renegades: your early novels, including *Waiting for the End of the World,* and the more recent *Save Me, Joe Louis* and *Ten Indians.* How hard was it to open your writing up to the demanding dimensions the Haitian trilogy required?

BELL: After I worked on this project for a couple of years, I realized that I couldn't do it in one book because it was too complicated. So I decided I would have to devise a structure where I could write novels that would be free-standing, and I think they are. You can read *Master of the Crossroads* without reading *All Souls' Rising,* and it still makes sense and you can follow it, but at the same time they all go together to make a larger whole. There were three critical divisions among the white people, a few among the mixed-blood people, still more among the blacks, and all of these different groups had to be somehow represented in characters, so I'm committed to a cast of thirty right there. I'd never tried to do anything on that scale before. Most of my other novels had centered on the lonely individual in some way. Keeping it all in balance was one of the more difficult aspects of it all.

DS: Did it make it easier to have real-life characters mixed in with characters of your own invention?

BELL: I didn't want to say anything about the real-life characters, the historical figures, particularly Toussaint himself, whom I admire a lot. I found that I was reluctant to handle him as a fictional character, so the solution was to surround him with a lot of people I made up that I could manipulate more freely. Through them, and their efforts to figure him out, you get an outline image of what Toussaint was like.

DS: It's like a kaleidoscope of portraits. Each time you enter another character's consciousness, you see Toussaint a little differently.

BELL: Toussaint was a person with a lot of apparent contradictions. He was in many ways a real accommodationist. He was trying to create, out of this initial period of anarchy and destruction, a reorganized society that would be based on racial harmony and in which basically everybody would cooperate. He was not somebody who wanted to wipe out all the white people or all the colored people either. He wanted to build a society where everybody would have a functional role, and he was actually close to doing that two hundred years ago, which is pretty interesting since we still can't do it here and now. On the other hand, he was capable of great ruthlessness and a lot of political and military chicanery. People who threatened him mostly ended up dead, often in consequence of things that he set in motion from a long distance away.

DS: The Haitian revolution was unbelievably violent, so you had to write about bloodshed, and you did so in *All Souls' Rising* with vehement detail. In the second novel, you achieve a balance by alternating private moments of tenderness with depictions of brutal violence.

BELL: I didn't want *Master of the Crossroads* to be quite so horrific as *All Souls' Rising.* It was important to do that once because there were terrible events and the magnitude of the atrocities is part of the meaning of the story, but I felt it would be a good idea to concentrate less on that in the second book, which is actually more about efforts to stabilize the situation and organize it. In this book, a strategy emerges out of the initial chaos of the first four years of the revolution. So, it's much more a book about military campaigns and pragmatic politics then about a senseless bloodbath.

DS: Another theme that unifies the beautiful and the gruesome is the practice of Vodou. In fact, the title itself refers to an essential element in Vodou beliefs.

BELL: I thought of that title fairly late. In this volume in particular, I've had to really grapple with the personality of Toussaint Louverture and figure out how he could have done all the contradictory things he did. In Vodou, the crossroads is considered to be a boundary between the world of the living and the spiritual world, and there's a particular spirit, Legba, who is in charge of the gateway, the passageway. There are many stories about how Toussaint got the name Louverture, which in French means opening. We assume that he chose it at a certain point for political purposes. I think he was trying to make an association between himself and Legba—such associations are normal in Haiti—to say that he was embodying the spirit of the crossroads and controlling the passage. The other dimension involved is that Legba has a kind of sinister alter ego, a more diabolical figure—in Creole, Mait' Kalfou, which translates into English as "master of the crossroads." By having those three levels of resonance in the title, I was able to refer to all aspects of Toussaint's personality at once.

DS: The other interesting point about Toussaint's many-faceted persona is that he is a devout Catholic who goes to church and is raising his children to be Christians. Yet you make it clear that he also practices Vodou and draws strength from both faiths, and political cachet from both.

BELL: I believe that's true. He made some efforts to suppress Vodou late in his career, because I think he understood the political ramifications of it were not good once he was in power. Its organization is cellular, and you have a lot of independent congregations that are not hierarchical, but networked, almost like terrorist cells. And it still works that way. Power transitions in Haiti have always worked through those networks, and it's very difficult for people in power to deal with because of the cellular quality. They can't be controlled from the top, and you can't kill the leaders because anyone could be a leader. Most of Toussaint's biographers have treated him as a Catholic. I think he was also Vodun; I don't see how he could not have been. For most Haitians, there is no contradiction involved in that they see it as two sides of the same coin.

Catholicism tends to be practiced by the majority in conjunction with Vodou.

DS: One of the *loas* is based on the Virgin Mary. Vodunists include saints and Catholic figures in their pantheon.

BELL: That syncretism occurred in a lot of Caribbean slave societies. It helped achieve conversion to Christianity, although in Saint-Domingue, they really didn't care about it all that much. It's one of the reasons, I think, that the African strain in the Haitian religion is stronger than most other places. They had a polytheistic pantheon from the African religion, so they just attached that to the cult of the saints. And that still goes on in Haiti and other places.

If you want to read the whole thing from the point of view of depth psychology, you'd say that these are the archetypes of the collective unconscious, and they always seem to take the same basic forms and the same series of manifestations. If the names and the images change, so what? I think the people of Haiti understood that from the very beginning.

DS: How do you feel when you're in Haiti?

BELL: I don't have many dreams when I'm in Haiti. There's no need to dream because all the contents of the unconscious have been moved around to the outside. But I did have one dream there. It's set in the deepest part up on the central plateau in this little town where I had inadvertently gotten stuck for the night. The dream was thirty seconds long and involved me diving to the bottom of this very deep body of water with a kind of panache, and there were people up top that I wanted to impress, and presently I realized I was stuck there. This dream was a message that I was going very deep into something that I might not come out of so easily.

DS: How has your immersion in Haiti affected you?

BELL: I think it's basically been good, in the religion and in the way a lot of the culture works. Others would debate this because not all Haitians feel this way about it, but I feel that there is a very strong possibility to abolish your ego and be free of the tyranny of the self. They have a formula for that that works rather well, and I think that's the goal of a lot of religious observance. And it's in that context that I've had more success with it than anywhere else.

DS: In *Soldier's Joy*, a charismatic religious figure named Brother Jacob tells Laidlaw that it doesn't matter whether God exists, what matters is love. You've made a similar remark about your experience of Vodou in Haiti, writing about one of your visits, "I knew during the journey my whole psychology would alter itself, and that I would enter completely into magical thinking. I would not know if it was reality that changed or my perception of it. I would know that it didn't matter."

BELL: That's right. That's why I made all the trips down there pretty well. I know people who can't make that transition. Foreigners who go to Haiti become very frustrated and crack up.

DS: Do you plan on writing any nonfiction about your experiences?

BELL: I've done a lot of literary journalism. I've done some regular journalism, not a whole lot. But I've written lots and lots of nonfiction about Haiti. So the question is, will I publish it? And I think the answer is no. I had a commission for a couple of years from the *New Yorker* to write a Haiti piece for them, and they never published it, but they did pay my way down there several times. I've basically written a book from all this called "Soul in a Bottle," and I thought it had, potentially, artistic status similar to fiction, but it's never really going to be finished, and the early parts have got a lot of mistakes in it, and it's very, very strange. I doubt if I'll publish it, for a lot of reasons, but it's been interesting to write; it kind of organizes my thoughts.

DS: I can't imagine how you do this much writing. These are immense books, and I know that a lot was cut before *All Souls' Rising* was published.

BELL: There were probably 100 to 150 pages cut out of that, and there were entire subplots involving characters that basically disappeared because the editors felt, correctly I think, that it was just too damn complicated. They were also concerned that it was too long, that people were going to be intimidated and wouldn't pick it up. So the simplest thing for me to do was just surgically remove whole subplots with the characters in them. It all went back together very well. I took out the weakest parts. There was one character I had difficulty getting right, and I took him out, and everything that was connected to him, and sutured up the gaps. What was cut is kind of interesting because it's about the urban situation, which otherwise doesn't get covered much in the book.

DS: One can only assume that you never sleep.

BELL: I work quickly, that's a simple answer. I don't revise much as a general rule. I have some sort of facility for organizing things ahead of time.

DS: Your novels do feel as though they were written that way: they flow, no matter how complex they get, smoothly and seamlessly. You write often about music, and it feels to me that music is your template.

BELL: I am an amateur musician, and I listen to a lot of different stuff. I think my models tend to be musical, not explicitly as though I'm going to write something in the form of a fugue, but in that my sense of organization in a piece of fiction is musical—themes and harmonies and those kinds of things.

DS: You've even written a book about narrative design.

BELL: That's true. I forgot about that.

DS: I'm grateful to you for writing vividly about the Haitian revolution. It's a subject that's actually quite relevant to Americans.

BELL: I feel it's part of our history. It's an important part of the history of the hemisphere. If things had gone differently, we would be living in a very different world now, because Napoleon's plan began with the restoration of slavery in Haiti, which was supposed to take three months. Then they were going to sail on to Louisiana, which was French at the time, and start invading the U.S. If that had occurred, we would have a rather different society here now, and our French would be a lot better.

DS: Haiti has suffered so terribly; it's been ruled by one tyrant after another, and it's remained mired in terrible poverty.

BELL: It hasn't helped to be a pariah state for two hundred years. Every colony and nation surrounding Haiti remained slave societies. The English were in Jamaica, and the French had actually successfully restored slavery in their other Caribbean positions. Slavery didn't end in the U.S. for another sixty years, and Haiti was considered a menace. People were terrified of it. Slaves in the American South knew about the existence of Haiti; Nat Turner knew about the existence of Haiti. Our relationship to Haiti in the nineteenth century was like our relationship to Cuba in the twentieth, and so, sure, they got no help. The Haitians were completely isolated.

DS: You have one more Haitian novel to go.

BELL: I've written about five chapters of it. I'm carrying the notebook around in my suitcase. I'm halfway into this little chapter that describes the first shots fired when Napoleon sent a huge army to depose Toussaint Louverture and restore slavery, which is their secret agenda. I have a bunch of characters who are fixing to sail into the harbor of a little town on the border with the Spanish colony and have a firefight and kill a bunch of people. I'm hoping to finish it so that it's out in 2004, for the bicentennial of Haitian independence.

Peter Carey

Born in 1943 in the small town of Bacchus Marsh, Australia, Peter Carey has lived in New York City since the early 1990s. The author of eight novels and a recipient of Australia's major literary awards, Carey is a wily storyteller who convincingly inhabits the complex worlds he conjures even as he stands a half-step to the side to allow the reader a glimpse of the apparatus at work behind the scene, namely the literary influences and historical figures and events that inspire him. Carey has been described as a literary treasure-hunter for his sure sense of a good yarn with a wealth of allusions and meanings.

Carey won the first of his two Booker Prizes for *Oscar and Lucinda,* which was made into a film in 1997. In *Jack Maggs,* Carey re-imagines a character from Charles Dickens's *Great Expectations,* the Australian convict Abel Magwitch, and explores Australia's history as a penal colony for the British Empire. Carey then delves even further into Australia's soul in *True History of the Kelly Gang,* a fictional portrait of Ned Kelly, the controversial Australian folk hero who is remembered as a hybrid of Robin Hood and Jesse James. Written in Ned Kelly's voice, the novel takes the form of an autobiography and a true confession written on the run, to an infant daughter he'll not live to raise.

True History of the Kelly Gang earned Carey his second Booker Prize in 2001, and it was then that Carey came to Chicago and appeared on *Open Books.* In his next novel, the many-layered *My Life as a Fake,* Carey turns to yet another curious chapter in his homeland's colorful history, an infamous literary hoax perpetuated in the 1940s. Then, in his first nonfiction book, *Wrong about Japan: A Father's Journey with His Son,* Carey extends his study of the monstrous, of how real life is transformed into fantasy, and of the dangers of cross-cultural assumptions as he explicates his son's passion for Japanese comics (manga) and the films inspired by them (anime) and chronicles their journey to Tokyo in search of the artists who create them.

DONNA SEAMAN: You've created a unique hero based on a true-life figure, Ned Kelly, a still controversial nineteenth-century Australian folk hero and outlaw. When did you first become enamored with Kelly and why?

PETER CAREY: It's complicated because Ned Kelly is such a dominant figure in Australian folklore that it seems as if I've always known about him. Ned Kelly has been part of one's life in some way. I do remember two cultural things that affected me. There's an Australian painter, not well known in the United States although very well known in Britain and Australia, called Sidney Nolan, who painted this extraordinary series of narrative, not quite naïve, paintings about the story. It was actually only the second exhibition of paintings I'd seen in my life, and I was about nineteen or twenty, so they made a big impression on me. The figure of Ned Kelly is represented in an iconographic way through the armor that he wore on the last free day of his life. I mean, here's a guy, he's twenty-four, twenty-five, and most of his life he's not wearing armor, but at the very end of the story, the gang—there's four of them—are wearing crudely fashioned breastplates and huge cylindrical things around their heads with visors. And Sidney Nolan represented the gang like this, with Kelly in the center, with, as we say reverently in Australia, a "buckethead."

DS: The novel opens with this strange scene.

CAREY: When Kelly comes out at the last stand in Glenrowan, the police are all around the little shanty where the gang is holed up. It's early morning, there's mist on the ground, and it's winter. The police don't know what they're looking at, and what they see is this headless monster with a long neck walking into a hail of bullets, and the bullets are bouncing off him. For quite awhile many of the police are just terrified. It seems like some supernatural being. To put this scene in full context, you also have to remember that Australia started the European part of its life as a penal colony, and this does make us very, very different from the United States, although we seem to be the same in certain ways. That's a foundation moment, just like the *Mayflower* is a foundation moment, although the convict seed is meant to be some sort of curse over the land, and we are meant to be cast out and second-rate, the descendants of convicts.

But Ned Kelly, whose father is Irish, will prove himself to be braver and more resourceful, to know the country better, and, basically, to be more decent than all of those forces of the police and the colonial administration. And yet, I think there was a sense for a great majority of the Australians at that time, and still today, that there is some shame in this heritage. There were all sorts of newspaper articles in Australia that seemed to suggest some sort of controversy surrounding this book.

DS: They don't want an outlaw for a folk hero, even though he's a Robin Hood figure in some ways.

CAREY: Yes. They don't want to be embarrassed. If you're a diplomat, if you're the prime minister, you really don't wish, I guess, particularly if this has been weighing on your mind for a century or so, to be represented by a criminal. But at the same time, I didn't invent the notion that Ned Kelly is a popular figure, I've grown up with that. So there is nothing controversial about what I've done. We are the people who admire Ned Kelly, just as the song "Waltzing Matilda" is the song of our heart.

DS: We sang that in school when I was a girl in New York State.

CAREY: I wonder why you did? Because in the narrative in the song, the swagman (the hobo) who steals the jumbuck (the sheep) is arrested by the trooper (the policeman) and then commits suicide rather than go into custody. Now this is our song, our unofficial national anthem. It's fine to have the "Stars and Stripes," which is a wonderfully triumphal and very moving song. But this is Australia's true song, so you can imagine, can't you, why the prime minister, or a diplomat, might not want to stand with his hand over his heart while he sings about the guy who committed suicide rather than go to jail. But this is seriously a deep part of us, as is the Ned Kelly thing. And this produces all sorts of wonderful traits in our character, and some things that are not so great, but it is real. I was interested in this from the beginning because I'm living in New York now, and there I was looking, once again, at these paintings, which is a long way back to where this conversation started. But, my point is, I was looking at the paintings and thinking, "Who are we that this should be our story?" And that there is so much that we had not imagined about it. We thought we knew the story so well, but what about the emotional life?

DS: You tried to fathom that by having Ned Kelly, in effect, write the novel, which takes the form of a series of letters that he writes to his baby daughter when he realizes he's not going to be around to get to know her. Early on, you establish the fact that as a boy he was somewhat contemplative. He wants to farm and raise horses and live a quiet life. But he's forced by poverty and prejudice and a very wild mother into a life of crime, which he does accept. But he also loves to read, and he has a lot to say, and you conjure up an evocative voice for him.

CAREY: Not long after I first saw those Kelly paintings, I read a transcription of a letter that Ned Kelly himself had written, and I, as a young would-be writer having just read Joyce and Beckett, suddenly discovered this less literary voice, but still a very Irish voice, unpunctuated, passionate, with great stream of sentence. This is like Ned Kelly's DNA. Much, much, much later, when I'm in New York and looking at these paintings, I think, "That's how I would write the book." I didn't doubt it for a second. This is his voice.

DS: And he wants to tell the truth. He knows that he's misunderstood and that he's a victim of circumstances. There's much compassion in his telling, which is so affecting. There is very little punctuation. His grammar and expressions are down-home, and he takes great care not to swear. He's considerate and gallant, and yet he lives such a rough and dire life.

CAREY: The letter that he wrote, the historical figure, is public rhetoric because it was written for the judge. It's for the government. It's for the people. It's like a soapbox speech, for all its wonderful language. But a novel can't work like that, can it? I had to figure out who he was writing it for, and I thought, "He's such a male figure in our culture, you would automatically think he's writing it for his son." And having a contrary aspect to my nature I suddenly thought, "No, I want it to be to his daughter. It will be a daughter, not a son." And then that immediately affects the way he's going to talk to her. This is certainly not postfeminist.

So, as you say, he has two conflicting passions. He absolutely wants to tell the truth, and he swears that he's going to tell the truth, may he burn in hell if he speaks false. On the other hand, he wants to behave well. Women were always so impressed with how gentlemanly the historical Ned Kelly was. People were always impressed with him, you know, from the bank managers he robs, to their wives. He wants to report how it is, yet not expose his daughter to actual curse words, so he develops euphemisms. One of these I stole from nineteenth-century Australian literary culture, when the writers had to deal with the great profanity of the common people at that time. Everyone would say "bloody this" and "bloody that," but they'd use the use the word "adjectival" instead. I like this usage because it gives the prose a very nice bit of inventiveness in a line such as, "Stand back against the adjectival wall."

DS: It's interesting that Ned Kelly was appealing to women. You make a very strong case in this book for his mother being every bit as flinty as a man. She's a real fighter, a hell-raiser, and causes Ned a tremendous amount of grief. She, in effect, ruins his life.

CAREY: Yes, it's a weird thing. First, I do believe I'm very close to the historical character. This is a wild woman.

DS: From a wild clan.

CAREY: Oh, yes, the brothers. If you want to figure out her character by sheer triangulation you only have to look at those around her and see who they were. Mrs. Ellen Kelly at one stage takes one of her husbands to court to sue for child support, and having won the case then proceeds to ride wild gallops, as they are described, up and down the main street. I think she's arrested for that. And also her husband dies when Ned is twelve. And we know that, generally, when you have a mother left on her own with her children, the eldest boy will take the position: he will be the man, and the mother will be pleased. She will need him and together they are a survival unit, these two. So all of that's not surprising. This is historically so. The father dies, and not too long after he's dead, the mother goes where she's always wanted to go, further north where her sisters are. So all the kids, with Ned as the oldest, go up there. When this has been written about in Australian history, even though he's a criminal and so on, he's really a hero. But when you think of a hero, your hero doesn't get jealous of his mommy or his mommy's many lovers. But if you think about how they live in this tiny hut and the only privacy are these little curtains, and here's a twelve-year-old boy, well, obviously, he's got to feel things about that. He's going to be combative and competitive. This is not something that is normally written about in his history.

DS: The conflicted emotions Ned suffers over his mother and her lovers show what fine stuff he's made of, how sensitive he is, how he's a bit of a romantic. And he loves the land, which is a key factor in the book.

CAREY: I recognized that this is a story about people who want to live on the land with the soil and the rain and the horses. These are the dominant things in their lives. So among the most important research I did was to go to the high country and spend time with people who know about horses. I hate to ride myself, but I'm a novelist, so you spend enough time with people, and you ask the right questions, and in the end you've got to produce something that is satisfying to somebody who can really ride very well. And, indeed, I had people read this who were farmers and horseman, although they never criticize enough, frankly, when one wants a lot of criticism.

DS: That physicality comes through, and Ned's struggles are mirrored in his suffering in the rain and the cold, his having to walk for miles and miles.

CAREY: Those folks were tough. They were even tougher than I made them. The land is rough, the weather demanding, and they lived out in the open, sleeping without cover.

DS: And his own family turns on him. But even though they betray him, and even though he lands in jail because of their accusations, when he writes to his daughter, he defends them. He says that they were often drunk, or "shicker," and that "they thieved and fought and abused me cruelly," but, he continues, her "ancestors would not kowtow to no one and this were a fine rare thing in a colony made specifically to have poor men bow down to their gaolers." Ned Kelly's story becomes the story of one man's fight against injustice.

CAREY: I think he ends up realizing that he represents a lot of people. He starts off not really understanding that and mostly feeling his own injustices. But a time comes when, I think, he suddenly sees how he is seen and how he is understood and who he represents. Not that this is intended to glorify any of these people. I do think theirs is a criminal caste, but he does sort of elevate himself and comes to see what he might mean to people, and that his strong feelings might actually be shared and understood. Australians of the time did express their admiration for him, and he really does become heroic because he is the child of a convict demonstrating that he's smarter and braver and more resourceful and more decent than the oppressor. That means a lot to everybody; he feels that and knows it.

DS: There's a rather amazing and hilarious fight scene that is pivotal to both his humbleness and innocence, and his strength and fortitude.

CAREY: Yes, that's a famous fight. You know, I did try to touch on all the key incidents in his life; sometimes I laugh and say that it's almost like the stations of the cross. So, yes, there is a scene in the book where he fights a man called Wild Wright. He fights Wild Wright because he's gone to jail for having supposedly stolen a horse, which he didn't steal, which this man, Wild Wright, had actually lent to him. And eventually they become friends and allies. But first the fight. Wild Wright is much bigger and older and heavier, but Ned is strong and fast.

DS: I want to know if Kelly really wore his long johns under his boxing trunks.

CAREY: There's a historic photograph of Ned, and as far as I can figure he is wearing long johns with silk shorts over them. It looks vaguely ludicrous. So one of the things I try to do in the fight scene is explain how he gets himself into this rig, and why, even if it was thought to be found more normal in his time.

DS: Yet he is kind of feral, and you imagine him as terribly modest, which is very funny, and subtly revealing of your simultaneous sympathy for your characters and awareness of the absurdity of it all.

CAREY: Humor has always been an important element in my work. Everyone complained that an earlier book of mine called *The Tax Inspector* was too dark. But I thought, it's actually full of humor. It seemed to me that humor really was the book's life force, and its light, and that when people were talking about it being too dark they were missing out on recognizing what else was going on.

DS: Humor is often a component in serious literature. The humor in your interpretation of Ned Kelly is found in the ludicrousness of his predicaments, and how he always unquestioningly adapts himself to whatever bizarreness transpires.

CAREY: The weird thing about this historical figure, this feared outlaw, is that he is so trusting. No matter what terrible things happen, and how much injustice he was subjected to, he really believed that if he could only explain what had happened, justice might be done. And throughout his life he believed people. He even believed the policeman who betrayed him. It's incredible.

DS: Another paradox is your novel's title: *True History of the Kelly Gang*. Does it take a work of fiction to get to the truth of Ned Kelly's life and of others like him?

CAREY: Historians are not allowed to invent, of course. This history, as it is known to us in Australia, basically comes to light illuminated by the police flashlight. It consists of police reports, court cases, those sorts of public records. We know about other things as well, but we really don't know about the emotional life. We are used to saying things like, "Ned Kelly was a friend of Constable Fitzpatrick." And Constable Fitzpatrick is the guy who gets shot in the hand and precipitates the whole event where they flee to the bush. But how was Kelly a friend to the policeman, and what did that mean? All of these things are totally lost. This sort of history is like a series of wood buildings that rot and are eaten by wild ants and collapse to the point at which they can never be reclaimed except through the imagination. And the novelist can also look at things like the whole business of the mother-son relationship, and examine the evidence—if we are going to use the wood hut analogy, that would be a few hinges and nails lying around—and construct something which seems not unreasonable. I feel very confident that the broad gist if not the detail of the mother-son thing is correct, because it's the one thing that really explains Ned Kelly's actions.

DS: Why do you think so many writers are writing fiction about real-life figures? Have you noticed that? I can think of many examples.

CAREY: You should get William Shakespeare here and grill him about it.

DS: So this is nothing new?

CAREY: That's what I'm saying in a sense, and a bit defensively. Of course, when people start to talk about the nature of history and truth, you start to think about Richard III, and about which Richard III we remember. Was the real Richard III deformed? I think not. I think I know why Australian writers continue to go back to the past: I think we tend to go back to things because we are trying to get our history right. We've lived with lies and silences as Ned Kelly would say, and so we obsessively return and try to find the whole truth.

DS: Americans may be doing the same thing. We're also a young nation that has glossed over the reality of our rapid growth. Ned Kelly's story reads like an American western; he's a Jesse James–like figure. And the poverty and the prejudice are also implicit in America's real-life stories and its literature. Russell Banks's work comes to mind.

CAREY: Yes, *Cloudsplitter* is what I started thinking about when you were talking.

DS: That's a prime example of a writer feeling the need to go back and try to understand the past on a deeper level.

CAREY: So the stories need to be retold, and what a privilege it is to be able to do that.

DS: It's a great boon for readers. Certain people love to read history, and prefer it to fiction. But a lot prefer fiction, so novels about historical figures are a sly approach to bigger truths.

CAREY: That's funny. I always feel so resistant to the notion that I'm an historical writer. Historical fiction sounds so dull. To me, a writer is someone who makes things up, and so the nicest thing anybody ever said to me about my work was when Jonathan Miller and I were on a television program. We were talking about *Oscar and Lucinda,* and he said, "Oh, I see. It's really a science fiction of the past." And I don't know how to explain that exactly, but it feels exactly right to me. In particular, I would not really distinguish necessarily between writing in the future or the present or in the past, it's all the same. People have more opinions about the past, so you have to be careful you don't get called out.

DS: You begin the novel with a quote from Faulkner: "The past is not dead, it's not even past."

CAREY: I know best what that means within Australia, and I even feel that it was really written for Australians who think, "Oh well, this white, Celtic male, this bearded bush ranger, has no relationship to the new multicultural Australian . . ." Which is what was expressed to me by a young woman friend of mine from Sydney who curled her lip when I told her I was writing about Ned Kelly. But then we had a long conversation about it. So in Australia that quote really has to do with that particular issue.

DS: Your novels don't feel historical because they are written from today's perspective, and because the drama, and the humor, is so fresh and immediate. It doesn't feel like the past.

CAREY: I think there is something crucial about the texture of the language. And if there had been no James Joyce you couldn't write like that. And if there had been no Faulkner you couldn't have written like that.

DS: Will you always be an Australian novelist even if you stay in New York?

CAREY: I don't know. I guess. For a little while during the period just before I wrote this book, I was feeling, perhaps, some pressure from my Manhattan friends, many of whom are writers. They were saying, "When are you going to write about us? What about this place?" I thought, well, this was sort of a test of skill, or of empathy or something. So I did start to write a novel that is set in New York, and it was about a subject that really made me suitably irate, and that is litigation. I had what seemed like an idea that would involve me passionately, but it was about the same time that I went to the Met and saw the Nolan paintings. I said to my wife, "When I finish this New York book I'm going to write the book about Ned Kelly," and she must have been watching me. I'm often rather depressed when I'm working; I feel as though everything is going to be a failure and so on. After a week or so had passed, she knew something was wrong, and she said, "There's no reason, really, why you can't write the Ned Kelly book first." I said, "Really, do you think so?" I started this book the next day, and I was insanely happy.

Anchee Min

Anchee Min's journey from a labor farm in Maoist China to America's bestseller lists is an astonishing one and provides the foundation for her commanding books, each a portrait of a resilient and courageous woman. Born in Shanghai in 1957, Min grew up during the terror of the Cultural Revolution, when her family barely had enough food to survive. Because this world was the only one she knew, she eagerly purchased Mao posters; loved the propagandist operas that became the closest thing to pop music for her generation; happily worked on her school's politically correct "Blackboard Newspaper"; and became a Red Guard. But none of her zeal prevented her from being sent, at age seventeen, to a collective labor farm near the East China Sea where she slaved in rice and cotton fields until 1976, when a talent scout working for Madame Mao chose her for her "proletarian" good looks. Min was taken to the Shanghai Film Studio and trained to act in a propaganda film under Madame Mao's direction. When Mao died, his widow was promptly denounced, arrested, and sentenced to death. Branded as one of her followers, Min was sentenced to eight more years of hard labor. In 1984, seriously ill and desperate to leave China, she managed to get accepted at the School of the Art Institute in Chicago and emigrated with the help of her friend, actress Joan Chen.

After teaching herself English by watching *Sesame Street* and *Oprah*, Min wrote her shattering memoir, *Red Azalea*, in which she candidly recounts the story of her stolen youth and the crushing conflict between the tyranny of the labor camp regime and the thwarted sensuality and romantic sensibilities of the young inmates. After *Red Azalea* became an international bestseller, Min turned to fiction and continued to write about the plight of young people and women subjected to the oppression and aberrations of the Cultural Revolution. She also began to develop another key theme in her work, the treacherous interweaving of friendship and rivalry among women as exacerbated by arduous circumstances. In her first novel, *Katherine,* a woman remembers the dangerous allure and naivete of an attractive American university English teacher. In *Wild Ginger,* a stark and tragic love story set in 1969, Min portrays a circle of teenagers driven to extremes by the divisiveness engendered by propaganda and fear, and by the eroticism of pain.

After writing about the inner lives of ordinary—hence powerless—people struggling to survive in a totalitarian world, Min decided to investigate the lives of two of China's most powerful—hence most reviled—women in her most resounding novels. *Becoming Madame Mao* is a meticulously researched, complexly structured, and nearly operatic interpretation of the life of a heretofore little understood and much despised figure, one who played a major role in Min's life. Min in no way minimizes Madame Mao's crimes, but she does make Jiang Qing thoroughly human. Min then reached to the more distant past to extend her mission of telling the truth about China's long tradition of demonizing women and retrieved the long-concealed, true story of the life of the Last Empress of China. *Empress Orchid* is a lavishly detailed historical novel about an impoverished young woman who, against all odds, becomes one of the emperor's concubines and, ultimately, his successor to the throne. After conducting risky and clandestine research in Beijing, Min internalized every aspect of the opulent and smothering world encased in the Forbidden City during the waning years of the besieged Ch'ing Dynasty, and she writes convincingly through Tzu Hsi's eyes, bringing back to life a remarkably intelligent, strong, and radical woman. And there's more to be told: Empress Orchid ruled for forty-seven years, a reign Min will fictionalize in her next novel.

Anchee Min appeared on *Open Books* in April 2004.

DONNA SEAMAN: I have to tell you how impressed I am by how you became such a powerful writer after immigrating to the U.S., especially because, as I understand it, you didn't speak English when you arrived.

ANCHEE MIN: Right, me too. See how American I have become? I'm not ashamed to say I'm impressed with that.

DS: Why did you decide to write your memoir, *Red Azalea,* in English?

MIN: I decided to write it because I wanted to get a better job than working as a waitress in a Chinese restaurant in Libertyville, Illinois. First I thought I wanted to be a secretary. So I went to the placement office at the school to try and get a job, and they gave me a typing test. I scored minus 13, so I said, "Can I work for you without pay until I qualify?" She said, "No, this is America. If we hire you we have to pay you." I knew that speaking good English was crucial. So I took English/Writing 101, and the teacher told me I was a lousy writer but that I had wonderful material. I kept writing, and all I knew to write about was my life back in China in the labor camps.

DS: You could have written your memoir in Chinese, but it seemed important to you to write in your new language. Can you explain why?

MIN: I had just come from China, and my mind was still very brainwashed. When any personal thoughts came up, I would suppress them. But when I spoke English, there was a freedom in the expression. I think that started when I began to study *Sesame Street* and *Mister Rogers' Neighborhood.*

DS: You taught yourself English by watching television?

MIN: Yes. Then one day I understood someone who was speaking English to me, and I found myself in tears because he said, "I am so glad that you're there and that you're proud of yourself." And I thought to myself, "I was told for twenty-seven years that I was a bolt in a communist machine, and here I am allowed to be myself." And Mr. Rogers said, "The best thing you can offer to people is your honest self." I think these things slowly transformed me through my writings.

DS: It's difficult for outsiders to grasp what went on during the Maoist years, the Cultural Revolution. Each of your books focuses on individuals, women in particular, and their strategies for survival; I wonder if you felt that the only way to express the enormity of what happened in China was to portray individual people rather than write a panoramic epic?

MIN: Yes. When we were living in it, it wasn't that bad actually. I felt good. There was a high sense of honor involved in being a proletarian, that was part of the brainwash. Now, looking back, I can see that the whole generation was deprived of understanding. Mao told us that we should feel happy because there are people living worse lives than us. For example, we saw pictures of skinny, starving children, and we were told that they were American children. So although I was so poor our family ate out of trash cans in the vegetable markets and I was infested with tapeworms, I believed I was better off—even though my classmate in elementary school died one day because a tapeworm went through her appendix. My belly was so full of tapeworms that I would sit in the classroom and groan. The tapeworms were trying to come out of my throat and come out of my rear end. But we felt that we were lucky; American children were living a worse life than us. So when Mao said the Americans are in Vietnam slaughtering the Vietcong, and China was going to be next, we were all very scared and very determined to protect our country. So I felt honored to be able to go to the Shanghai garrison to be trained to do combat with Americans. And my dream, I think it was everybody else's dream, too, was to be sent to Vietnam, to tie grenades on my body and to jump into American soldiers and blow them into pieces, and myself, too. And I imagined over and over that my remains would be sent back home, wrapped in the communist red flag, and my parents and family would be sad, but proud.

In the garrison we recited Mao's quotations and practiced with the bayonet. We had a dummy made of straw with a U.S. soldier's helmet on it, and I would go, "Kill, kill." And the drill goes on for six hours a day. Even in my dreams I was fighting and killing Americans, and they instructed us, "If you don't kill them, they are going to kill you." We saw movies of how American soldiers scooped the Vietcong children's eyes out. But today I'm happily married to a former U.S. Marine, a Vietnam veteran. On our wedding night he said, "I hope I don't have flashbacks." I said, "I hope *I* don't have flashbacks."

DS: It's just incredible what a life can hold. Listening to you describe your childhood several things come to mind. One is that children are honorable, and when adults tell them that they are on a mission, they try to fulfill it with all their heart and soul.

There is propaganda in the U.S., but compared to other places, it's of a much, much milder form, and a multiplicity of viewpoints and the voice of dissent are always being expressed.

MIN: Also, you were raised to ask questions. My daughter was born in Chicago, and I found that what I appreciate most in American schools is that you raise children to ask questions. In my case it never would have occurred to me that I should ask questions. When I first came to America for school, I was shocked when the instructor at the Art Institute asked me, "What would you like to learn?" I thought, "You're suppose to tell me what I should do or should learn."

DS: Did you realize that many people here would be astonished by what you revealed about China in your memoir? Did you intend to enlighten us?

MIN: No, not at all. What was driving me to write *Red Azalea,* and what drives me still today, is what you call survivor's guilt. I survived the labor camp and left my friends to die. Nobody would ever speak for them, and everything would be forgotten. And I'm here, eating McDonald's, drinking Coca-Cola, and having a good time. I just couldn't live with that. And also, in the broader sense, I was driven to write about the role of women, and about Madame Mao and Empress Orchid, or Tzu Hsi. Many people ask me, especially my own people, "Why do you want to shame China? What do you think of Madame Mao? Is she a good person or bad person?" I say, "That's not my focus. My focus is on how this woman, Madame Mao, was transformed from an early feminist who would not let them bind her feet into a murderer responsible for millions of deaths."

DS: You make her real. You make it clear what suffering can do to a person, how it can radically alter them, how the imperative to survive can warp us.

MIN: It's the complexity of human nature. Empress Orchid was the most important ruler in Chinese history in a culture that believed that women were grass born to be stepped on. Yet she ruled for forty-seven years and single-handedly held together a falling dynasty until she died.

DS: By writing these two novels, *Becoming Madame Mao* and *Empress Orchid,* you've dramatized two essential eras in China's long history, and portrayed two strong and powerful women, both of whom started out poor and abused. At one point, Empress Orchid thinks that for a woman to survive she must be audacious. Both she and Madame Mao were—and both acquire unheard-of power through intelligence and through love. But unlike her predecessor, Madame Mao is so damaged and her world is so damaged . . .

MIN: It's great that you use "damaged." And yes, they contrast in comparison because Madame Mao didn't survive that ordeal spiritually. Empress Orchid, on the other hand, did, and I focus on the fact that although she did not manage to revive China, her struggle was heroic. And it is the struggle that matters, not who wins. It was the process. It was the effort of that struggle.

DS: The two novels are different stylistically. The voices and the structure of each book reflect the women you portray. *Becoming Madame Mao* contains a remarkable back-and-forth narrative in which sometimes we hear her voice and sometimes the narrator's voice, and because the narrator knows the future, the narrator frequently looks ahead and cues the reader to what will come. *Empress Orchid,* on the other hand, is a lucid, straight-ahead, first-person account. I wonder how you ended up choosing these approaches.

MIN: I began by reading their writings, their memoirs and letters, documents, decrees. In reading Madame Mao's letters and her articles, I realized that she had a very strong voice, especially when she was in Shanghai in the early 1930s, when she was in her twenties writing about women's rights. I started with that voice, but after a few chapters I found that I got tipped off-balance because her voice was so powerful. I thought readers might be misled. I needed a narrator to guide the reader through what happened in history. So we see what Madame Mao sees and what she wanted to achieve, and the narrator shows us whether or not she did achieve her goals, or if the truth was the opposite of what she said. With *Empress Orchid,* I didn't have that problem.

DS: So you didn't let Madame Mao seduce us?

MIN: Exactly, precisely.

DS: Your contemporary novels *Katherine* and *Wild Ginger* are full of conflict and anguish. They're devastating really, and must have been painful to write. As I read *Empress Orchid,* I thought, Anchee Min is having fun. Was it a relief to go back to another time and tell a story with more triumphs than tragedies?

MIN: Yes. The novels *Katherine* and *Wild Ginger* are largely based on my own experiences. I chose not to plot too much because I feel life, as is, is so fascinating and powerful that my task was just to try to hold the water with both of my hands and not let it drip. But *Red Azalea* was my life. It was much easier to write in terms of construction, but it was much harder because of the emotional experience. Often I found that I could not sleep. It's very hard to describe the pain. Many times I just wanted to stop. And I found that in the first draft I had a tendency to portray myself as a victim. In fact, I found that many autobiographies easily humor you, you know, implying "I didn't do anything wrong." I found that was not true. A Cultural Revolution is not made by one Mao; a billion support it. As long as we don't step forward to take the responsibility, we will not learn the lesson. So that was the hard part, to portray myself as history, and as the truthful self, instead of saying "I'm not guilty," or "It's not my fault." So you see, it's not a flattering picture from the beginning to the end, although I do give you a reason. For example, I denounced my favorite teacher at the age of eleven. The situation was that I wanted to prove to the party that I, Anchee Min, was able to sacrifice my love and that I would be able to sacrifice myself for my country. And I was praised. It's like here if the principal tells you you're a straight-A student and you're going to Harvard. As you said, you'll be seduced.

DS: And by telling the truth, and by portraying yourself not as passive but as fully participating in your life, you enable us to put ourselves in your place and understand that we would have done the very same thing at that age under those circumstances.

MIN: I'm very glad for your response. With *Madame Mao* and *Empress Orchid*, I tried to make sure that every character and every event existed in real life. Then, when people read it, they are not just inspired or entertained, they are educated at the same time without suffering through very boring, long, heavy-duty history books. I want you to have fun and learn something at the same time, and I, too, have a good time. I learn so much from doing research.

DS: Are you free to travel to China and conduct research? Certainly for *Empress Orchid* you had to have direct access to materials in the Forbidden City.

MIN: Yes, but I was denied public library entrance because of my status.

DS: Your books are banned there I assume?

MIN: Right. I would say "rejected by the publishing house." It's a compliment. They didn't denounce me because they love it themselves. It's just policy. China wants to get the Olympics in 2008, and the government is very sensitive to any negative description of China that would harm that opportunity. So they wouldn't grant me an entrance pass. But, you know, I was a former communist. I knew which door to knock on, who to bribe.

DS: And you found incredible documents. It's astonishing what you discovered.

MIN: I knew that I should not trust the government documents or the officials. I learned in my textbooks that Empress Orchid, Tzu Hsi, was the enemy of the human race, and that she was responsible for the destruction of China's two thousand years of empire tradition.

DS: One woman ruined everything.

MIN: It's always the woman. It's a tradition in China that every downfall of a dynasty is the fault of the concubine, and the model example was Madame Mao. When she got sentenced to death, China felt good. And you still had her husband. You had the husband Mao's picture on top of the gate in Tiananmen Square, and the nation moved on. So we execute history, and history executes the Chinese women characters, one after another. Although it is changing. Now it doesn't matter that people believe that Empress

Orchid was evil. What matters is that she was the center of Chinese culture. So today you will see restaurants named after her, fashions based on her, more than twenty movies and TV series made about her life, including one that just got banned. It's called *Going Republic.* It shows that she was the person responsible for the opening of China and that she wanted to establish a parliamentary system.

DS: She was a visionary.

MIN: But giving her that credit threatens the current government. So some sixty TV episodes were banned. And it doesn't really stop there. My books go underground. I don't really care about copyrights for this particular reason. I knew from the publishers that people in China loved *Red Azalea* because it's about the life they lived and were not able to say anything about. It's about everything they can't talk about: sexuality, suppression, and the consequences of all that went on during the Cultural Revolution.

DS: Including horrific loneliness and every form of deprivation.

MIN: Yes, it's deformation of the human soul.

DS: In your work you struggle between loving what is beautiful and refined in Chinese culture and hating the brutality of China's political regimes. In *Empress Orchid,* for instance, you describe with great detail the Forbidden City, an amazing world-within-a-world of opulence and beauty, but you also describe how terribly the empress suffered within those elegant walls.

MIN: Many of us used to lead a dual life. On the one hand, Empress Orchid was the ruler of China. On the other hand, she was not allowed to breast feed her own son because she didn't have a drop of royal blood. And then there were the eunuchs. I was surprised to find that more than fifty thousand young boys were sent to Beijing by desperate parents who had them castrated in the hope that they would be one of the few selected to work in the Forbidden City. And An-te-hai, who became the chief eunuch for Empress Orchid and who was so knowledgeable and so sweet and kind—his biggest dream was to get his penis back before he died so that he can be buried in one piece, so that if he came back as a dog he wouldn't be a crippled dog. You know, I found all these details. I read accounting books, records, the history of grand tutors, the memoirs of the generals who dealt with the emperors, and the history of maids. Those are the forgotten places where I found some of the material that really tells the difference between the official version and the historical facts. For example, none of the historians have researched the record of Anhwei province where Orchid grew up, or her formative years from birth to seventeen, her life before entering the Forbidden City. War was what formed her. What I found was that she did not starve because she was the daughter of the governor of a small town called Wuhu, but the friends that she played with on the banks of the Yangtze River were so destitute they ate earthworms for dinner, and parents were forced to sell their children to pay off debts. It's like my friend whose tapeworms got through her appendix.

I also found that there is a comparison between the local opera, homemade opera, the opera that Empress Orchid grew up with, and the opera she finally learned to love, the Peking opera in the Forbidden City. I was able to understand something important about her because the opera she grew up with, the one that influenced her, is opera truly for the people. The homemade tune is for everyone; it has rhythms and lyrics and melodies that anyone can easily follow and remember. When she enters the Forbidden City, the opera she hears has no regular beats. It has unique and distinguished beats. It takes time to learn the lesson and to learn to appreciate it. But once you're hooked you're just as obsessed with it.

DS: Opera is the subject of many scenes in *Empress Orchid,* and it plays a major role in *Becoming Madame Mao.*

MIN: Opera plays a major role in the entire nation, in our life, in my life, in everybody else's life—although right now, it has become all karaoke. But whatever the form, Chinese people love to sing. It's a survival skill, mentally. We were so poor we couldn't afford anything, but we could afford our voices. We could afford to sing, and only when we sing opera do we escape the life we're living, and only in the operas do we get to live the life of the hero and heroine.

DS: The unbridgeable distance between ordinary people and royalty comes across very powerfully in *Empress Orchid.* The Forbidden City is isolated and rarefied and esoteric, and ritual and tradition determine every single thing its inhabitants do, no matter how personal.

MIN: Yes, and she is from the poorest province of China and she can never really leave that background. I think she's the only person in the Forbidden City that has real senses and has seen real life. But that was to her disadvantage.

DS: Even after she becomes empress, she's not fully in control.

MIN: Yes. When she became the ruler she was not allowed to select her own ministers. Imagine, you're managing China, you're saving China, and you're dealing with the worst people. How do you make them work for you when they hate you?

DS: Your novels are full of drastically adversarial relationships. It's understood that men are going to betray each other and the women who love them. So it seems that your women characters are hurt the most when other women betray them.

MIN: I found that this part of history has not been explored. In the Forbidden City, the Emperor expected all his concubines, all three thousand, to love each other. He said, "I'm falling. China is coming down, collapsing, and there is nothing I can do about chasing away the barbarians who are using explosives to blow up the palaces. But I'm in control in Forbidden City." He did not care to know what it meant that three thousand women depended on one man's affection to survive. And that if they didn't get to mate with the Emperor and have a child with him, they were doomed: they would never be a mother, and never be touched by another man. So rivalry was life or death among them, and they would put anybody down who was trying to get close to the Emperor. So my villains are women, too. And you will see that society forces them into a small cage and locks them up. And it's a deformation, the process of it, just like binding feet.

My grandmother had bound feet. Starting when I was seven years old, I spent four months of the year with my grandmother in the village town right next to the Yangtze River. I drank, swam, and washed my chamber pot and the rice in the same river without getting sick. At night we didn't have electricity, and she tried to save the candles, so we would go to bed early and she would tell me stories. Her bed was so small we couldn't sleep side by side, so I ended up sleeping at her feet. And I studied those bound feet. They looked like rice cakes. I asked her how that was done. "How did your mother, my great-grandmother, have the heart to wrap your feet like that?" She said it was out of love because her mother wanted to show that her daughter was not born to be a laborer. She should be born to be carried around in the palanquin because men thought that was most sexy, women on high, high heels. You reduce your feet to a point so your buttocks sway when you walk.

DS: But you're basically helpless. You're hobbled.

MIN: Right. My grandmother said, "The hardest thing, the suffering, is not the moment my feet got bound, it was when I grew from four years old until seventeen years old." The infections, the toes that curled underneath the sole. It makes me wonder what kind of psychological impact this deformation caused this generation of women and their daughters. On the other hand, because of such desperate suppression, the women who fought it were incredibly strong. Survival of the fittest in Empress Orchid's case, Madame Mao's, and my own.

DS: And now? What changes do you see when you return?

MIN: Oh, yes, change in China. I can give you one example: the changing of the banners across Shanghai's busiest street. In the 1960s, the banner said, "Long live Chairman Mao, Long live the Cultural Revolution." In 1972, "Welcome President Nixon." I was ordered, along with the entire school, to stand at the corner to welcome President Nixon. There was no school that day. Everybody was ordered to gather along the street that his car would drive down. The entire city of Shanghai, 17 million people, was clapping with two red, wrinkled paper flowers in our hands that say, "warmest welcome." We were practicing, and we were told to be quiet until we heard the clapping sound rolling towards us. So we hear from many, many blocks away the sound of thunder, and we know it is our turn to sing. And I stretch out my neck and try to see this person even though I knew I probably wouldn't see him because the window would be black and with the curtain and everything. But to my surprise, I saw this face and I knew this face. You know why? He was on the shooting dummy; he was on our targets. I thought to myself, "The enemy." I had been trained to shoot the enemy with the big nose. And here he is smiling at us.

Then, in the 1980s the banner says, "Let's build 18 million toilets in Shanghai." And nowadays it says, "Borrowing is good." Do you see the change in China?

DS: Yes, the old enemy, capitalism, is fueling the new revolution. It's yet another time of rapid transition, just like Empress Orchid's era. Your novel ends just as her rule begins, and I understand that you're writing a second novel about her?

MIN: The sequel, yes. *The Last Empress,* which will be about how she ruled, about her struggle to hold China together and make reforms, and about how she manages the balancing act as a politician, a strategist, a mother, and a lover.

DS: This project must have taken over your life.

MIN: Oh yes. Sometimes I get so tired my husband would call my daughter and say, "Lauryann, come here and translate. Your mother is a machine. The translating machine is down. She is too tired." But she couldn't understand me. Also, I wanted to keep a Chinese flavor in the prose, and that's a big task.

DS: You've succeeded. *Empress Orchid* does have a Chinese sound and sensibility to it, and yet it reads like a classic historical novel in the English and American tradition. I wonder if you deliberately wrote a traditional English-language historical novel, if this is what you strived for?

MIN: I'm embarrassed to say that my English is not good enough for me to really read the good historical novels. I wanted to. It's my dream to some day sit down and read English that's not related to my research and really be able to enjoy it. As to readership, I was very pleased when it got on the *New York Times* bestseller list. I am surprised because I didn't think it really fit the popular mass market category.

DS: But the story is so compelling, and you were able to tell it in a way that even readers who don't usually read literary fiction, readers who just want story, would be hooked. And what a story. The particulars are unique, but the emotions and drama are universal. And a character like Orchid's mother-in-law, the Grand Empress, is such an intimidating and horrifying figure that everyone could relate to Orchid's suffering at her hand.

MIN: But when the Grand Empress curses her and yells at her, she insults her by saying, "You are illiterate." In China the worst thing you can say to a person is "You're such an illiterate." And now I wonder, will American readers get that?

DS: That's an interesting comment on illiteracy in America. So, you will tell the story of the second phase of Tzu Hsi's life. What about telling the second phase of your own story? Will you write more contemporary novels reflective of your life? Will you write a second memoir about your life in America?

MIN: Ah, well, as I've said, I do identify with the struggle to survive of both Tzu Hsi and Madame Mao. I thought that I would either die in China because I was considered Madame Mao's political debris or that I would kill myself because they were slowly killing me. I was coughing blood, and they were sending me to Tibet, knowing I had intestinal infections. I passed out on the road on the bicycle. They couldn't care less. They just wanted to finish me. But my other choice was to come to America, which to me was like going to the moon because it was soundless. I didn't speak English and knew nobody, but I was daring enough to give it a try.

I am considering writing another memoir, but you know, sometimes the more you write the less confident you are. I'm at that stage. Am I ready to comment on America? Do I know it? I don't have much distance. I need to develop a distance and a little bit of maturity. But my life has been very interesting. I've almost gone through the typical American life. I've been married and divorced and remarried; I'm raising an American child. My daughter said to me after she read Amy Tan's book, "Mom, I think I'm pretty fortunate. You're not as bad as their mother." She used to tell me, "Blah, blah, blah. I know all about your labor camp. I don't want to hear it."

Kate Moses

Kate Moses was born in San Francisco in 1962 to a British father and an American mother, a union mirrored in the marriage she so perceptively dramatizes in her first novel, *Wintering*, which is a lyrical portrait of the American poet Sylvia Plath and her husband, the British poet Ted Hughes. Before Moses transformed herself into a novelist, she worked as an editor and as the literary director for an arts group. She also cofounded *Salon*'s popular "Mothers Who Think" website, and with Camille Peri co-edited the American Book Award–winning anthology, *Mothers Who Think: Tales of Reallife Parenthood.* She and Peri have put together a second collection, *Because I Said So: 33 Mothers Write About Children, Sex, Men, Aging, Faith, Race, and Themselves.* Motherhood, in fact, was the path that brought Moses to Sylvia Plath.

By writing about Plath and Hughes, Moses bravely entered a contentious realm. A steady stream of biographical and critical works, many hagiographic in nature, have been written about Plath, who became a tragic and iconic figure due to the revolutionary power of her work, the shock of her suicide at age thirty in 1963 when her children were still very young, and Hughes's harshly criticized handling of her literary estate. But Moses eschewed speculation, gender politics, beatification, and vilification, and instead focused on the poems Plath organized into a manuscript titled *Ariel* not long before she died—because Moses discovered a simple fact lost in the furor over Plath's legacy: When Hughes published *Ariel,* he didn't follow the table of contents Plath left behind. Not only did he reorder the poems, he also omitted some poems altogether, and added poems Plath hadn't envisioned as part of the collection. This revelation is the impetus for *Wintering,* in which Moses follows the story Plath's poems tell in the order she intended them to be read. This approach provides a unique view of her final months, and a genuinely poetic work of fiction. Interestingly enough, a year and a half after *Wintering* was published, a restored edition of *Ariel,* structured as Plath intended it, was published in a handsome volume that includes a facsimile of Plath's original manuscript pages.

Kate Moses came to the studio in June 2003.

DONNA SEAMAN: When and why did your fascination with Sylvia Plath begin?

KATE MOSES: It began when I was pregnant with my first child, who's now fourteen. I had been introduced to Plath when I was in college, but in a very cursory way. I think I was handed some mimeographed poems, you know, "Daddy" and "Lady Lazarus," and told that these were written by a woman who committed suicide at thirty after taping her children up in their bedroom upstairs. At that point in my life, her anger and her despair were far too scary for me. But years later when I was about to become a mother myself, I came across a poem of Plath's called "Morning Song," about a woman who is waking in the night to nurse her baby daughter. And this poem struck me as not only completely unlike the Sylvia Plath I had expected, but also as an uncanny and original portrayal of the complicated emotions involved in going into motherhood. I went out and bought Plath's collected poems and took them with me to the hospital to give birth, which may have made the nurses think I was kind of an odd case. But it's Plath's motherhood and her ability to see her life in a new light through her children that compelled my interest and made me become a reader of her work—although I never expected to write about her.

DS: When the advanced galleys for *Wintering* came out, I sighed. I had already read a novel about Plath, Emma Tennant's *Sylvia and Ted,* as well as many gossipy and speculative nonfiction works about Plath and her husband, Ted Hughes, and her suicide, and was he culpable, and what had he done to her work. So when I first saw your book, I thought, "Are we entering a cult phase? Is Plath the new Virginia Woolf, so to speak, in terms of almost compulsive interpretation of a life both stellar in its artistry and tragic in its suffering and conclusion?" But when I started reading *Wintering*, I realized right away that you were creating a completely different Sylvia Plath. Your focus on her as a mother and someone who loved the domestic arts is much more inclusive and illuminating than the view of Plath as a wronged and furious warrior poet. But I'm wondering why, even though you focus on her last month, even her last days, you don't include her death in the novel.

MOSES: It was very much a conscious choice for a number of reasons. One of them was because her death is probably the best known fact about Plath, and I think in many ways it's too available to us. We probably know more than is decent about her death, and what drove me to write the story told in *Wintering* was Plath's struggle to live, not to die. I saw that, in putting the poems of *Ariel* together, she had been telling herself a story, a story of how she might be able to get herself out of this emotional and psychological mess her life had become after her marriage to Ted Hughes broke up. The story she told through her assembly of the manuscript of *Ariel* did not end with her death. It actually ended on a note of very fragile optimism that she could make it through to the spring. The last line in "Wintering," which, in her vision of the book, is the last poem, is: "The bees are flying. They taste the spring."

And in reading the poem as Plath intended, I realized that it presents an image of Plath that we don't recognize. We recognize her as that warrior, that furious suicidal warrior, and not as a woman who, in fact, was juggling all these elements in her life, and juggling them alone, and quite heroically.

DS: Yours is a redeeming vision of her. We lost a sense of Sylvia Plath as a human being with a body as well as a mind. We picture her as cerebral, as isolated from life, at her desk and deep within her depression. In your novel, *Wintering*, you linger over her incredible domestic industriousness. In scene after scene, there's Plath dirty and sweaty in the garden. She's forever planting, weeding, watering, harvesting. And she's painting furniture, making curtains and clothes, and cooking. You reveal that she worked exquisitely hard on everything she did, and held herself to high standards.

MOSES: I do think you're right. In some ways, Plath's humanity has been stripped away from her as she's become mythic and iconic. We've lost sight of the fact that she was a real person and, in fact, a woman who was struggling with these children by herself under incredibly awful circumstances. At the end of her life, she had no telephone, the weather was terrible, and she was basically cut off from any support system. She was in a hard place.

DS: And she had been betrayed. You track exactly what betrayal can do to a person's soul.

MOSES: One thing that I found interesting for myself, one of the questions I was asking as I approached her as a character, was "Why couldn't she make it?" Why did she make the choice to end her life? She had her children, and most mothers can understand the thought, "You stick around for the children, if nothing else." But she didn't just have the children. She also felt that she had attained the creative artistic maturity that she had wanted all her life. So she had this manuscript that she knew would make her name, and she had the kids. And she was trying to remake her life. So why didn't it stick? One concern I had was not just trying to answer that question for myself, but wondering if readers would be able to forgive her, in a certain way, for taking her own life. And many women, in particular, have come to me and said, "Now that I understand what her life was like at that time, I get it. It seems horrible and tragic that she killed herself, but it doesn't seem completely, unreachably mysterious any longer."

DS: What a compelling story it is. It's full of archetypal struggles as well as an artistic quest. Plath struggled with her inner demons and with her mother. At one point, she ended up hiding beneath her family's house in a strange sort of living burial.

MOSES: She did. Actually, it was awful. She turned twenty years old and basically had a nervous breakdown. Her mother, trying to help her, lined up a doctor who gave Plath electroshock therapy. But contrary to the most basic practices for that kind of treatment, she was given no painkiller to start her off. She didn't even have something to bite down on. She then got no support after the treatment, and no therapeutic help. Nothing at all. Later she said that, partly, the reason she tried to kill herself was because she couldn't bear the thought of having to go through yet another treatment. She would rather die. So she took an overdose of sleeping pills and crawled into the crawlspace at the foundation of her mother's house. In fact, she only survived because she had taken such an enormous overdose that she got rid of it herself. She got violently ill and was unconscious for three days before she was found.

DS: In *Ariel,* the Plath book you base your novel on, she revisits this terrible trauma in her Lady Lazarus image, and casts it as a re-birth, a resurrection. And she derives some power from this just as she is starting to derive power from her poetry. You do a fine job of illuminating the artistic process and how it can transmute suffering into beauty. This is your first novel, but it doesn't feel like a first book, nor does your approach to Plath's work seem like that of a novice. So I wonder what writing you had done prior to this.

MOSES: I decided when I was four years old that I wanted to write stories, that I wanted to tell stories, and that's all I ever wanted to do. That was my only dream. But I didn't have anything in my life that set me up to know how to do that, how to accomplish it. I didn't know anyone who could tell me, "You could go to school to learn how to write." I was very naive, and off on my own, but I did end up becoming a writer. I started writing short stories and trying to publish them when I was in my twenties. The first story that I sent out was not only published, it also won a tiny little prize, and so was published with an interview of me and a photograph. A few days later I was in the grocery store buying carrots, I remember, and a woman came up to me and said, "Are you Kate

Moses? I saw your picture in the newspaper. You wrote that short story." And I fled the store. I dropped the carrots and ran. I was exposed, and I literally did not try to publish another piece of fiction until *Wintering*. Instead, for many years I have been writing lots of nonfiction, but that's a very different animal. In fiction, you are baring yourself. It's all on you. There is nobody else who is your accomplice when you're writing fiction.

DS: There is an element of nonfiction, at least in the structure and impetus of your novel. You did do research, and you discovered something that inspired you to write about Plath.

MOSES: Yes, once I realized that Plath's book, *Ariel*, had never been published the way she had intended it to be, I knew I was compelled to tell that story. And I knew that it would reveal a side of her that no one paid attention to.

DS: It is surprising that this hasn't been addressed: the fact that Plath left behind a complete table of contents for the book, which is the result of a great deal of thought about how one poem plays off another, and what sort of arc they form when read in succession. Ted Hughes had her outline, and yet he chose to alter the order of the poems in the published version of *Ariel*, and he left some poems out altogether.

MOSES: It is quite amazing, considering how every stone has been overturned in terms of Plath, and yet this incredibly important detail about her as an artist and a person had never been explored.

DS: So in your novel, each chapter title is the title of one of the poems in *Ariel*, and you follow the order she intended.

MOSES: Exactly. The chapters in *Wintering* follow the story that Plath was telling herself, which was an alternate story of her own life, a way for her to find her way out of the labyrinth of her emotional distress. This has been overlooked by scholars, which was both shocking and very exciting to me. But I also realize that I'm not Sylvia Plath; I can't try to emulate her. What I can do is try to imagine how she thought and felt and saw the world, and express that in a way that seems true to her. And so I don't think that my writing style, my sort of long-winded lyricism, is actually very close to Plath's at all. She was razor-edged and very terse.

DS: One of the wonderful benefits of your novel is that it makes any conscientious reader go back to Plath's poetry, which I'm sure you hoped would happen.

MOSES: Oh, yes, she burns her words down like diamonds.

DS: The lines are short. They are over before you know it, and you have to go back and reread them immediately. So much is going on in each line.

MOSES: That's exactly it. She's packed so much into her word choice. She was very precise. And at the same time, if you look at her journals, she's constantly playing with different ways to say things, and different personas she can take on as the writer—even as the character in her own life. So what I tried to do stylistically in *Wintering* was to reflect the more informal risk-taking that you see in her journals, where she's trying different things in response to the many sensory experiences and intellectual experiences that constantly flashed over her brainpan. Which, I think, is probably why *Wintering* ended up being so dense, but also because I think that's the nature of Plath's imagination. It was utterly dense. It never stopped. Her doors of perception were wide open all the time.

DS: That's a very difficult way to live. For people of Plath's sort of artistic genius, madness lurks on the edges. They are vulnerable. Comparisons between Sylvia Plath and Virginia Woolf are apt on some levels. They were feeling everything all the time. I think of them as porous.

MOSES: That's the perfect word for it. There's also a psychiatric term, hyperacusis, which means extreme awareness of the physical aspect of your experience. What you're seeing and hearing and tasting and feeling is with you constantly. And, as you said, it's both an incredible burden and an incredible gift, and Plath was able to make art out of it for a time.

DS: I assume that you read everything, all the biographies, the letters, the journals.

MOSES: I tried to read everything. I'm sure there are some things out there that I didn't find.

DS: How hard was it to pull yourself away from all that reading, from being the great absorber of Plath lore and information, and turn to writing? Was the synthesis of all that material difficult for you? Did you have thousands of notebooks and index cards?

MOSES: I did. It actually required every cell of organizational skill I had in my body. From the start, I found I could not just set about researching and then be finished with it and write. Researching and writing were going on in tandem. So I set up a schedule for myself where basically I focused on an individual poem for about a week, and I just read and reread that poem and let every word become as precise as possible. I spent a lot of time with my abridged OED looking things up and pondering obscure allusions that she used and finding out what different words meant that I didn't have in my own vocabulary. Once I had the poem sort of laid bare, then I would spend another week trying to figure out why she put this poem in this particular spot in her manuscript. What story was it telling to her? I tried to let things rise to the surface. Then I took a few days of just kind of mulling it all over. I did that with every poem. So the research was going on constantly, and I would find in one poem the resonance for a poem seven poems down the line. So I was churning out massive amounts of notes, and I had to keep on top of it all the time or I would have been hopelessly lost.

DS: This description of your process explains why the novel works the way it does. You have internalized Plath's poetry, and made her distinctive language your own. As I read *Wintering*, certain words and images would appear, and I would think, "Oh, that's in this poem or that poem." But you've expanded it, you've made visible all that she concentrated inside her concise poetry. You perform a sort of literary jazz improvisation by taking her poems and riffing on them in longer phrases and within a more fully realized context.

MOSES: That's interesting that you say that because I described it to myself—as I was working—as "listening." I was listening really hard to the music that she was creating with her words, and also to the tonal qualities of that music. I was trying just to catch the tone. When I could hear it as I was writing it—*if* I could hear it, since I'm basically tone deaf—but if I actually felt that I could get into harmony with her, I knew I had it. Somehow I had gotten on to the wavelength that I needed to be on.

DS: Another aspect you bring out are the social mores of Plath's time, especially the expectations for women. Here's this poetic genius living in the 1950s and early 1960s when women were expected to be domestic divas, and she was terribly conflicted about her role as wife and mother, and her need to write. And Plath felt that she had to be perfect at everything. She had to be the perfect homemaker in, as you say, extremely difficult, if not impossible, situations. She and Hughes and their children were living in the English countryside. They were poor, and both were writing powerful work, and she tried to make a paradise out of their modest home. And every task was just horribly laborious, and the work was endless.

MOSES: It is amazing. I had to laugh at one point because one of the documents I looked at very closely was her 1962 daily date book, or calendar, in which she never says anything like, "Today I wrote the poem that will make my name." Instead, she was writing down when the trash needed to be put out, when their daughter, Frieda, needed a haircut, when she needed to wash her own hair. And then there was the day when she was preparing for her mother's first visit to Court Green. And, of course, she wanted everything to be perfect for her mother. On the same day that she was making clothes for Frieda, she was also painting the sewing machine to make it decorative. My Lord, she could not stop.

DS: There is something heroic in your effort on Plath's behalf. I feel that you've enhanced our understanding of her work and her life. But I have to say that sometimes fiction about revered writers and artists seems parasitic to me, as though a writer is attaching herself to Virginia Woolf or Frida Kahlo, for example, to draw on their powers. This can trivialize the achievements of the artist in question rather than illuminate them. And suffering women artists in particular seem to attract us in a morbid way. Plath is such a controversial and cultish figure, and since Ted Hughes's death, there's been a storm of new writings about his role in her suicide and his performance as executor of her estate, and myriad other personal matters, which are often sensationalized.

MOSES: That was a huge concern of mine. I did not want to become a part of the dogs who "are eating your mother," as Ted Hughes wrote in *Birthday Letters*. I only felt there was a reason for me to tell this story if it was revealing of Plath as an artist and as a human being in a way that was important to her artistic legacy. The reason to write this novel was because so little attention has been paid to Plath's *Ariel* manuscript and her artistic intentions. In some ways, I really did feel that I was trying to recreate a moment in her life when she had a very clear vision artistically but her personal crises overran her artistic vision so it couldn't ultimately be realized. I do think it's important to think about the intentions of any artist. If you take a Beethoven sonata and move the notes around, it's not going to be the same work. In the case of Plath, the *Ariel* that we all know was published after being reassembled, or assembled in a different format, by Ted Hughes. Not that it isn't still a very legitimate work. It is, but you must read it a different way. You can say that this is chronologically the emotional landscape of her work. But if you look at Plath's assembly, she wasn't looking at it chronologically. She was actually putting it together as a particular story, and we lose that if we don't read the poems in that order. As you were saying earlier, the poems have resonance to each other, and they say different things. They are not the same work of art in a different context.

DS: In the Sylvia Plath and Ted Hughes debate, whenever people lay too much of the burden on Ted Hughes, and even demonize him, I object because it diminishes Plath's integrity and legitimacy as a human being. It was her life. They were her problems. She struggled with them in her way. I greatly appreciate your portrayal of Hughes, and your understanding that however much they loved each other, a marriage between two creative geniuses is nearly doomed to failure. And he certainly suffered long and terribly.

MOSES: Oh, absolutely. I can't imagine how he ever got out of bed in the morning, frankly, given what he lived with. And I think, too, that it's essential that you offer compassion to people who are the survivors of such a tragic loss. To judge Ted Hughes's actions as harshly as they've been judged is vastly unfair. To make him the cause for her suicide in effect infantilizes her. She had more power than that.

DS: I wonder if you had some concern about tangling with the Plath and Hughes camps, and Plath's literary estate, since a tempest continues to rage.

MOSES: There were some things that I did very purposefully so I wouldn't have to take that world on because I was well aware of the reputation of the Plath and Hughes estate. They are for the most part very skeptical and unsupportive of any critical work about Plath or Hughes that does not match their own estimation of events. I also did not want to be accused of appropriating Sylvia Plath's words or appropriating the lives of her survivors, so I knew from the start that I would not quote from their work at all. Yes, her vocabulary resonates throughout *Wintering*, but her writing is never quoted, and it's all very carefully distanced, so that you might be picking up the rhythms of the poems, and, as we were saying, the music, but not the poems themselves. In terms of the children, because I'm a mother myself, I felt very uncomfortable about the idea of taking from Frieda and Nicholas Hughes, Plath's and Hughes's children, their mother's words about them because I really feel that is their true legacy. That's all they have. They were so little. What they have is what she wrote about them. So from the start, I decided that I would make them completely fictional and base them on my own children. And I checked in with my kids.

DS: Yes, you were also writing with a son and a daughter to care for.

MOSES: Yes, but the children saved me because I had to reinvest in my daily life with them, with my family, everyday at 3:00 P.M. I actually wrote most of the book on my dining room table because I didn't have an office until about three-quarters of the way through the book. So at 3:00 P.M., Sylvia had to go away. She had to go sit on the sideboard and make room for homework, and that was really good for me. There was a strange pull of yearning to be in this luscious writerly place in my head. I knew that the kids were keeping me from getting so deeply into it that I couldn't pull myself back out.

DS: I believe that, when you're involved in something creative, time spent away is crucial. That's when the subterranean working out of things gets accomplished. It's the classic scenario: you get up, you walk away, you start doing something else, and then, suddenly, something comes to you unbidden.

MOSES: My best writing times were always on the carpool drive from my house to school after I had spent the whole day working and struggling over something. Suddenly while I was in the car, I would be scrambling for a piece of paper. I was one of those bad drivers that everyone wants to avoid because I was trying to multi-task while I was driving.

DS: You help readers envision Plath tending the garden or working in the kitchen, her body busy with one task, her mind writing poetry.

MOSES: Yes, think about the poem "Cut": "What a thrill— / My thumb instead of an onion." She took this kitchen accident, in which she basically sliced off the top of her thumb, and realized that it was emblematic of the artistic release that she was feeling. And something about the combination of pleasure and pain was how she recognized that she'd made it. That she was actually the genius she had always hoped to be.

DS: One can't help but wonder if she could have sustained the intensity of her last works had she stayed alive?

MOSES: I thought a lot about a phrase from "Kindness," one of the last poems she wrote, which was not intended for *Ariel* but ultimately was published in it. It has the very oft-quoted lines, "The blood jet is poetry. / There is no stopping it." That sentiment, that idea, has reverberated in my mind a lot. On one hand it means that artistry was her life force. But at the same time, if the blood jet is unstoppable, what does that leave you with? I think Plath was too acute and too much a perfectionist as an artist not to know that she was writing on both sides of the fence, that poetry was both the gift and the tragedy of her life.

DS: Who besides Plath have you been reading?

MOSES: I read a lot of fiction and poetry by women, and actually a lot of memoirs too. I think my early reading education was lacking in writing by women, and I felt that I didn't have any models. So I've been playing catch-up for the last twenty years, and I'm sure I'll keep playing catch-up for rest of my life. I love Gish Jen and Lorrie Moore. I think there are so many incredibly talented women writers right now who are breaking the old sound barriers of what women were supposedly interested in and what was important. And I think that we find that the old idea that the domestic isn't important has been washed away because, in fact, there's no one topic that's more important than another as long as you're doing it with great imagination.

DS: Where do you go from here?

MOSES: I'm starting on another novel, which like *Wintering* is very much about the creation of a self, but it's set in 1989, which was a great year for revolution. Remember Tiananmen Square and the fall of the Berlin Wall. The Rumanian government fell, and the Soviet Union was falling apart, and that big earthquake happened in northern California. So I'm finding not a well-known person this time, but instead, a little person who has big things happening around her, rather than a huge personality with little things happening around her.

DS: This sounds like a good change. *Wintering* is claustrophobic. We're in a very few rooms, we're in a garden, a car, but mostly we're inside Sylvia Plath's head. A tough place to be.

MOSES: Exactly. You know, it was a rich place, but also a dark place. And so, yes, I'm going from a tiny burning under a microscope focus to looking at a much wider canvas, so we'll see how that works out.

One wonderful benefit for me as a writer is that because I tackled the giant in *Wintering*, I survived that heart palpitation of "Oh God, can I do this? Who put me in charge? Who do I think I am?" And ultimately, I feel that the Sylvia Plath in *Wintering* is not Sylvia Plath. She is a fictional fragment that I hope is in some way truthful to the real Sylvia Plath, but she could only be a partial picture. And being able to do that lets me know that it's worth taking the leap again.

SECTION THREE: WORLDS IN TRANSITION

There is much to be said for tightly focused novels that elucidate the workings of a character's consciousness and the intricacies of personal relationships. But most great and enduring novels illuminate life at both the micro and the macro levels, placing characters within a richly imagined social realm (often a world embroiled in violent change) and then critiquing that world and the plight of individuals within it. These novels enable us to appreciate what is universal and unchanging in the human spirit, and what is beneficial and destructive in our endless inquiry into the nature of the universe and quest for better lives, whether we define progress materialistically, politically, or spiritually.

The novel itself coalesced as a vital literary form just as the industrial age took hold and science and technology began to alter every aspect of life on earth. In this crucible Charles Dickens wrote, and George Eliot and Tolstoy, and Proust, James Joyce, D. H. Lawrence, Aldous Huxley, and George Orwell—all writers prescient in their perceptions of how profoundly extreme changes in our physical world, and in our relationship with nature, change the nature of our psyches, our beliefs and desires, expectations and values. Rapid and revolutionary changes in everything from medicine to agriculture, to how we travel and communicate, have not ceased over the past century and a half, nor have their impact on our inner lives. It comes as no surprise, therefore, that the complicated symbiosis between humankind and its inventions continues to intrigue, inspire, and goad novelists. Now that our astonishing and irresistible technologies are causing potentially dire changes to the biosphere, now that we live under the threat of nuclear annihilation, the stakes are even higher, and the artistic challenge for novelists trying to address such grim and thorny matters without turning didactic is even more daunting.

Some writers choose to write science fiction, the genre that came into its own in response to the war-stoked technological surge that brought us jets, rockets, television, computers, and nuclear weapons. Drawing on both their love of storytelling and a fascination with science, science fiction writers try to get ahead of the curve and imagine where we and our machines are heading, and how, given our past, we'll behave once we get there. Other writers choose to work on the cusp between mainstream and science fiction, writing what is called speculative fiction. This inventive form explores the ramifications of social trends, technological advances, and environmental change without sacrificing the psychological or aesthetic lushness of classic literature, or attention to what we think of as reality. This hybrid form lures readers who habitually avoid science fiction into reading novels that address the impact of technology and such attendant issues as the ethical questions raised by biotechnology. It may also seduce die-hard science fiction fans into reading outside the genre.

I have enjoyed talking about the fine line between social critique and story with three writers of conscience who manage never to overwhelm story with ideas, and yet who excel at satire. Margaret Atwood is uniquely adept at walking this literary tightrope, most notably in *The Handmaid's Tale, The Blind Assassin,* and *Oryx and Crake.* T. C. Boyle performs this balancing act in many of his short stories and novels, including *Friend of the Earth* and *Drop City.* And newcomer Alex Shakar flirts with futuristic visions by creating a world much like our own, only more so, in *The Savage Girl.*

Margaret Atwood

Margaret Atwood was born in 1939 in Ottawa, Ontario. She spent her childhood summers in the wilderness of northern Ontario and Quebec, where her father, an entomologist, conducted field research. Her family moved to Toronto in 1946. After graduating from the University of Toronto, she won a Woodrow Wilson Fellowship, which took her to Radcliffe College, where she earned her M.A. She then entered a doctoral program at Harvard University, though she never completed a dissertation. Returning to Canada, she worked briefly for a market research company, then taught at the University of British Columbia. Atwood began publishing poetry and criticism, and winning prizes, in the mid-1960s. She has published forty books—so far.

Readers all over the world have come to trust Atwood not only to tell a bewitching story, but also to shrewdly, even mischievously, assess the state of society and unveil the true nature of our follies and crimes, our dreams and transformations. Atwood is especially incisive in her rendering of the lives of girls and women. She rapidly attained a must-read status with her early novels, namely *The Edible Woman* and *Surfacing,* and the short story collection *Dancing Girls.* She then dissected women's friendships and rivalries in *Cat's Eye*—which also considers women in art, the art of autobiography, and the perils of interpretation—and in *The Robber Bride,* which enfolds arch variations on fairy tales with peppery inquiries into war, fashion, and immortality. Atwood dramatizes nineteenth-century notions of class, femininity, sanity, and criminality in *Alias, Grace,* and questions the nature of inheritance, privilege, fantasy, and storytelling in the *The Blind Assassin,* winner of the Booker Prize.

A versatile fiction writer who takes a different approach in each of her short stories and novels, Atwood is also a poet, a children's book author, and an electrifying essayist and critic. A writer of conscience, she seeks to balance the demands of art with those of social responsibility, literature with commentary. Atwood considers this high-wire act, and many other facets of the writer's calling, with candor and wisdom in *Negotiating with the Dead: A Writer on Writing*, and she has collected her essays and other prose works in *Writing with Intent*. Free to write overtly about political matters in her nonfiction, Atwood takes a more subversive approach to complex issues in her fiction, most famously in the futuristic novel, *The Handmaid's Tale*. A magnet for awards, including the Arthur C. Clarke science fiction award, *The Handmaid's Tale* was made into a film in 1990 from a screenplay by playwright Harold Pinter. Atwood presents another galvanizing work of speculative fiction in *Oryx and Crake,* the primary subject of our conversation.

Atwood is sharply attuned to the way the practice of science, with its much trumpeted claim of objectivity, can engender a hubristic sense of omnipotence and detachment from the reality of life. The potentially dire consequences she explores in *Oryx and Crake* are integral to her ongoing fascination with power and powerlessness. And one form of power that particularly intrigues Atwood is the power associated with the telling of stories, whether it's the story of the self, a community, or a belief system. This fascination with how stories are told, who listens to them, and how they are understood resonates at the very heart of Atwood's work. Improvising on classic literary motifs while creating eroticism, suspense, and sly humor, Atwood seduces her readers into asking what it means to be human, and what sort of future we're inadvertently setting in motion in the dizzying present.

Margaret Atwood appeared on *Open Books* in May 2003.

DONNA SEAMAN: You've written that *Oryx and Crake* came to you in an epiphany.

MARGARET ATWOOD: That makes me sound a bit loony, but you do have ideas for books that come quite suddenly. I was in Australia, in point of fact, on a little expedition that I sandwiched into a book tour there. I was looking over the side of a balcony at a small Australian bird called the red-necked crake, the bird that gave its name to one of the protagonists of the book, and at that moment I had the "ah-ha" experience: Ah-ha here comes a novel. And there I was without any implement such as a typewriter or a computer, but I had the ever-ready ballpoint pen and shred of paper. So I began the book, and I continued it partly on a boat in the Arctic, where I went that summer and where I wrote the chapter about Jimmy and Crake in high school.

DS: As in *The Handmaid's Tale,* which I would place beside George Orwell's *1984* and Aldous Huxley's *Brave New World,* you take current social situations and technical capabilities to one possible and harrowing conclusion, imagining in *Oryx and Crake* dire consequences of our present-day biotechnologies. Did one particular, so-called advance in this field catch your attention and trigger the novel?

ATWOOD: Not really. I'd say a whole bunch of them. It's rather chilling to note that since I finished the book, more things have been happening, including the ability to create a virus from scratch. A man actually made a polio virus from the bits, and when asked why he did that, which you and I might take to be a question about why would you do such a dangerous thing, he took it to be another kind of question, and said, "Because it was a simple virus and easy to make."

DS: Were you working on *Oryx and Crake* during the anthrax scare?

ATWOOD: I stopped working on it. I glued myself to the screen. First of all, I was in the Toronto airport waiting to get on a plane to New York on the very morning of September 11. I was within fifteen minutes of boarding the plane when they said this thing had happened to tower number one. I thought, in a naive, silly way, "Oh dear, someone has had a heart attack. There's been an accident." And I cheerfully rebooked myself for 3:30 that afternoon and thought, "I'll just stay at the plane station," cause there's no point to going back and forth. So I was sitting there watching when plane number two went in, at which point I said to myself, "That was not a heart attack; I think I'll get into a taxi and go home," which I did in a pale condition. My agent, my publishers, and my assistant were all down there because we were going to meet up and do the paperback launch for *The Blind Assassin,* and I was going to go on book tour again. All of that got cancelled and postponed, and I stopped writing and I watched with very large eyes. Then the anthrax thing came along, and that was somehow even more applicable to the book.

DS: The questions of who would do such things, and why, must fascinate you, as a storyteller and novelist.

ATWOOD: Just think about who would get into an airplane, or on a bus, and blow themselves up to achieve some end, to fulfill some overriding idea, to prove a point that they feel is more important than whatever destruction they may cause.

DS: Is your mad scientist character, Crake, among such zealots, or is he more complicated, less certain?

ATWOOD: I would say that he's more complicated. Most people who do that kind of thing, either terrorism in which you get away unscathed yourself, or the kind in which you don't, assume that it will benefit the group they represent. Crake is more complicated in that he is fed up with the group of which he is a representative, namely human beings. He thinks he can improve on that.

DS: *Oryx and Crake* riffs on many classic motifs. There's the castaway in the wilderness; as the novel opens your hero, who calls himself Snowman, as in Abomidable, is living in a tree in a blasted landscape strewn with wreckage. Then as the reader begins to understand that there's been an apocalypse of some sort, the story takes on a kind of postnuclear war storyline, the sole survivor theme.

ATWOOD: That vision of the postnuclear world began to appear in fiction in the 1960s. There's a wonderful postnuclear book called *Riddley Walker,* in which the author, Russell Hoban, has invented a new language and other things, and people are essentially living in the Stone Age, although they're excavating iron from holes in the ground. I like that book a lot. Of course, people of my generation were brought up on such books as *Robinson Crusoe* and *Treasure Island,* an all-time favorite. And I had a tree house as a child. We built it. It was a bit ramshackle, but it's an appealing idea for children to be able to go up in a tree. You're hidden but you can see, and people on the ground can't get at you, or so you fondly believe. So maybe it's just a recreation of a childhood fantasy.

In any case, a tree is the logical place for such a person as Snowman to consider what's running around on the ground. Some are the ordinary things, such as rats and what have you, but some are experiments in animal husbandry and alteration, of which we already have some on earth—note the luminous blue fish reported in the *Wall Street Journal* last week, and the luminous green rabbit which has been around for some years, which did make it into the book. In the novel, we also have a rakunk, which is a blend of racoon and skunk, and I'm all in favor of it. I think it would make a very nice pet, not smelly, not destructive like racoons, very cute. But there are some others that probably were mistakes, for instance, they made a snat at one point, a blend of snake and rat, and multiple-organ pigs. In our world, scientists are now growing transgenic, knockout pigs in the hope that these pigs will produce kidneys and livers that will be of use to you and me, should we want a kidney or a liver. They might even be able to be customized for us, so that we can accept them without complications. This may actually work, but in my book, the pigs have become multiple-organ growers, so they're quite big, and they're also very smart. And these scary pigs have gotten out of the lab.

DS: Those are the pigoons. They pose quite a challenge to Snowman, and they connect to his past. As the novel progresses, Snowman is not only coping with his current, extremely trying circumstances, he's also coping with a tide of painful memories. It seems that his parents were involved in creating the pigoons. They're an interesting couple. They live in a high-tech, high-security compound, the ultimate gated community, which the father, an enthusiastic member of the establishment, compares to the castles of old.

ATWOOD: Well, that's what such places are like. They're to keep you in and "them" out, "them" being anybody you don't want to let in. In the case of a place growing animals like the pigoons, you wouldn't want anybody coming in and sprinkling hoof-and-mouth disease over them just to eliminate the competition.

DS: This is a corporate kingdom.

ATWOOD: You bet.

DS: Jimmy's mother—Snowman was Jimmy in his former life— rebels. She rejects the "moral cesspool" that she finds herself in. She eventually leaves and becomes a fugitive, a figure in the book who becomes a moral touchstone.

ATWOOD: In a way, although she does some immoral things. She puts, for instance, all these interests of hers over and above her son. She even gives away his pet rakunk.

DS: And she abandons him, and puts him in danger. But I felt that you made her case clearly: she's been broken, and she's been driven away.

ATWOOD: She has a case, and she's in a corner. Because once you're in, you're in. It's very hard to get out.

DS: Survival becomes the main impetus here, as it so often does in your work. Oryx, the female protagonist, epitomizes this. Her story is so powerful, I wondered what the source was.

ATWOOD: I tried not to have anything in the book that was not backed up by newspaper and magazine clippings and book references, all kept in the big, brown research box we store in the cellar, and to which we keep adding daily as it turns out. There have been a lot of stories about children like Oryx—about the child sex trade, the smuggling of young women from country to country, people in poorer countries selling their children in order to feed their other children. There have even been scandals involving such people living in garages and other places in the United States under the guise of being maids or something like that. So it is a widespread practice and it's enormously lucrative. A lot of people are making money out of it.

And Jimmy and Crake, when they are adolescent boys, do what a lot of adolescent boys do, which is they surf the Net, and some of the things that they surf are live-time execution shows for which there is a considerable lobby now; some people think this would be a great idea. And they also look at porn sites, and that is where they first see Oryx, on a child porn site.

DS: Another of their pastimes is playing computer games, and they play quite a variety, including one called Extinctathon.

ATWOOD: Yes, it's played with animals that have gone extinct in the last fifty years. They also play Blood and Roses, which is a game in which you pit human atrocities against human achievements, and they play one called Barbarian Stomp, in which one side is barbarians and the other side is civilized societies, and you get to replay history, but you have to use civilized societies and real barbarians and see if you can alter history by having a different side win than the side that did win.

DS: The world you conjure in *Oryx and Crake* is one in which the profit motive has run amok, and corporations have replaced government and all other systems that were meant to be ethical systems. This has an unnerving ring of truth to it.

ATWOOD: The book to read on all of that is Jane Jacobs's *Systems of Survival*, in which she says that there are actually two ethical systems that people have always used. One has to do with those whom she calls guardians, who are supposed to be in charge of policing the rules and regulations societies have. They're not supposed to engage in trade, or take bribes, or any of those things. The other set has to do with the ethics governing commercial transactions and people who are doing trade, and they're quite different. She says that monstrosities happen when the two mix. I would say that monstrosities also happen when you sacrifice one and have only the other. When you sacrifice the entrepreneurial part of humanity, which is involved in inventing things and selling things, you sacrifice that dynamic. When you put it under state control you get something like the U.S.S.R. If you sacrifice all government and take away all watchdogs and people regulating things, you get something like the world in my book, in which it's no-holds-barred competition with every dirty trick that you can think of thrown in. That's why you have to have unscalable walls around your commercial enterprises because you'll be raided. Where do we draw the line?

DS: Crake admits to Jimmy that the medical industry became concerned that there weren't enough diseases left for insiders to continue getting rich. Their solution? Invent and introduce new diseases to keep the industry healthy.

ATWOOD: And we hear of a new disease every day. It's as if all of the old diseases have split into about ten new diseases. A lot of stuff used to be called consumption. We didn't know what it was. Or brain fever. I always liked "brain fever" in the nineteenth century. Or they'd say, "He went into a decline." Now we know that these declines and brain fevers could be one of a hundred different things. So we do have a lot of diseases already, but what if we were able to cure and treat and get rid of them? And what if, at the same time, the medical profession were completely privatized and run on the profit motive? Then you would have a secret hankering, in fact it would be an almost irresistible temptation, to introduce a few new diseases here and there of the lingering kind, the sort that kill people slowly so that their money and their life end at about the same time.

DS: How diabolical. This sort of imagining, of speculating, of extrapolating, is what makes *The Handmaid's Tale* and *Oryx and Crake* and *Riddley Walker* and *1984* so powerful. Is fiction the way to approach such conundrums, the best forum for addressing complex issues more evocatively than one can in nonfiction? And more people read a novels than a book like Jane Jabobs's, brilliant as it is. Are you motivated in any way by this?

ATWOOD: I am a natural fiction writer and I'm not a natural writer of books of philosophy. In fact, I couldn't write a book of that other kind. So I just do what I can, not because I think it's a way of saving the world. I doubt very much whether this book will do that. But because novels are always about individuals in situations, and because you don't understand the import of a discovery, or of a social change, unless you can see yourself in it, or see yourself as an individual person with your life being affected by it, they may have a strong impact. That is why I set *The Handmaid's Tale* in Cambridge, Massachusetts. All of the things I write about had been done or were happening elsewhere, but they weren't happening here, where we are. It's when you take such things and have them happen to people like you that you realize what it would be like.

DS: So you seek to awaken empathy.

ATWOOD: Yes, to be unable to say, "That's them. This is us. We're different. It would never happen here."

DS: Nature is always a powerful and provocative presence in your work, but this is your most overt grappling yet with the state of nature now. I wonder if in your obviously vast reading you've looked at other contemporary novels that address questions of nature in a new and incisive way. I'm thinking of T. C. Boyle's novels *A Friend of the Earth* and *Drop City*. Barbara Kingsolver's *Prodigal Summer* and *Poisonwood Bible*. And Annie Proulx, who has always written about the wild, and who takes on industrial agriculture in *That Old Ace in the Hole*.

ATWOOD: I'm glad that such recognition is happening. And yes, I read books on this subject, although not necessarily novels. I am of the Rachel Carson generation. Remember *Silent Spring*? I have known people like Carson all my life because my father was a biologist and one of the early people involved in environmental organizations and doing that sort of thinking. He was an early member of the Sierra Club, for instance, and the Ontario Naturalists. Other people involved used to come over to the house, so I really grew up with it. I was familiar with that kind of writing in the early days, and it's much more prevalent and much more recognized now. People are much more environmentally conscious, and therefore stories about environmental issues make not just teeny little backpage mention in the newspaper, but have moved up much closer to the front. Help is on the way.

As for genetic engineering, there's another book that is of great interest, a nonfiction book, *Enough: Staying Human in an Engineered Age,* by Bill McKibben. It has just been published, and I've noticed it in airport bookstores, so it must have made some waves. He goes into, in some detail, the changes biotech people are contemplating: what has already been done, what can be done, and what the effects might be. By a great coincidence, I've just finished doing a review of it for the *New York Review of Books.* Who knew he was writing it? Not me. Who knew it would be published at the same time as *Oryx and Crake*? Certainly not me. But along it came and I'm finding it very handy. I can say, "You may think I'm crazy, but read this book."

DS: Our perceptions of our relationship with nature have always been part of the stories we tell about ourselves. To see this focus developed so keenly and deliberately in both fiction and nonfiction, now, at a time when this subject is so urgent is quite intriguing: a sign of raised consciousness, and hope, perhaps. I think the synergy between writers such as yourself and McKibben is important and significant. Interestingly enough both the science writer Michael Pollan, and Ruth Ozeki, a novelist, have recently written about genetically engineered potatoes, he in *The Botany of Desire,* she in a novel titled *All Over Creation.*

ATWOOD: Oh, goody. Let me read that. Insects have already adapted to one of the grains that they've engineered to be repellent to the insects that eat it. It turns out that the insects like the genetically engineered grain better, and they get bigger eating it then they did before. It's the doctrine of unintended consequences. As my father, an entomologist, always said—at which point I would excuse myself and go off to read Sherlock Holmes—the insects can reproduce so much faster than we can think of things to sprinkle on them, sooner or later they will become resistant.

DS: We need truly to understand the connections between things, the fact that there are no borders in nature. You can't keep genetically engineered crops in one place. The wind carries seeds and pollen; birds and insects carry seeds and pollen. Ecological awareness needs to be taught more effectively.

ATWOOD: Of course. What we got at school was the collect-the-autumn-leaf project. You were supposed to press them between two pieces of wax paper and glue them into your autumn leaf book. We didn't go into nature in a very systemic way in those days. People are now looking at the biosphere as a total system, and children are being taught that. You can't be too horrible about it, though, because it just makes them discouraged.

DS: That's true, and you've reminded me to remark on the fact that *Oryx and Crake* is as funny as it is powerful. Snowman loves language, loves books. He says that he's not a numbers person, as the more successful of his peers are, and consequently he's sent to the rather shabby Martha Graham Arts Academy. I found this section of the novel hilarious.

ATWOOD. The arts academy is not getting funding anymore. In the future, art is just a frill. And I can't say that what they have to eat in the cafeteria is very nice. Whereas Crake, who is a numbers person, goes off to the Watson-Crick Institute, and they get real shrimp. So Jimmy has a rather thin time at the Martha Graham Academy, except for the young women who want to be artists and actresses and who enable him to have a more sexually fun time than the guys at the Watson-Crick Institute, where sex is supplied on demand by Student Services so the students won't get distracted by having to have relationships.

DS: There's also a great deal of humor in Snowman's relationship with the curious tribe of people he lives near, who, unlike him, can run around unharmed beneath the brutal sun in this post-ozone era. They have no conception of the past, of the lost world. Snowman serves as their guru, reluctantly, yet as responsibly as he can. He finds himself in the difficult position of having to provide them with stories to explain their origins, their cosmology. Eventually the reader finds out that these are people designed by Crake, and their growing need for story, for an explanation of their very existence, provides an ideal way for you to talk about what it means to be human.

ATWOOD: Crake has made them in the hope that they wouldn't have such needs, but he hasn't managed to get rid of their curiosity altogether, and they do start asking questions, like "Where did we come from?" At that point, Snowman has to tell them something, so he does. He has to put it in terms that they can understand, so he creates for them a mythology. It goes on from there because they keep wanting to know more about it.

DS: He gets himself trapped, as liars do, in all sorts of corners.

ATWOOD: No mythology that I know anything about is completely consistent internally. They are all a bit ambiguous. The one he makes up is no different, except that he finds himself featuring in it somewhat against his will.

DS: He's telling them a story, and he uses the expression, "I was toast." Then he stops because he realizes he's made a mistake: they don't know what toast is. At that moment, you open up a portal onto civilization as he struggles to explain about grain and flour and baking and electricity.

ATWOOD: They don't know what any of those things are. Explaining anything in real terms is just hopeless. He can't do it, so he says other things instead. At one point, they want to know how Crake was born, because he's made Crake their creator. Snowman decides he can't have Crake being born because that would open up a whole other set of questions about Crake's childhood, Crake's mother. So he just says Crake came down out of the sky.

DS: In addition to looking after the people of Crake, Snowman's other occupation is to try to stay sane. He's grieving. He's lost everyone and everything. He's in danger, and he's anxious to tell his own story.

ATWOOD: But he knows that if he tells it to these people they won't be able to understand it at all. So he tells it to himself and we get to listen in.

DS: Often in your novels, the telling of one's story is intrinsic to survival. Is story the essence of self?

ATWOOD: I think actually it is. Or it's very close to being the essence of self. You probably know the books of Oliver Sacks about people who have lost their long-term memory; they exist only in the present. They're still a person, but not a person like you or me. Such people can't look back. They're just in the now. Most of us, who haven't lost our memories in that way, build who we are on who we have been, and on decisions that we have made and relationships we've had and things that have happened to us. We are, in a sense, the accumulation of the many stories that make up a story, but we're also constantly revising our story and getting a different perspective on it.

I was talking to a man recently who was talking to another man who works in palliative care, and he asked him what it is that people are left with at the end of their life. And he said, "They're left with their stories." And that is really all. No matter how rich they have been, they're not going to have wealth anymore. They're not going to have possessions anymore. But they have their story, and even if they have lost their memory of that story, other people know their story. So there's the idea of passing on the story, so that someone else will then be able to tell it.

There's a moment in a television play called *Playing for Time,* which aired some years ago, in which Vanessa Redgrave was portraying a violinist who had been put in a concentration camp. An old man gives her a sausage and he says, "I want you to have this instead of me because you may be able to survive and then you can tell this story."

The function of the witness is to tell the other person the story. That's probably why people write diaries and journals and leave them lying around for other people to stumble on later and why people in dangerous situations often write things and hide them, or smuggle them out. That feeling that you have to tell what you saw and what really happened is a very strong, human impulse. We are a narrating animal.

T. C. Boyle

Thomas Coraghessan Boyle has a remarkable gift for simultaneously defining and commenting on the zeitgeist of paradigm-alter-
ing times. He's a daring, provocative, and prolific novelist and short
story writer who exposes the obsessions, innovations, ironies, failings, and paradoxes of each milieu he portrays with vivid description, convincingly human yet iconic figures, and rollicking stories
spiked with humor and steeped in compassion. Boyle works large,
grappling with complex social conundrums related to family, class,
work, immigration, mental health, sexuality, gender roles, technology, and most resoundingly, our view of nature and our place
within it.

Born in 1948, Boyle grew up in Peekskill, New York, on the
Hudson River, where he lived the rock-and-roll life as a teenager,
singing and playing drums in a band and running wild. He attended the State University of New York at Potsdam, then taught
high-school English back in Peekskill. After having a story published in *North American Review,* Boyle was accepted into the
Iowa Writers' Workshop and received a doctorate in nineteenth-
century English literature from the University of Iowa. His stories
began appearing in the *Atlantic Monthly, Esquire, Harper's* and
Penthouse, and his first book, *Descent of Man,* is a short story collection. He began teaching at the University of Southern California in 1977.

Boyle has written six books of short stories, which include
Greasy Lake, Without a Hero, and *After the Plague.* His ten novels, many of which involve fictionalizations of real-life people, include *The Road to Wellville,* a high-jinx portrait of turn-of-the-
nineteenth-century health maniac John Harvey Kellog, which was
made into a film directed by Alan Parker; *The Tortilla Curtain,* a

tale about illegal immigration and winner of France's *Prix Medicis Etranger; Riven Rock,* a historical novel based on the life and psychosis of Stanley McCormick, heir to the millionaire inventor, Cyrus; *A Friend of the Earth,* a tale about an ecowarrior; and the 1960s saga *Drop City.* A master fiction writer and an audacious satirist, Boyle is a risk-taker and social critic with a sharp wit and a supple imagination.

For all his love of the solitude of writing and solo walks in the wilderness surrounding his home in Santa Barbara, California, Boyle has made public appearances, both in person and on television, an integral aspect of his literary life, and he attracts large and enthusiastic audiences wherever he goes. In keeping with his zeal for connecting with readers, he also maintains a lively website and continues to teach. A trickster who loves to toy with the interview process, Boyle joined me on *Open Books* while he was on tour with *A Friend of the Earth* in 2000, and again with *Drop City* in 2002. We had planned to talk once more, about *The Inner Circle,* the novel inspired by Dr. Alfred Kinsey's pioneering sex research, but circumstances conspired against us. So here are two conversations with T. C. Boyle, a keen observer and intrepid satirist of our densely populated, technology-addled, precarious, and precious world.

DONNA SEAMAN: *A Friend of the Earth* begins dramatically twenty-five years in the future during a ferocious rainstorm, a consequence of global warming. We meet a seventy-five-year-old ecowarrior named Tyrone Tierwater, and it doesn't take long for the reader to recognize that this is a work of ecofiction, one that reminds me of the work of Edward Abbey. Are you a fan of Abbey?

T. C. BOYLE: Yes, of course. Abbey began the whole idea of monkey-wrenching, with his novel *The Monkey Wrench Gang,* which inspired people like Dave Foreman of Earth First! The reason I've chosen to set this novel in the future is because I'm having fun with what appears on the front pages of the paper everyday. Every day, it's something worse. I'm having fun with our doom, with the slow degradation of everything that makes life worthwhile. I've never set a book in the future before. I've never read science fiction. I don't know anything about it. I'm more of a satirist—but, I hope, one with a heart—and I'm just trying to sort out my feelings about all the extinctions we're causing.

DS: You go to the future, and yet as you often are, you're inspired by real-life figures, in this case Julia "Butterfly" Hill, who lived for two years in the branches of a California redwood tree.

BOYLE: Half the book is set in 2025, and the other half flashes back to when Ty Tierwater, his wife, Andrea, and his daughter, Sierra, were members of a radical environmental group called Earth Forever! And yes, I was writing the book when Julia Hill went up her tree, and she did become an inspiration for these sections of the book. The book was finished before she came down; she stayed in her tree for two years. Sierra Tierwater stayed in her tree for three years. I don't want to give too much away for those seventeen or eighteen people in the world who still haven't read *A Friend of the Earth*, but she comes down a lot less gracefully than the actual Julia "Butterfly" Hill.

DS: Not only is this novel about the degradation of nature, but it also tells a passionate father-and-daughter story, that of Ty and Sierra.

BOYLE: I have a daughter, and I was thinking of her, of course, when I was writing the character of Sierra, especially in her Goth phase. My daughter is also a vegetarian. She became a vegetarian at the age of about eleven. Her aunt lives in Venice Beach, and my daughter was seen in close communication one day with the "Meat-is-Murder" guy. After that, no more meat.

As I said earlier, I love satire. I love writers like Evelyn Waugh or Kingsley Amis for the pure joy and fun and hilarity of their books. But I also think that most satire has a limitation: it has no heart. It tells you that this is ridiculous and you shouldn't behave like this, but what next? So I'm trying to do both. I'm trying to address a serious concern of mine, and I'm also trying to create some human characters to complicate my view of this concern and provoke the reader and move the reader, as well as make the reader laugh.

DS: You complicate things for yourself. I think many people read in the hope of finding things simplified.

BOYLE: People can read the latest thriller or vampire novel if they want things simplified. But I think really great literature should be as captivating story-wise as those popular genres, but it should do a lot more for you, that is, provoke you to think. Earlier today, I was on a show where the host asked me, "So what is your message?" I don't have a message, except that things are really bad. I write all my stories and books as a way of ordering how I feel about various things going on in the very mysterious world we live in.

DS: In *A Friend of the Earth,* you delve, not uncritically, into various aspects of the environmental movement.

BOYLE: Ty, like most people, had thought about the environment in a vague way. He was vaguely worried about the headlines in the paper, but like all of us he just lived and breathed and ate and tore up the environment without really knowing about it. It was his wife, Andrea, who was in the forefront of the movement. She got him involved. Then, as is often the case with such people, he became over-involved, obsessively involved, crazily involved, so that he could not shut it off. When the novel begins in 2025 after a series of storms, he's out there cleaning up, a grumbling grumpy old man of seventy-five—not really old though, one of the young old, not the old old. The phone rings, and it's his ex-wife coming back to see him because she has an agenda. I should also say that, unlike most of my books, this one has what you might call a happy ending. Okay, the world is destroyed, everything is extinct, everybody is miserable, but at least we have a love story.

As far as addressing the question of the environmental movement, I am an environmentalist. I wish that we could save the environment, not only for our own species but for all the other creatures. However, I'm not writing a tract, and I don't have a platform. I'm trying to create believable realistic characters. I think it's very difficult to paint somebody as a truly saintly character because nobody is truly saintly. So yes, I do poke some fun at these characters and at some of the environmental extremists, and I'm poking fun at their enemies, corporations like Coast Lumber.

DS: You orchestrate amazing and dismaying confrontations. I'm thinking in particular of the powerful scene, a flashback to 1989, when Ty and Andrea and Teo and Sierra cement themselves into a trench to prevent loggers from cutting down a forest.

BOYLE: I begin the book in the past, in 1989, with this scene, which is based on a real event in which some environmental activists cemented themselves up to their shins across a logging road to prevent the logging trucks from getting through. I had Tierwater, Andrea, his fourteen-year-old daughter, and another radical, Teo, do this. I do like it as an opening. It's mysterious. You don't know what's happening. It's night. You're wondering, what are they doing? What's coming next? But as I worked with it, I wanted to hear more of Tierwater's voice because he is narrating in a third-person mode. It's not me, it's him. He gives it color because he's cranky. He's been through this, he's looking back. So I came up with the idea of writing the current sections, those set in 2025, in the first-person. I stepped back from that chapter and wrote the prologue, and then the book went straight through. That was the little key that made it work for me.

DS: You're writing about how we've driven so many animal species into extinction, and yet nature remains an undaunted force. It is a power that kills people via both murderous storms and a bee sting.

BOYLE: Since the beginning of my career, since my first book, *Descent of Man,* I've had a very cold and Darwinian view of human nature. We are an animal species in a biosphere, in an environment. Of course, everyone says, "Save the earth." The earth doesn't need saving; it's our species that needs saving, and the various species we're driving into extinction. A lot of people don't understand how severe the crisis of extinction is. In all the books that I've read in preparation for this, such as *The Sixth Extinction* by Richard Leakey, there is not a ray of hope; it is so utterly depressing. We are in the middle of the sixth extinction according to Leakey, and we are slowly destroying the habitat of the remaining animals on earth. We have depleted the forests and the seas; what are we going to eat? There are six billion people. Where does that leave us?

DS: We're probably in the sixth wave of denial.

BOYLE: Two years ago, when I was putting together my collected stories, I included one from my first book called "The Extinction Tales." In it, I tell encapsulated versions of various animals that have gone instinct, and I was bemoaning the fact then that there were 3.5 billion people on the earth and that's why these animals were going instinct. That was only twenty-five years ago; now we are six billion. That is the problem, and it is a problem without resolution except that any animal species will be curbed by its environment. It sounds cold. It sounds hard to refer to you and me and our loved ones as animals, but we are. It also seems cold to talk about six billion people without mentioning that one third of them are dying now because they have no resources and no food, the sad facts of desertification, for instance. And we do do things that are very admirable to help stop it, but the effort is so small compared to the largeness of the problem. And as you say, no one really wants to talk about it. Most people don't even know that the problem is monumental. It's impossible.

DS: It really is a puzzle. As Ty says, "To be a friend of the earth, you have to be an enemy of the people."

BOYLE: Which is a cold way of looking at things, but that is what environmentalists do, and must do.

DS: As wilderness vanishes and animals go extinct, our changing perception of diminished nature is changing us psychically and spiritually.

BOYLE: It's interesting. I've just been reading Sven Birkerts's book of essays called *Readings*. He's a literary critic, but in this one essay he's musing about the way we are dominated by time, our various busy schedules, and the piles of information thrust at us. I had been thinking a lot about this myself lately. We don't have contemplative time even to read a book, let alone take a walk in the woods. I spend a lot of time in the woods by myself, or out in the backyard of my house by myself doing physical labor. What I love most is to walk in the Sierra Nevada after work, just to go out there and not have a thought. I'm not resolving great problems of art. I'm not solving the problems of the human race. I'm not even solving the problem of what to cook for dinner. I have no conscious thoughts. I'm like a child in nature. You just see the next bend of the river or the next tree. You are suddenly aware of sound. It's so silent in the Sierra Nevada in winter that I became aware for the first time in my life a couple of years ago that you can hear crows' wings creak as they fly over. That is wonderful. To have an experience like that is amazing. To be out of your own conscious mind is a great experience, and I think that's what nature gives us. If we don't have any nature then maybe we'll have a more difficult time getting to that place. I'm starting to sound like a new-age guru or something, and I'm not. It's just a personal experience that I treasure.

DS: I think that solitude, quiet, and communion with nature are necessary for everyone. Everyone benefits from time spent outdoors, and I think it's especially important for artists. Silence and openness to nature are part of the creative process. And I often think about how crucial nature is to literature. All the classic tropes and metaphors are based on the natural world, metaphors about flowers, trees, birds, rivers. Everyone used to know exactly what these allusions meant from direct experience. But now children are growing up with no understanding of how vegetables grow, or where fruit comes from, so much so that these comparisons, traditional poetics, may become purely abstract—a dead language.

BOYLE: I hadn't thought of that with regard to the impoverishment of experience in language. Have you observed this as a phenomenon, that people's metaphors are no longer so much oriented toward nature as toward K-Mart, for instance, or automobiles or TV?

DS: Yes—fast food, sitcoms—I am starting to see that. And I'm also noticing that in some instances literature is losing its exquisite specificity. I remember reading, say, Katherine Mansfield, or Faulkner, and being amazed at how many flowers and trees they name precisely, and at the beauty and resonance embodied in the exact naming of living things.

BOYLE: It took me all my life to know the names of animals and plants. You will notice in my last couple of books, for instance in *Riven Rock,* Katherine loves science and she always names the scientific names of things. I'm fascinated by that. My experience of nature as a child was much purer than it is now because I didn't know the names of anything other than that's a bee, that's a sticker bush, that's a tree, that's a rock. You see the generality like a Wordsworthian child walking in the woods. You don't know specifically what anything is called and you don't care. Now I know and I care what things are called. I love to name them. The wider your experience, the wider your ability to create analogies and metaphors and so on.

DS: I think that the urge to express ourselves is one of our species' more benevolent qualities. I often have the sense, as have many poets, including Mary Oliver, that we evolved to recognize and praise beauty and experience, to pay attention to life. I believe, almost along the lines of Buckminster Fuller, that if a child was raised in a box, she would find certain things beautiful and could even write about them in a way that a boy living on a mountain, say, would understand.

BOYLE: That's a great observation, and I think it's true. The impoverishment of nature, though, will make every child grow up in a box. Many urban people now, and if they are listening they are probably gritting their teeth because they enjoy where they are living, but nonetheless the condo dwellers and the urban people, it seems to me, are living lives that are somehow impoverished by the fact that their only environment is unnatural and man-made.

DS: People seem willing to give up so much of nature. They're putting televisions in cars now so people don't have to look out the window.

BOYLE: People say, "So what are you going to do?" So I dug a pond in my backyard. I dug it by hand, by the way, we didn't use any diesel fuel for that, just food fuel, and we dug it for the benefit of the butterflies—I live in the butterfly preserve where the butterflies come each winter to gather—and for the benefit of the frogs and the toads and whoever else in the animal world who might want to use it except people. I don't want people back there. I want it to be a private nature preserve. And I think that is kind of the dilemma of environmentalism. It's an elitist movement of people who have plenty to eat. The joke, as Tierwater expresses it in this book, is "What is the definition of an environmentalist? Someone who already has his mountain cabin."

DS: Do you think fiction plays a role in raising environmental awareness?

BOYLE: Oh, absolutely, and it would be even a greater tool for raising awareness if it weren't for the fact that nobody knows how to read. That makes it difficult.

DS: You teach writing, don't you?

BOYLE: Yes, I do. I am a committed teacher. I am one of the very few lucky literary writers who has attracted a large audience, and I make enough money so that I'm doing just fine. So I continue to teach because it's part of my life. I love it, and I want to spread the word.

DS: Do your students read, or do you have to make them read?

BOYLE: That's interesting. These are kids who really want to be artists, but when I ask them to list their ten favorite works of fiction and the writers thereof, some aren't able to do it. Others list admirable and great writers like Joseph Conrad and Shakespeare. They are not aware of what is current. I tell them, "You didn't list any current writers. What if I ask you to list your ten favorites CDs and the artists who made them, or your ten favorite movies, or ten favorite TV shows?" They could do that in a snap. They could probably list a hundred. I think that says something to them. Invariably in a Q&A session after I perform my stories on stage, somebody will say, "So how do you do it? What's your secret? What's your advice to writers?" And the advice is: read. You have to read as much as you possibly can of all literature, but particularly of current literature. All arts are an assimilative process. You have to put it in, in order to get it out. And the beauty of art is that we crave an individuality. We want to be important. It's a mysterious and horrifying world, particularly in the absence of God and with science crushing us with these facts and these miseries. We want to be individual, and art allows you to be individual, good or bad. Whether it's good art or bad art, nobody else could have made it because no matter how many billions of us there are nobody is you and nobody has had your experiences exactly. So there's a rush; there's a real charge to making art. I want to communicate that to the students, and I want to be their coach and let them express themselves in their own voices and in their own modes, and discover new ways of expressing themselves in their own very individualistic voices.

DS: If writing students aren't reading contemporary fiction, who is?

BOYLE: The core audience for literature is great in this country. My readings are well attended. People are literate; they read widely; they trade novels with each other. I just feel that the percentage of people who could be part of this audience has shrunk, especially in contradistinction to Europe where I think the percentage of people who revere writing and writers is much higher. The real audience appreciates and understands what you're doing in every turn of phrase. They find books illuminating, and in some way that is a one-on-one communication between reader and writer. After all, the process of writing involves bringing up the subconscious mind and forgetting that you're working, or that you are even existing, and so, too, to read you have to get in the same mood. Many people listening to us now will have had the experience of picking up a book to read and not being able to focus or concentrate and tossing it aside thinking, "What a piece of crap. Why did I waste my money on this?" Then six months later, they'll idly pick it up again and get riveted by it and read it all the way through and live in another world.

It really does take the same focus to create a book as it does to recreate it as a reader. That's the magic of literature that some of the arts do not provide us with, film for instance. I'm a big fan of film. I love it, but its limitation is that it is directed and it is one version of a work. Whereas to read *A Friend of the Earth,* or any book, you create your own version. You've directed the movie of it, and that's a very special experience that I hope people will continue to have in the future—although once you read this book you realize there is no future.

DS: I can't imagine navigating our world without books. I love the intimacy of reading. And while they take you away from the ordinary, they put you in touch with the sublime. This is different from the escape that people seek in television.

BOYLE: Others would argue that TV has been a boon, in that it allows people to have some kind of entertainment or communication with the world, especially in isolated areas. I suppose in the past before electricity, we went to bed early, and we were always very bored. But on the other hand, maybe it is not so bad to have a slower pace of life and not to be slave to the machine, which I am. I love my car. I love my stereo. I have to listen to books on tape when I'm driving down the street. I'm sitting in my hotel room and I have to have a TV on, all of that. But still, the time when I'm up in the mountains with none of that, with just a book and my own being, is very precious. And I wonder if we'd all be a lot more calmer and have less road rage and air rage if we could have more contemplative time. Books give you that, being in nature gives you that, and I guess in *A Friend of the Earth,* I'm bemoaning the fact that we have less and less of it.

DS: I actually think that as things get worse, more and more people are going to turn to books. They're going to realize that they need to know more and that books are the place to go.

BOYLE: I do believe you're right. I'm not very optimistic about much, but I think you're right in that there is a kind of reaction against the domination of machines. I have every possible machine because my chief purchaser, that is my wife, is very technological, and also she is an acquirer of the first degree. Those of you who know my story, "Filthy with Things," know whereof I speak, but I do not like to be trapped by them. I don't have a cell phone. I can't imagine having to always be in contact with everybody. Then again, I do have a webpage, and I love to be in contact with the fans. To talk to my readers is so rewarding for me. But I don't have to turn it on, and I warned them from the beginning that I'm not always going to be communicating with them. I think you do have to say no. I, by the way, have not answered the telephone in about twenty years without an intermediary because it might be my aunt, whose object in life is to talk someone to death. My object in life is that it's not going to be me. But let's not get into that. I just don't think you always have to answer the telephone. I don't think you always have to be in touch or informed. Why do we need so much information? Why is it so important?

DS: Can you tell us a little about what your readers can look forward to reading in the future? You're always working, I know that.

BOYLE: I have said many times that writing is an obsessive-compulsive behavior, and I can't stop and I don't feel right unless I'm writing. Also, as we discussed earlier, it is my way of ordering my thoughts and feelings about the world. Especially in the short stories, I now write about very current things. A collection of sixteen recent and new stories titled *After the Plague* will be out soon. Currently, I'm about ninety pages into a new novel set thirty years in the past. I've gone into the future. Now I'm going into the past to hippie times when there was a back-to-the-earth movement, so that I can examine that and think about, "Was I utterly naive? Could anyone ever put the brakes on this consumer rush? What would it be like to go back to living in nature? Is it possible? Is it conceivable?"

[T. C. Boyle Returns]

DS: Since you were here last, the short story collection we spoke of, *After the Plague and Other Stories,* came out.

BOYLE: It came out the week of the 9/11 attacks, and I found myself first in New York and then in Washington, D.C. As you know, normally when I'm on stage I give a funny performance because my theory is you can't laugh and snore at the same time. But that was impossible. The crowds that came out to see me were very, very muted, and I read two stories from that collection that are non-comic, stories about violence. And I said to the audiences, "I feel terrible, we all feel terrible, but at least for this hour you're not going to be thinking about what happened on that day."

DS: And here we are in the studio as we go to war against Iraq, so I was happy to be rereading your new novel, *Drop City,* this past weekend, as an antidote to news and spin.

BOYLE: I think one of the reasons the novel has caught on so and has become a bestseller is because it takes us to a time when there was also war protest. *Drop City* is set in 1970 when we had a back-to-the-earth movement; we were distrustful of consumer society, and there was a very unpopular war going on. I think people are embracing the book for that reason. It's not that I'm prescient. It's just some weird concurrence of events.

DS: When I was reading *Drop City*, that's just what I thought—that we need this. I've always felt frustrated by the way the 1960s and early 1970s are trivialized and mocked, because that was a time of great awareness of injustices, of bravely voiced objections to war and discrimination.

BOYLE: Sure. I grew up then. I was a young man during that period, and I never really wanted to address it in my fiction because, as you say, it not only had been trivialized, but we've heard about it ad nauseam. Give us a break already, who cares? The closest I came to dealing with that period was *World's End*, which I wrote in the mid-1980s and which was published in 1987. It comes up to 1968, and it doesn't really deal with any of the politics or culture of the day. Again, I felt it was too much in the news. However, a long, long period has gone by, and now that I look back thirty years, it seems like ancient history. *Drop City* is a historical novel like my other historical novels. In fact, you might find this hard to believe; I had to do research. So it was really fun for me to go back and examine this period in light of what we've become today. Look at the failure of the dot.com boom and the stock market. No one in the last half of the 1990s really thought about the consequences of greed and putting all your eggs into the basket of making more money. All the ads on TV were for e-trading so you could get rich, but what are the consequences of that? Why do you want to be rich? It seems totally antithetical to what *Drop City* was about. Maybe I wrote it partly in response to that.

DS: In *Drop City*, you don't gloss over the naiveté of the back-to-earth movement, or claim that everyone involved in utopian visions for hippie communes was a good person. Everything, good and bad, that goes on in any community went on in the hippie world, too.

BOYLE: Absolutely. And as I say, the book has been widely embraced, but of course, I have my critics. And mainly the critics have been people who were in hippie communes and feel that I should have portrayed this community as very beautiful and loving. But that doesn't make for very good drama. My depth of thinking on the hippie period, when I was very young and a hippie, was pretty much summed up in a scene later on in the book. This book takes us to Alaska because until 1970 you could homestead there, and it was the last time anybody was ever going to be able to do this. So my hippie group goes to Alaska, and there they encounter the locals. One of the locals, a main character in the book named Pamela, is having a discussion with one of the hippies named Star. They find that they have a lot in common. They want to be back to the land. They love nature. They want to live off the land. And so they have a discussion, and Pamela says to Star, "All right, I understand. We both have a lot in common, but what does face paint, LSD, and bell bottoms have to do with going back to the land?" And Star thinks for a minute and shrugs and says, "I don't know, it's just hip I guess." That was sort of the depth of my philosophical reasoning during that period.

DS: I'm glad you've brought Star and Pamela to our attention because, as so often happens in your fiction, your women characters are the heroes. There's a scene early on when the Drop City commune is in its original location in Sonoma County, California, and things are not going very well. They are having a lot of problems, and one of the men, Alfredo, says, "It's all about the chicks," meaning that the guys depend on the women to do pretty much everything.

BOYLE: That's right. I found in going back and doing research and reading about the communes, many were incredibly sexist even though we were having the great period of women's liberation.

DS: Star's story reveals the dark side of so-called free love.

BOYLE: Absolutely. She feels that the onus is placed upon the women because if they aren't willing to make love on demand with anybody in the commune at any time, whether they are attracted to him or not, they're considered uptight like their bourgeois mothers. You know, "Come on, get with the program." She has that recognition in the first chapter from her point of view, so we start from that point and see where it will take us. I think many of the people who know my work and haven't read this yet may be very, very surprised by what happens in this book. When I first started to talk about this book on the last tour, people thought, "Okay, Boyle, hippies, Alaska. They will be lambs to the slaughter. This will be a hilarious black humor book." But, you know, I want to defeat your expectations. I want you to open each of my books and be totally surprised by where it's going to take you.

DS: Is this a departure for you stylistically, too? The descriptive passages in *Drop City* are extraordinarily vivid. You write about nature with such energy, you've reached a new level in poetic writing.

BOYLE: I try to challenge myself each time out to do something new. As far as the nature descriptions are concerned, I really wasn't aware of it so much, except that the book is set in nature and it's about nature, so obviously you have to set the scene. The last half of the book flowed very quickly; I must have written it in a period of three or four months, a lot of it while I was on my mountain, which we've talked about before, up in the Sierra Nevada right in the middle of the Sequoia National Forest. So I was writing about an Alaskan landscape, which I had visited the previous year, in a very wild California landscape. Further, Alaska was a new place to me, and I was very excited by what I saw there.

DS: I think one of the jobs only fiction does is to create a texture of being, to articulate what exactly it's like to be alive in a certain time and place. That interests me more sometimes than storyline and character.

BOYLE: Wow, that's great. My job as a fiction writer is not to write a history, or geography; it's simply to seduce you into believing this story and enjoying it. And one of the ways I try to, as you say, create the texture of being alive in this book is to give you very strong third-person points of view from five main characters so that the point of view is shifting and you can see one character through the eyes of another, and then have that reversed the next time that character's turn comes around. There are many ways of achieving that, but this is the one I relied on in this book.

DS: I know that you're a big admirer of nineteenth-century fiction. Charles Dickens comes to mind, naturally, and I wonder if his work was a model for you in any way.

BOYLE: Yes. I was just talking about this last night, with my daughter, the beautiful and talented Kerrie Coraghessan Boyle, who is sitting right here with us. We were talking about the difference between the nineteenth-century novel and what we're doing right now with a work like *Drop City,* in which you have a very focused third-person point of view with very little omniscient narration. I think the difference between *Drop City* and a Dickens novel is that Dickens would freely enter the minds of characters page to page, even line to line. One character will observe another and we will get that character's thoughts, and then we will be privy to the character to whom they are speaking and that character's thoughts. I don't see that being done so much anymore, and I can't quite say why. A book like *Drop City,* for instance, uses some of that technique, but once you're in one character's point of view, you will not get the other character's point of view at all until you move to their section. I guess it gives the characters more control over the book and the author is much further in the background because the author never comes in and explains. There is no exposition on the part of the author, or very little. It's always focused through the character's point of view.

DS: What different challenges do you face when writing first-person and third-person novels?

BOYLE: There is a different joy in doing first-person and third-person. Third-person can be very close, or more distant. If it's more distant, the author participates more, and the author can give you exposition and tell you about the town of Boynton for instance, which you do learn about mainly through point-of-view of characters, but also it's fudged a little. The author is coming in to give you some information that you need. Right now, I'm working on a book which is a first-person narrative, and it's just flying. I got it more than half done in only about four months, which is quite extraordinary for me because I work rather slowly. I think it's just because I'm completely liberated by doing a first-person narrative after having done this close third-person point of view of *Drop City*. I'm just having a lot of fun with it. It's called *The Inner Circle*, and it's set in the 1940s and 1950s in Bloomington, Indiana, around the sex research of Dr. Alfred C. Kinsey. After writing about the concept of free love and this whole opening up of sexuality and bringing down the barriers in *Drop City*, I wanted to go back and see where that came from.

DS: I really am amazed by how much you write and by the scope and depth of your concerns. Has your writing accelerated with each book?

BOYLE: I guess it is accelerating as I become more and more dedicated to what I'm doing. I don't know if it's healthy psychologically because it's a monomania. You know, I really don't want to do anything else, and I just want to follow it to see where it will go. I never know what I'm going to do or what I'm going to say. I don't even know how I think about most issues on a deeper level unless I write about it. So I just can't wait to get onto whatever is next just to see what it will be.

DS: Do the short stories percolate while you are working on your novels?

BOYLE: When I get toward the end of the novel, they start percolating up. Right now, I don't want to know about them at all. However, if I discover something really amazing today while I'm out on my book tour, I might make a little note and that might become a story down the road. But right now, I'm not really thinking much about stories because I'm totally invested in this new novel, which has to be finished first. But yes, once I get toward the end of it, I will start thinking a lot harder about what the next stories are going to be.

DS: Do you dream about your writing?

BOYLE: Very rarely. When I'm in the middle of a long novel, I will probably just say the names of the characters to myself as I drift off to sleep. It's like counting sheep. Once in awhile, very, very rarely, I've awakened with a dream which I've used as a story. I think it's only happened twice in my life. But more typically, a lot of times the dreams that I have in that waking period in the morning—where you awake, you have a dream, and you fall asleep back and forth—I edit the dreams and actually edit the dialogue of the characters in the dream. Then I know it's time to get up and go to work.

DS: Habits of mind. I dream about what I'm reading, and I had dreams related to *Drop City*, which is, at heart, about a utopia and about how a utopia begins as a dream but can easily turn into a nightmare.

BOYLE: Well, America started as a utopia. The Pilgrims came and religious groups came and founded their own utopias. And throughout our history, and in our recent history, there are many, many attempts at it. You know, horrible ones like David Koresh's. There are many religious utopias. And, yes, the whole hippie ethos was a utopian ethos. So I am certainly concerned with that as I am in many of my other books. Many of my books deal with small communities set against the society at large, and I guess this is probably the fullest expression of it so far.

DS: *Drop City* is also about the last vestige of the frontier.

BOYLE: I did write this to let us reflect on how we got where we are and what that means, especially in terms of the environment and environmental destruction. Environmental regulation posits a society that wants to preserve the environment for the good of everybody, and that is diametrically opposed to the rugged individualism that made this country.

DS: Another ethical conundrum that comes up among the hippies is the idea of our relationship with animals, which is something you've written about before: the idea that animals must die for us to eat, and the different perspectives of the vegetarians and the meat-eaters.

BOYLE: Yes, they find out that, unfortunately, if you're going to live off the land, you may be forced to kill other animals. Those of us who eat meat bought in stores, like myself for instance, find it very sanitized, and we are very far removed from the actual hunting, and killing, and skinning, and so on. And that intrudes at the end of the first section of the novel when Ronnie Pan, who wants to live off the land, kills a deer out of season, a puny poor little doe, makes a mess of butchering it, and feeds it up to the vegetarians and the whole group. Some refuse to eat, and others realize, "Hey, it's free food, let's eat it." On the other end of the spectrum, of course, are the Alaskans Sess and Pamela, who make no bones about having to kill animals in order to survive.

DS: But Sess is a good shot, and he knows what he's doing. These are important distinctions.

BOYLE: I guess I'm providing lots of grist for the graduate students of the future, and I was a grad student myself and I am happy to do it for them. From the very beginning, I've been very concerned with us as animals in a state of nature and with what that means. And I guess I'm playing it in many different ways through many different stories and novels.

A *Friend of the Earth* is a real cry of despair, and it's misanthropic, too, because you know who the enemies are: They are us.

I really have no solutions. In fact, I had to go around the world with that book, and say that it was a representation of everything I had read by all the environmentalists and they don't give us any hope whatsoever. And audiences sat there in stunned silence, and the questions were, "What can we do? Is there any hope?" I hope there is, but in my view it's over already. So maybe in *Drop City* I'm going back to a time in which it seemed as if we could live in harmony with nature and in which our ideals could be fulfilled without destroying everything that sustains us.

DS: Reading *A Friend of the Earth* gives me hope because we can bring imagination to the situation, and that in itself is a belief in other possibilities.

BOYLE: You can actually think about the situation on a deeper level. I do think the environmental movement, which sprang up during the period in which *Drop City* is set, has been great. Until the George W. Bush administration, we were making tremendous strides in cleaning up our rivers and really understanding how important nature is to us, even in limiting suburban sprawl. But if that gives me hope, what defeats it is the fact that throughout the world we are insanely overpopulating. This is extremely depressing for the writer. You know, we were talking about Dickens and his era. In those days, the British empire was eternal; God was in his heaven; we knew why we existed and what it was all about. Literature handed itself from one generation to the other. Now though, not only do we face the fact that culture and literature will die— the species will die. We now know the planet itself will be incinerated, and we don't have God anymore, so what is there? It is just utterly depressing to face. My way of dealing with it is to absorb myself into writing fiction and making it art. It puts me into a subconscious, tranquil, meditative state, and it just helps me feel better about my own life and about the life of everybody else.

DS: But Dickens was concerned about environmental matters, he was already writing about industrial pollution, about soot and the black fogs in London.

BOYLE: Oh, of course. He wrote about the travails of industrial society and child labor and all of that. *Hard Times* is a whole book about the horrors of manufacturing. My point was not so much that Dickens was unaware of it, but that, at least, he believed in progress, that things could be changed, that you could write a socially conscious novel and change things. In fact, I shouldn't be so negative, because *The Tortilla Curtain*, which I wrote in 1995, is about illegal immigration, and it has been influential in helping people rethink the issues involved. I am a socially conscious novelist, so, yes, I am certainly trying, and maybe I do have a progressive instinct in me.

Alex Shakar

Born in Brooklyn in 1968, Alex Shakar earned his B.A. in literature at Yale. While working towards his M.A. in English with a creative writing concentration at the University of Texas, Shakar wrote the seven stories that became his first book, *City in Love*. Set in New York, and evincing a deep love for the city, Shakar's inventive tales riff on Ovid's *Metamorphoses* as they track the mythlike adventures of a museum guard, an artist who makes sculpture out of junk, an actor, a young girl, a police detective, an astrologer, an options trader, and a writer. The collection won the University of Texas's Outstanding Master's Report and garnered Shakar back-to-back James A. Michener Fellowships. *City in Love* won the 1996 National Fiction Competition and was selected as the Independent Press Editors' "Pick of the Year."

Shakar was working toward a Ph.D. in English and creative writing at the University of Illinois at Chicago when he wrote his first novel, *The Savage Girl,* which secured him a coveted university fellowship. This was only the first in a torrent of accolades, as Shakar's second book was widely and positively reviewed. A laser-fine satire that tells an emotionally authentic story, *The Savage Girl* is set in Middle City, a megalopolis on the steep flanks of a smoldering volcano. All day and all night a conveyor belt feeds trash into the molten crater, while on the streets, roller-blading "trend-spotters" troll for clues to the population's incipient desires and obsessions, longings ripe for exploitation by wily marketers. Shakar's tale of the profit-motive run amok in an edgy and decadent world not so very different from our own offers moments of prophecy, knotty moral quandaries, and bright patches of humor.

Shakar is currently on the fiction faculty at the University of Illinois at Urbana-Champaign. An occasional commentator on National Public Radio's *All Things Considered,* he is working on a novel tentatively titled "The Missile Shield." Set in New York City six months after the World Trade Center attack, it portrays a family struggling with questions of faith.

Alex Shakar came to the studio to talk about his novel in November 2001.

DONNA SEAMAN: In *The Savage Girl,* we meet two sisters, Ursula and Ivy. Ursula is an artist, and she's always taken care of her younger sister given the amazing dysfunctions of their parents, especially their creepy plastic surgeon mother. Ivy was on her way to becoming a supermodel, but she's had a spectacular breakdown. As the novel opens, Ursula has come to Middle City to look after her sister. She has also taken a job as a "trendspotter," working for Ivy's ex-lover Chas—once a philosophy professor, now a scary marketing wizard. The setting is striking: Middle City is a menacing megalopolis spiking the side of an active volcano. Where did this place come from?

ALEX SHAKAR: It's funny, I've just been on a reading tour, and everywhere I've gone, people recognize their own city in Middle City. I guess I came up with it for a lot of reasons, and some of them I'm still discovering as time goes on. But the one thing that I wanted to do was to give the novel a fantastical setting so that when people picked up the book and started to read, it would seem like an Alice in Wonderland-type book—something that they wouldn't feel immediately implicated in. But then gradually, I hope, as the story goes on, you realize that this world is eerily similar to our own. The volcano itself was something I did intuitively, without really understanding why. But as I continued writing the book, it became pretty clear to me that it was symbolizing the way that our culture just kind of paves over everything. I found the image of people going about their daily business while living on a semi-active volcano quite powerful, so the volcano is like the gun on the stage that doesn't ever quite go off, but it always has an aura of menace.

DS: The time frame is ambiguous. There's a sense that this is taking place in the future, and yet everything is exactly the way it is right now. Did you mean for us to wonder about this?

SHAKAR: Yes, I did. It does feel like the future, but there is nothing you can point to in the novel which is futuristic.

DS: In keeping with that futuristic flavor, the novel flirts with science fiction: it is and it isn't. Is that another intentional ploy?

SHAKAR: It is. The trendspotters are obsessed with finding the future, and I wanted to suggest the idea Sartre had, about how we all live in the future. You know, we all live with this expectation that we'll always be living. As though we're not only not living in the moment, but also that we're always projecting into the future. In the world of the novel, this is true to an almost chaotic extent.

DS: When you describe Ivy's modeling work, before her first dramatic breakdown, I was reminded of some of the more outrageous fashion spreads in the late 1980s and early 1990s in which thin and glamorous but louche women were being threatened by ferocious Doberman pinschers and German shepherds in blasted out urban landscapes with burning cars and broken glass. Were you thinking of those images?

SHAKAR: Yes, definitely. That's where the "Savage Girl" comes in. The savage girl of the title is a mute and homeless girl who lives in a city park and hunts pigeons for food and dresses in neo-primitive tatters. Ursula is fascinated by the savage girl. At first, she isn't sure why, but gradually it dawns on her that it's because the girl seems so autonomous from the consumerism that Ivy seems so ruled by and so broken by. But as the story progresses, Ursula ends up using the savage girl as a marketing image. I wanted to explore the ways in which our culture, our specialty and marketing industries, seize upon violent and sadistic images.

DS: Ivy's suffering, her craziness, is rooted in the insidiousness of commercialism, which co-opts every experience. She's interesting, too, because she's considered beautiful, and beauty is power in this culture; yet her beauty nearly destroys her. Ursula creates beauty —she's an artist, and a compelling narrator. You write well from a woman's point of view. Was that a deliberate choice from the outset?

SHAKAR: No, it took me awhile to get around to it. Ursula wasn't even a character in the early draft of the book, and neither was Ivy, actually. Both sisters kind of emerged as I went on, so I kept writing and Ursula became more and more central to the story. In retrospect, it's obvious to me why that was, but at the time it was mysterious. I think that men are increasingly experiencing the same kinds of conflicts about beauty, glamour, and body image that women do, although women's bodies are still the ground zero in this whole thing. They are still the thing that catalyzes the exchange. And I have to say that it was a real learning process for me to write from a woman's point of view. Most of the time, I was writing to the similarities between women and men, and not to the differences. And I did have a lot of women readers. My girlfriend and other women writers would read the manuscript and then talk to me about the issues that it brought up for them, and that really helped me try and nail it down.

DS: The world you create, a thoroughly cynical, artificial, and advertising-driven society, is just one breath away from our own, but that separation helps us see what it means to turn everything into a commodity, however useless it is. Ursula works with a product called "diet water," and you can't get anymore absurd than that. But even diet water can be successfully marketed. And here's where your evil genius, Chas, comes in.

SHAKAR: Ursula ends up working with Chas, the head guy, and Javier. Chas and Javier are similar in that they both believe that our purchases say something pretty deep about us, but their similarities end there. Javier believes that products are things we use to give ourselves beauty in a way that enables us to express what's best in us, and even develop into the kind of people we want to be and the kind of world we want to be in. He's young and idealistic and romantic, and he believes that beauty is the PR campaign of the human soul. Chas is older and more cynical. He believes that products are mere surfaces, quick fixes that we use to give ourselves an illusory surge of power, but which leave us all the more empty in the long run. When he takes Ursula to a supermarket he tells her that surfaces are all that people have.

DS: And he teaches her about a term and concept you coined: "paradessence." Chas explains, "That's what consumer motivation is about, Ursula. Every product has this paradoxical essence. Two opposing desires that it can promise to satisfy simultaneously. The job of a marketer is to cultivate this schismatic core, this broken soul, at the center of each product." That's some heady stuff. Did you read marketing texts and ponder marketing theories?

SHAKAR: I did a lot of reading of marketing textbooks, looking for the kind of theories that I wanted to give my philosophical trend-spotters. I ended up having to invent most of them myself, but I did find one book that I thought was incredible. It's called *The Strategy of Desire* by Ernest Dichter, who is the father of consumer motivation research. He wrote this book in the 1950s, at the height of the cold war, and in the introduction he talks about how he compared and contrasted Soviet propaganda and American marketing. He said that if you look at a propaganda poster and at an American ad they will look pretty similar, but they are actually polar opposites of each other. The purpose of Soviet propaganda is to make its citizens feel content, feel happy, feel like they belong to the society, feel like their lives are meaningful, that they are doing good, that they are a part of a great society. The purpose of American marketing, on the other hand, is to create discontent in its consumers, to make them want new cars, younger spouses, and so on. It was this dissatisfaction that was going to win us the cold war by making our economy grow. And you know, eerily enough, he was right. The creepiness of thinking how dissatisfaction is cultivated in each of us made me look at everything around me in a totally different way. I started watching commercials and reading magazines and going to supermarkets and paying attention to what was having an effect on me and how. I think that's when I started coming up with these ideas.

DS: It is paradoxical, as your hero, Ursula, realizes. Because she's an artist and because she's honest, her first drawings of the savage girl as an advertising icon are too realistic. Chas objects to their grittiness, and instructs her to sanitize them.

SHAKAR: And once Ursula learns how to harness this marketing tool of paradessence, she's able to make the savage girl into a very powerful marketing image because it's bursting with contradictions. In her drawings, the savage girl is both voluptuous and strong. She wears high-heeled moccasins. She wears pastel war paints.

DS: But Ursula thinks she can beat the system by working within it.

SHAKAR: That's a good thing to point out. Ursula tells herself that she's using this image as a kind of guerilla campaign against consumerism itself—that she wants people to see the savage girl as an image of resistance to consumerism, which is what the savage girl means to her. I think this is how most trends start out. They begin as a form of rebellion, as resistance movements. And then they're co-opted.

I was working on this novel in a coffee shop in Chicago a few years ago, and all summer trendspotters kept coming in. I would watch them as they handed out questionnaires and asked people to fill them out. People from Puma sneakers came and said, "Draw your ideal sneaker and we'll pay you ten dollars." Stuff like that. This was at the height of the economic boom, so companies were actually paying people to do this stuff pretty frequently. One day two women came up to me and I thought, "Okay, this is my chance. I'm not going to tell them anything about me. I'm not going to give anything away, and I'm going to really milk them for material." They started asking me questions, and at first they were asking questions my research led me to expect. Like, "Where would you go on your ideal date? How many pairs of designer jeans do you own? What is your favorite store?" But then they started asking me, "What is your philosophy of life? What are your goals in life? What is your world view?"—really deep and abstract questions. So I started getting carried away, until one of them stopped me and said, "By the way, those are nice shoes you have on. What kind of shoes are those?" I answered, "Oh, these are Australian sheepherder's boots." And they just stopped and they looked at each other. And I felt so humiliated because I realized in that moment they found the one product that I romanticized and had made part of my identity.

I thought about it and I realized, I've never been to Australia. Who told me these were Australian sheepherder's boots? A salesperson. Then I started to think about what these boots meant to me, and how the trendspotters saw this, too, because the boots were really scuffed up. I had been wearing them for years, and they obviously meant something like getting back to the earth, some sort of rural, rustic image of autonomy. And sure enough, a year later these shoes were everywhere. I don't claim responsibility for this, but I did begin to think about how trends start from the ground up. They start out as subtle movements that have political or spiritual or emotional content and meaning. But by the time they come at you from the top down, they mean something quite different.

DS: Ah, this is the source of the scene in the airport where Ursula accosts a guy who is quite hostile to her marketing-related questions until she asks him about his unusual boots.

SHAKAR: Yes, he is wearing what he was told by a salesperson were Mauritanian jungle boots. The joke is that there are no jungles in Mauritania.

DS: Your characters are under a strange form of pressure, and everything seems to be on the brink of disaster, although you do leaven your dark vision with humor. For instance, someone has a screensaver that consists of a sequence of images of the destruction of Middle City by everything from Godzilla to the sandaled foot of God. You also have a fine time with the Savage Girl trend. Once the savage girl image starts catching on, companies start selling war paint as make-up, and offering "savage makeovers." It's hilarious, and yet very sad.

SHAKAR: That was important to me. Once I realized that this was a book about consumerism, I wanted to make sure that it wasn't a dry, one-sided critique. I really wanted to show what we find irresistible and beautiful and empowering about consumerism as well as what's insidious about it. I thought that the book would be incomplete if it didn't contain both of those views and, moreover, both of those views in the same moment. So hopefully, by the time you finish reading this book, you'll look around—and people have told me this, which is why I feel I can talk about it—and anything you look at you can either see as beautiful and/or horrific and insidious. I think increasingly a lot of us have that split feeling about everything that's going on around us. That's what I was trying to get at.

DS: This is also a very literary book, so I wonder what writers you read and who you were inspired by.

SHAKAR: I read all kinds of stuff. I read a lot of nonfiction. But in terms of literary novels, I like books that entertain me and involve me emotionally but that also leave me feeling as though I've learned something either about myself or about the world or about people. So I like Don DeLillo a lot. I think he's really been carrying the banner in terms of writing penetrating books about our culture. When I was younger, one of my favorite writers was Faulkner, especially *The Sound and the Fury.* I thought his treatment of all those different points of view, including various levels of intelligence and sanity, and his trying to collapse them all into one book, was incredible. I love a novel called *Hopscotch* by an Argentinean writer named Julio Cortázar, which is sort of about Bohemian expatriates in Paris. It starts out with chapter seventy-three and then you go to chapter one. So you never know how far into the book you are. It's a wonderful book because it's very intellectual, yet at the same time it manages to be emotionally gripping. So that sets the bar for me. Realizing that a novel could do both of those things if it was good meant a lot to me. And I like all kinds of writers from the nineteenth century, Dostoevsky especially, for his ability to achieve such a manic pitch from all his characters.

DS: Do you feel that it's part of a novelist's job to reflect society, and to look for its undercurrents and critique its failings?

SHAKAR: I don't know. When people talk about engaged literature it makes me uncomfortable because I think that the definition they are using when they say it is very narrow in a political sense. I really think most writers do engage the world, but they do it in different ways. Personally, what intrigues me is where the rubber hits the road, you know, where the social hits the psychological and the personal. I hope to write a book that shows how these two things interact, how the world around us influences who we are and the decisions we make on a day-to-day basis. That's where I was coming from with this book.

DS: The novels I find most interesting do exactly what you're talking about. They are deeply and candidly psychological. The characters' perceptions are altered and so, consequently, are the readers'. And while I treasure fictional depictions of various social institutions, it has to relate back to an individual and to the workings of a particular mind.

SHAKAR: Yes. It was really difficult to write a book about an industry, especially about the pop-culture industry that pretends to make fun of itself all the time. It's hard to write a satire because in a way satire has been co-opted by the advertising industry and by Hollywood. So the question for me was how to write a book that's a satire of these things and still have it be effective. Then, it was so strange, the products that I created, like diet water, and the kind of people I imagined, including a woman who wants to be a performance artist and who has all this plastic surgery to make her look like Betty Boop, seemed way over the top. I thought nobody would believe this. But it fit so well thematically, and it seemed so right for the story that I was telling, that I kept it in. Then, lo and behold, by the time the book comes out it doesn't seem farfetched at all. Smart water we've got. Vitamin water we've got. Oxygen water. And plastic surgery is more common and elaborate all the time.

SECTION FOUR: BETWEEN WORLDS

The history of America is a mosaic of the stories of immigrants, and American literature abounds in tales of displacement and exile, cultural collisions and prejudice, questions of identity and belonging, tradition and assimilation. Powerful fiction is forged when writers dramatize the traumas, confusions, and follies of cross-cultural experiences. The decision to leave home—sometimes under duress, and even when the journey is by choice—is fraught with unruly emotions and difficulties. People in exile long for lost landscapes, scents, foods, music, slant of light. The pressure to fit into one's adopted society often leads to dilution, or even abandonment, of traditions and values, which can make an immigrant feel liberated, but which may leave a stranger in a strange land feeling cut off from the past while still not wholly knit into the present. Even after living in America for many years, an immigrant can still be singled out as a foreigner, as suspect, untrustworthy, and unwelcome. The need to adapt creates a divide between the generations as American-born children outpace their immigrant parents in the process of assimilation. And once each wave of immigrants feels settled, they may resent and resist the next wave. Immigration, it seems, is a study in fortitude and irony.

Every classic storyline, from the coming-of-age tale to love stories, the family saga, the up-from-poverty epic, is expanded and given added weight and complexity when applied to the lives of immigrants. As writers reflect on both the world left behind and the one newly-arrived-in, what is lost and what is gained, their fiction runs the gamut from intensely personal narratives to socially satirical romps. Diasporas have always been part of human life, and now, more than ever, people are on the move all around the world.

Each of the writers presented here considers not only the enduring themes of immigration, but also how immigration has changed in our times as they offer incisive perspective on lives lived uneasily between worlds.

Sandra Cisneros writes of the complicated relationship between Mexico and the United States. Chitra Divakaruni tells the stories of immigrants to the U.S. from India who still have strong ties to home. Aleksandar Hemon's tales of exile illuminate the Bosnian War and the obliviousness of most Americans to its causes and consequences. Jamaica Kincaid meshes the personal with the political and the historical as individuals embody the tragic legacies of the colonized Caribbean. And Chang-rae Lee tracks the convoluted paths of Korean immigrants in America and the unexpected configurations a family can take over several generations as love and marriage bring together people of disparate backgrounds. Their stories about people attempting to bridge a divide between worlds celebrate both cultural distinctions and human universalities in the struggle to belong.

Sandra Cisneros

Sandra Cisneros was born in 1954 and grew up in Chicago, a place that plays a significant role in her work. Chicago was the setting for her first book, *The House on Mango Street*. A uniquely concentrated, poetic, and potent take on the rite of passage we call "coming of age," and a lancing view of urban life and the immigrant experience, *The House on Mango Street* has had an enormous impact on readers of diverse ages and backgrounds. Since its publication, it has been included on countless high-school and college reading lists, hit the two million mark for copies sold, and opened the door for Latina literature. Cisneros has become a speaker in great demand, and her warmth, openness, and concern with social justice have won her legions of fans who feel that she has spoken not only to them but also for them.

Cisneros bridges the divide between girlhood and womanhood in her second book, *Woman Hollering Creek,* a collection of funny, candid, and provocative stories about Mexican American girls and women. By turns ironic and angry, romantic and critical, Cisneros links the everyday with the cosmic with characters who play Barbie and ask saints for help, and she spins stories that explore family bonds, cultural imperialism, romance, and sexism. She is outspoken about womanhood, sexuality, and social mores, and she explores the mythic dimension of femininity, as well as the conflict between the pressure to be a good girl and the desire to be a sexy woman, in her bold and caustic, erotic and shrewd poetry, collected in *My Wicked, Wicked Ways* and *Loose Woman*. Cisneros is also the author of a children's book, *Hairs/Pelitos*.

Cisneros has received numerous awards, including the American Book Award and the Lannan Literary Award, and fellowships from the National Endowment for the Arts and the MacArthur

Foundation. When Cisneros appeared on *Open Books* in 2003, we spoke primarily about her novel *Caramelo,* a many-faceted, multi-generational family saga that weaves back and forth between Chicago and Mexico, and addresses the complications of private life and the influence of cultural icons. At that time, the paperback edition was bringing the adventures and discoveries of young Celaya "Lala" Reyes to an ever-growing audience.

DONNA SEAMAN: In the final chapter in *The House on Mango Street*, which was published in 1984, the narrator, Esperanza, is preparing to leave Mango Street in an unnamed city, but one that resembles Chicago, and she is speculating that friends and neighbors will wonder where she is going and why. She thinks, "They will not know I have gone away to come back." This line seems prophetic, and indeed, twenty years later, you've returned to writing fiction that is set in part in Chicago, and to the coming-of-age story of a Mexican American girl who can't wait to leave her discouraging neighborhood. Is there a connection between Esperanza and *Caramelo*'s narrator, Celaya?

SANDRA CISNEROS: People think *The House on Mango Street* is autobiographical, and it was to some degree when it began. But I was working on Chicago's South Side, teaching at an alternative high school in the Pilsen neighborhood, and the book changed during those years when I was in my twenties and formulating my politics and my Chicana feminism. Esperanza was really every woman that I came in contact with in the barrio, every Latina. I was a very frustrated English teacher who felt helpless and impotent in my attempts to change the lives of my students. Esperanza was every woman who was questioning our way, asking, "What was our route? What were our politics going to be as Latina feminists? How did our feminism differ from our sisters who were white, and what kinds of things were we looking at?" We were looking at issues of housing, violence, and immigration, which were not necessarily at the top of the list of issues cited by the white women's feminist movement.

Esperanza is connected, in a sense, to Celaya and *Caramelo* because, as a young woman, I thought the worst thing that could happen to me would be to get married and get stuck in the Midwest. I really disliked Chicago intensely, and that's because I didn't live on the Gold Coast or in Lincoln Park. I lived in Humboldt Park, which isn't exactly a swanky address. I just couldn't think of anything more miserable than spending my whole life tethered to someone and his family and being anchored here. Even though my family is here and I love them and I visit them often, it was a very hard town for me as a working-class artist. I'm not working-class anymore, and I certainly earn a lot more than I used to, but it would be hard for me to live here knowing what I know and seeing people that I see.

DS: You've made Chicago's problems a key element in your fiction.

CISNEROS: I always tell the truth about the politics of Chicago and how I feel about the city. A writer has to write their truth—what they know—and this is the truth I know.

DS: In *Caramelo*, you express objections to drudgery and oppression, especially in the lives of poor women. Lala is the only daughter in a family with six brothers. Her mother is a servant not only to her children and her husband but also to her mother-in-law, whom Lala calls the Awful Grandmother. Many stories unfold within the complex structure of your novel, and several themes emerge, including a protest against women being accorded the status of second-class citizens. Lala learns that women actually do have options if they think creatively, even as she realizes how difficult it is just to find the space and solitude one needs in order to think about one's life. She never has her own room, which brings to mind Virginia Woolf's *A Room of One's Own*, and it's so poignant to see Lala struggle to make spiritual space for herself even when she has to sleep on the La-Z-Boy recliner in the living room of a busy household.

CISNEROS: We need space to think, yes, and poor people in cities need that spiritual uplift the most. They are also the ones who need to see flowers and need to have concerts and need to have the arts because their lives are so hard. The arts sustain you and keep your spirit alive.

DS: Lala not only hopes to stay free of the drudgery of marriage and unwanted children, she also rejects the notion that a woman's life has to be domestic.

CISNEROS: She wants to do things like train dolphins or teach blind children how to read. I tried to be specific so that people wouldn't assume that I was writing about myself, so that no one would think that Lala was going to become a writer.

DS: The novel begins with a road trip as the Reyes family drives from Chicago to Mexico City. It's wonderfully frenetic, and show-cases one of the literary techniques you use so avidly, which is to make lists, to catalogue everything in a household, everything in a suitcase. And you make the objects you name meaningful and significant.

CISNEROS: I like to name things because naming tells you so much. When I meet people, I pay attention to what we call trivia, all the little things everyone notices. When we step into an elevator, we check someone out for three seconds, then we turn around. But if you had to write a little sketch of that person, there's lots of things you could say. This usually doesn't come across in writing. For me, because I was trained as a poet, writing is about naming things and itemizing. So I got in the habit of making lists—I did it in the stories in *Woman Hollering Creek*—and there is a certain pleasure in doing so. You know, naming all the things that are in your mother's living room, naming them all, and when you talk about homes like my mom's, it's jammed-packed with things. So sometimes when I was depressed and in a funk and I couldn't write, I would find myself complaining in my journal about how crowded my old bedroom was with stuff. One day, I wrote down everything that was in my bedroom, and that's what I borrowed from later when I wanted to write about what kind of a house Lala lived in and the things that were in there. I just went to my journal and there it was.

DS: Speaking of meaningful objects, the reigning metaphor for the novel is a *caramelo rebozo,* an intricately woven shawl.

CISNEROS: Yes, a rebozo is a Mexican shawl. You sometimes see Frida Kahlo wearing one, so I think it's more familiar now to non-Mexicans because they have seen Frida wearing these long, long strips of cloth. They were created in Mexico from a mix of many different cultures. The fringe work, we think, comes from the macramé of Spanish shawls, and long textiles were created during the time of the conquest because Indian women weren't allowed to wear Indian clothes. They were mandated to wear non-Indian clothes so, I guess, they could be assimilated into Spanish culture. But they didn't have money to buy Spanish clothes, so what they did was make, on a back-strap loom, long strips of cloth. At first the fringe was very short, but over the years it became longer and more and more elaborate. Originally the embroidery came from the Manila galleons which carried Chinese embroidery, then the macramé came from the Spanish mantillas, and they include Arabic knotting, so it's a little bit of this and that.

I love collecting these shawls, but I never put them into my writing before. This time I thought, "I'm going to throw in my love of shawls because people are losing regard for the shawls, and so many young people don't even know the history of the shawls. So I'll make the grandmother the daughter of makers of Mexican shawls. And I will weave into the story the shawl's history and im-

portance. This way another generation will be introduced to them."
In a way, I'm preserving the shawls. That's why I wrote about them,
but what I didn't realize was that the rebozo was going to become
a very important metaphor for the many strands of stories that get
woven together. I think that's the magical thing about why we
write. We put something in because we love it, and if you trust your
heart, and if you trust the thing you love and include it in your
work because it is one of your passions, it will find a way of making
a pattern and tying itself to all the other elements.

DS: The caramelo rebozo is made from a blend of tones.

CISNEROS: Right. The shawls have different names depending
on what they look like. The caramelo, for example, means caramel,
but it also could mean candy. So the striped shawls that look like
candy, peppermint or taffy with licorice stripes, brown and white,
those are called caramelos.

DS: I couldn't help but picture those colors as skin colors because
of how vividly you describe each character's eyes, hair, and skin,
and how beautifully you evoke the multiplicity of backgrounds that
Mexican culture embraces.

CISNEROS: People don't realize that about Mexico. Most people
think that all Mexicans have dark hair and dark skin, but that's not
true. If you go to Mexico, you will see that we have people of all
ranges as in the United States. We have African Mexicans, who
were slaves, and settled and intermarried. We have Irish Mexicans,
who were in the Mexican-American War and defected, and because they were Catholics, they intermarried. We have French
Mexicans, who were part of the occupation when the French
crown was dominating Mexico. Then you have green-eyed German Mexicans, and Lebanese Mexicans like Salma Hayek. Jewish
Mexicans, freckle-faced Mexicans. And you have to remember that
Mexico is comprised of many Indian cultures.

DS: Most Americans have a simplistic view of our neighbor to the south and don't now how very entwined our histories are.

CISNEROS: When I began the book, I was upset over the fact that my father's life would dissolve with his memory, that his history and his contribution to the United States, and the contribution of all the people of my father's generation who immigrated to America, who live and die here, will be forgotten. When we talk about Americans in American history we don't talk about them. In order to write about my father, and about others like him, I had to write about one hundred years of history, although the chronology I provide goes all the way back to 1519. I didn't intend to write a history book, but that's what it turned into, a history of the two countries and the way that they look at each other. And I wanted to write a book that wouldn't be dismissed as a piece of literature and just literature, so I included the chronology and lots of footnotes to back up my points.

DS: That's so interesting. I think the novel's power is in its imaginativeness and lyricism, the fact that it is a work of art, but you offer a very intriguing observation when you write, "Life is more astounding than anyone's imagination."

CISNEROS: That's true. When you think about the density of a person's life, all the coincidences and the extraordinary little miracles that happen, it's astonishing. If you wrote it down as it happened, no one would ever believe you.

DS: And you tried, didn't you? That's why you worked so long and hard on *Caramelo*. That's why you struggled.

CISNEROS: It was like pushing a Buick with my forehead. It was so hard. Every day I would go to bed exhausted and in tears, and it seemed like the Buick hadn't even budged. It was the most dreadful project. I thought, "How did I get into this? Help!" I felt like there was nobody who could save me from myself. Every week, I just felt exhausted, that I just couldn't do this.

DS: I know how hard you worked, and yet when you read *Caramelo,* it is scintillating—funny and fast-paced. There are no signs of authorial distress.

CISNEROS: I certainly hope no one can tell. But I had to labor over every page, and on some days I didn't get any pages. A good day for me is a page and a quarter. I don't write with an outline, and I don't write from left to right, and I don't write from up to down. People would say, "How much do you have to go?" And I would say, "I don't know." I write the way a filmmaker makes films. I do little scenes, and I don't know if each scene will be in the beginning, the middle, or the end. I don't know what's going to wind up on the cutting-room floor. So when the book was finally in galley form, a bound advance copy with a temporary cover for reviewers, I was amazed. I thought, "That's my book?" It was so fat. I thought, "No wonder this took me so long: I wrote three books."

DS: It is an enormous book. It covers more than a century of one large family's complex history in great detail. You conjure scenes on the streets of Mexico City in 1910 and 1911, for instance, in which you detail every smell, every sight, every sound. You must have done a phenomenal amount of research.

CISNEROS: Many people helped me to write *Caramelo* by allowing me to interview them and by loaning me their memories. Every single person is a walking Smithsonian or a walking library, an incredible trove of treasures. And when each person dies, all those stories die with them. We felt that after September 11 when we read all those obituaries that tried to sum up the incredible richness of a life in one paragraph. So my kind of research is almost like that of an anthropologist since it involves so much personal contact. One person just died who helped me a great deal: my father's cousin Enrique Arteaga Cisneros. He was the family archivist, and he was instrumental in helping me to shape the Mexican part of the book.

DS: Another subtle theme in *Caramelo* involves the importance of storytelling and the curious truth that no one person owns a story, even that of their own life. Lala and her grandmother frequently debate about the way the novel is progressing. The Awful Grandmother says, "I thought you were telling my story." And Lala replies, "I am, but it's my story too." There is no separation. You're suggesting that each person is composed of all who went before them.

CISNEROS: That's right. It's a very Buddhist point of view that we're all interconnected and that we're all connected to every single thing in the universe, whether it's a pebble or a feather or the sky. The grandmother wants the novel to be about her, but Lala understands that we're all interwoven like the threads in the shawl, so in order to tell the grandmother's story, she is going to have to tell her own story, too.

DS: They argue about details and time frames, and their arguments inspire the reader to consider the vagaries of memory, the elusiveness of truth. Within any household, every family member has a different version of what goes on there.

CISNEROS: And then there is so much we don't know about our families and each other's stories. I'm interested in what doesn't get told; that's where the real stories are. That was the wonderful thing about having the grandmother's intrusive voice come in and correct things. I think when we are writing about families we can't help but hear our family members, living or dead, saying, "That's not how it was." So I let her speak and bicker.

Somebody said my book was postmodern, but that's just the way we speak. You know, it's oral storytelling. When we tell stories, we often tell the ending first. "I'm going to tell you about when I almost died," he says, then tells the story even though he's already given you the punch line and the plot. Then he interrupts and says, "Oh, but first I have to tell you . . . and then I forgot to say . . ." The good storytellers can take you on these side detours and bring you right back. They give you just enough, and you keep listening. To me, that's a key to a good story. Do you want to hear it? Are you quiet? Do you listen because you can't wait to hear the next sentence?

DS: You've also included the stories of historical figures, real people from the past such as Josephine Baker.

CISNEROS: I got to weave in people I love, like Josephine Baker, because I read a lot of biography and because I prefer history as it's revealed in a person's life, by trying to understand how a certain person was affected by historical events. It was fun. I didn't know that this was going to happen. I just left myself open. When you're writing the way I do, you use everything in the kitchen to make the stew.

I really wrote this book like a blind woman; I was feeling my way. I put in all the things I loved and all the people I feared were disappearing, people from my father's generation involved with music or film. I threw everything in, and I just trusted it would find a place. So, for example, if I read in the newspaper that a Mexican movie star had died, I would just weave her into the story.

DS: One historical figure I was quite surprised and very pleased to discover in *Caramelo* is Maria Sabina.

CISNEROS: Maria Sabina, yes, the wise shamaness. She's the woman who introduced the sacred mushrooms to a German anthropologist, and then all kinds of people came to visit her—world leaders, rock stars, the rich and famous. But she died as poor as the day she was born. She was such a pure healer that she didn't charge, so people took advantage of her. But what a visionary she was. I admire Maria Sabina very much. Not many people know about her unless they're poets or poetry people because a lot of her chants have been transcribed and are very beautiful.

DS: You gently lead your readers to spiritual places.

CISNEROS: I didn't intend to, but maybe that's just where my head is at now. I've really gone on great searches for the spiritual in my forties. There has been a lot of death and loss in my life in the last decade, so I've been forced to make this spiritual search. I also suddenly felt that I was being put in a position, whether I liked it or not, of being a role model and a spokesperson. I was a little startled by this because it wasn't in my life plan, but obviously it was given to me for a reason. So I asked for spiritual enlightenment so that I could be responsible in this role. But when you ask for spiritual enlightenment, you're asking for the plague and you're in for hard knocks because that's how you get spiritual enlightenment. But I didn't know that; I was very naive. I said, "I want to be wise because people are looking to me to say wise things, and I need to guide the community with my writing, so please make me wiser." It was the worse decade of my life. All these sad things happened to me, all these exploding cigars. But you know, those exploding cigars happen to you so that you can graduate to the next spiritual level. That's the only way it happens. Otherwise, you would stay exactly where you were and you would be very happy. It's only when there is change and great difficulty and conflict that we move out of our place of comfort and grow.

DS: I believe the making of art can be a spiritual endeavor, part of a person's spiritual growth. Of course, that puts a great deal of pressure on the creative process.

CISNEROS: I really feel I was given this gift to walk a path. Even if in real life I'm not that sort—or I'm not that wise, or I'm not that generous—when I write, I have to be. So people confuse the book with me. Me, I struggle with things like anybody else, but when I'm writing, I'm doing a sitting meditation. If I'm patient enough, then that wisdom will come through the writing, but you really have to sit there for a long time and be very, very humble for it to come. I think if you muddy it for reasons of creating art for ego, for money, or for fame, then you may get money or fame, but I don't think you'll get happiness. I really believe that. Maybe somebody can prove me wrong because I only know my own life, but I feel as if you will get a lot of grace if you do the work you are meant to be doing in this lifetime on this planet. And we get guidance every single day of what that work is, but people aren't quiet long enough to hear what they are supposed to do. They don't ask either. If you ask, it will be given to you.

I don't feel that the light I write from comes from me. I really feel that it comes from some higher energy. People think I have the gift, but everybody has the gift, every single one of us. That's the most wonderful thing, and I tell young people this all the time. Think of service work for your community, whatever your community may be. Just say, "I have some work to do for the specific community I come from. What is the most important work I could be doing? How can I give of myself, of my own time?" I think when we volunteer and give our time, which is the most expensive thing we have, then we get that light. I see that happening now with the stories I wrote for my father. I've been reading them to immigrants, and when immigrant readers come up to talk to me, when you see that your writing makes a difference to people, that's more rewarding than a positive book review. These are people who work really hard. They don't have a lot of money, yet they bring me flowers, earrings, a little necklace. It is so touching to get gifts from people who don't have money, who work with their hands, who are so moved by stories about their lives.

I write by myself and cry and laugh all by myself in my office, and I meditate everyday when I write. I hope these stories will honor all the people I'm writing about. I always pray that I will get some sort of affirmation when I perform. And it happens. Someone will come up to me afterwards and say, "Oh, I felt like you wrote that for me." Someone says, "You wrote to me twelve years ago, and I read *The House on Mango Street* when my life was falling apart, and now I've got this wonderful job and your story saved my life."

DS: I'm curious about how you went from being Catholic to becoming Buddhist.

CISNEROS: The amazing thing about Buddhism is that you can be a Catholic Buddhist, a Methodist Buddhist, a Jewish Buddhist. Buddhism forces you to look to your past and go to your roots and embrace things that you might have wanted to discard but that you realize are a part of you. It made me go back to my Catholicism and take the parts of Catholicism that worked for me and weave it in with my Buddhism.

DS: There is an oft-repeated refrain in your novel that I think of as a quintessential Buddhist thought: "Just enough, but not too much."

CISNEROS: It's based on the instructions for how to dye a black rebozo in the old days when they used natural dyes. In order to dye cloth black, you had to use iron, so you threw in wagon wheels and horse shoes and all kinds of iron scraps until the water got really black. And to get a true black you had to dip the cloth several times and leave it soaking, but if you did it too much, the cloth would come apart. So it had to be just enough but not too much. And that became a metaphor for many, many things.

Chitra Divakaruni

Born in Calcutta, India, in 1956, Chitra Divakaruni and her family lived in many places, including Bangkok, Delhi, Bombay, Kuala Lumpur, Darjeeling, Singapore, and Madras. In 1976, Divakaruni came to the United States on her own to continue her education. She earned her master's degree at Wright State University in Ohio, and her Ph.D. in Renaissance literature at Berkeley. Two intensely emotional experiences induced her to write. Stunned by the death of her grandfather, and stranded in her grief far from family, she began writing poetry in an effort to preserve memories and sort out her feelings. Then, while working as a volunteer at a women's shelter in the Bay Area, Divakaruni was deeply affected by the plight of a battered and frightened South Asian woman. In response, she helped found Maitri (Sanskrit for "friendship"), the first West Coast hotline for South Asian women, now a thriving organization serving women-at-risk. This frontline involvement inspired Divakaruni to start writing fiction about the difficulties facing South Asian women living in the United States, a subject that has become the wellspring for her short stories and novels.

Divakaruni's first book was a poetry collection, *Black Candle,* and she has continued to write and publish poetry. But she felt that fiction was the form she needed to concentrate on, so she enrolled in a fiction-writing class at Foothill College, where she was teaching twentieth-century multicultural literature. Her teacher, Tom Parker, was so impressed with her short stories he sent them to an agent. Soon Divakaruni found herself writing what became *Arranged Marriage*, a short story collection that portrays young Indian women immigrants in America caught between homesickness and the pull of tradition, and the longing for liberation and the fear and promise of life in a new world. *Arranged Marriage* garnered a number of prizes, including the American Book Award. Then Divakaruni gave birth to her second son and suffered serious complications. After her recovery, her near-death experience and a deepened sense of spirituality have found their way into her work.

Mistress of Spices, Divakaruni's first novel, is a mystical and romantic fable about a young woman versed in the healing properties of spices who works her magic on immigrants from India in a rundown shop in Oakland, California. In her second novel, *Sister of My Heart,* Divakaruni intermingles realism and mysticism as she tells the enchanting story of two young cousins born within hours of each other. As close as these sisters of the heart become, they are different, and their divergent paths dramatize the contrast between the old ways and the improvised lives of immigrants. Divakaruni continues the entwined stories of Anju and Sudha in *The Vine of Desire,* linking her tale to India's ancient epics. In between these two novels, Divakaruni brought out a stellar collection of short stories, *The Unknown Errors of Our Lives,* in which she extends her cast of characters to include several generations in families divided between India and the United States, which enabled her to delve even more deeply into questions of inheritance and obligation.

Divakaruni has written two books for young people, *Neela: Victory Song* and *The Conch Bearer.* And she has continued to define her role as a writer bringing into alignment disparate worlds: India and the United States, the old and the new, male and female, parents and children, the secular and the spiritual, public and private. She fulfills this mission with grace, insight, and humor in the astute and involving novel *Queen of Dreams,* which dramatizes the ancient art of dream interpretation, the struggle to live a creative life in an increasingly corporate society, and the consequences of post-9/11 fear and loathing. A writer on a mission, Divakaruni sets out to both enchant readers, and to arouse their empathy. Chitra Divakaruni appeared on *Open Books* in June 2001.

⌐⁓

DONNA SEAMAN: You gracefully use descriptions and metaphors to convey emotional states—the pattern in the fabric of a sari, for instance, or in the short story "Silver Pavements, Golden Roofs," the image of snow on a character's hand. I wonder if this stems from writing poetry.

CHITRA DIVAKARUNI: That's correct because I came to writing first through poetry, and poetry is my first love. I love writing prose, but I really have learned so much because I came to writing first as a poet. Words matter a great deal to me, and I pay a lot of attention to the choice of the right word and the sound of the word, and the rhythm of a sentence and the rhythm of a paragraph. I obsess over all these elements.

DS: The central theme of your work is the immigrant experience. How much has your life influenced this facet of your work?

DIVAKARUNI: Immigration was a transformational experience for me. It changed me in ways I really could never have imagined. It gave me a whole new vision of my own culture, things that I appreciated, as well as things that I questioned for the first time. It also gave me an unusual vision into America because I do see things that people who have lived here all their lives don't. I think, in a way, immigration made me into a writer, and therefore in my writing, I go back to that experience over and over again. I realize that that experience is very different for different people, and that is one of the main themes in *The Unknown Errors of Our Lives.* In *Arranged Marriage,* my first short story collection, I was very concerned with the immigrant herself, or himself, who wants to come to America, who is excited about the opportunities and all the possibilities. But now that our community here is an older and more established one, I'm also interested in the experiences of a group I call the reluctant immigrants, our parents. People who never really wanted to leave India, but who came to America because they were lonely without us. What is America like for them? It is a whole different experience.

DS: Marriage and family life are at the heart of your work.

DIVAKARUNI: I think that comes out of my cultural background. Family is central to the traditional Indian upbringing, which is the way I was raised. We are taught as children that family is the first thing in your life. You are members of a family first, and then you're an individual. Now having lived in the West for a long time, I don't agree with that completely, but family still remains very, very important to me.

DS: Your characters' definition of family includes myriad relatives, the classic extended family, which makes its absence all the more acute. You portray young Indian women who come to the States to go to school, or to get married, and they think they're going to be free and liberated, but instead they're unmoored, lost, terribly lonely.

DIVAKARUNI: That is at once the attraction, but also the pitfall, of living an individual life: you have a lot more freedom, but you are more isolated. Many of my characters discover that. Ironically, they miss the things that drove them absolutely crazy in India, where the extended family would know everything you're doing, and interfere all the time in your life. But here when you open the door to that empty apartment, you kind of wish they were there.

DS: "The Blooming Season for Cacti" is a profoundly sad and complicated story in which a young woman comes to the U.S. in the wake of a tragedy. This isn't a journey of hope, it's an exile in mourning.

DIVAKARUNI: In some ways she is escaping from her past. I wrote that story some years after the riots in Bombay, terrible riots between Hindus and Muslims in which a lot of people were hurt and killed. So many suffered, particularly women. This character lost her mother during the riots and has come to America hoping to heal herself. I'm so aware of the complexities of the lives of people who come here. We often assume that when people come to America it is the beginning of their life, and we erase the fact that they had any past. We don't think about it. But it's amazing, all the difficult pasts that people carry with them to this country, lives and losses that all of a sudden have no validation. No one wants to hear about it. Everyone says, in effect, "Why don't you just get on with your life?"

DS: I've noticed that there is a strong alignment in your work between characters who are mothers and the home country, your motherland. In "The Intelligence of Wild Things," for instance, the narrator tries to convince her brother to go home to visit their mother, who is ill. As the story unfolds, it becomes obvious that the connection to family and to place is profound and organic. Your characters are often pulled back to India against their will.

DIVAKARUNI: Which may have to do with where I am in my life. A lot of my friends, not necessarily Indian, and not necessarily immigrants, are feeling the same way. They have older parents now, and often their parents live in a different part of the country than they do. And they are worried because their parents are getting old, and they are getting sick. They are struggling with the notion of putting them in homes, which is very painful for everyone concerned. So it's a generational thing that I'm dealing with, which is made more painful by the fact that for many of us, here we are half the world away from each other.

DS: As poignant as your stories are, they are often very funny—I'm thinking of "Mrs. Dutta Writes a Letter"—and humor is a marvelous way to keep readers reading. It's a real challenge to write fiction about the sort of conundrums that can be called "issues" without being dogmatic. Do you find that that's the case?

DIVAKARUNI: Yes, I have to make a real effort. Anytime I start a story by saying, "Oh, I will send a little message out to the world about this matter," it falls flat. I cannot do it. I have to start with a character, with a scene, and with an image in my mind of the character doing something that is very essential to her situation. In "Mrs. Dutta Writes a Letter," there's a moment late in the story that has a connection to my life. My mother had come to visit, and because all of my siblings are in this country, we were trying to decide if she could move here. She had lived here for many years, then she went back to India, and now this was going to be a trial visit to see if she could come live here again.

Early in the visit, she went into the bathroom for her shower, and I heard this noise in the bathroom. It was kind of like a thump, thump, thump. It sounded strangely familiar, but I couldn't figure it out. After awhile, I knocked on the door and said, "Mother, what are you doing in there?" There was a long silence, and then she opened the door and said, "I'm washing my clothes." She was beating them out in the bathtub, like we traditionally do in India. I said, "But mother, I have the washer and dryer. Why don't you let me do them?" She was very firm, and she said, "No it wouldn't be the same." And then after it was done, she took her clothes out into the backyard and laid them out on the bushes, and I followed her out there and said, "Mother, don't do this." And she said, "I have to do it." This happens with Mrs. Dutta, only her daughter-in-law has absolutely forbidden her to drape her clothes over the back fence into the neighbors' yard, so she does it in secret, which leads to all kinds of problems. It seems to me so significant that, after that visit, my mother decided to go back to India. And I kept thinking about how the washing of the clothes was so symbolic of what she was feeling. Doing the laundry by hand was a way to regain control over a life in which she lost all autonomy. And as I looked around at other friends with their parents, I felt this was true of many of the parents, of many of the older generation, especially women who are independent and proud of being independent. It is so painful for them to lose control of that. In some ways it's more important than family because it's as though they're losing their self.

DS: Mrs. Dutta says that there is no word in Bengali for privacy. And in "The Intelligence of Wild Things," the narrator thinks about a word, *abhimaan*, which, you write, means "that mix of love and anger and hurt which lies at the heart of so many of our Indian tales, and for which there is no equivalent in English." This makes me think about how intrinsic language is to culture and how much language untangles and defines our emotions.

DIVAKARUNI: That's right. The question posed by that story is, "If you don't have a word for it, can you really feel it? Do you know how to feel it?" I often bring words from my language, Bengali, into my stories because I want to bridge that gap and I want to, through the inclusion of these words—hopefully in a context where the emotion can be understood—bring these emotions to the English language. *Abhimaan,* for instance, describes how, when someone you love very much has done something to hurt you, you are really upset and you withdraw from them but you still feel a lot of love towards them.

DS: Her family's predicament reminds your narrator of classical Indian tales. You also allude to Hindu lore in the title story, "The Unknown Errors of Our Lives," in which a young Indian woman living in the U.S. teaches herself Bengali so that she can write to her grandmother. And when she starts to paint, she uses classical Indian stories as inspiration. That's a lovely way to have a younger generation cycle back and rediscover a source of strength in their ancient culture.

DIVAKARUNI: In my own life, storytelling has been so important. I was very fortunate that my grandfather was a great storyteller. He was the first storyteller in my life, though I don't tell my mother that, and his stories are the ones I remember. For all my extended holidays, I would go to the countryside to be with him, and he would tell me wonderful tales that I have never seen written down anywhere. So I believe that storytelling is a wonderful way of connecting with people. I see that with my children. A lot of times, if I want them to do something or I want them to learn something, and I talk to them, they won't even hear me. But if I tell them a story about it, well, they're listening closely, and asking what happens next. Then when I talk to them about the story, they understand the lesson embodied in it perfectly. So I use storytelling in my own life and in my characters' lives. I think storytelling can be quite magical. It can help us connect with things that we might not logically understand at all. It can sometimes be a way of expressing the inexpressible.

DS: Every tradition has created stories to reflect its values and beliefs. Philosophers, artists, and scientists alike believe that we're hard-wired for narratives.

DIVAKARUNI: And in some ways as we learn through stories, they also heal us. I think there is something very healing in a story, something very compassionate and embracive. The best stories are those that invite us in and are not judgmental.

DS: Compassion is the key word. I believe that writing imaginatively about life, and about the consciousness of others, is empathic: even if you have some preconceived notions, when you open yourself to the story, those all fall away.

DIVAKARUNI: That's true for reading and for the writing process. I sometimes find when I am writing that I had a lot of prejudicial ideas, and as I write and try to create a character, I can see that I'm not being fair to that character. Hopefully, I can then let go of this prejudice I wasn't aware I had and treat the character with respect, with clarity, with empathy, understanding the fact that from that character's viewpoint there is a whole different world going on in there. But without writing, I don't know if I could have understood a quarter of the things that I understand. I'm not saying that I understand much, but I understand a whole lot more than I did before I became a writer.

DS: I feel that way about reading. I frankly don't understand how people function without reading literature. I don't see how they can begin to understand the way other people think, how minds work.

DIVAKARUNI: That's right. How can you get under someone else's skin? How can you ever be sympathetic to someone who's different than you if you haven't read?

DS: Reading your work, I feel you're also learning as you go along and that you're surprising yourself. I'm traveling along with you when I read, and at certain moments, I experience both my discovery and yours.

DIVAKARUNI: I worked on many of the stories in this book for quite a few years, and some started out with different endings. I will come up with an ending, but I'll put it aside for awhile, and then I'll go back and ask, "Is this the right thing for the story? Is this what this character would do?" Not necessarily the most predictable thing—you don't want that—but rather, would the character do this? So I do learn as I go along. I find that when I want a story to have a particular ending, it doesn't necessarily work for the story, so I have to allow the story to surprise me, and allow the characters to do their own things and surprise me. Sometimes unexpected and interesting characters will enter the story halfway through. For example, in "The Unknown Errors of Our Lives," the knife woman suddenly comes in. She was quite a delightful surprise. She knocked on the door and there she was.

DS: So much goes on in a short story, and the beauty of the form is that you can hold it in your mind in its entirety. A short story is like a film or a painting or a poem. What happens when you write novels? Do you have to change your writing habits?

DIVAKARUNI: I try to do the same, but because of the length of the novel, I think of it like stitching a tapestry: you have to do it slowly and painstakingly and there's a lot of detail that you have to fill in. But it can take just as long to work on a short story. A page of a short story, a page of a novel, the feel is different. It's like painting a watercolor, and the challenge here is not the filling in of detail but the brightness of touch, the subtlety, the nuance, the suggestion, the ellipses. I think in a short story what you leave out is as important as what you put in, and that's not the case in the novel. I think in the novel it's definitely what you put in.

DS: A reader lives in a novel. You're in there for the long haul. You welcome tangents and subplots and asides that don't connect in an obvious way.

DIVAKARUNI: A story is a more tightly unified whole. So, it's a different experience, and the pacing is different. A novel has a slower pace, but a pace that you have to keep up. In the short story, you have to achieve that speed quickly. You only have a page to get right into the story.

DS: Like a sprint instead of a marathon

DIVAKARUNI: Exactly.

DS: I'm pleased when a short story collection gets treated with the same respect as a novel, because there seems to be a persistent prejudice against short story collections, which I cannot understand.

DIVAKARUNI: I can't understand it either. It can't be from the artistic angle. It must be from the marketing or financial angle because—and this, too, surprises me—more people buy novels than they do short story collections. I would think with our fast-paced modern life and our fragmented time we would go for the short story because you can sit down and read one from start to finish.

DS: Did you feel pressured to write novels?

DIVAKARUNI: No, and my publisher and my agent are both quite wonderful. But when I announced that my next book after *Sister of My Heart* would be a book of short stories, there was a moment of silence on the line, and then there was a little sigh, and then they said, of course we will support you. But I knew they were wishing for another novel for sales purposes. But now that I'm working on the next novel everyone is very excited.

DS: I assume that you still write poetry.

DIVAKARUNI: I do, I do. I write poetry because it fulfills a different need in me.

DS: I can imagine. Certainly I get different experiences from reading different types of literature. But whatever the form, I find that reading beautiful language is good for you.

DIVAKARUNI: I think language heals you. In my current novel, there's a character who, when she gets really upset, repeats words that she loves to herself, and they calm her. The sounds of those words calm her down. To return to short stories, I think the other misconception about the short story is that it's a "literary form," which can be code for inaccessible. I do want my stories to be accessible. Without compromising on the art, I wanted them to be accessible because I want people of many backgrounds and many communities to read them. And I want readers of all ages to read them, because the stories span three generations, the immigrant, her parents, and her children.

DS: Anyone can enjoy and find something surprising and moving in your stories. And what a skill it is to write that way. Your essays are also remarkably lucid. Some people get academic when they write essays, but you stay open. You wrote a piece for the *New York Times* about reading hundreds of novels for the National Book Award. Did reading those novels all in a row change the novel you were working on?

DIVAKARUNI: It absolutely did. When I was judging the National Book Award, I was reading so many books, one immediately after the other, it made me begin to see the novel form in a different way. I could visualize the novel more clearly. I saw that the novel had to expand, it had to open up like a bell. I saw that it's not enough to have a good strong story and keep it going. You have to do more. By the end, the novel has to be more than that story, more than those people, more than just that milieu. It has to really be a wider world into which the reader can be drawn in a very powerful manner. Of course, all this time, I was halfway through my own novel when I was doing this. I was convinced that my novel was doing just fine. And then when I went back to it, I said, no it wasn't doing fine. With my newfound understanding, I went back and revised the whole novel. One never knows how much one holds up here in one's head and translates into one's writing, but at least it gave me a perspective that made me revise everything.

DS: That was generous and rather brave of you to participate in such intense reading. All those voices. It must have been be a challenge to hear your own.

DIVAKARUNI: It was, but you know, reading has always been so important to me. People have said, and I really believe this, that reading has saved their lives. I think reading saves my life all the time. I always think of a quote from Kafka; he said that a book should be an ax to shatter the frozen sea inside you. So every time I go to a book, I want to be open to that experience. I don't want to block myself from that, because I think books do change us. They change us as readers and people in the world, but they change us as writers also. And I particularly want that to happen, to learn from books how to be a better writer.

DS: Do you think that most readers welcome that cathartic experience, or are they looking for what we call escape?

DIVAKARUNI: Part of it is that the reader has to be open. But I think part of the writer's responsibility, or at least the writer's aspiration, should be to write a book that, even if you come to it with the hope of escape, it forces you instead to embrace a new world.

That's my goal. I want my books to seduce readers into the world of the book so that they will come out changed and more thoughtful in exploring questions that they wouldn't think of. And feeling a connection to people whose lives are very different than theirs—people who may look very different, may eat different things, but, ultimately, deep down, are they really that different?

DS: Do you have a large readership in India?

DIVAKARUNI: I do have a readership, but I will tell you a little story that will clarify the point. When I took my boys to India, to my little village, I encouraged my boys to write in a journal. They are too little to write it physically, but they tell me things and I write them down. So after we came back, my son said he wanted to write about the trip. I was delighted. I said, "Tell me what to write," and he said, "I went to India with my mother, the famous author Chitra Divakaruni. She was not so famous there."

DS: How do you feel about being labeled? If I were to say that you're a feminist writer, how would you respond?

DIVAKARUNI: I think one has to think about labels intelligently because as human beings that's one of the ways in which we understand things and classify things. If we didn't have labels, how would we find anything? How would we distinguish among writers? It would be like books without titles. So as long as we understand that that is the nature and the use of the label, it's okay—As long as we know that one writer or one person can have many labels and belong to many categories. I'm a woman writer; I'm a feminist writer; I'm an Indian writer; I'm an American writer. I may be all kinds of other things. I'm an immigrant issuist writer and a writer of color. I'm all those, and ultimately, I'm simply a writer. As long as we don't use labels to box people into little categories and refuse to let them out, then we are using labels intelligently.

Aleksandar Hemon

Born in 1964, Aleksandar Hemon grew up in Sarajevo, the son of an electrical engineer and a comptroller for a public utility. Certain of his literary calling at a young age, he majored in comparative literature at the University of Sarajevo and found work, first at a radio station, then as an editor at a newsmagazine. Hemon also endured a year of mandatory service in the Yugoslav army, an experience that engendered his highly critical view of military culture, which was affirmed all too horrifically as tensions escalated between Bosnians and Serbs. Hemon came to the U.S. as part of a cultural exchange program for journalists in 1992 just as the Bosnian War erupted. Stranded, depressed, and anxious about his family and friends, he applied for political asylum, and eked out a spare existence working low-wage jobs. He focused all his energy on learning English, and read Nabokov, whom he reveres and to whom he has been compared, for inspiration. His efforts paid off when he was accepted into Northwestern University's master's program. Sensitive to the struggles of immigrants, Hemon took a job teaching English as a second language at a technical institute, which is where he met his American wife, Lisa Stodder. Hemon then enrolled in Loyola University's doctoral program.

In his galvanizing debut, the short story collection *The Question of Bruno,* Hemon exposes the emotional torment of oppression and exile in a set of interlocking stories set in Bosnia and America. Hemon handles English as though each sentence were an incendiary device. He fractures narrative form to embody displacement and isolation in tales sharply attuned to the different perspectives of the powerless and the powerful, the legacy of tyranny under Stalin and Tito, and the daunting challenges facing immigrants. In his first novel, *Nowhere Man,* Hemon continues the story of his hero, Jozef Pronek, who first appeared in his stories. He loops back to Jozef's boyhood in Sarajevo, during which Jozef coped with the longings and bewilderment of adolescence by starting a Beatles tribute band, then follows Jozef to Chicago, where he struggles with the continual revision of identity and dreams that immigrant life demands.

Haunted by the violence in his homeland, fascinated by the ever-changing mesh of memory and experience, shrewdly observant, and adept at conjuring both universal states of mind and specific cultural biases and conflicts, Hemon creates a vigorous, nearly surreal physicality and a supple, often sly psychology that express a sardonic affection for humanity. Creative and audacious, big-hearted and scathing, Hemon is a fearless critic of society, a wry tragedian, and a commanding satirist. His work has appeared in the *New Yorker, Granta,* and *Esquire;* he contributes to *Slate,* and writes a column for *Dani,* the Bosnian magazine he once worked for. In 2004, Hemon was awarded a MacArthur Fellowship.

Aleksandar Hemon appeared on *Open Books* in October 2002.

DONNA SEAMAN: The first thing that struck me when I was reading *The Question of Bruno*—especially the novella that introduces your protagonist, Jozef Pronek—was the vigorous physicality and psychological heat of your descriptions of objects and places, and the freshness and potency of your English, which is wholly unlike that of an American-raised writer. Pronek is a native of Sarajevo visiting the U.S. for the first time, and through his eyes sights that are familiar to me became new and strange. Are you consciously attempting to induce American readers to see their world and hear their language differently?

ALEKSANDAR HEMON: I'm addressing all readers as part of a general literary strategy. I'm not targeting Americans as Americans. I'm targeting readership: not because readers need conversion by me, but because that's what I like when I read. I write books that I would like to read.

DS: Books that make you see things differently.

HEMON: Yes. Beginning with very small things. For instance, in *Lolita,* Nabokov compares cars on a parking lot to pigs in a trough. I find this beautiful because it makes me realize, suddenly, that cars in a parking lot could be the most common visual image in North America. Wherever you look there are cars in a parking lot, and this instant conversion from the mundane to something meaningful and something fresh and visionary is what I like about literature.

DS: And that's exactly what you achieve. You write about an airport and turn it into a human body. You render places and circumstances we take for granted, and are oblivious to, metaphoric and, consequently, more alive and significant. In *Nowhere Man,* which takes place in Chicago, you call attention to urban wildlife, pigeons and mice and cockroaches, creatures we would prefer not to have to deal with, but must.

HEMON: Yes, cockroaches are a part of everybody's experience. I've lived in apartments packed with cockroaches. They were cockroach vacation spots, some of the apartments that I lived in. But they are on a range of life, if you wish. I don't know why that is interesting to me, but our life with all those little creatures is fascinating to me.

DS: It comes across as a fascination with survival, a focus on life thriving in the most unlikely circumstances—behind a stove or in a really filthy basement, the persistence of life, which is at the heart of the immigrant stories that you tell. Jozef is displaced in *Nowhere Man,* and of course, the title itself, courtesy of the Beatles, cues us to the feeling of arbitrariness and weightlessness. You also make a correlation between the exterior reality of someone displaced by war, and their interior sense of alienation.

HEMON: Yes, and I tried to work that into the structure of the book. I tried to convey the sense of Jozef's discontinuous life by depriving the reader of a stable narrative position. Otherwise, the world conveyed is at least implicitly a safe and stable, fixed third-person there, or even a first-person there, and a kind of continued narrative. It suggests a sort of harmony made out of chaos. It's one of those old jokes about what art should be creating: order out of chaos. But to create order is to deny the reality of chaos, so I had to maintain a bit of chaos.

DS: Indeed, the novel does not proceed chronologically, and there are two main characters in *Nowhere Man*. There's Victor, an American of Ukrainian descent who remains enigmatic, revealing little about himself except for his obsession with Jozef. The scene changes from the Ukraine, to Jozef's musical Sarajevo boyhood, to Chicago, to Shanghai. Ultimately, you spin a web of stories that reveals how connected we all are, a web that reveals how catastrophic events, such as war, affect you even if you're not directly involved, a web of stories that reminds us that we are tied to strangers, and to their suffering. Did you consciously form this web?

HEMON: Yes. Every human being is part of a social network, although American individualism wishes to deny that. If your life is stable and nice, you're not aware of that network, you take it for granted. And I'm talking about people beyond your immediate family or beyond your five or ten closest friends. When I found myself in Chicago in the early 1990s, I had this sense of displacement, and I became aware of things I was missing. For example, I found in some ways I was missing acquaintances more than friends because with friends I retained a connection, however impeded, and sure enough my best friends before the war are my best friends now. I see them regularly. What I was missing was a network of acquaintances.

Sarajevo is still a relatively small city, so living there you meet a lot of people and they become people you know. So you walk into a bar and see someone familiar. You walk down the street and you say "Hi," to ten people. You recognize the faces of twenty-five other people. I realized that there was this whole social network that I was a part of, and that I took for granted—that there were people who I didn't even talk to for years, but I could talk to them at any point in the future. I assumed that they would be there, and their lives, common social practices, and customs, as well as the lore of the city, all sustained me. Then suddenly I was displaced from all that, and I realized that I would have to work on building a new acquaintance network. So now, after ten years, I have a barber, I have a butcher, I have a bar, I have a vet, I have a steady set of soccer buddies, which adds up to a hundred people, maybe, and I consciously work on this network. I had this need to connect with people on a level different from the intimacy and closeness you have with friends or family. And that's something that you need to have. One has to have a sense that his or her life is connected with other lives, not directly but indirectly, and this is what a war shatters.

DS: You dramatize this loss in *Nowhere Man* to profound effect. Every outing is lonely and treacherous for someone in exile, and language becomes an incredible barrier, making even the most casual small talk, that social lubricant, impossible. As a refugee or immigrant, you are unknown and you can't be understood.

HEMON: My wife and I used to teach English as a second language, and we had students who were literally rocket scientists and only attained level two in their ESL course. All the students had rich, complicated lives. Most were from the former Soviet Union, a lot of them were Jewish, and they had stories to tell, but they were often treated as second-rate human beings. Their "bad English" made them seem, to some, retarded, and they were treated as incomplete human beings. Add to that the widespread belief in the U.S. that people who lived in Bosnia or the Soviet Union are idiots because they don't come from "real" countries. They didn't have a free market or democracy and they couldn't read, say, Philip Roth, freely. So they're kind of half-human beings because of the language barrier and because no one expects them to have full and complex lives.

DS: There is a great deal of sorrow associated with exile and sur-vivor's guilt. Jozef and other characters know that people they've left behind are suffering terribly, while they're safe in the land of many cars and fast food. The way you get at this most powerfully, in my opinion, is through humor, and language difficulty is a sub-ject you handle comedically especially well. Language confusion arises when Jozef gets a job canvassing for Greenpeace in the sub-urbs of Chicago. Is this based on your own experience?

HEMON: I did work for Greenpeace in Chicago's suburbs, but none of those scenes are reproduced exactly from what I experi-enced. I worked for about two and a half years, and I calculate that I spoke with about five thousand people, so it certainly was a crash course in American middle-class life.

You know, humor is a tricky thing. When I go to Saravejo, peo-ple tell stories about being under siege, and more often than not, they tell them as funny stories, but these were not funny events. They had to have survived to turn their experiences into funny sto-ries, so it's a way of coping, a very important way of coping. Humor allows the storyteller to avoid self-pity, and humor allows the reader to engage with so-called dark things; they're more willing to imagine painful events. So humor is very important to me. The worst fear of mine in relation to the response of readers to my book is that they won't think some things are funny. When I read some-thing to an audience I think is funny and people don't laugh, I'm mortified. Suddenly I have a sense that they are not hearing me, and suddenly I feel isolated from the audience.

DS: I've read that you already wanted to be a writer when you were thirteen, and that Kafka's work particularly appealed to you. I'm sure you've thought countless times about what your life would have been like had you been able to stay in Sarajevo. I can't help but feel that you still would have written with an outsider's point of view, even if you had stayed in Bosnia. Do you have any sense of that?

HEMON: I don't really think of myself as an outsider in a meta-physical sense, I really don't. I'm just outside of the mainstream.

DS: Most artists are to some extent.

HEMON: Yes, although some are in the center of it. In fact, they kind of produce it. I'm outside of the mainstream of American culture, and I was also outside of the mainstream Bosnian culture. But it was not a metaphysical situation because in Bosnia I was embedded in the network I talked about earlier. So I could not have been an outsider because my parents were mainstream and I got along with them. You know what I mean? It's a very closely knit society in many ways. When I was younger, I thought I was a rebel and I could change my parents by playing loud music. But I don't really have the sense of being a physical outsider. There's not even an outsider culture, strictly speaking. If I'm an outsider, it's more due to the perception of people who think of themselves as insiders than due to my feeling of being an outsider. I mean, outside of what? I'm where I am, and that's the center of my world, and not just my world, but a world I share with a large number of people and in which I'm perfectly comfortable.

DS: You've done some journalism.

HEMON: I wrote for newspapers and a radio station, but I was hardly a journalist in the classic sense because I did not get along with facts.

DS: But you are a keen observer, and there is an immediacy to your work: the sense that you want to connect with readers, to share your sensibility. This brings to mind your character Victor, someone who is very drawn to literature, and yet I think he feels let down by it. He also strikes me as an American who's not comfortable in his life.

HEMON: Yes on both counts. Feeling uncomfortable in one's life is a common occurrence in America. Victor is a product of a so-called mixed marriage. His father is Ukrainian and his mother is Irish. His father was severely displaced because he experienced World War II and had some kind of anger problem, while his mother is pure South Side Irish. And Victor is someone who tries to find answers in literature for personal problems, to treat literature, as well educated as he is, as a kind of self-help manual. In some ways, that's a perfectly understandable way to approach literature because you look for other people's experiences and compare them to yours. But at the same time, it's the wrong approach because it leaves hidden a lot of things about literature, not to mention the fact that it's a wrong approach for self-help because you don't get it there. There's no help in literature because it concerns other people and other people's lives. Victor has trouble engaging with the world at the most basic level. He thinks he can engage with the world through literature, but the way he engages literature just sets him apart from the world, and it's kind of an impasse he struggles with.

DS: I'm reminded of an essay you wrote about a professor you had who turned out not to be the man you thought he was. He could quote Shakespeare in English and you revered him, yet he was actually involved in a Serbian atrocity. We often assume that art and literature enoble us, and make us better people.

HEMON: Of course. You can spend your entire life in museums and listening to Beethoven and still be a murderous bastard. There's no contradiction there. There is no reason to believe that literature makes anybody better. Now, I do think the desire to be made better through literature is an admirable one, but it's a doomed project. And if it does make you better, it makes you better, I believe, at the most basic level, the level of perception. This is why I'm a stickler for details. When I was in college, I wrote a thesis on James Joyce's *Ulysses*. He's a maniac for details, and I started writing down all the things that I thought were noticeable or significant, and I noticed frequent occurrences of the color red. I had no idea what it meant; I still don't really. But I suddenly started noticing red things around me, and how red they were, and the newness of red, and all that. And I think that's what art does.

Our senses are assaulted at all times by people who want us to buy something. You can't walk the street without ads screaming at you, "Buy this, buy this because life is going to be great if you buy this." There's a war for human senses in the United States, the western world, everywhere for that matter, just at different levels. So to live in a society and to be a good consumer and citizen, you have to be numb. You have to dull your senses. So at a very basic level, the political significance of literature, the way that literature can make you better, is the way it brings you back to your senses so that you suddenly start seeing things again and hearing things and, if you think of your engagement with language as a sixth sense, that too reawakens. All the arts do this, they sharpen your senses.

DS: Your take on history and on today's events is so vivid. I wonder if you have any interest in writing more nonfiction?

HEMON: I don't. I have no interest in nonfiction as a category. It doesn't interest me at all. I don't read biographies, and any book labeled as nonfiction I lose interest in because of its label. Nonfiction is for cowards.

DS: Now there's a throwing down of the gauntlet.

HEMON: Because I think fiction provides challenges.

DS: For both the writer and the reader?

HEMON: Yes. Nonfiction often has this kind of confessional appearance. In other words, I'm going to tell you about myself. I'm going to tell you about my experience, and I'm not going to embellish anything, and you are just going to sit there and listen to what I have to say. It's just boring. It's a one-way street of communication. Fiction engages people at a different level. And I don't want to talk about myself.

DS: You don't want to share observations or express opinions.

HEMON: Right. I do write nonfiction pieces for this magazine in Sarajevo, and occasionally it is solicited, but my overwhelming instinct at all times is to tell stories. Whatever opinion I have, I seek a story that can convey it, that way it lasts longer, in a sense. If I write an op-ed piece for the *New York Times*, people throw away those papers, and rightly so. You read it and then you say, "This is good. This is smart." Then you throw it away. Nobody keeps it. I wouldn't, and it's not insulting. In fact, I like that aspect of writing for papers. That aspect of journalism is a different challenge, how to engage the reader who might or might not read one of the many articles in the magazine, and who might or might not throw it away the same day. But fiction gets to you; I firmly believe this. It gets to your brain through your senses, first and foremost, including the language sense. And this is why it has the possibility of staying around for a longer time, because human perception does not change every five years. The way that people feel cold now is the way people used to feel cold many years ago, many centuries ago.

DS: The body still aches and hungers.

HEMON: Yes, in some ways the body is the universal experience. And I think that thought in fiction can get into the brain through the body.

DS: This reminds me of how in *Nowhere Man* you write about just how completely hideous military life is by describing all the vicious bodily discomforts caused by it.

HEMON: The Army, by definition, is devoid of thought. To be a soldier you have to stop thinking, and there are mechanisms that make that happen. The way the Army explains this to you is through bodily discomfort. I remember my body in the army. I was eighteen at the time and I was a conscript. But I don't remember my thoughts because I had none. I had hatred for my commanding officer, which is hardly a thought, it's a feeling.

DS: I think the real distinction we're talking about is not just between fiction and nonfiction, but between literature and journalism, between imaginative writing and strictly reportorial or op-ed composition. The sensuousness of fiction, poetry, and other creative writing, the mysteriousness of the feelings it describes, this is why you can read the same work over and over again and always discover something new and resonant.

HEMON: In one of Kafka's unpublished stories, the underdog character watches two people talking on the street and has no idea what they are talking about, but one of them, the narrator says, holds his hand with the palm facing the sky, "As if he's balancing the weight of the world on the palm of his hand." I'm not sure what exactly this means, but this scene is indelibly stuck in my mind for the rest of my life. That image is central; I imagine the whole world around that. Such a rare thing. This is what literature does.

Expressing opinions, on the other hand, is easy, and opinions are a dime a dozen. Talk shows produce ten dumb opinions per second, and they are instantly forgotten. What I'm saying is the common experience of our lives is based on this pace, and the material world that we share. Thoughts come and go, you know, but you remember yourself and other people in a place in a time in a sea of sensory experiences that are shared with other people, and this is what literature captures. And this is a challenge. It's not only recording it, it's transforming it into an experience that is beyond itself. I believe that literature has transformative possibilities and duties, in fact, beyond the merely descriptive. It discerns a sort of intensity. Seeing cars in a parking lot is hardly an intense experience, yet Nabokov saw it as something meaningful. That's the challenge.

DS: You excel at transforming the ordinary and bland into images of electrifying implication. In *The Question of Bruno,* Jozef goes to a drab hotel room where every object is bristling with energy and attitude. A place meant to be anonymous is seething with feelings and intimations.

HEMON: The dominant trope of history and the dominant trope of art, is the trope of geniuses—great men, mainly men, who you know are great because we're told they're great and involved in great events. The rest of us who are not great and are not geniuses do not get to participate in great events, do not get to decide whether to start a World War III or not. So I'm stuck with parking lots and hotel rooms and the streets of Chicago, which are beautiful to me, but which are hardly uncommon. They are hardly products of a genius mind. So you can deny this experience, which means you deny a large part of your life, or you can try to transform this life and its commonness, as it were, into something that is beyond itself. I want to engage with the blandest of things because that is my life, and I want to try to transfer them into an experience that is worth sharing. Otherwise I'm stuck at the bottom, while geniuses like George W. Bush run the show.

DS: The best way to fight back is be aware, to pay attention, to remember.

HEMON: I believe that to pay attention to the world in a political sense and also a global sense and a philosophical sense, you have to pay attention to the smallest things. You have to see the hair on the table in front of you and how it shimmers if the light hits it at a certain angle. If you don't see that, you don't see the global situation.

Jamaica Kincaid

Jamaica Kincaid is a persistently autobiographical writer whether she's writing about family, colonialism, or gardening, and her work is charged with a sense of urgency as she seeks understanding of the past and of how it shapes the present. Born Elaine Potter Richardson in 1949 in St. John's, the capital of the small Caribbean island of Antigua, she loved to read as a girl, consuming British novels by the armload and lingering most intently over the works of Charlotte Brönte, whose influence on her work is manifest. But she also became highly sensitive to the racial prejudice and deep-rooted chauvinism inherent in her British-oriented education. Initially, her mother encouraged her ardor for reading, but things changed drastically after Kincaid's father became too ill to work, and she had to leave school at age thirteen to help care for her three younger brothers. Furious at having her education interrupted, she left Antigua for the United States when she turned seventeen to work as an au pair for a family in New York. She was expected to study nursing and then return home, but she went her own way, eventually meeting with success as a freelance journalist. To mark her break with her past, and to cover her tracks, she changed her name in 1973.

Famously flamboyant, Kincaid came to the attention of writer George W. S. Trow, who introduced her to William Shawn, editor of the *New Yorker*. Recognizing her unique talent, Shawn invited her to write for the "Talk of the Town" column. Ultimately, Kincaid wrote eighty-five pieces over the course of twenty years, the best of which are collected in *Talk Stories*. Kincaid became a *New Yorker* staff writer, and much of her fiction debuted in the magazine, including her breathtakingly witty and unnerving first story, "Girl." A three-page, one-sentence exchange between a mother (the first of many daunting mother figures) and her nearly silenced daughter, it forms a sardonic duet that exposes every paradoxical aspect of womanhood. This bravura performance became the first story in Kincaid's first book, the impressionistic story collection *At the Bottom of the River.*

Kincaid achieved a more forthright, though no less lyrical, narrative style in her first novel, *Annie John,* a coming-of-age story rich in cultural and political undertones. Here her signature voice emerges with its deft interweaving of inner and outer realms, its exacting yet poetically resonant descriptions, and its incantatory musicality and stream of consciousness. Here, too, Kincaid establishes an ongoing theme of a young woman's liberation from her mother and her refusal to abide by sexist mores—personal quests for freedom and autonomy designed to embody the need for colonized lands and cultures to throw off the yoke of the imperialist nation, the so-called motherland.

Kincaid hadn't been back to her homeland in almost twenty years when she was awarded a Guggenheim Fellowship in 1986 and made the journey to Antigua. Outraged by what she found there, she wrote her first nonfiction book, *A Small Place,* a blazing indictment of island life, from the obliviousness of tourists to the harsh realities Antiguans contend with, to the inability of Antiguans to establish a compassionate and rational society. The book enraged many, and the Antiguan government attempted to ban it. Kincaid then carried her anger like a torch to her next novel, *Lucy,* a scathing tale about a West Indian au pair employed by a wealthy New York family.

Kincaid's obsession with her painful conflicts with her mother finds its most intense and cathartic expression in *The Autobiography of My Mother.* This gothic and tragic novel about a woman whose mother died giving birth to her, and who is subsequently raised without love and refuses to become a mother herself, opens out into a stunning condemnation of slavery and colonialism, and a haunting elegy for the massacred tribes of the Caribbean. Kincaid then returned to nonfiction to recount the story of her youngest brother, Devon, and his fight with AIDS. The result was the unsparing memoir, *My Brother*, an unforgettable reflection on illness, fear, prejudice, family, and destiny.

Plants have been a lifelong passion for Kincaid, who can't help but view plants and gardening through the lens of imperialism. Her thorny and revealing gardening essays are in *My Garden (Book)*. Plants also occasioned the life-changing trek Kincaid chronicles in *Among Flowers: A Walk in the Himalaya*, a remarkably candid and poetic travelogue. Freed to some degree from her preoccupation with mother figures, Kincaid turns to the figure of the father, and the father's role in the forging of a self, in her novel, *Mr. Potter*, the main subject of our conversation when Kincaid came to the studio in late 2002.

DONNA SEAMAN: Whenever I read your books, I find myself in awe of your narrative voice, its intensity, its clarity. Where does this poetic and incantatory voice come from?

JAMAICA KINCAID: I'm really happy to hear you say that. You know it's true that, when I'm writing, it's very clear and right to me, and then when the book is out in the world and I'm reading it as a reader, I often wonder how it will be experienced by someone who hasn't written the book, which is almost everybody else, because I can see that it doesn't do the thing that a conventional narrative does, which is a thing even I like. I don't really know how to explain it as a style, because even though it is deliberate, I choose to do it—I always choose to write in a certain way—still, it's not as if I can do something else. This is how writing seems to me, that in writing the way I write, I require that language itself be a character. I require that language, ordinary words, have a personality, and even have their own life. So that, just for instance, the way the book begins . . .

DS: The book begins with "And," so that readers know we've entered at mid-stream.

KINCAID: Yes, I did want to do that, to imply that there were some things before and things after, but I started with that juncture, a simple statement, and a simple description of it being midday, which is repeated a great deal because that's a way of making midday into its own personality. It has its own psychology, or I would like the reader to think that.

DS: I feel as though I read your books with my whole body. They sort of take over. They're tremendously atmospheric and very musical.

KINCAID: I rather like you saying that. I read that way as a writer. I find reading very active. When I was little, we'd recommend books to each other and the highest thing we could say was this book is sweet, and of course the word now is used in a different way, but we meant it as if it were something you could taste and feel and wear. We loved books. So I like hearing that. I think I aspire to do that. And I like that writing is work. I think that I like all the things people say are pleasures to be work because I like working. I like reading because it's working, and I have actually turned reading into a job.

DS: It's interesting to hear you talk about reading and writing this way because Mr. Potter is a working man, a chauffeur. And you mention early on that he can't read and he can't write. The narrator in the book knows what a tremendous loss this is, that this means he can't really understand himself and he doesn't know much about the world. This is such a serious deprivation to consider: being aware of all that Mr. Potter is missing reinforces the power and pleasure of the prose.

KINCAID: I know that literature was oral before it became written, but I have this great belief that you don't really know something until you can separate it from yourself, and I think that one of the great vulnerabilities of cultures that do not have writing is that they are very dependent on there being a continuation of memory. And when you have things just repeated, just memorized, there is no interpretation, and there is no change. The thing grows more powerful if it's removed from the individual, if it can be put apart from the individual and weighed by the individual. If it has many interpretations, it becomes a less essential source of power. If everyone can own it individually, and have their own interpretation, then everyone is powerful. But I started to say something about the vulnerability of people who do not have things written down. When the people who have things written down arrive and conquer, they destroy the vessels that carry the things that are not written down, and then the whole culture is lost. But if you have things written down, there is a good chance that in the writing down you may survive—because as I say, it's just not that vulnerable.

DS: I think you need both, but it's true that cultures that depend more on storytelling and oral tradition are on the brink of extinction.

KINCAID: I do believe you need both, but I just prefer reading and writing. I love oral things, but I'm glad that I can have Homer on the page.

DS: I've always felt that the oral tradition is very present in your prose. It seems rooted in the traditional use of repetition, which helps people remember what they're hearing. You often use this device; you write refrains.

KINCAID: I've been thinking about this, and I think the thing I keep forgetting—a great thing that shaped my young childhood imagination—was reciting poetry, written poetry, but I had to recite it a lot, and recite it without understanding it. It was just a question of memorizing it. I'm a great believer in memorizing, by the way. I can no longer do it, but I think my young imagination was very much shaped by repeating and reciting things that were written down. So in some way, I have managed to make one thing into the other. I've managed to make the written word into the oral word, and, I think, vice versa.

DS: In *Mr. Potter*, you're writing about family, and you write about family a great deal. And I believe that you weave a great deal of autobiography into your fiction.

KINCAID: I always do. I have a tremendous amount of autobiography in fiction. I don't really have a separation. I think whatever has happened to me is always front and center. That's just my way.

DS: That fluidity seems intrinsic to the purity of your work. You're not setting things up, you're drawing on the facts, feelings, and truths of your life. I know, for instance, that Potter is one of your names.

KINCAID: That's right. Elaine Cynthia Potter was my name before I changed it to Jamaica Kincaid. When I use facts of my life in my writing, it's as if I've gone to the store and bought a ball of thread. So that I have red thread and yellow thread and blue thread to crochet or weave something. I regard these facts in the writing in a very impersonal way. They are facts about myself, but when I am writing them, it's never really about me. I just never found other facts apart from myself compelling to work with, and you're making me realize, or making me admit, that when I'm writing, words are an essential tool. They are not just words. I'm really not able to write about people's love affairs, and their driving to pick up their children, and, you know, the tiny betrayals and the little moral crises. I really hope to one day because it seems to be the thing that everyone can do. And I don't know why in the dickens I can't do it, but I just can't.

DS: You start with what you know most intimately, and then transcend the autobiographical. Your narrator becomes an everywoman who is able to see her past as ancestral, as connected inexorably to the past of her homeland, the Caribbean, her people, the world. This is the exact opposite of the postmodern way of bringing the writer into the book. You're turning yourself inside out to vanish into the universal.

KINCAID: You know, I think of Mr. Potter as a very modern person in a way, the way he is alienated from himself, isolated from himself. And he makes you realize how alienated all human beings are. The minute a person begins to think of themselves in any situation, they are immediately isolated from their surroundings. That's modern, and so perhaps the very existence of a human being thinking is modern from the very beginning, you know, from the Stone Age. The minute a person said, "Is this a stone?" might be the beginning of modernism. Not James Joyce at all, but the inner questions, "How do I feel about this? What shall I do with it? How does it make me feel about what I'm doing with it?" Maybe that's the beginning of modernism. In some ways we don't like to think of people like Mr. Potter as having these modern experiences. But the modern experience is not about the motor car and air travel. It's about the relationship between the individual and the world, but not just the world, the individual and God, or the individual and anything.

DS: It's interesting how, in the novel, you start out talking about the sun and the sky, then you focus in on Mr. Potter's white shirt against his skin, and how he's dressed and how he walks, and then suddenly we're in this sort of cosmic realm: everything opens up and becomes connected, there's the sea, the earth, the deep past. As happens so often in your work, you're tapping into a spiritual realm.

KINCAID: I don't know how to admit this, but I really did want to place this person in the middle of the beginning, and in the beginning. It's really the reason the book begins "and." In the beginning there was this vast emptiness that you take for granted and then there's this little man in the middle of it who can't read and can't write.

DS: You're so protective of him.

KINCAID: I like him very much, and much to my horror it's been said that it's an angry portrayal. It isn't angry at all. I thought it was very sympathetic.

DS: Tender.

KINCAID: Yes, I thought it was very tender.

DS: And compassionate. The curious thing, though, is that you and the narrator think you should be angry with him because he did not love his daughter, or any of his daughters.

KINCAID: It's just a fact. That part of the story is true. This person really did have all these children. But it's a very common situation, in the world where I come from, for a man to have many children with many different women, and never to have to admit it because nothing is expected of him. And lo and behold, many of the children grow up, sometimes all of them, to be very nice, productive people. They have grown up in fatherless houses, and they don't seem to be prone to more evil-doing than, say, members of the Bush family.

DS: There's a provocative take on the history of conquest and genocide woven into *Mr. Potter,* a theme connected to two rather loaded characters: Mr. Potter's employer, Mr. Shoul, who may be of Lebanese descent, and Dr. Weizenger, who seems to be a Czech Jew in exile from the Holocaust.

KINCAID: Yes, I don't say that Mr. Shoul is Lebanese anymore than I say that Dr. Weizenger is Jewish or Czech. I just say where they come from. But you can infer.

DS: This approach is subtle and somewhat unnerving. There's a scene early in the book in which Mr. Potter has gone to pick up Dr. Weizenger, who has just arrived on the island, and he takes him and his wife to their new home, and they stand there, stricken with awkwardness. They can't begin to understand anything about each other. This feels to me like a scene out of Beckett. There's a reason they've come together, but it's lost in inarticulate sadness.

KINCAID: You see, the thing about Mr. Potter's existence is that, even though he was born in 1922, his life began in 1492 with those murderous actions that came out of Europe. The thing that almost no one points out is how these same murderous actions came marching back to Europe during the twentieth century. It doesn't really happen in isolation. It's not just some new thing the Germans invented. It has a lineage, what they did. But no one likes to say this, and Europe doesn't say to itself, "Oh, I see, we've been doing this all along, but in somewhat different form." You would have thought that set of circumstances, what we now call the Holocaust, would have brought something to an end, but it seems not to have.

DS: All of your work is rooted in your awareness of this terrible, seemingly endless chain of genocide. It's your signature theme.

KINCAID: Yes, I try. It's very irritating to a lot of people, but I plan to keep it up, I'm afraid.

DS: It's a crucial subject, and you're right, it is something we turn away from. But you keep pulling us back to it, even in your writings about gardening and plants. I was quite astonished to read your essays about imperialism in the garden.

KINCAID: The more people are annoyed at me for it, the more I realize that what they don't like is that I bring it up in what they think is a safe place, because what could be more untroubled than the garden. But my goodness, the whole of creation ends in the garden, and it's in the garden that trouble begins. It's where good and evil become known, and we know how troublesome that is.

DS: Let me ask you about another theme in your work: the conflicts between men and women.

KINCAID: Again, that seems so universal. In the world we recognize, this world we want to be in, where women want to run corporations and bomb people, where women want access to these things, to power, it's as if everything, for it to be valuable, has to be transformed into a man's realm. Even knitting, if it were to become valuable, would have to be transformed into something that made a billion dollars or could enable you to see in the dark or something.

DS: We don't genuinely value femaleness.

KINCAID: That's right. I think we don't. What we think is valuable is what is men's.

DS: Still.

KINCAID: Still, and I don't know if a new generation of women will figure that out, but certainly we continue to transform the world of value and even of equality into the masculine realm. In the place I'm from, it's not a battle of the sexes so much as a domestic irritation, because the realm of the female is very valuable. Where I'm from, women have enormous influence and enormous power.

DS: It's certainly true that the women in your fiction are extremely powerful.

KINCAID: And complete.

DS: Here we are talking about gender and society, and genocide, as though these are discussed topically in your work. Actually, these matters are deeply embedded in descriptions of landscapes, and how a person walks, and the blare of the sun. You write not about issues, but about the state of being.

KINCAID: State of being? Yes, I'm very interested in the state of being, because it's so mysterious to me, and I think that it must be the most common form of godliness—that each person's state of being is holy. I'm not a particularly religious person, but it seems to be clearer and clearer that, when I am writing about people, I'm very aware that they are some kind of extraordinary creation. I can't really explain them. In my writing, I try very hard to understand what a human being is. And the only human beings I have known are people who normally aren't thought of as human beings: poor black people living on an island who came there as slaves, or some who are descended from master and slave, who occupy a place that is full of the most horrendous crimes in history.

You know, those islands were occupied by people before 1492, and those islands were depopulated within fifty years of the arrival of a new group of people. I'm always so aware that the people living in this place are witnesses or testaments: their existences are testaments of something terrible. And I think, when I am writing about them, whether it's in *The Autobiography of My Mother* or *Annie John,* and certainly by this time when I'm writing about a character like Mr. Potter, I think "how can I explain what a human being is?" The terrible irony is that these islands are really beautiful, that incredible, murderous things happen in such lovely places. They aren't harshly beautiful like the desert, they're paradisaical. That's what is so peculiar.

DS: Yes, you write often about that paradox. For instance, in *Mr. Potter,* the sun is always beaming, which makes tourists happy, but in fact, the island is in the grip of a terrible drought, and the islanders are suffering. To go back to the question of the holiness of individual lives, I wonder if you feel that literature has a moral imperative?

KINCAID: Yes, I feel that way completely. Whatever sort of people writers write about, a car salesman or a person that sells computers, I think that's a holy person. Let's say there's a scene in a contemporary novel in which people are coming home from work after dealing with a lot of stress, and they meet more stress at home, and then instead of doing yoga or something that would relieve the stress, they suddenly think, "Oh, I'll have a drink." You know, something like: "I made myself a martini." If I were to contemplate a person doing that, I would have to contemplate the origins of martinis, for instance, or what gin is made of. If someone made a meal, I'm afraid I would wonder about the origins of potatoes, then I'd have to talk about the Andes and how is it that the Irish came to depend on this thing that grew in the Andes. And I would wonder, as I often do, "What did the Irish eat before potatoes?" I can't help it. So, to me, the life of a car salesman is either the most joyous thing or the most sad thing, or the most beautiful thing, and maybe all of that.

DS: This a poet's way of looking at the world, and there certainly is poetry in your prose.

KINCAID: I do read a lot of poetry, and I would have loved to have been a poet. I think it's the noblest thing in the entire world. Of all the forms of writing, of all the things you can do, of all the things you can be, to write poetry and to be a poet I think is the most blessed, wonderful thing. I just have never felt that I was deserving of it. And so I have just never done it, but it's the only thing really worth reading if you have the spiritual stamina for it. And I don't have it as much as I like, but I do read poetry and I do love poets.

DS: That's a perfect description: the spiritual stamina. I have to bring the right sort of energy to poetry. You have to be really sharp, and open.

KINCAID: That's true. Good poems put you through something. To read Gerard Manley Hopkins, Shakespeare, Derek Walcott, is to enter a world of great mental activity. The poet's tool cupboard is as big as the ocean.

DS: I feel that each book you've written has meant a great deal to you, that you don't approach them as projects.

KINCAID: That's true. The only sort of project I have is the garden writing.

DS: Is that a release for you? Does it require a different sort of energy?

KINCAID: Yes, it's a different kind of energy, but it's not a release. I'm not an historian or a philosopher, but I end up looking at history from the garden's point of view. I write about the origins of dahlias, or how the color in European gardens changed after 1492, because so much of what's in a European garden comes from exploration, from the Old World of Asia and the New World in our hemisphere. I was reading the other day about how European landscape painting changed because of Captain Cook's first journey around the world. He had taken not only scientists but also artists, and they had never seen landscapes like that before. So when they returned to Europe, apparently, they had a big influence and changed European painting.

DS: Do you know what your next book will be?

KINCAID: No, it depends on which one I finish first. I'm always writing two or three things at once.

Chang-rae Lee

Chang-rae Lee was born in Seoul, South Korea, in 1965, and immigrated to the United States in 1968. He grew up in Westchester, New York, attended Yale University, and earned his M.F.A. at the University of Oregon. After returning to New York, Lee worked for a year as a Wall Street analyst. Once his writing life was underway, he switched to teaching. He became the director of the creative writing program at Hunter College and is now on the faculty at Princeton University.

Lee's first novel, *Native Speaker*, was a literary sensation. A portrait of a Korean American, Henry Park, who works for a private intelligence agency in New York City, it explores questions of identity, race, alienation, emotional accessibility, the nexus of private lives and politics, and the dynamics of a marriage cruelly tested by the death of a child. *Native Speaker* won the PEN/Hemingway Award and the Barnes & Noble Discover Great New Writers Award, and was selected as an American Library Association Notable Book of the Year.

In his second novel, *A Gesture Life,* Lee transforms what seems at the outset to be a tale of suburban angst into a searing examination of the psychosis and horrors of war. Franklin "Doc" Hata has earned a sterling reputation in pretty little Bedley Run, New York, as the town's sole Japanese American citizen and the always considerate and helpful proprietor of a medical supply store. But Hata is assailed by painful memories: musing over his poor Korean family and how they gave him up for adoption to a wealthy, childless Japanese couple; and about how he fell in love with a Korean comfort woman during his service in the Imperial army. Exposed so brutally to humanity's capacity for evil, Hata has lost the ability to succumb to passion.

Reserved and solitary, devoted to habits of being that help him keep emotions at bay, he is wholly unprepared for the emotional complexity and chaos that he inadvertently brings into his orderly life by adopting a Korean orphan, the daughter of a Korean mother and an African American soldier. Lee's story of a good man whose soul has been cauterized would resonate in even the plainest of prose, but the sheer glory of his writing—its spiraling structure, perfect pitch and pace, the intensity and exactitude of every suspenseful scene—makes this a true work of art. *A Gesture Life* won the Anisfield-Wolf Book Award, the Gustavus Myers Outstanding Book Award, and the Asian-American Literary Award, and it was designated as a Best Book of the Year by the *New York Times, Los Angeles Times, Christian Science Monitor,* and *Esquire.*

In his third novel, *Aloft,* Lee portrays Doc Hata's opposite, Jerry Battle, who is, or should be, a quintessential insider. Frank, self-deprecating, funny, and acutely observant and articulate, Jerry is heir to the American dream. His Italian immigrant grandfather started a masonry business which his son, Jerry's father, turned into a lucrative Long Island landscaping company that Jerry, in turn, managed until handing it over to his ambitious son, Jack. But not even close family ties, job security, and plenty of money can protect Jerry, a widower at fifty-nine, from life's cruelties.

Flying has been his salvation. The only time Jerry feels serene and free is when he's aloft and above it all. Not that Jerry is ever in the thick of things; he's always somewhat airborne and out of reach. As he meanders into memory and reverie, and offers caustic commentary and antic reportage on unfolding events that alternate between the absurd and the catastrophic, the reader comes to understand that Jerry is not so different from Doc Hata after all. He, too, habitually avoids dealing with emotions, a restraint exacerbated by the tragic death of his Korean wife, Daisy.

A great deal happens in the deceptively placid suburban world Lee conjures, some of it profound, some of it hilarious. As he glides between comedy and tragedy, he neatly parses our complex feelings about race, ethnicity, assimilation, sexuality, political correctness, age, and dignity. And he is profoundly concerned with the nature of love and the giving of care, writing discerningly about family, illness, sacrifice, and loyalty. Chang-rae Lee first appeared on *Open Books* in 2000, and we spoke again in the spring of 2004.

DONNA SEAMAN: You were born in Seoul, Korea, but your family immigrated to the U.S. when you were just a toddler, and you grew up in Westchester County, New York, the plush yet melancholy setting of much of your novel, *A Gesture Life*. Even though you grew up in America, you're exquisitely sensitive to the traumas and confusions associated with immigration, of trying to fit into an alien culture. I wonder why this looms so large in your imagination and if this attunement to outsiderness is a factor in your becoming a writer?

CHANG-RAE LEE: Westchester is a particular landscape I keep returning to because it's a place of wishes and dreams for an immigrant family, especially an immigrant family that's landed in New York. And we all know what it looks like: there are suburbs like it all across America. But it's also a place of prosperity, of quiet, and of a certain kind of standing. It can also be a place where certain folks, certain immigrants, in this case a man called Doc Hata, can hide, where you have a kind of veil. Property grants you this. And also you're not seen in the same way that you would be seen in an ethnic community in the city, where you're among others like you. Instead, you're always trying to belong. So it's always like being a newcomer, even if you've lived there for thirty years, as Doc Hata has. And I sort of feel the same way. I live now in a suburb in New Jersey right across from New York, and it's not as if I'm ever pained by living there. There are no incidents, racial or otherwise, that I have to deal with. But there is always a little bit of a distance that comes about for no reason at all, and sometimes things don't seem quite real.

DS: Franklin "Doc" Hata, the hero of *A Gesture Life,* is a retired businessman and the only Japanese American in the suburb in which he lives, and his story is an incredibly subtle one. I note your title's allusion to being correct but distant, polite but cryptic. And not only is he veiled and in hiding, he has developed habits of being, private rituals, in an effort to keep his life orderly—to keep painful memories in check, as we learn. One of his habits is swimming in his backyard pool, and you have him read a story that the reader will recognize as "The Swimmer" by John Cheever. I take it, then, that you want us to know that we're in Cheever country.

LEE: Yes, it absolutely is "The Swimmer," and it is Cheever Country. I thought it would be a delight to throw that in there because I've long been a Cheever fan, but probably for different reasons than a lot of Cheever fans are Cheever fans. I read those stories with an anthropological interest. As we recall what happens in "The Swimmer," this younger man, or at least he starts out as a younger man, is swimming across the county in people's pools and slowly coming to the realization that he's losing his mind and his life and everything around him. It's a wonderful story, and one that I will always, always remember, and take to heart. But when Doc Hata reads this story, he is, in his own way, a little dull to it. He muses about the point of it all, and he wishes that its meaning and its theme were clearer. But he is moved to the point of thinking, "Well, what would someone think of me swimming in my pool in my backyard, this older Asian gentleman in the suburb." And I just loved the picture of him swimming in his dark—he describes his pool as being slate-sided—pool, seeing him in that black water. I really like the idea of him escaping everyday reality physically, and, of course, spiritually.

DS: When we meet Doc Hata, he's at a major transition point in his life, but it's all rather mysterious. We know nothing about his past, but we feel its pressure. As I continued reading, I felt your novel was like a bud, tightly closed but packed with life, and then it slowly unfurls.

LEE: I really felt that I needed to start very, very small and very, very quietly and with a very small perspective on things. And I think my editor was a little worried about how small I started. I think she thought, "Gee, will anyone continue to read this story because it just seems like he's just this nice little gentleman in suburban New York," which is not such a sexy story. But it felt like it absolutely had to be that way because of who he is—that he's not so forthcoming about his life and himself—and because he's the one telling the story. It's not someone else telling his story who can reveal anything at any time. This is the challenge I had as a writer, to write the story of a man who didn't really want to tell you his story, but to have him tell it anyway.

DS: There's so much tension in the prose, and the reader is quickly intrigued with Doc Hata because we sense that he's holding so much back.

LEE: I think what I liked immediately about his character was not so much what he did in his life—and I didn't know quite all that when I started—but his voice, the measure and the rhythm of his voice. And I thought I could get a lot in there, but very slowly. He's porous in some ways, and there's a lot that he can hold, but you have got to squeeze him.

DS: Hata is more than twice your age. Was it somehow liberating to write from a point of view of someone older?

LEE: Yes, and I liked the idea that no one would ever say this was autobiographical. I was accused of that in my first book, as all first novelists are. And I think maybe Asian American novelists are accused more than others, so that was a nice side benefit of writing about an older man. But his voice suits me, too. I think maybe my own nature, at least at this point in my writing life, is found in the natural pace of his thinking and the way he gets to things. He makes very clear observations, but he's not rash.

I worried that Franklin Hata was too fastidious. He is a very difficult person and frustrating in some ways. He's like so many people I know, and I've been saying—and this is absolutely true—that he's the person I don't want to become, that I'm always afraid of becoming. Because he's so neat, and so protected that he seems absolutely content and perfect, while of course, he's the furthest thing from that.

DS: Observation drives the story. And memories, including his memories of serving in the Japanese army and his relationship with a comfort woman he refers to as K. You've said that K was the first character you thought about when you were planning this novel.

LEE: Right, she was my focus, and she was my intent from the day I found out about comfort women and what happened to them. I couldn't believe all of this had occurred. As a Korean, I didn't even know about it. To me and other Koreans, it's a holocaust. We are talking about a hundred and fifty thousand women, girls really, who were used this way. I was just so set and so passionate about this woman's story. I thought, "This is going to be such a sad and beautiful tragic story," and I couldn't believe I was going to write it. I had all these great intentions, and I did write it. I worked on it for two years, and did all the research associated with it, but I found that it just wasn't working out in the way that I wanted it to work out. Maybe my expectations were too high. Maybe my wish to honor the subject was too much. You know, art fails when it tries to do those kinds of things.

I think, too, that part of the problem was that I had met some of these women. I actually spent an afternoon with some of them in Seoul, and I couldn't get their voices or their faces out of my head. Their presence was so powerful. My prose never seemed to equal that, so I thought, "Why am I doing this? Someone else can do this, I can't do this." So one day out of utter despair I decided, I'm not going to write this book anymore because I'm not adding anything to anything. But I did think about this one guy, this medic, who showed up in a scene. He was literally a guy who comes in, delivers something, and leaves. But my mind's eye was following him out of the examination room, out in the camp, and then into his life. That's when everything started to expand for me. Then I began to think about all the complications, moral and otherwise, associated with a man who has had an experience like that, of caring for a comfort woman. To think about what his character was then, and what it would be afterwards. And to think also about him maybe having a prosperous life, a life that on the outside was absolutely wonderful. You can see how it became so much more ornate.

DS: K haunts Doc Hata, but his adopted daughter, Sunny, is the one who really puts him to the test.

LEE: When I read *A Gesture Life* at bookstores, some readers said, "She's just so relentless in her bitterness and her hatred and her hardness towards him, and it seems like he has given her everything. So why is she so angry at him?" It's hard to explain. I can see how they could feel that way, but for me, she is there because she calls his bluff emotionally. She is the sort of person who can really see through all of his, as you say, habits of being. His MO is to always soothe, to be a good citizen—to try and fit in and not ruffle any feathers. Sunny, of course, chooses to do the exact opposite. Although she's not happy about it, she is willing to let her father have the perception that she's a little promiscuous, that she's involved with shady characters in town. I think it's mostly because she feels like she's been put into the role of a daughter who's been adopted not out of love or need, but as a part in his facade.

DS: When she first arrives, she's a bone-thin, skeptical seven-year-old orphan who has traveled halfway around the world to this gentleman who wants her to be a perfect girl, a doll. And Hata confesses when he first meets her that he's a little dismayed at her appearance, and then he realizes that not only is she of mixed race, but that she's born of war.

LEE: Yes, she's not the pure Korean or Asian that he thought he was going to get, and I think it's clear that Sunny recognizes this disappointment in his face, and that it tips the ship a little bit. If she is hard, I think she's hard in her youth. Later on, when she returns home, and she's older and has a son, she is, if not warm, at least willing to get along. I think it gives Doc the opening through which he can explore his life again. I've realized that without Sunny, there is no book. Even if there is the whole war story, even if we have all his memories, without her presence in the present time, I don't think he can actually go through what he needs to go through. That's because Sunny doesn't know anything about his past. In fact, no one does. I felt that was right. I felt that he would never, ever tell anyone about that. Although, of course, he does have to tell us about it.

DS: That's the movement of the book, Hata's finally coming to terms with his past, including his own adoption. Did you see adoption as an echo of immigration, another form of displacement, or way of losing connection to your heritage, your roots?

LEE: In some sense it's never having roots, because the roots that you can point to aren't yours. I think a lot of adoptees, particularly Korean ones, feel that although they are from Korea they have no connection to it. When they can look at their families here, it's quite apparent that they don't have a blood connection, the same kind of connection that most of us take for granted, and to some extent enjoy. Yes, for me, adoption is a very clear instance of belonging and not belonging. For Hata, that's a condition of his life, and yes, by adopting Sunny, and by coping with her antagonism, he has to relive his own adoption, and all his compromises and assimilations.

DS: I was struck by a passage in which Hata remembers his boyhood and discloses the fact that Hata is a shortened version of Korihata, which translates as "black flag."

LEE: Yes. The black flag, as I was told, was what a village would put up in Japan to ward off visitors if there was some kind of contagion within the town. It's really a "Keep Out" sign. And maybe it was put up sometimes just to keep certain people out, which I thought fit him very well. His name is a kind of warning to all those who might enter his life and his heart. And at the end, he laments the fact that everyone he's ever touched, at least he feels this way, has come to some great misfortune. So it's a flag that I think he's always carrying, both out of a wish not to hurt others, and also as a sign of the shadow he feels within.

DS: Can you name any literary influences?

LEE: I read so many people. When the book first came out, a lot of people said that the book, or the voice, reminded them of Kazuo Ishiguro's *Remains of the Day.* I had read that book and admired it, and I do admire and like his work. Voice and tone are so important to me. The tone that I was hearing was more from writers like Walker Percy and Richard Ford. I don't know why that is, maybe because they write about isolated men in suburban settings. I also didn't want to make Hata sound Asian in a very obvious way. I wanted him to sound very American because his thoughts are not like the way he talks. The song of his heart was one of melancholy and the kind of emptiness that gives a slight chill to everything that he says.

DS: Your prose is so lapidary and your psychology so nuanced, I feel as though your work falls inside the Henry James school of fiction. But when you write of war, I feel the overwhelming despair and helplessness, the profound frustration and sadness that Joseph Conrad evokes.

LEE: I was very conscious of the shift in voice in the war scenes. I guess there's less poetry in those, no flourishes. It's a little clinical, and it's a little more spare, and I think it's just because I couldn't bear to write it any other way. I tried to write that way in the suburban sections and it just didn't work. I didn't want his voice to completely change because that would be wrong for the book and no one would believe it, but there had to be a difference. So I asked myself, "What is the right kind of music for that?" It's a music that's quiet, and that sits back. I hope it lets what he's describing come through.

DS: Hata is very skeptical about beauty, yet he thinks about it a great deal.

LEE: He does. He describes it all the time, and yet he's always looking for the other side of it. That's what I tried to do with the sentences and what I tried to do with his voice.

DS: Beauty is often under siege. K, the only person he loves, is brutalized. Sunny is beautiful and plays beautiful music, yet she behaves in a deliberately unattractive, irritating, and self-destructive manner. And Hata almost destroys his beautiful home.

LEE: Beauty is a real curse in his mind and in his experience. It only brings sorrow and malfeasance, yet he can't help but have beautiful things and people around him.

DS: And be drawn to them. And he himself is elegant.

LEE: Yes. I had hoped that he was an elegant older gentleman.

DS: He dresses perfectly. He's very tasteful, so much more refined than everyone around him, which seems indicative of deep loneliness to me. That's what the reader feels, that his perfection is a trap, isolating and claustrophobic.

LEE: Yes, and for me there is also a component of beauty that is straight from Mishima's sadness, his spare lyricism, because beauty is waning and it can only be sullied in this horrible world of ours. There are lots of things running through my head, and his head, concerning that.

DS: I can see how Mishima would interest you. Clearly, he's an artist who found life to be torturous on many levels.

LEE: Oh so beautiful and oh so awful.

DS: And the pressure in his work to do the right thing is excruciating.

LEE: Duty is the force and prerogative of living, which is such a burden, and Hata has that burden. He is a creature of duty. I know about this from growing up in my family, too. I'm Korean, and in a Confucian society, duty is a big part of life. Duty is really the only thing that makes things work. One's fealty to duty and honoring of duty is crucial, without that, there's nothing.

DS: Speaking of duty, you teach writing as well as practice it, do you not?

LEE: Yes, and I enjoy teaching. I actually do. Sometimes it takes up more time than I would like to give it because I would like to be writing. But even if I didn't have to teach, I think I would. I remember so clearly, when I did a graduate program, the same sort of program that I'm directing now, how fortunate I felt to have people around me who cared about my writing and gave me advice and counsel and mentorship. It always reminds me how just plain lucky I am to be able to write and do that for a living.

DS: Does teaching keep your writing more vital?

LEE: Yes, because I always see these young writers and their struggles and their excitement and their eagerness. I like working with that. What I think I enjoy most about it is the academic aspect, when we talk about craft and technique. But in the end, what I'm always inspired by is the passionate nature of these writers.

DS: Did you have a teacher who was especially inspiring?

LEE: My great mentor was, and still is, Garrett Hongo. He's such a wonderful poet, and memoirist. He's such a beautiful writer. We talked about writing and literature, of course, but I also just learned a lot from him about how to be an artist. How to think about the work and how to commit one's self to the work. You know, those are the things that you find out on your own, but it's wonderful to see them in practice. It never hurts. It's wonderful to find an inspiration.

DS: A writer has to feel that what they do matters, because it's so hard and it can be so lonely. When you describe having spent all that time writing the first version of *A Gesture Life,* and then having to set it aside and start over, I can just imagine how crushing that was.

LEE: That was the worst day of my professional life.

DS: And it takes a lot of courage to go on. Many people want to write. The urge to write is very common and rather wonderful, although I hope that it includes the desire to read as well. But there is a great difference between that nascent longing to express one's self in language and being able to actually do the work. To maintain that sort of conviction, you really do need to have someone to talk to about it, or you're not going to make it.

LEE: I agree, and I think as a fiction writer I was particularly lucky in hooking up with someone who is a poet. I started out writing poetry and writing creatively when I was in high school. I've always been drawn to poetry, first as a reader. I think Garrett Hongo encouraged my own love of language and obsession with language in a way that maybe a fiction writer who is more interested in story wouldn't have.

DS: That's the great divide between popular fiction and literary fiction. Pop fiction is all about story, action, and the concrete, exterior world. Literary fiction is more internalized, the language richer, more poetic, with descriptions that help explicate ideas. What's so notable about your work is an acute sensitivity to language, and to the workings of the mind.

LEE: I try to do that. So much of writing, for me, is language. I know I've heard some novelists talk about how they've always wanted to tell stories from the time they were young, and I never quite feel that way. I never felt myself to be a storyteller in that mode, and my imagination doesn't run that way. It really runs more towards the human voice and then what that might suggest about a story. The voice suggests the story, not the other way around. Even if I wanted to sketch out the plot beforehand I couldn't. Even as much as I tried to think about what might happen, what really happens always confounds and surprises me. I have in the past written out little things that I would like to see happen, but I never end up following them. I have copious notes, but I never look at them again. That's the strange thing about it. I'm always asked, "Do you carry around a little notebook?" Sometimes I do, but then I never look at it, so what's the point of it? But it's very frightening when you write a novel like that because you feel as if you are completely unorganized.

DS: Did you have fun writing *Aloft*?

LEE: I had a lot of fun writing *Aloft*, for a lot of reasons. On the writing front, the daily grind, I wouldn't say that it was easy, but it did feel as if the language, and the cadences and the rhythm, were coming to me in a way that felt more natural than ever before. I was surprised by this, given who the protagonist, Jerry Battle, is. But I just felt that I was in a certain zone with the language that I'd always dreamed about.

DS: Do you think that writing about someone whose experiences don't parallel yours freed you in some way? Opened a door onto that zone?

LEE: The other books don't parallel my experiences. In fact, *Aloft* may have been easier because in a strange way Jerry's life does parallel my life. Not, of course, in the outward outline, but the daily rhythms of his life and my life. I didn't feel like I needed to reach for anything. I was imagining within a world that I was very familiar with—family life, suburbia.

DS: There's always been an element of social critique in your work. In *Aloft*, I felt that it attained the level of satire.

LEE: Oh, definitely. But it's the kind of critique that's both within and without. Jerry is not revolutionary in any way. He's not trying to upset the cart, but he is trying to feel all the little bumps and shocks of that cart as it goes along. He's someone who's probably too far gone in terms of accepting his realm. There's no other world out there for him. He's not going to go to a commune. But I did want him to look at everything in such a way that he developed a deep seam of worry. He definitely sees his son, Jack, who is putting the family landscape business in jeopardy, as a product of our culture.

DS: I think the "house that Jack built" is a riot. That gigantic, overly designed, status-symbol mansion.

LEE: Right, and Jerry is awestruck by and proud of that eighth wonder of the world.

DS: Your depiction of a multigenerational family is so compelling, especially as measured within an evolving family business that sharply mirrors changes in society.

LEE: I wanted the business to decline in fits and starts, to decline, that is, with the appearance of expanding, which goes straight to the heart of what Jerry is thinking about the culture. There are some basic, fundamental things that aren't going right. The dot.com bubble is a great example of this. But also, Jack's enterprising intentions are bringing everything down, and he's forgotten everything that really built the business, which was literally brick and mortar. And that's no accident, the fact that it used to be a brick-and-mortar business, and now Jack is enamored of the virtual. There's a decline in the family, too. Immigrant families are so centered, people work so hard and stay close together. But with generation after generation, we've all separated from one another, often because of prosperity. Jack is separated from his family members by that huge, honking house. And the telling detail in that house, and about what's happened to the family, is that he needs a kitchen in his bedroom suite because the main kitchen is just too far away, and he wants everything right there.

DS: Another telling detail is the library without books. To me, this seemed indicative of the fractured state of the stories we tell, our break with the past, our loss of tradition.

LEE: Yes, it's a beautiful library, but what does it house? House design magazines. Nothing substantive. So yes, the house is very central to the novel. I needed a house that would fall apart, and I like the idea that in the end they all end up in Jerry's old ranch house.

DS: You also satirize our materialism and status-seeking in a hilarious scene in which Jerry, in effect, duels with a rival to try to get his lover, Rita, back. Their epic "battle," to pun on Jerry's last name, consists of a tennis match in which Jerry bets his plane and the other guy puts up his Ferrari.

LEE: To go back to your question about having fun, my other two books are pretty darn serious. They don't have much levity. They don't have a lot of release through humor, but rather through the end of violence or the end of sadness. But there's very little quirkiness. They're straightforward and serious. In this book, I wanted to change gears. I wanted Jerry to riff, and make fun, and have an entertaining perspective on everyday matters. So I found it fun to write about a silly pissing contest, a tennis match with a plane and a Ferrari. It's outrageous, but that's the sort of thing I did have fun with. I think it's been good for me to write this book. I felt like I always had range, but given the subject matter and the characters in the first two books, I wasn't interested in revealing it. Here, because Jerry is Jerry and he feels at liberty to talk about anything and anyone in any way, it gave me that same levity.

DS: I wonder if the character Paul, a very serious and somewhat esoteric Asian American writer, embodies you in some way. Perhaps your old self.

LEE: He is a part of myself, and I wouldn't say an old part. Of course, we only see Paul through Jerry's point of view, but how he sees Paul is how I feel that the culture sees me: as a semi-exotic, on-the-margins fellow who does all he can to write about his subjects, but the subjects, as Jerry says, aren't the hottest ticket. I am poking fun at myself, but I do worry about being seen this way.

DS: Yet as much fun as you had, and as hilarious as certain scenes are, this is a sad and tragic novel.

LEE: Yes, and Jerry is ultimately a really sad and pathetic figure. But I wanted him to have a certain amount of likability so that he'd be charming enough to keep you reading, so that you'd feel insinuated into his personality.

DS: And he does act. He does come down to earth, if you will. He does liberate his father from the old people's home, and at the end, he gathers his family to him.

LEE: And that's what he's desperately been trying to avoid, having everyone living in his house. It's not a happy ending, but he's now accepting that maybe this is a better way to live—together instead of all apart, independent, or so-called independent. And I think that's one of the problems in our culture, that we all think that we're independent agents and that we don't really need anybody. But of course we do.

DS: It's so circular, the way you show us how the immigrant family starts out tightly knit together, due, in part, to being poor. Then as people become more prosperous, they go their separate ways, but then life delivers its blows—illness, age, and death—and people draw back together. You reveal both how much society and the exterior world have changed from generation to generation over the course of the last century, and how people are still the same inside.

LEE: I think what we figure out about Jerry is that he is a lot like everybody has always been. He's a lot like me. My favorite fan mail this season was from a fifty-two-year-old black female bookseller in rural North Carolina. She wrote that she'd never written to an author before, but she wanted to write to me because she really thought that she was Jerry Battle. I thought that was great. She said, I never would have thought I'd be connected to a guy like that before I read the book, but the more I read it, the more I thought, I am Jerry Battle.

DS: You can't ask for a stronger affirmation as a writer than that. Your observations and way of thinking are so profoundly literary, I wonder what you would be if you weren't a novelist.

LEE: If I weren't a novelist, I would either be a food writer or a chef or restaurateur because I'm obsessed with food. I've been writing for food magazines, and will continue to. Food is definitely the largest part of my life. Being a writer means you're home a lot, and you certainly can't write all day, at least I can't. The rest of the day is this incredibly frightening void of indolence, so one has to do something. I like to make bread and cook.

SECTION FIVE: WORLDS WITHIN WORLDS

The most haunting and subtle works of fiction describe the complex workings of the mind, often through arresting metaphors that reveal the connection between the world within and the world without. To explicate the psyche, the relentless reportage of the senses, the interplay of memory, reverie, fantasy, thought, and feeling—this is what literature does best. The reward for reading fiction is the chance to enter the world of a person wholly unlike the writer and, perhaps, the reader. Richly psychological fiction offers invaluable insights into human nature, from the wildness of sexuality and the convictions of love to the thickly braided ties between parent and child, the subtle yet often devastating emotional legacies that are passed down unwittingly from one generation to the next, the catalysts for violence and self-destruction, the chemistry of grief, the solace of beauty, the inspiration for altruism, and the mystery and toll of creativity.

The writers we read over and over again not only capture the ephemeral workings of the heart and mind, but also create compelling characters, entrancing stories, and vivid settings, and conduct penetrating inquiries into the nexus between individual and society. By nesting the illuminated inner world of their characters within a sharply delineated outer world, novelists are able to trace the ways that world shapes a personality and forges a soul. Psychologically acute novelists tend to write poetically, revealing as much about the human condition in the nuance of language as in the twists and turns of the plot. These writers recreate the texture of life so precisely we call their work realism, until they dig even deeper into the unconscious to present scenes so transporting and otherworldly, yet laced so intrinsically into the story, we call their fiction magical realism.

Stuart Dybek summons up both the earthiness and romance of Chicago, a city on a great lake that is at once a city on the make, to quote Nelson Algren, and Dybek's own "Dreamville." Ward Just dramatizes states of mind that encompass everything from innocence to cynicism, grief, and fear in settings as disparate as Vietnam and Illinois. Alice McDermott's novels mesh the intimacy and conflicts of family life with the dynamics of close-knit communities as her characters struggle into selfhood. And Joyce Carol Oates imbues her fictional worlds with the dark forces of sexual predation, obsession, and loneliness, as well as the resiliency, determination, and strength of survivors who triumph over the bleakest or most harrowing dilemmas.

Stuart Dybek

Stuart Dybek is a poet and a short story writer whose work is inspired and shaped by his memories of growing up in Chicago, and by his love for music. The eldest of three sons, Dybek was born in 1942 in the working-class neighborhood known as Pilsen and attended Catholic schools. Books and humor were his primary passions as a boy, although he spent most of his free time hanging out on the street with friends. Dybek was the first in his family to go to college. He graduated from Loyola University Chicago (where he had quickly switched from pre-med to English), then enrolled in the Iowa Writers' Workshop. His first published story, "The Palatski Man," appeared in 1970 in the *Magazine of Fantasy and Science Fiction.*

Dybek's vision of Chicago underlies his down-to-earth, funny, and erotic books: two poetry collections, *Brass Knuckles* and *Streets in Their Own Ink,* and three works of fiction, *Childhood and Other Neighborhoods, The Coast of Chicago,* and *I Sailed with Magellan.* As versed in realism as in surrealism, Dybek has created a mythic city of brick and asphalt, desire and dreams, a checkerboard of ethnically defined neighborhoods in which human life in all its striving, absurdity, and beauty dominates, while nature, in all its determined wildness and glory, persists in the city's weedy seams and in the vastness of Lake Michigan. Dybek's linked stories and poetry are as essential to understanding life in Chicago as works by Nelson Algren, Gwendolyn Brooks, and Saul Bellow, yet Dybek transcends his earthy precincts, spiriting readers away to more mysterious, archetypal, and profound realms. Not only does Dybek masterfully evoke the intricate web of urban life, he also elucidates the complex relationship between people and place in painterly descriptions of city streets, the chimerical lake, and the white-cap-raising and trash-spinning wind, thus showing our ability to discern and be transformed by beauty, however unlikely its manifestations and harsh its settings.

Dybek's work has appeared in the *New Yorker,* the *Atlantic Monthly, Harper's, Poetry,* the *Paris Review,* and *TriQuarterly.* He has been the recipient of many awards including a Whiting Writers' Award, a Pushcart Prize, several O. Henry Prizes, and a PEN/ Bernard Malamud Award. A professor of English at Western Michigan University, Dybek was in his hometown in late May 2004 when we spoke, making one of many appearances associated with the selection of *The Coast of Chicago* for One Book, One Chicago, a city-wide reading and discussion program sponsored by the Chicago Public Library.

DONNA SEAMAN: Your stories are so poetic, the imagery and metaphors so rich and fully integrated into character and story, I'm curious what form you started writing first, poetry or fiction.

STUART DYBEK: They were always simultaneous, and continue to be written in tandem, so to speak. I kind of "collect" in poetry. Writers often keep little journals, and I call mine "A Great Thoughts Notebook," with tongue firmly planted in cheek. In there a lot of stuff gets recorded in a sloppy verse line, and imagery is emphasized. Then I loot it for both stories and poems.

DS: In talking about the early stages of writing when you aren't sure what form a piece is going to take, you've referred to pieces-in-progress as "unidentified written objects."

DYBEK: Yes. It very seldom happens that a piece starts out as fiction and ends up as a poem, but it has happened to me frequently that a piece starts out as poem and ends up as a story. Ray Carver wrote both fiction and poetry. People, most of whom much preferred his fiction, used to say that he didn't think he could write fiction if he didn't write poetry, no matter what anyone else thought about his poems, which, I hasten to add, I do like.

DS: There's an intriguing tension in your stories between what we call reality, or observable life, and other dimensions of being. And I think you bridge the divide between the tangible world and the unconscious, or the hidden world, with images. *I Sailed with Magellan,* for instance, is brimming with images of water, birds, and flowers. Is this is a conscious choice? A deliberate strategy?

DYBEK: I don't think it started out consciously. And to this day I remain a big believer in taking advantage of accidents—which are often an indication of what your un-reflected-upon-instincts are—but without drawing it out too much. For instance, for my first book of stories, I had written a bunch of stories and they didn't seem to have much coherence. I really hadn't even thought of them as a book. Then a local library asked me to do a talk, and they asked me to give them a title for the talk, and while I was happy to do the talk, I hated the notion of giving it a title. I always have a hard time coming up with something snappy. I worried about that excessively, and somewhere along the line I came up with *Childhood and Other Neighborhoods.*

Initially I was just proud of myself for having succeeded in coming up with a title for my talk, but later on I became kind of fond of it. Then I realized that it could be the book's title. So that was an accident. A second accident was this: Once I had the title, it made me realize that from the stories I had, I could sort out neighborhood stories, which also meant Chicago stories, because I had several stories I had written that didn't have a darn thing to do with Chicago. So all these many years later, people kindly rank me in the Chicago Tradition, but it was only an accident that I decided to gather Chicago stories around this title.

The other problem I had at that time was that a bunch of my stories were what you might call realistic and several were unrealistic, and I had never thought about putting them together. But when I looked at what I had, now that I was going to do Chicago stories for the first book, I realized that I had almost equal amounts of each and that by just completing the design and writing a couple more "unrealistic stories" I could have a sequence: an unrealistic, a realistic, an unrealistic, a realistic. There never was an overarching strategy, a conscious decision, but once that I did that, it made me aware of the whole notion of counterpoint in writing. I was very aware of how important counterpoint was in music, but it never really occurred to me before that it was a tremendously important mechanism that writers of all kinds use in order to create compression and resonance—that when you take two things that are unlike and you put them side by side, a current jumps between them, as in positive and negative, and that this current is often what the reader supplies where there is silence. So the reader is participating in bringing these two things together, and what's happening is that stuff is getting said that you haven't had to write in language. You're able to say it by just the arrangement of two images, or two stories, or two whatever.

So I became very conscious of the notion of counterpoint, so much so that when I was working on my next book I was looking for another kind of counterpoint. This time, I had written all of these short-shorts, these prose-poem-like stories. So the counterpoint in *The Coast of Chicago* became the counterpoint between the little vignettes and the longer stories.

DS: Music is a key element in your work. Not only is your writing musical, but music also plays a part in your characters' lives, and music is part of the cityscape in which they move.

DYBEK: It's become a real subject for me, and an unavoidable one because of the role music plays in my own life. In my personal life, aside from writing, music has an almost religious aspect to it. So it sneaks in and bleeds into the writing the way a person's religion might. Music is transformational, transcendent. A lot of what we ascribe to religious experience any number of people find in music, and so as subject matter in a story it often signals that there will be some transcendent moment, or at least a reach for a transcendent moment.

DS: A profound sense of place is also key to your work. You grew up in Chicago, and you're considered a Chicago writer, part of the

Chicago Tradition, as you say, which includes Theodore Dreiser, Nelson Algren, James Farrell, and Saul Bellow, a literature known for its gritty realism and focus on the underdog. Yet if you look closely at Chicago literature, you do find poetic prose, highly imaginative interpretations, and surrealist or magical or otherworldly passages. You detect the writer's awareness of the fact that this pragmatic city is actually a land of fantasies and dreams. I wonder if you perceive of this aspect of Chicago literature, and if you feel that Chicago-based literature has changed over the years.

DYBEK: My perception of it now is certainly different than what my perception was when I was a younger guy at any earlier point in my own writing, when I was still in a kind of apprenticeship. My perception then was that the Chicago Tradition was, in fact, a realistic tradition. I could see where Algren tried to make departures, and certainly Bellow was capable of tremendous lyrical flights. He's a spectacular stylist, and he can write anyway he wants. But the tradition itself seemed to be pretty much linked to social realism, and that was something I admired it for. I never ever sat down and thought of myself as a "Chicago writer" by the way. I was just trying to write stories. But the stories I wrote initially were imitative in that they were realistic stories, and I found it very hard to have what seemed to me to be an individual voice writing in that totally realistic mode. I had a nagging feeling about this lack of distinctive voice, but I didn't know how to get it. Finally, what happened was yet another accident: I ended up writing a story I hadn't sat down to write, and it had to do with music.

I've told this anecdote before, so I feel a little sheepish about repeating it, but I always write to music, and I always have. It's a way of heightening concentration and "getting in the mood." When I first started doing it, I listened mostly to jazz, which was the first music I really fell in love with. But by this point in my early twenties, I was writing to anything that interested me, and what was interesting to me at the moment was Eastern European composers, Bartok and Kodály in particular. I absolutely love cello. So I was listening to their cello stuff, and I had taken on loan from the library a very beat-up LP record of Janos Starker playing Zoltan Kodály's "Suite for Unaccompanied Cello," which still amazes me to this day. And under the spell of that music, I wrote a kind of unrealistic Chicago story. At that point, the only writer I knew who even nodded in that direction was Bernard Malamud. So that was a little personal breakthrough for me.

At this point, speaking now in the present, sure, I don't think that Chicago writing can any longer, or in any sense, be strictly identified as coming from social realism. There are just so many independent voices of different ethnic and racial backgrounds, and a lot of them bring the folkways of the culture that their parents or grandparents lived in to their work, and all of that has enriched the palette.

DS: I agree, and yet so much of Chicago literature is rooted in the city itself. The neighborhood is a theme of Chicago life that continues to inspire most contemporary writers, from John Mc-Nally and Joe Meno writing about the far South Side to Sandra Cisneros writing about Mango Street, Ana Castillo writing fiction about neighborhood gentrification, and Joseph Epstein and Adam Langer writing about Rogers Park. The neighborhood is a crucible of the self, even as young protagonists dream about discovering the wider world, which is often associated with Lake Michigan. You write about the lake and other aspects of nature so evocatively, which reminds me of a line in a story titled "Blight" in *The Coast of Chicago*. A line that I think can serve both as your credo as a writer and as a key to your questing characters. Bijou, the guy with the car, tells his friends, "I dig beauty." This turns into a big joke, but it truly is a reason for living, and your characters often find and treasure beauty in the most unbeautiful of circumstances.

DYBEK: I think that's really accurate. I still feel that, even though we live in this postmodern world, art in general, certainly literature in particular, can be beautiful without being ornamental. So as a writer, it's often a goal to try and risk writing something beautiful. In the stories themselves, imagination often becomes a survival skill for characters in a world of sometimes severe limitations due to class. One of the reasons that Chicago neighborhoods are interesting is that they are paradoxical. There is an enormous amount of richness in this little unit called neighborhood, but at the same time there are dangerous limitations inherent in it as well. So how does one enjoy the richness and make that part of life without also suffering the limitations. For many of the characters—and as you said, a lot of them are young—imagination helps them survive, and it's imagination that also leads them to a perception of beauty.

DS: And this perception of beauty provides an unexpected portal into other realms.

DYBEK: That's right.

DS: In *I Sailed with Magellan,* Perry, the main character, loves what he calls the "unsanitary canal." It's actually a harshly industrial spot, but because he's an imaginative guy, he transforms what's in front of him into a place of strange and haunting beauty. Of course this vision is difficult to share, which makes him feel like quite the misfit.

DYBEK: I think that's true. In the earlier story you mentioned, "Blight," one of the things that happens is that the neighborhood has been made an official blight area, but in all different ways, the story tries to demonstrate the notion of beauty as being in the eye of the beholder. Well, I suppose I've just reduced my story to a cliché, but what the heck. I wrote it, I guess I can destroy it, too. So to continue, one element of that is the ecstatic. These kids are always looking for the ecstatic moment. And, in fact, when Bijou utters that line, "I dig beauty," a remark that he then gets maligned for, for the rest of his days, he utters it in a total ecstatic moment, when he's just carried away. Then there's a story in *I Sailed with Magellan* called "Orchids," in which one of the ways the guys make fun of each other is to keep telling each other, "You're getting carried away," or "Don't get carried away." But, of course, what they want to be is carried away.

DS: I'm interested in the evolution in your fiction, from *Childhood and Other Neighborhoods* to *The Coast of Chicago* to *I Sailed with Magellan.*

DYBEK: In the first book, *Childhood and Other Neighborhoods,* the kind of stories that were providing the nonrealistic side of what I talked about earlier as counterpoint are, to my mind, essentially grotesque. Grotesque is frequently identified by the merging of humanity with something else, often the beast. And there's actually a story in there called "Visions of Budhardin," in which a guy is merged with a papier-mâché elephant. So while I also wanted to imply counterpoint in the next book, I didn't want to repeat the grotesque-realistic counterpoint. What was kind of interesting to me at that time goes back to your earlier question about poetry. I asked myself what the difference was between verse and poetry. And one of the things that occurred to me was that when people ask me about "poetic fiction," a lot of the time what they are really talking about is something that might happen in a story that would earn for you, or trigger for you, a lyrical moment. And in order to express that lyrical, or even ecstatic, moment, you change modes. You go from the realistic mode to the lyrical mode. Without going too much farther on that, I will just quickly say that in our society we mainly associate poetry with a lyrical mode. That is, it is associative; it isn't cause-and-effect, the way a story is. If you put a story in a chronological line and you say first this happened and then this happened, there is an implicitness in that, a cause and effect. Whereas if you go from the image of rain to the image of a lake, because of the association of water, you're thinking in an associative way, as you do in dreams. And lyrical time is different from narrative time.

As soon as I began thinking along those lines and realized there were different modes a writer could write in—even though I hadn't articulated this quite clearly to myself—I realized that I wanted the counterpoint to the realism in *The Coast of Chicago* not to be grotesque but to be lyrical. So in that book, there are all kinds of different versions of lyricism. "Chopin in Winter" has one kind of lyricism, and some of the little interconnected vignettes, like "Lights," have a prose-poem like lyricism, and "Pet Milk" has got a very romantic lyricism. One of the things you do in a lyrical mode, or one way you can use a lyrical mode, is to eroticize the city, and that book has various versions in which the city itself is eroticized—whether it's a kiss going across the city in "Night-hawks," or on the El-train in "Pet Milk." The city is constantly being eroticized there.

The basic reflex was similar in *I Sailed with Magellan.* I wanted to continue to explore writing about this city, and I want to continue to explore writing about this neighborhood, but I didn't want to continue repeating these kinds of formulas. I don't want to repeat the lyrical-realistic counterpoint anymore than I wanted to repeat the grotesque-realistic contrast. So I was looking for sameness and yet difference. I also wanted to try to write a book that was more unified in conventional ways because, for me, there were underlying unities in those first two books. I mean that unities were present in the kinds of choices I made with the first two books as to what to include and what to exclude, and once I had decided what to include, what I then needed to write in order to complete it felt, on a gut level, like some kind of design. I didn't necessarily expect that the reader would tease that out, but I did hope that the reader would feel that there was a coherence.

In *Magellan,* I really wanted the reader to be a little bit more aware of what the coherences were. How could you not be aware that a character named Perry Katzek appears in every story, or that each story has within it a song? There were what I would call conventional unities in it, unities that approach a form that is sometimes called a novel-in-stories. Some critics debate exactly what a novel-in-stories is, but I have no huge desire to join in that debate. And I really did still want some interplay between the real and the non-real, so the last story I wrote for the book was "Breasts" because I really wanted to add that one, underlying counterpoint moment.

DS: Your writing is full of music, but it's also gorgeously visual, and I picture each of the books you've just discussed as works of art, with the first being a collage in which you've juxtaposed many images and styles. *The Coast of Chicago* is more patterned, fit and jointed together like an inlaid floor rather than pasted together. And *I Sailed with Magellan* is a tapestry, each tale woven seamlessly into a greater whole.

DYBEK: One thing that I mention to students when I teach, and which I've always enjoyed saying for the sake of pure mystification, is that I find literature to be a really odd art form and that I live in a state of total envy toward all the other arts. I would give anything to paint or to play a musical instrument. It's the lack of the sensual. All the other arts come right through the senses. We see a painting with our eyes, but how do we read? Where does that all take place? It doesn't take place on a piece of paper or a computer screen. The medium, language, is the most abstract of all the mediums. And that mystery extends to the point at which if I read a story by Dickens or Eudora Welty I say, "Eudora Welty told me this story or Dickens told me this story," but who tells the writer? In other words, even though I could tell you that "Breasts" includes a few factual incidents, the story itself is not a recounting of those factual incidents. It's just so mysterious how stories piece themselves together.

I was in a hotel room in New York City just after 9/11. I had gone to New York to do a benefit. There were benefits all over the place at that point, and it was just a few days after and the city reeked of death. The ruins were still smoldering, and I don't know, maybe it was under the spell of all that violence, but suddenly, just totally unbidden, the scene in "Breasts" in which Joey Ditto kills Johnny Sovereign just came out of nowhere into my mind. I wrote feverishly on hotel stationary.

The same thing happened with the wrestler in that story. I was sitting on a curb with a great photographer Paul D'Amato.

DS: One of his photographs is on the cover of *I Sailed with Magellan*.

DYBEK: Yes, he did the cover. I think he's brilliant, a genius. So Paul and I had gone down to a summer fair in Pilsen, where I grew up. Paul had spent seven years taking pictures of that neighborhood. We were hanging out together. It's always fun to hang out with Paul; I just loved watching him take photos. I was sitting on the curb eating a taco, and Paul was right up on the action. They had erected a wrestling ring on 19th Street right under the El by St. Ann's church, and I was watching two guys with masks wrestle. And I was watching Paul photograph them, and suddenly one of the guys got tossed out of the ring right on top of Paul. For a moment I was afraid he broke Paul's neck. Then the next moment I was thinking, "Paul still has his neck intact, how's his camera?" But Paul is a tough guy. He picked himself up and laughed and dusted himself off. At that moment, I suddenly knew there had to be a wrestler in the story "Breasts," which didn't even have a title and wasn't even written. I'm talking about process now, not writing, and I'm always a little suspicious when the conversation turns to process because it's so very different than actually creating a thing. It always takes place in Dreamsville. You can talk about process, and then the actual thing never gets written, so what good is it?

DS: But it's essential. Lots of people have the chops. Lots of people can make sentences, but they don't have the stories to tell. They don't have the images.

DYBEK: It was just so oddly mysterious. I guess I'm back talking about accidents. Why would that come into your mind, and why would you know it was for a story that you hadn't even written yet?

DS: I think you're talking about artists' receptiveness to the world, their openness. I think of it as an aesthetic readiness.
    To go back to the abstraction of writing, I understand what you're saying about writing's lack of sensuousness, but writing is a physical practice. You do use your hands and your eyes to build words out of letters, sentences out of words, pages out of sentences. To my mind, writing encompasses every creative act. It does all that painting can do and all that music can do, and more. Language is the universal medium. You can read and write any-

where with the minimum of equipment. And literature's reach is infinite, its subjects and points of view limitless.

DYBEK: One of the things I've tried to do to emulate the other art forms, which I'm admitting to envying, is that I've tried to become very aware of the craft of writing. Because what I really want is a stained up old box of oil paints, and things like color wheels. When I first got interested in all this, one of my best friends was a painter. He was going to the Art Institute of Chicago, and I envied the way he bought himself a pair of real soft suede pants to impress girls. But that wasn't enough. He then had to take the pants that he had just paid some obscenely expensive price for, money he couldn't afford, and he had to spatter them with his paints so that he looked like an artist. What am I going to do, walk around with a piece of paper?

DS: Ink stains.

DYBEK: They'll just think you're an accountant or something.

DS: You're explaining something that mystified me in the story "Nighthawks," in which the library becomes some sort of miserable hell and the art museum is heaven.

DYBEK: There it is. That's it. One of the things I've done is try to pretend that all the things like metaphors and scenic construction and counterpoint and blah, blah, blah are like easels and canvases and canvas stretchers and gesso. Because I do perceive abstraction in language and concreteness and sensuality in all the other art forms, I've been attracted to writers who swim upstream against abstraction, that is, writers who set out to make an abstract medium as essential as they can. Sometimes they do it and play both sides of the fence, and those are often my favorite writers. The writer who comes immediately to mind would be somebody like Eugenio Montale, the Italian poet, and Yeats, another poet. Writers like that really intrigue me. In the great Yeats poem, "Sailing to Byzantium," he talks about "hammered gold and gold enameling." By the time you finish that poem it feels like a poem written not of words but of gold. So an unreachable goal for me—the attempt to turn a story into music, which of course you can never do, or to turn it into a sensually visual object, which of course you can never do—leads to the emphasis of imagery and rhythms and so forth. Not that those things aren't already a part of writing. Of course they are, but by energizing them and keeping your mind on them, one draws on one's love and emulation of other art forms. And I think it's really important. A lot of times, writers are asked, "Who are your influences? Who are you reading?" The question needs to be expanded to "Who are you looking at? Who are you listening to? Whose performances are you going to see?"

Ward Just

Ward Just has written fourteen novels, each distinguished by thoughtful and deep-feeling characters and incisive plots. Born in 1935 into a Waukegan, Illinois, newspaper family, Just worked as a journalist before becoming a novelist, and he remains fascinated by the quandaries of reportage, both for its own sake and because it is emblematic of our efforts to chart and navigate the fast-moving stream of life. Just writes of the valiant yet impossible effort to attain objectivity in the face of outrage and tragedy, the all-but-impossible quest for truth in a world of subterfuge and lies, and the bottom-line pragmatism that can engender oversimplification, sensationalism, and the avoidance of genuine dialogue both in private and public discourse. Just is fascinated by the interface between the political and the personal, power and the illusion of power, and he's a skilled writer about cultural collisions and generational differences and the psychological fallout of war.

Just has written a cycle of novels that reflect his Illinois heritage, beginning with *A Family Trust*, a saga about a newspaper family, and continuing with *Jack Gance*, a complex political tale about the Chicago machine and beyond, and *An Unfinished Season*. Set during the McCarthy era, *An Unfinished Season* is an atmospheric, bittersweet, and quietly devastating novel about a young man of privilege who spends the summer working at a Chicago newspaper, attending debutante balls at North Shore mansions, falling in love, and discovering that life is far more complex, treacherous, and unjust than he imagined.

Just's curiosity about the convolutions of Washington politics and society, the nature of dynastic families, and the way life has of derailing even the most empowered and vehement among us are the subjects of *Echo House,* a finalist for the National Book Award.

His stint as a reporter during the Vietnam War, during which he was wounded, is the subject of his nonfiction book, *To What End,* and the impetus for *A Dangerous Friend.* A harrowing dramatization of the earliest days of the conflict, and a trenchant inquiry into the abuse of power and the danger of ignorance, *A Dangerous Friend* won the James Fenimore Cooper Prize from the Society of American Historians.

Just and his wife, Sarah Catchpole, spend part of each year in Europe (where Just was a Berlin Prize Fellow at the American Academy in Berlin). Consequently, a number of his novels are set in Europe, including two of a loosely defined series of suspenseful portraits of creative individuals in crisis—tales that open out into considerations of the moral and political aspects of interpretation and expression—*The Translator,* where a German living in Paris with his American wife and autistic son becomes a literary translator, which seems benign enough until events conspire to involve him in a nefarious arms deal, and *The Weather in Berlin,* which features a filmmaker in his sixties, who became famous for an antiwar movie but who hasn't made a film in fifteen years.

A consummate storyteller and an even better conjurer of the workings of the mind, Just is a master at illustrating—through the quandaries of his compelling characters, his painterly imagery, and his piquant wit—the vagaries of memory and the burden of secrets, the immensity of solitude and the inescapable influence of politics and world events. His many fans are confounded by the fact that Ward Just hasn't yet become a more widely known and read author, but it's bound to happen. Amid a swirl of laudatory reviews, *An Unfinished Season* won the 2004 *Chicago Tribune's* Heartland Prize. Ward Just appeared on *Open Books* in July 2004.

DONNA SEAMAN: You grew up around Chicago.

WARD JUST: I did indeed.

DS: You're the grandson and the son of newspaper publishers.

JUST: That is a true fact.

DS: That's quite a legacy

JUST: That is a legacy.

DS: And you began writing as a journalist.

JUST: I did. I started out on my father's newspaper when I was fourteen years old during the summer break from school. I told a friend of mine that once. I said, "I have been writing in each of the last seven decades." He said, "I don't believe that. You can't go to work at a newspaper when you're fourteen years old." I said, "You can when your father is the publisher."

DS: Did you intend to be a journalist?

JUST: No, I always had it in the back of my mind that fiction was my natural métier. It just took me awhile to get there. You have to find things out. You have to know things. Of course, there are writers who can produce wonderful work, I think, without ever leaving their room.

DS: Proust, perhaps.

JUST: Yes, Proust, exactly. And I was thinking, too, of Henry James. One recalls the climactic winter season of 1907 or 1908 during which this was the conspicuous thing that happened to him, according to his biographer Leon Edel: he accepted 109 invitations to dinner. That passed for excitement in the life of Henry James. But you've got to be James to write from within a cocoon, or Proust. The rest of us need to get into the way of life, get into the way of things, and I really know no better way to do that than in journalism, particularly daily journalism. It's better than magazine journalism somehow because you're up close to things. Think for a minute of the police blotter and the weight of fact: the age and the address of the accused, the full name, including the middle name if there is one, and the sex and all the rest of it. Then the little thing down at the bottom, what was the offense? When I was doing this work in Waukegan at the age of fourteen, many of the offenses were D&D. D&D stood for drunk and disorderly. But think what a world is behind those two words, drunk and disorderly.

Why drunk? Why disorderly? Why that night as opposed to some other night? What was this man's history? It's a man because I can never remember in my brief career as a summer reporter a woman ever being arrested, God forbid, for being drunk and disorderly. I always thought that behind that mysterious D&D lay a whole world, a whole personality, a whole life, and you'd never know what it was. You'd have no idea what it was. All you had were the facts.

DS: You sought a lot of facts in a very dangerous place when you went to Vietnam at the height of the war.

JUST: I did go to Vietnam. I was thirty years old, and I was running from the *Washington Post*. I always thought my strength as a journalist was that I really had a high appreciation for, and I thought, a higher understanding of, ambiguity. The stories that I liked the best were stories that ended in a kind of nothing, and the reader would say, "But there's no wrap-up to this." My thought was that much of life is like that—that there isn't a wrap-up, there isn't a clean beginning, middle, and end. Anyway, I go to Vietnam, which is, if you like, the Mount Everest of ambiguity, and you were climbing the damn thing every single day. So I was there for a year and a half, and by the time I was finished with it, which was in, I don't know, the late spring of 1967, I thought I knew all I needed to know. I didn't need to know anymore. I certainly was not going to go to another war; it's much too dangerous, much, much too dangerous. I didn't want to do that. So I came back and covered a political campaign. I covered the Nixon campaign and that finished me. I said, "That's it, I'm out of here." About a year after that, I quit the newspaper business. I loved the newspaper business while I was in it, but after awhile it gets kind of boring. It got boring to me anyway.

DS: In *An Unfinished Season,* Wils, at nineteen, spends the summer working for a newspaper in downtown Chicago, thanks to the influence of his wealthy, North Shore businessman father. And he tells the editor that he learned that the best stories are the ones that don't have endings. The editor is appalled.

JUST: That's right. Wils says, "Look, the stories that people remember are the stories that remain mysterious." And the editor, who is a type you recognize, he's basically a self-taught thug, becomes enraged. His little arms are wheeling around, and he says, "You idiot," and goes on to denounce anyone who would find mystery attractive. He says, "All most reporters want to do is find things out. They don't care what they find. It doesn't matter to them. It's just finding it." And Wils says, "That's only half of it. If you're looking for something, the search is never-ending." That's the way he sees things. In other words, he is the most colossally unsuited person to ever be a newspaper reporter. It's just not his métier. He should go on and do something else.

DS: You're dramatizing the difference between the artist's sensibility and that of the hard-boiled reporter.

JUST: Yes. Although what I was really trying to do in that passage, and other passages having to do with the news business, was trying to deal the cards fairly. I did not want to stack the deck because during this period that I'm writing about, in 1953, the news business was much different than now, and the people who were in it were much different than they are now. Most of them were not educated people. They were self-taught. They were working-class stiffs. And that had a tremendous virtue to it, and one should not disdain or look down on some of the characters who were roaming the streets for Chicago newspapers. They were very, very streetwise, and that's no small thing in a town like Chicago. If you're a newspaper reporter, it's hard to apprehend the life of the city if you're living in Evanston or Winnetka. That's the simple fact of the matter. The reporters in those days had no choice. They didn't make enough money to live in Winnetka or Evanston. They had to live West Side, South Side, downtown, far North Side, and I think that gave them a connection with the city that maybe some of the modern reporters don't have. On the other hand, modern reporters have got a lot of other tools at their disposal, but I didn't want in any way to make it seem that the earlier guys were some how less capable. They were as capable, and in some cases more capable. They were simply capable in different ways. So that's sort of what I was up to with that long passage about the news business in Chicago, particularly the tabloid business.

DS: War is present in many of your novels. In *An Unfinished Season*, it enters the story via the father of Wils's girlfriend, Aurora. He's a psychiatrist who served on the Pacific front. The good doctor reveals some of his past to Wils, and Wils realizes that war never ends for those subjected to it.

JUST: At one point he figures out that maybe it's true that once you're tortured you stay tortured. What interests me generally in life are things that don't end, things that don't have a clear conclusion. I think that's what life is. I've read a critic or two now and again who would like to see things wrapped up neatly in books. I don't believe that happens often.

DS: To me that's a distinguishing trait between pop, or commercial, fiction, and more literary fiction, even the best of the hard-boiled fiction. And there's an edginess to your work; you do verge on the noir sensibility.

JUST: Yes, it's true. I tend to think that things often end badly. I don't promote that, but my life has told me that.

DS: But what you don't do is simplify things. You achieve a toughness of voice, a dark perspective, but you work on a deeper level, and you don't worry about convention.

JUST: That's what I'm up to. That's what I try to do in any event. You mentioned that war is present in a lot of my books; that's true and that's probably a generational thing. I was age six through ten during the Second World War. I remember clearly reading the *Chicago Tribune* and keeping up with the war news, listening to the radio. Then Korea came along. I was too young to get involved in that, and it was such a puzzling war. *An Unfinished Season* is set just as Eisenhower is trying to bring the Korean War to a conclusion. Such a sloppy war, it was so ambiguous. A police action— what does that mean, when you have the North Koreans invading the South, and then the Chinese invading the North? What was there about it that constituted a police action? That was just at the time of my life when I was beginning to understand these things. It does seem to me that for most of my lifetime, one way or another, war has been on the front pages of newspapers, so it's the fabric of one's mind. It's not so much the Vietnam experience that informs the little war riffs that go on in these books, but the fact that in my lifetime that's what I've seen and read a lot of. I can't resist repeating a line from the great poet Elizabeth Bishop, who observed that the twentieth century was "our worst century so far." Go to lunch on that, friends.

DS: And we find ourselves at the beginning of the twenty-first century in the same mess.

JUST: Yes, exactly.

DS: Questions of power and the keeping of secrets also figure in your work. Your novel *A Dangerous Friend* is set in Vietnam in the days just before the war, and it's about covert nation-building endeavors by civilians. The novel came out in 1999, but it seems also to presage the unregulated presence of civilian forces in Iraq, where we're making the same kinds of mistakes with the same hubris as in Vietnam.

JUST: The conceit of that novel, if you want to call it a conceit, coalesced because I had never seen a Vietnam novel that really dealt with civilians as opposed to soldiers. The civilians played a huge part out there, there was a huge AID team and a vast CIA operation. I'm mostly concerned not so much with the CIA, but the AID people, that is, the Agency for International Development. You know, they are distributing bulgur wheat and rice, and they are trying to build schools, and they are sending medical teams. All the time, nobody is speaking the language, and they are looking at the Vietnamese, who are looking back at them saying, "Why exactly are you here?"

DS: They've marched in to a complex place, an ancient civilization, that they know nothing about.

JUST: That's right. And the head of this group, of course, wants nothing more than to increase his budget and get more people, and more vehicles, and a bigger compound and all the rest of it because the whole AID industry is a kind of vast bureaucracy, and the more money you've got, the more people you can employ and the more power you have. That's what *A Dangerous Friend* was about.

DS: It made me think about how little those of us on the home front ever know about what's going on in situations like Korea, Vietnam, and now in Iraq.

JUST: I await the story of the aid workers and the civilian contractors in Iraq. I haven't yet seen the story that tells me what their lives are like, what they are actually trying to do, how much is succeeding, and what the Iraqis think. You only get bits and pieces of this.

DS: Your novels about war and reporting make me wonder how different news gathering is now than it was in the Vietnam era. It seems as though in the past, journalists were able to find things out; they were free to speak with people; they were willing to take risks to report the facts. It seems now as though there is much more stringent control of the media by the government. Many more events are staged, the media are corralled and monitored or, in Iraq, kept close to military authorities.

JUST: Iraq has got a particular problem that was not present in Vietnam: it's very dangerous physically to the point where no serious journalist is prepared to risk his life every other day. Some of the cowboys might think about taking unacceptable risks, but if you're going to be a newspaper reporter, you've got to be alive in order to write the copy. I thought a lot about the embedding process. As people may know, in Vietnam there was no restriction. You could go wherever you wanted to go, and the military would take you there. Furthermore, because there were no front lines in the war, there was just a series of fire bases where occasional battles would erupt. That meant you could go to these places and arrive safely. It was dangerous when you were there, but the danger was acceptable danger. Then when you wanted to leave, some helicopter would take you out.

The great value of that was that after six months' time you really could gain a sense of the whole country. And if you used your eyes and ears, you could really believe that you probably knew more about the country than any resident American official for this one simple reason: No one else but a journalist could look at it all the way around. No one other person could go visit the Vietnamese Army, the American Army, the AID people, the government people, the proud provincial headquarters, or drop in on the CIA. And if you just kept your eyes and ears open and you did not go into it with some vast bias ideological or otherwise, you could come up with a pretty clear picture of what was happening.

With Iraq, you're embedded. In Iraq, it would be very difficult if not impossible to pursue the matter the way we pursued it in Vietnam. The nature of the conflict is so different.

DS: You write a great deal about politics in your fiction. Have politics always interested you?

JUST: If you grow up the son and grandson of newspaper publishers, I am here to tell you that the common coin around the dinner table when it isn't the wretched circulation figures or the advertising budget or who are you going to fire out of the newsroom, is politics. Who is going to run for mayor and who would the paper like to see as the chair of the county board of supervisors, and what about the state's attorney? Is this Republican candidate solid enough? Lake County at that time was, and maybe still is for all I know, as they say, staunchly Republican, which really mattered, particularly to my grandfather, who I dare say was a kind of boss when he was alive. He pretty much hand-picked a lot of those candidates, and then supported them with the newspaper. It was kind of a little, tiny mini-version of the *Chicago Tribune* in the old days, and then my father became publisher. He was much more of a businessman. He found politics tedious, and he found politicians boring. They always had their hands out. They wanted money. They wanted an endorsement. They want this, they want that. My father, I do believe, was the best kind of Republican. He had no interest in social issues. He wanted to keep the taxes down. He wanted to keep the Reds out of government.

Needless to say, I kept to my own thoughts, or followed my grandfather. Not that I ever wanted to pick anybody or endorse anybody, but I love the political give-and-take. A guy on the stump. What was the basic stump speech? What were the constituents of that speech, and the way it might vary depending on who he was talking to, whether he was talking to a union group, a business group and so forth? I just love the back-and-forth of that.

DS: The theater of it.

JUST: Yes, frankly, the theater of it. Then when I went to work briefly, only for about a year, as an editorial writer for the *Washington Post*—that is what my grandfather did, he wrote editorials for the *Waukegan News Sun*—I said, "Okay, I'm going to fire up a few lines and let fly with the salvos." I specialized in editorials, but it just wasn't in my nature.

DS: You were destined to write stories.

JUST: Exactly.

DS: In thinking about your fourteen novels, I can see them loosely grouped by themes. For instance, there's a set about creative people that interests me very much. There's a woman painter in *Ambition and Love*, a male translator in *The Translator*, a filmmaker in *The Weather in Berlin*. I was wondering how and why you created those characters, and if their pursuits are metaphorical endeavors standing in for the quest for truth?

JUST: I'm not so sure *Ambition and Love* isn't at some level my favorite book.

DS: I love that novel.

JUST: Critics hated it.

DS: Not this one.

JUST: I am happy to hear that, Donna. Did you review it at the time?

DS: I did for *Booklist,* yes.

JUST: I tell you, that's absolutely typical of me. I only remember the bad stuff. I never remember the good things.

DS: We all do that. But I do love that book. In fact, I think about it often.

JUST: I was crazy about that book. The thought behind it is that there's a woman who is really torn between love of her art—she's an artist and a very good artist—and ambition for herself. And this means, is she willing to do anything to promote this art of hers, or is the making of the art itself so precious to her that she simply won't do the kind of things that you often have to do to promote yourself? Critics didn't understand that. Most of them thought it was sort of ambition for yourself as opposed to love for some man.

That didn't have anything to do with it at all. I was thinking about an artist, a writer, a sculptor, and asking them the question, "Will you do anything to push this forward? Is there nothing that you won't do to get your art noticed, and the fees for it to rise ever higher?"

DS: I think it's a very moving novel, and I'm sure it was misread because your artist is a woman—which is maddening, but still a fact of life. I really appreciate the women characters in all your novels.

JUST: Thank you. I spent some time trying to get that right, frankly.

DS: They are very intelligent. They are nuanced psychologically, and they are as edgy as the men and full of significant conflict. Many of your characters grapple with questions of ego and confidence and sacrifice.

JUST: Yes, all those things.

DS: In a world that seems to value nothing but power and money.

JUST: Precisely. And it seems to me, as we move forward into our wonderful century, a world increasingly indifferent to anything genuine. It really is the cheap stuff. Of course, there is nothing new about this, but it does seem to me somehow more conspicuous now than it might have been twenty or thirty or forty years ago.

DS: I sense your feelings about this in the passionate and gruff newspaper heroes you've portrayed, from Amos Rising to Lowell Limpett, compared to the news people we see now, and to the plastic-wrapped, corporate mass media.

JUST: Prettified.

DS: And shallow, as spin has been elevated above reporting.

JUST: Yes, we're at a period now where the spinmeisters, instead of being denounced, are quoted and consulted. I have a new thought about Washington: impropriety no longer matters because the improprieties are so vast. What really matters is the appearance of impropriety. You've got to stop the appearance of impropriety. Impropriety itself, well, we'll let that go. What a place. What a circus.

DS: Things seem so out of whack to me. For instance, and I don't mean to be too blunt here, but I'm always shocked that more people don't know who you are. Not that you don't have a lot of readers, not that you aren't a critical success, but I believe you should be much more widely read.

JUST: One of my wisecracks has come back to haunt me. A couple of years ago somebody said, "You know, you're very unappreciated." I said, "I'm not unappreciated. I'm appreciated quite a lot. I'm undersold is what I am." But the books are there. I'm sixty-eight years old, I'm still here, and I regard myself as a kind of survivor's manual.

DS: Many of your earlier books are back in print.

JUST: Houghton Mifflin has done a really great thing for me. I've got I think six or seven books from my backlist back on the shelves. *A Family Trust* is back from Public Affairs Press, and they just re-published *To What End*, which is a Vietnam memoir of mine. These have been out of print for thirty years. The memoir is doing kind of nicely. It's not making any money. God forbid if any book made money, but it's doing rather nicely. People remember it and they pick it up. So I'm thrilled to have this stuff back in print. That's all you can ask for, is to have your books available. You can't beat people over the head with them.

DS: That's my job.

JUST: That's right. I'm counting on you.

DS: To return to art, paintings seem important to you. You've written about artists, and Edward Hopper paintings appear in *An Unfinished Season.*

JUST: I live on Martha's Vineyard off Cape Cod, and there's a wonderful community of painters there. It's thought of as a writers' haven, although there are only three or four writers who live there fulltime. It's the painting community that's large, and as a consequence in the last eight or ten years, I've spent a lot more time thinking about art and how painters go about things. Then when my wife and I were living in Paris, we haunted the museums. We also spent a lot of time in Germany, and I really fell, as you might imagine from my work, for the German expressionists. So the French impressionists and Edward Hopper and the German expressionists are the painters who interest me the most. And in one way or another in the last four or five books I think they've made an appearance.

DS: Do you revise a great deal?

JUST: Yes. I work on a typewriter, and for what reasons I can't tell you, I decided to keep track of the reams of paper that went into the making of *Echo House,* and it was twenty. Twenty reams at five hundred sheets of paper a ream. I think it went through six or seven drafts. I'm endlessly rewriting and revising. I believe the secret to writing is rewriting. You will write a paragraph that does seem to be complete in itself and you don't have to horse around with it, but in my experience that's pretty rare. You run it through the typewriter one more time. You can change a couple words, maybe add a sentence, maybe take one out, and it will be a stronger paragraph. And the more you do that throughout the book, it will be a stronger book. And sometimes you will stop at a hundred pages and go back to page one because you've got to keep the whole thing in your mind as you're writing, and you can lose that if you've been turned away from it for too long. You've got to keep spinning the damn thing, you do.

DS: So you just keep retyping.

JUST: Yes, and keeping the papers. Occasionally I'll discard. I once discarded twenty thousand words from *A Dangerous Friend*. There was an ending that a friend of mine criticized. He was right, so I took the twenty thousand words and put it aside. There were nice passages. It wasn't that it was junk work. It was just that it didn't belong there; it belonged someplace else. So for the last seven years, I've been trying to find a place for those twenty thousand words. Waste not, want not.

DS: Right from the start, your books have been very rich, but I feel that they've grown more clarified. And in *An Unfinished Season,* you let yourself write even more lyrically than before. I wonder if the fact that your hero is so young, younger than most of your characters, freed you in some way.

JUST: You know, it's funny, I do think the fact that the protagonist, or the hero, is so young and I'm so old let's you sort of cast a light down. For me, it's a fifty year difference. I'm trying to write in the vernacular of the 1950s, but also with something of the present day to it, too. And when you're writing about that period, which is a very difficult period to write about, I think you do it more effectively the older you are, frankly, as opposed to writing about it when you are thirty-five or forty-five. I think you're better off looking at it later. Not that you are taking a more relaxed view of it, not the wisdom of age and all that, that's nonsense. It's just that you have a clearer light on it, and in some funny way it allows you to be lyrical because when the teenage years are not torturous, they are lyrical. There are moments of really high lyricism. When you're older it's not easier to do it that way, it's the intelligent way to do it.

DS: Yes, the perspective, the distance, is invaluable. This must also be why you so often write about the past.

JUST: The present is too much with us. And I don't know that I find the present time in some fundamental sense very interesting. Now we have terrorism. I'm going to use a neutral word: and we have a very "interesting" presidency. So there are those two things, particularly terrorism, but just because terrorism is present and a threat and one of those things, particularly if you live in a large city, that you think about most every day, it doesn't make it interesting. I don't find it very interesting. I don't find the terrorists especially interesting. People I find interesting are those Muslims who are caught between things, who really don't want to put a bomb in their pocket, but who are appalled at occupation and American materialism and all the things that they denounce. Those are the ones that interest me, how they are going to find their way along what seems to me to be a very, very fine line.

DS: Yes, that's a story. I hope you write it sometime.

JUST: That's it. I will. You have my promise.

Alice McDermott

~~

Alice McDermott was born in Brooklyn in 1953. Soon after, her family moved to Long Island, and it is her memories of working-class Irish Catholics who escaped the crowded city for the sea-caressed green of Long Island that have inspired her fiction. McDermott earned her B.A. at the State University of New York at Oswego, and her M.A. at the University of New Hampshire. She has taught at the University of California at San Diego and American University, and she's been a writer-in-residence at Lynchburg and Hollins Colleges in Virginia, and Johns Hopkins University in Baltimore. A Whiting Writers' Award winner, McDermott won the National Book Award in 1998 for her fourth novel, *Charming Billy*.

A psychologically acute storyteller and an impeccable stylist, McDermott renders the everyday tangible world—a city street, a cluttered living room, the body language of an aging relative—with exquisite specificity, and she meticulously elucidates the workings of the mind, the flickering of thoughts and surges of emotions. Yet her precision serves not to simplify and make comprehensible reality and experience, but rather to accentuate the mysteries of being, the vagaries of the psyche, the unreliability of memory, and the power of fantasies. Add to that her gift for portraying adults through the wise eyes of children and teenagers, her sensitivity to the recklessness of desire and our persistent longing for purity, her lashing yet tender wit, unfailing lyricism, shrewd humor, and keen interest in how the stories we tell about our lives become our lives, and you have fiction of the highest order.

McDermott's distinctive voice and viewpoint were already crystallized in her first novel, the wry and poignant *A Bigamist's Daughter*. This exceptional debut was followed by the suspenseful *That Night*, which was chosen as a finalist for the Pulitzer Prize and the National Book Award. *At Weddings and Wakes,* McDermott's intricately structured third novel, features a vivid and compelling cast of Irish Catholic New Yorkers and Long Islanders. *Charming Billy* is a meditation on grief, longing, charisma, and oblivion. And *Child of My Heart,* a departure in many ways from her previous work, is enchanting and unnerving.

Alice McDermott was in Chicago in late 2003 for the Chicago Humanities Festival, during which this conversation was conducted before a standing-room-only audience.

~

DONNA SEAMAN: Many of your characters are ardent storytellers, and in your novels, family lore is told and retold, polished and embellished until it attains the status of myth. I wonder if the perception that such oft-told family stories both nourish and smother us inspired you, in part, to become writer?

ALICE McDERMOTT: Certainly. But I have to first disclaim any reality in this. My family tells stories, but they are the worst storytellers you've probably ever met. My mother can tell a story that can go on for twenty-five minutes before it even has the gleam of a point to it, and she will include every detail that comes to mind. So my brothers and I were used to saying, after about fifteen minutes, "Mom, wait, why do we want to know this?" But certainly the tradition of storytelling—in the sense not so much of relating what happened but of manipulating what happened, and not telling a story once but telling it over and over again—is something that interests me in every one of my works. And it's a theme that keeps coming back. I think part of it, for me, is that any event, even something horrific, life-changing, and memorable, is still finite. The thing happens and it's over with. You get through it or you don't, but it's over. Story, on the other hand, is never over. There is the story that you tell right after something has happened, and then there is the version you tell twenty years later looking back through time at what happened. There's your version, and there's someone else's version. And it's that malleability in memory and story, and what it says about us and what it says about not only what we get out of story, but what it is that we're hoping to glean from the events of our lives as we retell them, that interests me the most because it is always changing. It seems to me there's more of our spirit in what we say about what has happened to us than anything that simply happens to us.

DS: You grapple with many of the paradoxes of storytelling, of auto-biography versus fiction, in your first novel, *A Bigamist's Daughter.* Your protagonist, Elizabeth Connelly, is working at a vanity press where she reads one ludicrous and heartbreaking amateur manu-script after another. I believe you had a similar experience, which is quite an education in how very difficult it is to tell a story well.

McDERMOTT: I think there was a little bit of superstition on my part as a first novelist writing about people who were writing bad novels—as if you could get rid of all your bad writing through them, so that maybe it would never creep back into your work for the rest of your career. It was a kind of exorcism. It amuses me now to look back on my younger self. I suppose I thought, "If I ac-knowledge that there is bad writing in the world, and I show the reader what bad writing is, then maybe I won't be blamed for it when I do it myself." And I did have some experience right out of undergrad working at a vanity publisher. It was one of those jobs you get out of the *New York Times* when you're an English major right out of the University of New York at Oswego at $115 a week. My job was just typing, but when I had free time, I was told to look through the folders of all the books that they'd published, and that piqued my interest. I then went off to graduate school and took a course in journalism, for which I had to write an investigative re-port. That's when I did a lot of research on vanity publishing. So when it came time to sit down and write my first novel, I thought, "One thing I know a lot about right now is how vanity publishing works, so let's see what I can do with that."

DS: Surely good writing inspired you, too.

McDERMOTT: Yes. You read somebody wonderful and you say, "If I spend my whole life trying to create something that comes anywhere near to this, or at least strives for it, I will have done the right thing." I can remember feeling that very clearly the first time I read Nabokov. I suppose if I have a literary god, he's it. The fabulous use of language. The compassion as well as the humor. The clear-eyed seeing of the world as it is, and yet also with a very informed and intelligent sympathy. The sympathy we all want for ourselves, he applies to the worst characters. Virginia Woolf is another one. You read *To the Lighthouse* and you say, "Ahhhh, that's what I want to do. I want to do one of those." Naturally, I had my Faulkner, Fitzgerald, and Hemingway phase—and Hardy. Poets have had as much influence on me as the prose writers. Poetry is a higher art, and it takes me two hundred pages to begin to approach what Yeats can do in eight lines. People like Wallace Stevens, Yeats, and Seamus Heaney and Adrienne Rich and Sylvia Plath. And Dickens. I went back to Dickens this summer. Every five or six years, I reread Dickens; he's so smart; he keeps getting better.

DS: What do you draw on that you knew intuitively from the start about writing, and what have you learned from writing?

McDERMOTT: Oh gosh, I don't know if there is anything I've always known how to do. It seems like it's always been a very long and constant learning process. I think the thing that I have perhaps gotten better at doing is trusting the story and letting the story happen, rather than keeping the reins on it or looking over your shoulder at the reader, or wondering, "Is this going to sell?" or "Is this what people want?" I've gotten better at just letting the story happen, which is one of the hardest things to do. When I teach, the most difficult thing to convince young, talented writers is that they are better writers than they know they are. I try to tell them, "You don't have to stick to your outline. When you write something that surprises you, look at it again. Get yourself in a place where the subconscious can come through." Seamus Heaney has a great line about poets. He says, "We must teach ourselves to walk on air against our better judgment." I think we need to learn how to do that as fiction writers, too, to trust the story, to trust the character, to not always be in control. To let things happen is one of the hardest things to learn. I think I'm getting a little bit better at that.

DS: You've mentioned that you work on more than one novel at a time. What are the advantages and disadvantages of that practice?

McDERMOTT: I've fallen into a really bad habit of working on two books at the same time. I don't recommend it to anyone who's writing fiction. It's not that I've spent half the morning on one and half the morning on the other. It's that life intervenes, things change, your focus changes. Something piques your interest, and you feel compelled to write about it, so you put something aside. And I'm a terrible procrastinator. I love to procrastinate; I need to procrastinate. If I have two things, one everybody knows I'm working on and one nobody knows I'm working on, I can sneak off and work on the one I'm not supposed to be working on and feel like I'm procrastinating even though I'm still getting some writing done. So it's rewarding in that way. The other part of it is, I always have two books going so I can jettison one when I need to. I don't want to ever have to publish something I'm not happy with, or that I don't think has come to full blossom, and having two gives me an option.

DS: One thing that strikes me about your novels is what you've kept back, what is not shared or said. As you work with different characters, do you consciously decide what they are going to reveal and what they're going to conceal?

McDERMOTT: I think so. People who write fiction don't always like to admit that one of the largest challenges is keeping yourself interested in your own story and your own characters. You think as a reader you want the writer to keep you interested. Well, the first reader of your own work is you, and that reader wants to stay interested. So, what appeals to me—or at least interests me enough to keep working at it—is the sense of "What are these characters saying, and what are they not saying? And how is what happened transformed by the telling of it?" What they say about it isn't perhaps precisely how they feel about it. So yes, for me it's a real balance between what's spoken about and what's kept back. Not to sound too terribly middle-aged, but time and again I'm struck that those of us living in the early part of the twenty-first century say too much. We reveal everything, and somehow in the revelation, things gets flattened out.

Things are as complex as we believe them to be. And, again, the speaking of it, the telling of it, the spilling your guts, the writing your memoir, gives an impression that all is being told. Yet I think we all believe that no, there's got to be something else, something that's not said. This may be part of my own Irish heritage—things best kept to yourself—but it seems to me that only in a fictional narrative can you have the full sense that there's a lot more going on, that there's a lot more being felt, that there's a lot more emotion. There's more truth in what's not being said than in anything that's being played out dramatically, which is probably why I don't have an awful lot of plot in most of my stories. There's not a lot happening on the surface, but I seek to retain the sense that our inner lives, the voices with which we speak to ourselves, have validity, and cannot be immediately translated to a public or even a spoken arena. I guess that's why the inner lives of my characters tend to be the most interesting thing for me, and the thing I most want to get at.

DS: Your characters have a resistance to disclosure. They'll say, "too much said," or "He didn't have to go that far." And *Charming Billy* is predicated on withheld truth, and a lie, and over the course of the novel, the reader puzzles over this and wonders how much damage the untold truth and the lie did.

McDERMOTT: Yes, in *Charming Billy*, characters try to change the truth, to change reality, to let story make another reality. A character, Dennis, sees what happened in the real world and says,

"It's not acceptable," which is what the fiction writer does for the most part. So there is a manipulation of what actually happened, and it's played out over time, raising the question, "Does 'actual' really matter?" Isn't it the belief that matters? Isn't the way we look back and recall as valid and as important as what really happened? Because once what really happened has passed, it doesn't have the weight of what we perceive to have happened. Because that's how we shape our lives, around the things that we believe and perceive to have happened. So that's very much on the surface. I'll never claim to be really subtle in my themes. I'm thick sometimes, and I don't get a lot of things, so I pretty much want to make sure it's out there.

DS: Faith is an important theme in your work, and your characters really struggle with it, often improvising on their Catholicism. And you refer often to the *Lives of the Saints* as sort of a story anthology from which people pick and choose lessons and role models. I wonder if religion as a particularly powerful form of storytelling interests you?

McDERMOTT: Oh definitely. And also, you know, when you write about something that's identifiable, you are labeled, and that helps marketing. So suddenly I find myself called an Irish Catholic writer, and the last thing I ever set out to try to be was an Irish Catholic writer. I went to twelve years of Catholic school. If anybody told me I should read a Catholic novelist, I said, "Oh, right." I have no interest whatsoever in reading anybody who calls themselves a Catholic novelist, yet that's how I've been labeled. And for me, the Catholicism in my work is not so much my attempt to understand the faith or to put it in any kind of context; it's the thing that provides my characters with a vocabulary for the inner life. These are not necessarily people who have been through therapy and have a vocabulary for all their feelings, their hopes and aspirations, the things that worry them in the middle of the night. But their faith gives them that vocabulary. I never wanted to define any particular religion at all, but I needed to have a way for my characters to put their lives in a context. This goes back to not having to say too much, because in that community, where there's a shared faith, a lot of shorthand goes on. The whole idea of an almost existential moment—of asking, "Is this life worthwhile? Does it come to nothing, or does it come to something?"—this is not the kind of conversation these characters have the time or the inclination to have. But they can have it within the vocabulary of their faith.

So although it's made me a cover girl for a couple of Catholic magazines, I never set out to be a Catholic writer or an Irish writer. I grew up on Long Island. My parents were first-generation Irish, but all four of my grandparents died very young. I never knew any of them. We lived in a community in which there were Irish, Polish, Jewish, Italian, Irish, Polish, Jewish, Italian households all the way down the street. All I knew was that grandparents had accents. It didn't matter whether they were brogues or Russian accents or Yiddish accents, or whatever; they just had accents. And I had no hyperawareness of being Irish. As a matter of fact, my father had no patience for people who were too Irish. He used to say, "They are more Irish than the Irish. You're American. If Ireland was such a great place, we wouldn't have left. This is a better place to be." So when *At Wedding and Wakes* came out, which was the first novel that used the Irish Catholic setting, and suddenly I'm seen as this Irish Catholic writer, my older brother called me and said, "What the hell do you know about the Irish?" My mother, in twenty-five years, never made corned beef and cabbage. But again, it's a context. As a fiction writer, I don't—and I think most of us don't—set out to copy down the world as we find it. We set out to take that material and make something else of it. We need details. We need specificity. We need place. But that specificity, those details, that place must be fresh rather than plugging directly into what's already there. We're not illustrators. We're not photographers. We work in oils or watercolor.

DS: Your novels are gorgeously descriptive. You offer detail upon detail as you describe a cluttered city apartment, the sensations you gather as you drive into the city from the suburbs, someone's attire. Every sense is addressed, but gradually one realizes that it's not the objects or the place or even the face under scrutiny that matters; it's the person observing them that you're interested in. This is Virginia Woolf territory, human consciousness.

McDERMOTT: Yes, the life of the spirit. You know, where else can it be recorded with authenticity and that kind of honesty except in fiction? There are many wonderful memoirs, and I have nothing against the genre, but more often than not in most memoirs there's an ax to grind. There's an individual ego telling the story. In fiction, the individual ego is as created as the story the ego is telling us. And the ego is there for a purpose, to play a role within a larger work and to make clear what those of us who do this crazy profession are trying to get at. Fiction can express what can't be approached, I think, in any other way, and that is the inner life, the private, singular voice that is our own. It's the voice with which we speak to ourselves, and that's the voice I think we're trying to get down on paper through a character whose life, plot, and details are all put into the service of the larger work and not in any way confined by "but this really happened." I feel sorry for journalists and memoirists: they are stuck with what really happened.

DS: An imagined world seems so arbitrary and amorphous. How do you start building one? Does a certain character coalesce in your mind, a certain situation?

McDERMOTT: I've published five novels, and started many more, and it's been different every time. Unfortunately, I haven't found the formula. The encouraging and discouraging thing about this profession is you always have to start all over again. Every time you start a new work, you're a novice. It doesn't matter that you told a story once. This is a whole new story. You are a brand-new writer putting down the first sentence. And every time for me, it's been something else.

As I said, *At Wedding and Wakes* was the first novel in which I had used the Irish-Catholic milieu, and I was pretty sure it was my first and last. Again, I had no particular interest in the Irish. The Irish in reality drive me crazy. They are lovely people, but of course, we have a tradition of not liking ourselves, which we are very proud of. And I really thought that was it for the Irish, but when I was working on another novel, I had this echo in my brain from *At Wedding and Wakes*. I realized that I had certainly hit a number of types in the Irish Catholic community, but that there was one central type that did not really appear in that novel. And that is the lovable drunk, the life of every party, the great guy who's drinking himself to death, and certainly there's such a character in every Irish American and Irish extended family. It interested me that this was a person who is fully a stereotype and that every instinct as a fiction writer tells you, "You don't want to write about a stereotype; that's not what we're supposed to do." But then the stubborn, Irish, anti-rule person in me says, "Okay, well, if you're not supposed to write about that, then that's what I'm going to write about."

The challenge I set for myself was, could I create a character who is a stereotype without taking the obvious path? The obvious path in this case would be to disprove the stereotype. "Oh, everybody loves him. He's a lovable drunk." While back home in his bedroom, he's a pornographer or a mass murderer or he really doesn't like anybody. No, no, no. What then? Ask, instead, what if this character were, indeed, to his bones everything he seems? He is lovable. He is fond of everyone he meets. He is drinking himself to death despite all the people who love him. How can you capture that, or can you? That was the challenge. Can you capture that and still render him as an individual and authentic to himself?

DS: Another frequent element in your work is your use of Long Island as a setting. Does this label you as a Long Island writer?

McDERMOTT: In fiction everything is put to the service of the larger story. I never intended to write about Long Island even though I grew up there. My intention was not to reproduce the place. My Long Island is not the one we grew up on. My Long Island is there because it's a tool for me. The geography, that hundred or so miles between Manhattan and the tip of Long Island, is a means of getting at what the characters want. In those hundred miles, you have the perfect metaphor of yearning. You've got a place immigrants come to, the fresh green breast of the new world—the sense that whatever they were leaving wasn't good enough, that they want something more. You start out in the city, and the next generation moves to the suburbs to get that green patch of lawn for the children, beautiful beaches, the ocean. It's the quintessential American success story.

DS: You set yourself the artistic challenge of trying to do something different in each book, and you certainly did that with *Child of My Heart*, which is very distinct. It's quite pagan, I feel, and kicks free of all that you've written before.

McDERMOTT: I'll say it's different. *Child of My Heart* came to me unlike anything else that I've written. Again, I was working away on another novel. There's always a novel in the works somewhere, and I was working on another novel, and September 11 happened and everything stopped. We all did that. Everything stopped; routine stopped. We had those numb days sitting in front of the television. Then, when I went back to my desk, literally to the sentence that I had stopped writing on the morning of September 11, I hadn't lost interest in the book, I just had been out of my writing routine, which I try not to have happen, and I needed a jump-start. I needed to restart my fictional brain, and I thought about an idea I'd been toying with. Somewhere in the back of my mind, I thought someday I would like to write about a relationship between a younger girl and a slightly older girl, that kind of infatuation that often happens with teenagers and slightly younger girls. It seemed to me that I had seen that in prep-school boy stories, you know, the younger boy infatuated with the athlete or the popular senior or whatever, but not with girls. So I thought, "I'll put that down. Maybe it will turn into a story, and then I'll be ready to go back to the novel for the long haul." But I was quickly taken over by this story, and I wrote the novel in six months. I can't even write letters or e-mail in six months. I've never written anything so quickly.

Once I had finished it and looked back, I realized—and this was not my conscious intention at all in the composition of it—that it had its roots in September 11. It is a book about mortality. It is a book about golden moments in childhood, in summer, those eternal moments that we know are really not eternal because they are always shadowed by a future. We understand that. It struck me, when the *New York Times* did all their pieces about the people who were killed on September 11, that many of the photographs they showed of the people who were killed were taken on beaches. It made sense. When do you take pictures? On holidays and during summer vacation. It was all Christmas and beaches. Young fathers and young mothers with their children having fun. We look at those photographs knowing the fate of that young father, the fate of that mother, and yet we can look at those photographs and we can still see and appreciate the joy of their lives at that moment. The tragedy doesn't totally overshadow it. The pain doesn't wipe out that moment. You look at them at the peak of their lives. They were happy. They didn't know what was coming. Now that we know what was coming for them, we still see that happiness. We can hold those two things in our mind. We can hold the tragedy. We can hold death in our minds, and we can recognize the joy of the moment at the same time. I think that's what I was trying to somehow capture in fiction in *Child of My Heart:* that there are the golden moments, and at the same time we understand that we are finite, that life holds for us all an end sooner or later. It holds it for us all, and that does not have to diminish our joy in the moment. Again, this is only something I could see clearly once I had gotten the story down.

DS: *Child of My Heart* is a fairy tale about the village beauty, a fifteen-year-old girl on Long Island. Children, dogs, cats, and men all love Theresa, who is sweet and affectionate and imaginative. But she is also wily and manipulative, a supremely confident young lady on a quest for knowledge, and the mentor she chooses is an abstract painter well along in years. He's the only adult she has any respect for or curiosity about. I wonder what led you to choose an abstract painter, besides the fact that Willem de Kooning lived on Long Island for many years.

McDERMOTT: Again, it was part of the mystique. I saw her right away, this fifteen-year-old girl who is telling her story in retrospect. So her story is filtered; she is making an artifact of her young self's consciousness. She is putting things together. She is only telling us certain things about her life and about the few days in which the novel takes place. But what I recognized about her right away was that she was an artist who had not yet found her art, although she does recreate the world. She recreates it for the children she takes care of. She recreates it for the reader in the telling of the story. So it just seemed right that she would be drawn to an elderly painter, the only adult in her universe who is doing the same thing she is doing. And he has to be an abstract painter because she doesn't want the real world recreated. She wants it remade so that it is almost unrecognizable. That's how she handles the world.

DS: It's very much a novel about the imagination. Daisy, her poor little cousin, understands abstract art immediately and tells us what it's about. She looks at one drawing and says, "This is a drawing of something broken," which now, in light of what you've said about September 11, makes perfect sense to me. And what a powerful perception, the recognition that things have to be broken to be reborn, remade, renewed. Stories do that, and there are many allusions to literature in *Child of My Heart*. You pay homage to all sorts of writers.

McDERMOTT: That was purposeful. I'm a little bit hesitant to say this, because there's something crass about tying anything else to September 11, but it is the circumstances under which the book was written that inspired that. It struck me how often in the days and months following September 11 I heard poetry and fiction quoted in public places. On the nightly news Peter Jennings was ending the newscast with poetry or a little bit of Mark Twain or E. B. White. I was hearing it on the radio, too. Poets were actually being asked to talk about how we deal with such a tragedy. This made me realize in an instant something I think that I didn't fully appreciate as a reader: that we read literature and we store it up somehow, so that when things happen in our lives or in public, events that we have no language for, we can use what we've stored. We can use that language, those images and stories.

When I was young my father used to always worry about how skinny I was. That's what fathers do, right? And he used to always say to me, "You should always have a few extra pounds just in case you get sick because then you can afford to lose a few." That's sort of a metaphor for what we do with literature. You know, things are going along, and it's only a happy and comfortable society that has the leisure to read literature, to read fiction and poetry to any extent. So life is good, and we're sitting on the beach reading our books, and somehow we're storing it all. Somehow that inner voice with which we speak to ourselves gets transformed by the language the poets give us. And it was an eye-opener to me to see how it comes back. And people weren't reading or talking about new poems about September 11. As a matter of fact, most of the poetry and fiction that came out immediately after September 11 was terrible. No, people were going back to the classics and to Auden. With that new awareness, I felt that I wanted to tip my hat to the books and poems that got into my head when I was fifteen. I knew that Theresa would have to be a reader because she's a lonely child and an artist without her art. And it's at that age, in the mid-teens, when you really fall into literature. So it gave me a good chance to think about those things. Some references I don't expect any reader to pick up on, and others are very obvious. To have a story set on Long Island with a character named Daisy is a giveaway. But it was a way of saying, "Yes, these are important. These books changed our lives and the way we see and remake the world."

Joyce Carol Oates

Joyce Carol Oates was born in 1938 in rural western New York, a harsh place bordered by Lake Ontario and Lake Erie that serves as the setting for much of her haunting fiction. In fact, many aspects of Oates's childhood press into her writing. She attended grade school in a one-room schoolhouse. The first books she read and loved were *The Gold Bug and Other Stories* by Edgar Allen Poe and Lewis Carroll's *Alice in Wonderland.* Her sister, Lynn, was autistic, a child bereft of words. Oates is a virtual Niagara of language. Her one-room schoolhouse education carried her far. She won the prestigious *Mademoiselle* fiction contest while attending the University of Syracuse on a scholarship and was valedictorian at her graduation. She then earned an M.A. at the University of Wisconsin and in 1978 joined the faculty at Princeton University, where she is currently the Roger S. Berlind Distinguished Professor in the Humanities. Oates also helps her husband, Raymond J. Smith, run a small press and publish the literary magazine the *Ontario Review.*

Already the subject of an in-depth biography by the time she turned sixty (*Invisible Writer* by Greg Johnson), Oates has written now and then about her writing life, most revealingly in the essay collection, *The Faith of a Writer.* Here she alludes to the universal impulse felt by all who encounter her work: the need to exclaim over how inconceivably prolific she is. How can one help but marvel? Oates has written more than thirty novels, not counting the many she's written under the name of "Rosamund Smith." She's written twenty-plus short story collections, and an array of novellas, plays, poetry collections, and books for children and young adults. Add to that a profusion of smart and scintillating essay collections about literature, art, and boxing. But as she observes,

"How do you write so much? is a question frequently asked of me. Less frequently asked is Why?"

Possible clues abound, but not even Oates herself is certain of the answer. But it is significant that her fiction evinces a fascination with men who prey on girls and women—stalkers, rapists, and murderers—and with brute lust and sadism, depravity and vengeance, betrayal and obsession. She handles these terrors and proclivities with clear-eyed realism and a gothic sensibility. The vulnerabilities, anxieties, courage, recklessness, and resilience of adolescent girls and young women intrigue her endlessly, as does the death of innocence, family matters, secrets of all kinds, race and interracial relationships, eroticism, and crime.

Oates's 1966 short story, "Where Are You Going, Where Have You Been?" is one of the most potent and indelible stories in all of literature. Oates's novel, *them,* a tale of Detroit during the racial violence of the 1960s, won the 1970 National Book Award. *Black Water,* a bleak tale based on the Kennedy-Chappaquiddick scandal, secured a Pulitzer Prize nomination. Her controversial fictionalization of the life of Marilyn Monroe, *Blonde,* was a National Book Award finalist in 2000 and a national bestseller. Oates's bestselling family saga, *We Were the Mulvaneys,* was an Oprah Book Club title. She's written about a girl gang in *Foxfire,* a serial sex killer in *Zombie,* and exactly what the title states in *Rape: A Love Story. Rape* is one of many of Oates's seemingly lurid tales that offers a redemptive twist as she reminds readers that the real power resides in the survivor, not the attacker, and that women possess an uncanny ability to recover and embrace life even after the most hellish ordeals.

Oates won the PEN/Malamud Award for Excellence in Short Fiction in 1996; her story collections include *I Am No One You Know,* a set of bold and bloody tales that explore the malevolent aspects of sexuality. The novel *The Falls,* set on her home turf in Niagara Falls and the nearby toxic waste site known as Love Canal, dramatizes the perverse connection between love and death. The recently published *Uncensored: Views & (Re)Views* is a collection of literary essays, reviews, and criticism in which Oates discusses a range of figures, from Thoreau to Plath to Doctorow. And new works in the pipeline at the time of this writing include a poetry collection, story collection, books for children and young adults, and several novels.

Oates appeared on *Open Books* in 2002, when her current book was the novel *I'll Take You There*. Set in the early 1960s on the campus of an upstate New York university, it tracks the misadventures of a white scholarship student who cannot fit in with her sorority and who carries on an obsessive relationship with a black philosophy student. A master at explicating the emotional valence of place and the turbulent weather of the mind, Oates pushes her characters to the edge, where the tides of myth, mayhem, and madness roll in.

DONNA SEAMAN: You've been devoted to literature, to reading, writing, and teaching for many years. I wonder, what does literature do for you? Why has it never lost its enchantment?

JOYCE CAROL OATES: I think that the first experiences I had with literature were so long ago when I was a child that I wasn't even thinking in terms of literature but just, I suppose, as a response to the imagination. Initially, we were readers. Children love to read and then tell little stories. So I think that the creative spirit is very deep in all of us, and it's absolutely natural and simply follows us through life.

Obviously when one becomes a writer, the imaginative processes become more sophisticated and complex and self-conscious. But still, I think that a component is always there of a childlike curiosity and wonder.

DS: Stories come to you in different forms and voices. I wonder how you know if you're going to write a short story as opposed to a novel?

OATES: It very much depends upon the characters and whether their stories are complex, whether I'm going to follow them through time. The novel is the great genre for taking a character through time.

DS: Do you find that characters return to you, that they keep talking to you?

OATES: My characters do haunt me. That's true. I think of them quite often, but they really only belong in a certain novel or a certain short story. To take them out of that would somehow not work. I'm the kind of writer who's very dependent upon setting: landscapes and cityscapes are about as important to me as the characters.

DS: In *I'll Take You There,* for instance, you write about what I think of as Oates terrain. You call it the snow belt in northwest New York, and I assume that that place has a deep resonance for you.

OATES: It does. It's a certain landscape found in upstate New York, and people who have lived there and who read my writing say that my writing conveys that area very faithfully. It has much to do, I think, just with the geography and the nearness to the Great Lakes. And of course Chicago is so characterized by the lake and by a certain kind of feel, I think, in the air.

DS: It's a severe land, and that comes through immediately in the beginning of *I'll Take You There.*

OATES: That's true. And that novel is sort of a memoirish fiction, a work that I think of as having a contour and a tone of memoir, but the elasticity and freedom of fiction so that it's both—it is and it isn't one's own life.

DS: I read a *Paris Review* interview with you by Robert Philips— who actually went to Syracuse University at the same time you did —and he mentions that you were in a sorority.

OATES: That's right, and I remember I said in that interview I would never write about the sorority because it was so trivial. What I wrote about in *I'll Take You There* is not my own sorority. The sorority to which the young woman belongs is not literally the sorority that I belonged to.

DS: Yet it seems that the subject was percolating deep in your subconscious until it became an important thing to revisit, a painful memory. You said that your sorority experience wasn't disastrous but merely despairing, yet you write about it now with such passion.

OATES: It was disillusioning. But in my novel, the young woman is yearning for sisters and for companionship and friends, and she tends to be an obsessive personality. I don't think I was quite like that. I had a warm and supportive family, which she does not have. So there are some distinctions between her and me, but the voice of the novel is virtually identical with my own. In many ways, she is me.

DS: This narrator struck me as another variation on a type of character you write about so evocatively—young women on the brink of genuine womanhood. That is a vulnerable stage in our lives, and you've written about it so many times with such insight. Why does this passage, this transformation, interest you so much?

OATES: I suppose I still identify with that quest. No matter how old we are, many of us still have the insecurities and the questions and curiosity of adolescence. Adolescence is a time in our lives when we are emotionally vulnerable and we're yearning for some sort of idealism. We are susceptible to moods, to depression and melancholy. In adolescence, emotions are up and down, up and down, you know, as a kind of exaggeration of adult life.

And then we become adults, and many people lose that capacity, that childlike and adolescent capacity for wonder, which I think is very valuable to retain—along with curiosity and a sense of humor. For many years I've taught late adolescents, one might call them, very young adults on the university level, and that age group is just so wonderful. They tend to be very funny. My students at Princeton are extremely self-critical, idealistic, and hard-working. I guess they are emotional. I don't see that much as a professor. But they're living closer to the edge of emotion than adults are. And also young people are very susceptible to influences. They can learn so much in just one semester; they can really improve. For instance, they can improve their writing. They can be guided; they can be helped.

DS: You've written a couple of young adult novels. What inspired you to write for this audience?

OATES: A young editor at HarperCollins who had always liked my writing invited me to write specifically for adolescents. She said that since I had written so many stories, and even novels, about adolescents, especially adolescent girls, why didn't I try to write a young adult novel. And it was, to me, an experiment.

DS: Your fiction often focuses on how profound a force sexuality is at that stage of life, and you often dramatize the negative sexual influences young women have to cope with.

OATES: I suppose that's true in the adult fiction, especially. The young adult writing tends to be a little more positive. I feel when I'm writing for young adults I'm allowed, without any strain or contrivance, to arrange for a happy ending. The plausible happy ending is what I aim for in my writing, but if it isn't plausible, then obviously I can't provide that.

DS: You seem very attracted to gothic and horror fiction. What appeals to you about these genres?

OATES: The earliest books I read were *Alice in Wonderland* and *Through the Looking Glass,* and the short stories of Edgar Allan

Poe. Lewis Carroll is very funny—kind of cartoon and antic, and very imaginative in an energetic way. Edgar Allan Poe is not usually funny. He's nightmarish and surreal. Poe is writing about interior experience, the psychological experience rather than the exterior, and Lewis Carroll seems to be writing about his own society, but he's parodying it and putting it into kind of a cartoony imaginary world. But both these writers are fantasists, and there are gothic elements in both writers. To me, the word "gothic" is a very complex signifier, and it seems to me to refer to the imagination as it encompasses the nighttime experiences as we dream, as well as our daytime lives.

DS: You've written often about the 1960s and the 1970s. I wonder if that era intrigues you in particular, or if that's just a setting that comes to mind without great deliberation.

OATES: It's hard to say. There seems to be an ideal time for certain stories. One novel I wrote called *You Must Remember This* really belongs in the 1950s, and it's of that era. It's about the Cold War and Senator Joseph McCarthy and his influence and nuclear experimentation and so forth. Then other novels seem to belong to a different time. I have a novel called *Middle Age: A Romance,* which is set basically in a place like Princeton, New Jersey, a suburb of New York City, at the present time. It really needs to be set in the present time because of the affluence and the way society has evolved. And so I guess there is just a specific time that seems appropriate for a specific story.

DS: I'm impressed at your grasp of these different eras. I'm thinking of *Blonde,* a profound interpretation of Marilyn Monroe's life in which you consider in great detail a particular and highly influential phase of American culture. I wonder how much research you do when you write?

OATES: That was my most ambitious novel in terms of structure and research, and the emotions that went into it, because it turned out to be much more difficult and much longer than I had planned. I had originally planned it would only be about two hundred pages or even less, but obviously I got so caught up in the life of the times as well as Norma Jean Baker's life. I did a lot of research into the politics and the popular culture of that time. I got very interested, for instance, in Norma Jean Baker when she was a little girl. She saw lots of movies, so suddenly it seemed to me very important that I see some of the movies that the little girl had seen, because obviously they would influence her. That was the beginning of my research, and one step of research leads rather innocently to another, until finally you have a thousand pages of notes.

DS: It's such a complex work, multi-voiced and multi-layered, and yet it fits so well into your ongoing inquiry into the difficulty women have in coming into their own at a time when women were overtly considered second class.

OATES: Oh, absolutely yes, especially girls and women from impoverished parts of the country.

DS: Class, in fact, is another theme that you write about with great insight.

OATES: I think I write about class because of my own background. I am from a working-class background, and very often my family did not have much money. When you're on the outside of society, or at least on the margins, you tend to look at things very differently than you would look at them if you were on the inside.

DS: Do you think your background sensitized you to yet another facet of American life you handle so perceptively in your fiction, race relations?

OATES: Probably so, because when I was in junior high school, I was bussed into the city. There were just a scattering of black children who were in the school, and it really seemed to me, you know, that psychologically, and literally, we were all on the margins. So I do identify with black children, and other ethnic minority children. In the 1950s it seemed that everybody was Caucasian, and everybody, at least at school, was middle class, and so it was very natural to feel that one was somewhat on the margin.

DS: We've talked about your female characters, but you write very strongly from male points of view.

OATES: I'm attracted to the masculine point of view because I did identify very much with my father and his world. He introduced me to the world of boxing when I was quite young, maybe nine or ten years old, and that's a world almost exclusively of men, so completely antithetical to the world of my mother and grandmother. It's not that I chose one world over another, but I saw them as quite completely different.

DS: I enjoyed your book on boxing very much and your book on George Bellows, an artist who painted boxers, in part because I've always been curious about the ritualized aggression of boxing. To watch a boxing match is to realize that we all have the same instincts, the same fascination with power, pain, and competition.

OATES: That's right. And because I was so young, I didn't have any preconceived notions. I didn't think that boxing was barbarous. I didn't have a feminist prejudice. I was just basically a witness to something very different from everything else in my life. My mother didn't go to the fights, and of course, my grandmothers didn't go either. It was a world, as I said, of men and boys. Just a few women would be there—you know, the mothers of the boxers. I'm speaking of Golden Gloves fights. I was never taken to a professional fight. It was all amateur fights. So, you know, it was a world that was very dramatic and very exciting, sometimes almost too exciting. Because when two boys get into the ring, both of them are just so thrilled to be there, but only one of them wins. And that harshness is shocking to a child, to see that you can be very prepared and have such hope and that it can be all over in about three minutes.

DS: Your mentioning your father makes me think about the protagonist in *I'll Take You There* and her tragic, enigmatic, and difficult relationship with her father.

OATES: When I was rereading the novel, I was struck by how unjudging she is. Basically she expects people not to be that nice to her, and I guess that's the way I am, too. I don't really expect things to go that well, and so when things don't go well for my character in the novel, she doesn't feel that it's unjust. When she falls in love with a young black man who's intellectually superior to her, as he is older than she is, she really feels that probably he will never reciprocate her feelings for him. And she really does accept that.

I feel that probably there's a kind of wisdom in that, because otherwise you go around in life being hurt and feeling resentful and always feeling that you're being judged negatively. There's a certain wisdom, maybe, in just accepting the fact that many people are just not going to reciprocate your feeling for them. But still you don't want to cut yourself off from them and run the other way, because they may have a lot to teach you about life.

DS: I was intrigued by the narrator's invisibility. The dreadful sorority housemother, Mrs. Thayer, never gets her name right. The reader's not even sure of her real name. And her lover has a very hard time understanding anything about her.

OATES: He is sort of bemused by her. She's just a little white girl who follows him around, and he's actually not that interested in her. But she is so dogged and so devoted to him that he finally comes around, and he likes her a little bit. It's almost as if she's like a younger sister. Then when he's in a very bad mood, he takes it out on her, and she doesn't run away, or lash out at him; she just accepts it. I'm wondering whether I would do that in the same circumstances. I'm not sure how I would behave. I never had a love experience that was so painful and so brutal. I was never personally rejected like that, and I'm wondering whether I would have accepted it the way she did.

DS: There's an interesting twist on her not being seen when, in the last section of the novel, she's not allowed to look at someone she dearly loves.

OATES: Right, it's a kind of fairy tale situation.

DS: It is. It's very intense, and I took it as emblematic of the artist's predicament—that as a creative and observant person you're often outside and separate from what you desire, and that your writing serves as a way back to it.

OATES: That's true, and she finds a little piece of broken glass or a mirror in the desert that she uses. She looks into a mirror to see a forbidden sight that is shocking to her, that she otherwise would not have seen. So the mirror is like the novel, where we're looking indirectly. I was thinking of Medusa the Gorgon with the snakes screwing out of her head in classical mythology. We can't look directly at Medusa; she's too terrifying. But you can look at her through a reflecting surface, like a shield. I was also thinking about my own experience. My father was very ill for several years, a lingering illness due to two kinds of cancer. He did finally die a couple of years ago. But it took a long time, and I remember talking to him on the telephone a lot. I became, in a way, my father's friend, or he became my friend. We had a new relationship at the time of his dying and decline because we were on the telephone a lot.

When I was with my father, like in the same room, he actually couldn't hear that well, but he could hear very well on the telephone, or maybe he had a special listening device. So strangely enough, when I was not in my father's presence, I could talk to him with a freedom that I couldn't when we were together. A lot of that went into the novel, but of course, it's different in a novel. It is fiction.

I almost never write about anything directly. I don't know why. It's either that I can't do it or I don't find it that interesting. For instance, the housemother in the sorority is based on a real woman who was British, and she was our housemother in my sorority. She had some of the characteristics of Mrs. Thayer but not all of them. What is different in the novel and which did not exist in real life is the young girl being so interested in her and wanting her to like her, in part because the girl doesn't have a mother. In fact I did have a mother and I had a grandmother, and I didn't really have those feelings about the real life of Mrs. Thayer. But I might have.

DS: That section of the book reminded me so much of Charlotte Brontë's novel *Villette* in terms of the intense scrutiny of another person under rigid circumstances, that obsessive need to try to understand someone who may never respond.

OATES: I suppose I identify with that kind of personality. Norma Jean Baker, who becomes Marilyn Monroe, had a lifelong, almost frantic yearning to know her real father. She never knew him. Some names were given to her, one name in particular of a man who might very well have been her father. She never saw him face to face, but she did try to telephone him, and he actually hung up the phone. I guess I have an interest in the kind of personality that seeks some kind of truth or acknowledgment from another. Even though we don't get that recognition, we do get other things. We learn other things about life in the process of seeking out that other person.

DS: That's a classic hero's quest, one in which you're in pursuit of something elusive, and you grow and change over the course of the quest.

OATES: That's right, and I think that in our culture girls sometimes have infatuations with older men that are based on the yearning for wisdom. It's a sort of projection of the quest for a father, for a really ideal father, a father that provides us with some sort of wisdom or knowledge that we're not getting from other sources.

DS: Given your interest in the longings and fortitude of girls and young women, your interest in the painter Balthus, who often painted provocatively self-possessed girls, makes sense. You've written the introduction to his remarkable memoir, *Vanished Splendor.*

OATES: There's a dreamlike quality to Balthus's paintings, and many people think of his paintings as iconoclastic because they're rather erotic. But in his memoir he writes that he thought of them as quite the opposite, that they have kind of a mystical dimension and that he's basing the strategies or the structures on Renaissance art—that he was concerned with purity. It was quite a surprise and very interesting to me.

DS: In your introduction you quote Henry James's famous order to look to the work, not the artist. And yet, as we're talking about your work, we end up talking about your life.

OATES: That's true, but many other people have lives like mine in upstate New York, but they're not interested in creating anything. So I think it's some mysterious component where some people are just so curious, and they want to do a little more with the world than just live in it or get a job.

DS: Yes, the imagination is universal, but the urge to take it seriously, to work artistically with it, is not common.

OATES: And I think most people would be just astonished, and maybe even pitying, if they knew how hard many artists and writers worked. If anybody knew how many times I write a page over or do a scene over and over again, most people would just back off, shaking their heads. They would say, "This is ridiculous. Why are you doing this?" I really feel that sometimes there's an element of the absurd in trying to get something "perfect," because there may not be an audience for it. Some of the things we work on may not even be published, yet there's a strong obsessive component in artists and writers that make us do things over and over again until we get them right, or what we think is right. Most people would feel that the effort was rather ridiculous.

DS: Balthus spent many years working on some of his paintings in absolute isolation.

OATES: I was so struck that Balthus could work for twelve years on one of his large canvases.

DS: That sort of devotion and involvement is far beyond the efforts most of us make, and I believe that the viewer, the listener to music, and the reader subconsciously recognize that level of conviction and commitment in artists.

OATES: One of the qualities that it provides is a sense of timelessness. If you work on something for twelve years, you're really divorced from the daily or the ephemeral, and it enters another dimension. Emily Dickinson wrote little scraps of lines on little pieces of paper and put them in her dress and apron pockets, and she created her very complex art out of these little snippets, little fragments, and her poetry also has that timeless quality to it.

DS: I imagine that you're working on many things at once in different stages of their creation. Is that true?

OATES: No, actually not. I tend to focus on one thing at a time. If I get to a section, say I've finished part one or part two of a novel, I always take some time off and write some short stories or essays or reviews or poetry, because I need that little space. It's like breathing space. But when I'm working on a novel, I tend to be very immersed and obsessive.

DS: For most people, to take a break would be to go for a walk or go to a movie. Your break is to write an essay.

OATES: And my breaks are just exhilarating. I've sometimes even written novellas. Even a novel becomes a break. After I wrote *Blonde,* I was so exhausted and worn out that I gave myself a holiday and wrote *Middle Age: A Romance,* which is actually about five hundred pages long. But in contrast to *Blonde,* it was so much easier; the emotions that went into it were so much more positive and exhilarating, and it was based on some experiences that either I or my friends had had in Princeton, which were almost commonplace experiences of middle age in contrast to the uncommon experience of Marilyn Monroe. She turns out to be so unique in our history. So that was a wonderful vacation for me.

DS: I understand that you also keep a diary.

OATES: Yes, I have a very long journal. I started about 1972. Most of it's in my archives at Syracuse University. There's a collection of my manuscripts and letters and journals at Syracuse University. So they have most of it. I have maybe one hundred, two hundred pages at home.

DS: Do you ever think about writing a memoir.?

OATES: I have written memoirist essays about my father, my mother, my one-room schoolhouse. I've done little things through assignments, and I do think I'll put them together into a book some day.

DS: What's it like to be in the thick of things and have someone write a major biography about you?

OATES: The biography by Greg Johnson has been out for several years, and it is very well researched. I particularly like the parts about my parents and my grandparents; the early chapters I like best. It was his first biography, and I was just so impressed with the degree of sophistication that he brought to it. He was exhaustive. There had been a lot of things written about me over the years, and there have been some books written on my writing, so the transition to the biography was probably not that different.

DS: How did you feel when your novel *We Were the Mulvaneys* was chosen as an Oprah Book Club title?

OATES: It was a wonderful experience to meet Oprah, this American icon, and to feel that Oprah is quite deserving of her reputation, her extreme fame. She's got a high-voltage personality. She's someone who, in a group, would shine, stand out. She just has a natural radiance. And the fact that she's also interested in serious fiction is just so wonderful.

DS: I wonder what your sense of the reading public is. You know, people are always so concerned that people don't read enough; that people don't have the time to read; that young people are not taught to read and understand literature. What are your impressions of our state of reading?

OATES: It seems quite various in this country. We have a problem with illiteracy, and I know that's very real. Since I'm a professor at Princeton, I'm not seeing those students. I tend to see students who are in the humanities, who are self-selected, and they are very gifted and interested in language. They are natural readers.

And I do have friends whose children just read books all the time, like a little girl who's nine years old who reads two or three books a day. So there are some people still reading. But as I say, I'm not really experiencing the wide range of America, and I know there are serious problems of illiteracy that are more prevalent than children who are reading two or three books a day.

DS: I suspect that the many well-known writers, including yourself, who are now writing for young people indicates an effort to try to reach younger readers so that literature isn't forgotten in the great buzz of TV and movies and video games. Reading is important; literature does something that no other art form does.

OATES: Literature is very inward. If I'm reading a book, I'm also thinking about it in different ways that I'm not necessarily thinking if I watch a movie or see television. You're so much on the outside of those forms. Television is particularly unsatisfying, or dissatisfying, I think, because of the commercial aspect: the repeated breaks for commercials. It's so discontinuous. Even if you were making an effort to watch something good on television, if it's commercial television, those breaks are so artificial. But when you're reading a book, say, by Charles Dickens, you just kind of lose yourself in it for a long time.

DS: Do feel that writers have a responsibility to people, some kind of social or moral role to play?

OATES: Some writers have very keen social consciences, and it has always been that way. Other writers are much more hermetic and interested in the aesthetics and private experience. I think it really depends upon our personalities. I've gone through different stages. I tend not to want to dictate how other people should feel, so I'm not that politically involved. But I do believe in the communication aspect of literature, and I personally don't believe in a private or hermetic art, really. Most of what I write is a reaching out to other people.

DS: You write in many forms, including plays. Drama is certainly about working with others, writing for others, creating a community of performers and audience members.

OATES: I'm always writing plays, and you're absolutely right. I was just at Bard College in upstate New York where some students performed a one-act play of mine that I had just written. I had never even heard a reading of this play before, and I was quite enthralled by what the actors did with the lines, and the way the student director directed them. It was such an exciting experience. These young people were so great, so creative.

DS: You often write about our more violent tendencies, so it's wonderful to hear you celebrate our finer qualities.

OATES: I think that one can have a tragic sense of human history over periods of millennia but still have great hope for individuals and families and smaller units. I don't see a necessary contradiction there. And when I'm working with young people, all my feelings of idealism are completely mobilized. I feel that the future is in very good hands, and I don't worry. It's when I stand back and look at the larger perspective that my sense of tragedy is predominant. Of course, history tends to be about public figures and impersonal subjects, whereas art tends to be about people.

PART TWO: Genre Crossers

Writers often work in different forms and genres in order to express different perspectives, take on different subjects, challenge themselves creatively, or just earn a living. Such versatility tends to strengthen a writer's work. Writers might bring elements of fiction to their nonfiction, thus writing narratives animated by the evolution of a character, enhanced by atmosphere, and quickened with drama. Conversely, writers versed in the demands of nonfiction may write fiction that is enriched by their knowledge of such fields as history or biology. By writing in different genres, writers attract a wider array of readers, and can serve as bridges between literary forms. It could be that few readers of Lynda Barry's popular, long-running syndicated comic strip, *Ernie Pook's Comeek*, routinely read novels, but after Barry pushed herself to extend her story-telling reach in her novel, *Cruddy*, she may have inspired some converts. Poets who also write about poetry, such as Edward Hirsch, bring their fluency in metaphor and imagery to their prose, and a scholar's appreciation for the poetic tradition and other art forms to their poetry, thus deepening the resonance of both genres—and keeping readers on their toes.

Alan Lightman's literary double life reflects the paths he has followed first as a scientist, then as a writer. In his essays, he writes straightforwardly about physics, scientists' lives, and the ethical concerns raised by technological development. He then addresses the same significant, even urgent, concerns in his fiction, but from more oblique angles, in more lyrical prose, and with more freedom to be inventive and follow his intuitions to startling conclusions. Barry Lopez performs a similar sleight of mind. In his acclaimed nonfiction books—works of natural history, travel writing, and ethnographic inquiries—he explicates our perception of nature and of our place within the web of life through in-depth studies of the relationships among landscapes, plants, animals, humans, and culture. He writes from an ecological viewpoint, combining his own observations from the field with the fruits of his extensive research. Then, in his hard-hitting fiction, Lopez adds an emotional and spiritual dimension to his inquiries, not to mention suspense, lyricism, and compassion.

Paul West, a dazzlingly prolific and protean writer, crossed an ocean and became an expatriate English writer living in America, where he crosses genres by writing both novels and memoirs. West makes the most of this double-barrel approach by composing elaborate, even baroque, and playful multi-layered novels, which flirt with nonfiction by featuring historical characters, and by writing nonfiction notable for its clarity and concreteness, as well as its emotional valence and wit. Colson Whitehead also blurs the line between fiction and fact, whether he's writing novels spiked with history, pop culture, and technology, or a love song to New York, pushing the reader to ask what is real and what is imagined, and to recognize how intertwined the two are in the alchemy of the mind.

Lynda Barry

Lynda Barry is the fanatically adored creator of the nationally syndicated comic strip, *Ernie Pook's Comeek*. An outrageously funny yet keenly sensitive, frank, and provocative comic about the traumas and absurdities of growing up, it features young Marlys Mullen, her sister Maybonne, brother Freddie, and a host of screwy cousins, neighbors, and other quirky characters. Barry has an uncanny ability to dwell in the anxious, inexplicable, intensely sad and beautiful realm of childhood and adolescence, capturing with thorny specificity life's grittiness and contrariness and the kaleidoscopic churnings of the mind. It may be that childhood remains so vivid and significant for Barry because hers was so difficult.

Born in 1956, Barry grew up in a tough Seattle neighborhood, the only girl in an Irish-Filipino family. Her father, a butcher, disappeared when she was thirteen. Her mother worked as a night janitor at a hospital, and Barry eventually went to work with her. But Barry wanted to stay in school, and with the help of a sympathetic counselor, she was able to attend a better high school, and later enrolled at Evergreen State in Olympia, Washington, an alternative college where she befriended Matt Groening, who later created *The Simpsons*. A painter, Barry started to draw cartoons as a cathartic exercise. She began getting published in alternative papers and then was offered her big break, a gig at the *Chicago Reader*. Barry now has a shelf of books to her credit. Her comic strips are collected in *The Freddie Stories* and *The Greatest of Marlys*. She is also the author of a short novel *The Good Times are Killing Me*, which became a hit Off-Broadway play, and a more recent, and similarly innovative book, *One Hundred Demons*, a high-voltage collection of seventeen illustrated tales that Barry describes as "autobifictionalgraphy." Barry is also a contributor to Salon.com and National Public Radio.

Cruddy, an illustrated novel, is a work of daredevil wizardry. Barry has always leaned toward the grim, gritty, and spooky, but here the grotesque and the traumatic reach nearly surreal heights, bringing Hunter Thompson and Tama Janowitz to mind. But Barry's affinity for the brutal and the gross does not overshadow her huge affection for her characters or her understanding of how difficult it is for human beings to feel at ease in their own skin, let alone within a family, neighborhood, school, or community. And Barry is doubly gifted. As an artist, she can convey a lifetime of feeling in a simple line, and as a writer she has perfect pitch for both ranting inner monologues and spiky dialogue.

Lynda Barry joined me on *Open Books* in 2000.

DONNA SEAMAN: *Cruddy* is a full-fledged novel that, in spite of its wild and wicked humor, is a work of serious literature. Your narrator, sixteen-year-old Roberta Rohbeson, is instantly recognizable as a Barry creation, yet the depth and complexities of her story seem like a departure for you. I understand that the creation of *Cruddy* was long and demanding.

LYNDA BARRY: It was really long. I had been trying to write a novel like *Cruddy* for almost ten years. For the first seven, I had the idea that I should know exactly what the book should be about before I wrote it. I had this idea that I would write a story about a rich girl and a poor girl who become friends, and the evil class system that makes their friendship impossible. So it was really bad. I'm a painter. That's how I started out doing stuff, by painting, and it didn't occur to me that what I knew about painting—that you just kind of start and on you go—I could apply to writing a novel. The way I was trying to write a novel would be to make a painting where you just paint the first inch from the top and then go down and do the second inch, and you just keep going down until you sign your name in the lower right-hand corner. Finally, when I was at my wits' end trying to write *Cruddy*, I got the idea that one of the problems was that I didn't know where the book was. When you make a painting, you know where the painting is. When you're writing a book, where is it? And really, where is a book? A book happens when you read it, right? So I figured out that I had to paint a manuscript, and I did the first manuscript, the first successful manuscript, with watercolor.

DS: You painted it?

BARRY: I painted it, eight hundred pages long. I did. I used Tucson red watercolor, and I painted it very slowly. It was really big handwriting, and then when I was finished, I'd take my hair dryer and [noise like a hair dryer]. There was something about slowing down that made the story able to come. As I was slowing down and concentrating on making the letters really pretty, I just figured the sentences would be pretty too. So I have really good handwriting now. After I finished that big fat crinkly manuscript, I copied it over on a manual typewriter, mostly because I just love the sound of typing, you know? I love that "ding," which I don't have on my computer. Although I'm sure you could program it. From there I copied the typewritten manuscript on a computer.

DS: Were you revising and changing as you did this?

BARRY: I was, but always in the context of the flow of the manuscript, and that's what made it so easy. It's sort of like the philosophy of riding a bicycle. As long as I was in motion while I copied those three manuscripts, and then copied it one more time, the revisions happened by themselves. I knew the characters better, so I didn't have to try to fix individual sentences, which is just like death. It's like trying to fix one part of your makeup after you have it all perfect. So, that's how I did it, and it was really easy to do. It was really much easier to write it slowly with a paintbrush then to try to type the first draft on a computer. On a computer, as soon as you start to have doubts, you go and pick at the sentences, and you could be there forever. Plus, you can just erase it when you're feeling bad about it. When you've taken the time to handwrite something with paint, it just looks too pretty to toss, although I did toss a lot.

DS: Your manuscript is a work of art; it's downright pretty, and yet it's called *Cruddy*.

BARRY: It is pretty, but it looks like it was written by a seventh-grader with dried blood, to tell you the truth.

DS: That makes sense: blood is a key element in the novel. Where did your gruesome tale spring from?

BARRY: If there was any influence in this book, it was Grimm's fairy tales. I think of *Cruddy* as kind of a fairy tale. It's kind of a dark, hilarious horror story.

DS: Let's talk about your characters, and let's start with the father. Here's his wisdom, which Roberta quotes frequently: "No matter what, expect the unexpected. And whenever possible *be* the unexpected." Are these words to live by?

BARRY: I think so. It's a good idea.

DS: Frankly, the father is one of the creepiest and most alarming characters a reader will ever come across in fiction.

BARRY: Yeah, he's horrible.

DS: He has Roberta pose as Clyde, an idiot boy who can't speak, and they take off, cruising on down the road, when she's eleven years old, and much of the story is told in flashback. And it involves a great deal of gore and mayhem.

BARRY: When I was trying to write about the poor girl and the rich girl as friends, it was really good and moral. And I've always thought of myself as the peaceful, loving, hippie chick. I never thought that I would ever write about murder or anything like that. But I was reading some D. H. Lawrence—because I've always felt that if I read, I have to read everything, even the classic stuff with really tiny print—and the main character was just thinking and thinking and not doing anything, and he drove another main character crazy and she hit him on the head with a paperweight. And I thought, "You know, I have to read more books where there's more hitting on the head with paperweights." So I started reading a lot of mysteries and finding that I read like crazy as long as there was a lot of action. Then, once I was writing the book by hand, it was like dreaming. That's just what it was like, and I didn't try to stop the creepy stuff. I had such a good time.

DS: *Cruddy* is intense. The book has such velocity, it's positively hallucinatory, and it seems incredibly real. And we're talking about things like dismemberment and eyeballs sitting on countertops.

BARRY: It's far out. And funny. It's horrifying, but I laughed my pants off many, many times while I was writing it.

DS: You mentioned Grimm's fairy tales, and like fairy tales, your novel taps into the archetypal vision of the dark side of life, the underworld. The epic battle between "the father" and Clyde is right out of Freud or Jung.

BARRY: Any kid can read the story of Hansel and Gretel in any library and get a pleasant thrill, yet if you read it in the newspaper, it would be so horrifying. Then again, I found stories full of horrifying things tremendously comforting as a child. Reassuring.

DS: It's true; children love gross stuff and scary things.

BARRY: Yes, they do like that stuff, and they also like real conflict and real danger, and then there's resolution. In a funny way, mysteries are similar, because the detective is usually an outcast, doesn't have family, is lonely, and is going into some crazy situation. But in spite of my love of Grimm and mysteries, I still didn't expect *Cruddy,* and I was really sad when it was done because I sure enjoyed it while it was rolling.

DS: It feels as if you were on a roll, a high. And the paintings are haunting and strangely beautiful, and quite different from your comics.

BARRY: Oh, thank you. They're finger paintings. When I started to draw them I didn't want them to look like regular illustrations. I'd read a chapter and find the picture in there and then just sort of draw it. If you look really hard at the cover, you can see my little fingerprints.

DS: It's perfect. Finger-painting is kind of cruddy. You just get right in there and muck around.

BARRY: Yeah, getting messy.

DS: Another thing that intrigues me about *Cruddy,* and about all of your work, is your ability to write so convincingly in the voice of younger characters. How do you keep in touch with that sensibility?

BARRY: You know what? When I was a kid I always wanted an imaginary friend, and I had friends who had them, and I wanted one really bad, so I pretended I had one. I had an imaginary imaginary friend. But I had always wanted one, and when I started writing fiction and comic strips, I always think of them as the same thing. I hear them talking when I'm falling asleep. Or in dreams. What's amazing to me about dreams is how detailed they are. In a dream, if you're going to be in a supermarket for just three seconds, you conjure up a whole supermarket with shelves and people wearing certain clothes. And so I have characters that just talk, and it's a blast. That's why I was laughing so hard when I was writing *Cruddy,* because for me it was more like going to a movie or dreaming. As I was writing it, it was like I was scratching away the blank part on the page. It was like the characters were always there.

DS: *Cruddy* runs on two tracks, past and present. In the present, Roberta is sixteen and she's hanging out with Turtle, an albino drug dealer, and they take a drug they call Creeper.

BARRY: Yeah, I got to make up a lot of drugs and alcohol. So I made up Creeper, and the father's favorite drink is Old Skull Popper.

DS: So, there is Roberta in the present, hanging out with her crazy friends, and then there is the story of how she ends up in the Nevada desert, a tale right out of classic horror movies, science fiction, or any nuclear nightmare scenario that you can imagine, not to mention the work of Hunter Thompson and Jim Thompson. And there is, indeed, a lot of movement and adventure. At one point, they end up at a true nightmare setting, a joint named the Knocking Hammer.

BARRY: Yes, a slaughterhouse, bar, grocery store, and camping area. There really were places like that in eastern Washington. When I was a little kid we used to go to a slaughterhouse just as a matter of course on Saturday. My grandma is from the Philippines, and she used to cook this dish that was made with pig's blood. It was illegal to sell that, so she had to get it underground. So we'd go to the slaughterhouse on Saturdays. They would give us little salami sandwiches, and then grandma would come out of the back room with these Skippy peanut butter jars full of blood.

DS: This in no way influenced your work.

BARRY: Actually, no. I don't think it did, really. That blood, to me, was all about food. It didn't horrify me. And at the slaughterhouse on Saturdays, they weren't slaughtering animals. But it was a place that was both a grocery store and slaughterhouse, so I think that might have popped up.

DS: The father is a real meat man; he talks about meat people ruling the earth. And, of course, he and others as violent as he is turn people into meat.

BARRY: Yeah, they do that a little bit.

DS: And they love their knives so much they give them names. Roberta's is Little Debbie.

BARRY: Yeah, she loves Little Debbie. When I was working on *Cruddy*, I was on a train heading down to Louisiana and I sat next to a guy who had been a butcher since he was fifteen in Mississippi, so I grilled him all about knives and the whole business. And he would say things like, "All you need is an eight-inch and a ten-inch and you can take apart a cow." He would talk about it that calmly. I was just thrilled.

Edward Hirsch

Born in Chicago in 1950, Edward Hirsch came to literature through his love for his maternal grandfather, Oscar Ginsburg. An immigrant from Latvia, Ginsburg worked as a stringer for the Yiddish newspaper, *Der Yidishe Tog,* or *The Day,* and wrote poems in secret. As a boy, Hirsch loved to read, but it was his athletic prowess that carried him to Grinnell College on a football scholarship. By the time he graduated, his poems had already been published in prominent literary magazines. He went on to earn a Ph.D. in folklore at the University of Pennsylvania. He soon extended his literary efforts, publishing interviews and writing reviews and essays about the lives and work of poets.

Hirsch's lyric poetry is as open and as deep as a Great Lake, and erudite yet welcoming. His poems are shaped by his boyhood in Chicago and Skokie, Illinois, his Jewish heritage, his sense of the sweep and sorrows of America, his belief in his membership in a global community, and his profound connection to the soul and legacy of poetry. He champions for the great poets of Eastern Europe, and he is also an active supporter of his fellow contemporary American poets, who struggle to be heard in our busy world.

A poet, literary scholar, and teacher, Hirsch is the author of six books of poetry, among them *Wild Gratitude,* winner of the National Book Critics Circle Award, and most recently *Lay Back the Darkness.* He has also written two books on poetry and art, the best-selling *How to Read a Poem and Fall in Love with Poetry* and *The Demon and The Angel: Searching for the Source of Artistic Inspiration.* He has received numerous awards, including the Prix de Rome, a Guggenheim Fellowship, an American Academy of Arts and Letters Award, and a MacArthur Fellowship. A professor in the Creative Writing program at the University of Houston for seventeen years, Hirsch is now president of the John Simon Guggenheim Memorial Foundation, the first poet to hold such a position. He also teaches at New York University.

I spoke with Edward Hirsch in the spring of 2002 when he came to town to lecture at the Art Institute of Chicago, and to talk about *The Demon and The Angel.*

DONNA SEAMAN: When I read your writings about poets and poetry, I feel as though I'm part of a larger whole, as though I'm entering a deeper realm, one that exists beneath every day surfaces.

EDWARD HIRSCH: I do feel that writing poetry is noble and that you're participating in something larger than yourself—that you've found an unbroken string that leads back to our roots, our most ancient culture. I feel in writing poetry, and in writing about poetry, that you are participating in that realm through language in what you might call the mutual-participation mystique. Making that connection is important to me, and I hope that when people read my work, both my poems and my writing about poems, they feel they're part of this enduring world culture of poetry and they realize what it means to be part of that.

DS: In *The Demon and the Angel,* you not only go beyond English, you go beyond language into other forms of expression such as music and painting. Can you talk about your understanding of the creative impulse that gives rise to these diverse art forms? A force you associate with the great Spanish poet Federico García Lorca, who serves as your mentor through much of the book.

HIRSCH: It's true, Lorca is my Virgil. But first I should say, writing *The Demon and the Angel* was a little illicit, and very exciting, because in the past I've only written about poetry. Writing about music and art felt shocking. I was excited and challenged.

DS: But you do write a great deal about poetry at the outset.

HIRSCH: I feel absolutely confident about poetry, so it grounds me and, I hope, grounds the reader as I establish my argument and then move out into other art forms.

DS: I was struck by the book's movement, its almost symphonic development. You begin by introducing two forces, the demonic and the angelic, two sides of the creative impulse. Then as you connect them and reveal their workings in art, the reader experiences a tremendous sense of intellectual and psychic connection. It's actually a very emotional experience.

HIRSCH: I structured this book differently than anything I've written before, and I've written short chapters that feel to me like a cross between a prose poem and an essay. I thought that would be appropriate to the subject because there is something improvisatory about it. It gave me the chance to do, say, four pages on Keats, or six pages on Paul Klee, or eight pages on Rilke, and then circle back to the main argument. It seemed to me a way to both write about something and to enact what I was writing about because you kind of steal some of the qualities you're defining to make your own structure and your own form.

DS: Lorca's teachings on duende are the heart of the book.

HIRSCH: Lorca wrote an essay that had a huge impact on me when I was in my early twenties. It's called "Play and Theory of the Duende," and it's actually a lecture he gave in Buenos Aires. I begin by saying I wish I had been at that lecture because it seems that on that occasion the spirit of artistic mystery, an electric force, entered the room. This is duende. It's curious that there is no exact equivalent for duende in English. All over Latin America and Spain, the duende is understood as something like a trickster figure, like the Yiddish dybbuk, a sprite, someone who causes trouble. But in Andalusia, where Lorca was from, the word is used a little differently. It refers to something equivalent to soul, as some sort of artistic inspiration, so that you'd say that a singer has duende, meaning that the singer has this ineffable force, this dark and potent quality.

For my part, I'm trying to account for something that seems to me ineffable in our experience of art when we are taken over by a mysterious power. We recognize that it's happening, but we don't know how to name it. Lorca gives a name to that experience, and so I want to import the notion of duende into our vocabulary, into the way we think about art. Lorca says that it's a mysterious power which everyone recognizes and no philosopher explains. So I attempt to locate it and talk about what it is as precisely as possible, to explain, for instance, that Billie Holiday had it and why.

DS: I'm particularly taken with a phrase you use to describe duende, "a joyful darkness."

HIRSCH: I wanted to account for something that is demonic but also joyful, and so I came up with the idea of "dark joy" because I think this force is life-giving and life-enhancing, and yet it's also tied to death. What Lorca means by duende, when he says that a singer has it or that a flamenco dancer has it or that a poet has it or that a particular performance has it—he means that something else takes over, some kind of haunting or possession. Something lifts off in the process of creating the work that leads an artist to the summit of the work, to somewhere that he or she hasn't been before. So it's a kind of demonic enthusiasm, a kind of dark force.

For Lorca, and this is the Hispanic part of the idea, it's tied to death—to being in the presence of death, metaphorically speaking. In other words, Lorca recognizes that in many great works of art there's an element of mortal panic and fear. There's some sense of our humanness, some sense of our strangeness, and some sense of our mortality. And he thinks that great works of art take their risks by being in the presence of this dark force, which, for Lorca, is tied to the spirit of the earth. Lorca was, let's say, weak on the idea of the muse and the idea of the angel, but those concepts are very much related, I think, to what he's talking about, that is, about possession. He didn't like the idea of the muse or angel because you call the muse down from above, and angels fly overhead. The duende he was sure about came from the very earth; it was an earthly force.

DS: That is an ancient perception. For millennia, the earth was seen as sacred, as the source of spirituality. The sky was too abstract, too distant, too cold.

HIRSCH: There is something archaic in this idea, and primal. I think Lorca sought ancient roots in Spain and Spanish culture, in bull cults that reach back to Mesopotamia and beyond. And I like the idea of a dark artistic connection to our earthly origins.

DS: Dance is as ancient as poetry. The act of stamping our bare feet on the ground, of tapping into the deep life force within the planet with our bodies, is as basic an impulse as speech.

HIRSCH: Lorca, too, saw the duende as coming up through the soles of the artist's feet. One of the things I find compelling about this idea is the sense that there's no hierarchy in the arts, that the same force is present in every form—poetry, *cante jondo* ("deep song"), flamenco music. This is Lorca's vision, and I follow him to write about painting, music, dance, sculpture, poetry. There's something very appealing in this equality of forms, something both ancient and contemporary about it, even something American.

DS: I was very moved by your characterization of an American spirit, what you call the American sublime, and how you work your way toward that as you write about quintessentially American art forms, specifically the blues, jazz, and abstract expressionism. But you also explore the duende's counterpart, the force you call the angelic, which you connect to Ralph Waldo Emerson, who is also one of your guides, a second Virgil illuminating the creative realm. And what a pair he and Lorca make.

HIRSCH: They form a peculiar duo, all right. The word "duende" traces back etymologically to the word "demon," and I think one of the reasons Lorca preferred duende to demon is because demon has an ethic, or sense, of foul possession in the New Testament, and Lorca didn't want to suggest that the force he cherishes is foul in anyway. But it turns out that the etymology of the word demon goes way back, long before the New Testament, when it originally meant a kind of dark possession without any sense of evil.

DS: It implied some sort of intermediary.

HIRSCH: Yes, some kind of intermediary zone, and this goes back even further to what the Greeks called the *daimon*. For the Greeks, the *daimon* was an indestructible inner spirit. The *daimon* would be the origin of all gnosticism. Empedocles, for example, believed that in reincarnation your *daimon* was the part of you that lived on. Your body died, but the *daimon* migrated. It was something indestructible and permanent inside of us, something immortal: a drop of immortality within each of us.

After I traced the figure of the duende to the demon and the *daimon*, they all seemed to me to be aspects of the night mind, aspects of something that was not daily and commonsensical, some aspect of reverie. For me, the demon inevitably inflected the counterfigure of the angel, and that's how I got to the angelic force, to the celestial light. One of the things I discovered in thinking about angels and writing about artistic uses of angels is that if you trace the figure of the angel—which in the New Testament is a figure who flies above, a messenger from God—back in culture to before the New Testament, back to the Hebrew Bible, you find a much more archaic idea of the angel, as exemplified in the story of Jacob wrestling with the angel.

It is a beautiful and mysterious story, and I was struck by how the Hebrew Bible's description of Jacob wrestling with the angel is not very different from the way Lorca describes the artist's struggle with the duende. Jacob wrestles all night with this unknown stranger whom he never sees, and the stranger wounds him. But at the end of their battle, Jacob forces his adversary to give him a new name, which the stranger does, naming him Israel. I see Jacob metaphorically as the figure of the artist struggling with the dark, creative force. For me, the demon and the angel become two aspects of our nature, two parts of ourselves: something inside of us that empowers us. So I write about moments of artistic possession and encounters with demons and angels as experienced by various artists and writers, including those who write about angels or paint angels.

DS: It occurs to me that the artist can't capitulate entirely to this power. The artist needs to maintain what you describe as a spiritual alertness. Artists feel possessed by the angel or demon of artistic inspiration—you discuss writers who have felt as though they were taking dictation from a creative spirit—but they had to be present in some way; they had to remain themselves and control the transaction. They must possess, as Jacob did, the presence of mind to clarify, benefit from, and preserve the experience.

HIRSCH: We don't know how to think about this experience very clearly, because it's not just a question of putting yourself into a trance, of being taken over by other forces, and letting the forces dictate to you what to do. There's some weird combination of artistic making and artistic possession, of putting oneself at the service of other forces, other powers, while also controlling one's art. I was trying to think about, for example, the way John Keats talks in his letters about "associative drift" but then writes in "Ode to Psyche" about a "working brain." Somehow the working brain works in tandem with associative drift.

We tend to see the aspect of making on the one hand and the aspect of the seer on the other, as though they're diametrically opposed. But I think there's another kind of vocabulary that we can bring to this, to think about the way that the working intellect, what Keats calls the working brain, operates in tandem with this other demonic force. And I love something that the Spanish Sufi poet and thinker Ibn 'Arabi says: "A person must control one's thoughts in a dream." That's what I'm trying to talk about. That gives me a name for it, because it's both controlling one's thoughts and it's also entering the dream state.

DS: You can compare this state of being to the shaman's experience in that the artist, like the shaman, travels between, and bridges, the human and spiritual, the light and the dark, even life and death. The artist and the shaman mediate these places.

HIRSCH: And with skill and control. I'm not advocating madness, for instance, or giving yourself over to irrational forces. There's also the craft that one brings to the making of art. You couldn't be a great dancer if you hadn't spent a lot of time working at dance. On the other hand, there's some element of the making of great dances that goes beyond mere craft. There's some other summit that is involved, and I'm trying to account for the way one develops an art through craft and then also hits peaks, the way an artist opens himself or herself up to something and is taken over to reach another level.

DS: Another way of thinking about it is to consider archetypes, to enter the collective unconscious, to use Jung's term. Each artist taps into that stream in his or her own way, so that one sees very similar images and symbols and metaphors in diverse artists' works, yet each expression is unique. I'm thinking of Rilke and Hopkins, for instance. Each poet wrote of similar states of mind, of similar revelations, yet their creative responses are uniquely their own.

HIRSCH: I think there is an element of anonymity to art, especially great art. It involves tapping into something that we all recognize, and yet there's also something peculiar, idiosyncratic, and strange. And in many works of art that I love, there's something that seems both unique, say peculiarly Rilkian, and also something that we all recognize that Rilke is touching on behalf of all of us. Freud calls this the unconscious, Jung calls this the collective unconscious, and there are other metaphors and names for what we are talking about. But I think they're all after the same thing, which is that a great artist will touch on something that is collective, that we share—but also come at it at an angle that is unprecedented, stylistically and spiritually. So there's a place for the individual, and there's a place for the individual's connection and overlap with the larger collective.

DS: Exactly. You explicate this with particular grace when you write about Frank O'Hara. He was a very stylish, very hip poet, maybe not the deepest writer in the world, but when he wrote about the day Billie Holiday died, he plugged directly into the electric current we're talking about. And you write about how Holiday had duende to an almost overwhelming degree—she's a perfect example of how difficult it is for an artist to live with that intensity, that creative force, flowing so hotly through her life. And you intuit that O'Hara channeled that force when writing about Holiday. He catches fire, as you do in describing it, as the reader does in reading it. This is an incredibly moving recognition of the duende's power.

HIRSCH: I love a lot of O'Hara's work, but in the poem "The Day Lady Died," he hits another note. It's not just cosmopolitan; it's not just charm; he finds a darker music, and in trying to account for how that happens in this one poem I feel that, yes, Billie Holiday lent him her duende. In its opening lines, this poem seems connected to O'Hara's other work; it's one of those "I do this, I do that" Frank O'Hara poems: first I'm going to go out to dinner with Patsy, then I'm going to buy a book for so and so. Then he's going to the bank and "Miss Stillwagon (first name Linda I once heard) / doesn't even look up my balance for once in her life." But then he sees the picture of Billie Holiday on the cover of the *New York Post* and the poem changes dimension. It just takes off. Suddenly, he is transported back to the moment when he was in the 5 Spot, a jazz club in New York, leaning against the door, and listening to Billie Holiday sing, and he ends the poem as she whispers a song "to Mal Waldron and everyone and I stop breathing."

It's just a fabulous end to the poem because the poem stops breathing, you stop breathing, and the spirit is transported to the audience. I felt that somehow when Billie Holiday took over that poem, something lifted off, that the duende had arrived. And this triggered my memory of an experience I'd had that I hadn't actually ever articulated. I was on a street in New Orleans watching a little girl dance, and I don't know quite what happened, but the accompanist hit a string of odd, extremely low notes, and suddenly she began dancing with another kind of fever. It was almost lunatic. But what struck me was that everyone immediately understood that we were not just watching a street dancer, that she was peaking, that she was hitting another note, that she was inspired. And she was moving more quickly than she had moved before, and with more power and control. And it went winging through the crowd, this electricity. Time stopped. Everyone stopped breathing. And that's what happens with art. You're suddenly aware that something amazing is happening, that you're a part of something.

DS: Something has broken through.

HIRSCH: That's it.

DS: You write that Lorca observes that the duende may reside as much in the audience as the artist. That it travels between the performer and those who watch and listen and read.

HIRSCH: I don't think that we could recognize it if we weren't part of it, or if the artist wasn't tapping into something on behalf of all of us. Lorca liked to invoke the duende before his poetry readings because he said only when the duende was present could an artist be sure of being loved and understood. Only then could one be recognized and the audience give up its intellect and undertake the hard task of understanding metaphor. And we can only do that if we're aware of it, if we're conscious and present, if the duende is available to us. So, I feel that it's a kind of ethic of communication, an ethic of participation.

In *How to Read a Poem and Fall in Love with Poetry,* I write about Martin Buber because I love Buber's idea that "in the beginning is the relation." In *I and Thou,* he writes that the relation precedes the word, because it's authored by the human, and in a way I feel that this duende is not just located in a singular artistic experience, but rather when the artist connects with an audience. And the audience can be a reader, someone watching a dance, or someone listening to a song, or it could be a group of people. I think it was easiest for Lorca to find it in spoken poetry, in dance, in music, because they were all performances. It's more palpable in a performance. But I also wanted to locate it in written poetry and in visual art. There are moments when you're with the painting or you're with the poem or you're with the piece of music on your own and you are transported. In other words, you bring your own duende to it, you bring your own spirit, you bring your own soul to it. I like this idea of a sort of electricity that passes back and forth between the work of art and the recipient of the art.

DS: You segue into a consideration of American art in the last third of *The Demon and the Angel,* especially blues, jazz, and abstract expressionism. And surely only you would say that singer and musician Robert Johnson is the Gerard Manley Hopkins of the blues.

HIRSCH: I turn to American art in the final part of the book, to the American experience, and I offer a counterargument to the idea that American art is all created in what Emerson called "the optative mood." We do have a kind of native optimism, and we do live in a kind of present without much historical consciousness, as we know all too well. But there is a darker side to our national temperament and to our art, and I wanted to recognize and write about this. So I look to Whitman's spectacular poem "Out of the Cradle Endlessly Rocking."

In that poem he remembers being a boy and going down to the shore. And he goes down to the sea, and he hears two birds singing, and one flies away, and then he begins repeating the word "death, death, death," in this incredible incantatory way. And then he very consciously says that from that moment he began to become a poet. He calls himself the "outsetting bard." And he very consciously ties his practice to that moment. So this alerts me, it clues me to the sense that in Whitman there is a dark undertone behind all the optimism—that, for Whitman, his own practice as a poet began with a recognition that we're mortal, that we live in the presence of death. And I then take that as a kind of authorization to go forward.

There are two particular art places where I locate this force most powerfully, although I think it exists in lots of places, but what I write about particularly are blues and jazz. That's where Robert Johnson comes in, and I like saying that the duende arrived in a Dallas warehouse on such-and-such a day when Robert Johnson sang certain songs. The earth should have opened. I just think Robert Johnson's songs, "Hellhound on My Trail," for instance, are shattering.

I see this force in blues and jazz, which are so deeply indigenous to American forms. And I see it in abstract expressionism, in particular the flip side of abstract expressionist painters' involvement with color: their use of black. I look at the way Pollock, for example, improvises with black. Pollock, who always insisted that what he was creating was not accidental, that it was purposeful, that along with tremendous spontaneity and improvisation there's also control. The idea that one must control one's thoughts in a dream relates perfectly to Pollock because he's putting himself in a kind of trance, but he's also controlling it. He's working with a demonic force when he uses the color black. I was just stunned to recognize how many of the great abstract expressionist painters— artists who turned away from surrealism and turned away from representation and turned towards a painting of process to something more organic—used, and concentrated on, the color black. I think hard about Mark Rothko and his use of deep blacks, and about Barnett Newman and Franz Kline—and especially about Robert Motherwell, who is a key figure here with his *Elegies to the Spanish Republic*, black paintings on which he worked for fifty or sixty years, and which tie his American practice to something Spanish.

DS: As did Miles Davis in *Sketches of Spain.*

HIRSCH: Exactly. I'm arguing that Davis and Motherwell, in a way, are turning to the culture of Spain to import some kind of force. They wouldn't have necessarily called it duende, but they were looking for some Hispanic power, for some Hispanic majesty, to bring into their work. At these two moments in Miles Davis and Robert Motherwell, something Spanish meets something American.

DS: I was thrilled to read your take on Martha Graham, a mythic artist to be sure. You talk about the body as an artistic medium, which also goes back to Lorca's sense of duende as a tangible force, and to Pollock, who added an element of dance to painting by working on the ground and on such an enormous scale. I'm also reminded of the critical writings of Albert Murray, who writes so insightfully about how the jazz artist is utterly present in the moment, about grace under pressure, and about how improvisation is rooted in craft.

HIRSCH: Yes, that's very American, that opening up to the present. And it is a great force in jazz, which has its roots in the blues, and there has always been an element of suffering in it, this element of pressure, of dark power. It feels to me almost as if Lorca had written his essay so that I could write about jazz. It feels like a direct connection, which is no accident because Lorca was in New York, and he did go to Harlem and hear jazz singers, and I think he refined his idea of duende after he heard them. I think jazz changed his idea of *cante jondo,* or deep song, that it made him realize that *cante jondo* wasn't strictly a rural form. Jazz opened him up to a kind of urban art that he didn't recognize until he came to the New World. So, in a way, he refined, deepened, and enlarged his ideas of duende by his encounters with black artists in New York.

DS: And by the suffering he saw there.

HIRSCH: And the suffering that he saw, yes, the inequality, the injustices. Jazz seems to me the perfect embodiment of this because of its opening to the dark spirit of the present. There are moments in Charlie Parker, for instance, where the pyrotechnics are spectacular, driven to some other level. In Louis Armstrong's "West End Blues," it's almost as if an orphanhood is calling out. In a way, Miles Davis is one of the best examples, because in some peculiar sense, Davis didn't actually have the chops of the other great musicians of his era. He didn't have what Charlie Parker had, and yet he had this other ineffable quality, and he had tremendous power, this soul, this duende. That spiritual power allowed him to reach the pinnacle of his art.

DS: It's the source, I believe, of the tension in his music. The trumpet is such a tiny vehicle for all that he's feeling. The music is forced through, compressed, concentrated. I always feel as though this is a perfect metaphor for the confines of the body, the limits of the conscious mind in the face of the great force we're discussing.

HIRSCH: Very much so, and I think that happens in Armstrong, too. That's why he scats along with his voice, creating a kind of dialogue with his instrument. But I think in Davis, certainly in *Kind of Blue,* there's also the sense of collaboration, of improvisation in response to other artists, creating something in tandem. It's not just solo, it's a response to other people. And those spontaneous sessions on *Kind of Blue* are some of the highest moments in the history of jazz, in the history of American music.

DS: It's interesting: We think of writers and painters as soloists, and yet what we've been talking about is the fact that the artist is not alone. When you're writing, you may be physically by yourself, but you're filled with all the poetry you know and all the music that you've heard. I think the image of a poet alone is a misnomer.

HIRSCH: You're absolutely right. You are alone in some sense, but you're also participating in something, and that participation connects you to something greater. In poetry in particular, it always implies a reader. The poem is lonely, and it's always reaching out for someone else. It needs the contact.

DS: The poem is lonely, and so are other people.

HIRSCH: Exactly. It's some kind of connection between strangers. And I think this is interesting: It's not just talking to the people around you. It reaches out to some future listener, to some future speaker, some future recipient, because the people around you, in daily life, may not be the ones who understand you the best.

DS: That's right; they may not even read your work.

HIRSCH: It posits a transcendence; it posits a future connection, and a deeper connection. I like to think of art as a connection between two people who don't know each other, who aren't physically present to each other, and yet who are able to connect and find this bond through the vehicle of the poem. Much of *How to Read a Poem* is about the mutuality of that relationship.

DS: Writing poetry is an act of faith.

HIRSCH: Yes, it's a real act of faith in human connection. A kind of faith that there will be a listener, that someone will find the poem, and, similarly, when you find such a message yourself, you feel deeply grateful for it, you feel understood in light of what you're encountering. I hope that everyone has had the experience that I've had where you read a poem so deeply that you feel almost as if you've written it, when, in fact, you're only responding to it.

DS: That's the thing about poetry. I often try to define to myself what's so different about reading poetry as opposed to prose, and what I conclude is that I feel as though my mind is somehow being calibrated to it—that I'm changed by it physically, that poetry alters my chemistry.

HIRSCH: I think it is a bodily art. I think it inhabits you. You know, poems communicate before they're understood. I think you feel it taking over. There's a kind of transport in it. You're taken somewhere else. And this is the root meaning of ecstasy: to be beside oneself. I feel like you are taken out of yourself and delivered back to yourself in some deep way by works of art that you especially respond to, that are especially meaningful to you, that especially call to you. You feel recognized.

DS: That feeling of identification happens throughout *The Demon and The Angel*. Because you're a poet, you understand the experiences of other poets and artists, and I sense your sense of recognition and affirmation in relating the presence of duende in the lives of others.

HIRSCH: There is a kind of *ars poetica* here, but I think it's unseemly to write about yourself in any way. You can't do that, but you wouldn't be able to write about this if you hadn't experienced duende. It doesn't have anything to do with the ultimate value of the work, but it does have to do with the fact that you have moments when you're writing in which you feel taken away; you feel transported. When you suddenly write something that is stranger and spookier and more self-revealing than what you have written before. You are suddenly in the presence of something that you couldn't have summoned up entirely by your will. This is humbling.

This interview previously appeared in TriQuarterly *117 in a slightly altered form.*

Alan Lightman

In his second collection of essays, *A Sense of the Mysterious,* physicist and writer Alan Lightman offers readers a glimpse into his Memphis, Tennessee, past. (He was born there in 1948.) He describes himself as a scientifically curious, book-loving boy who both wrote poems and conducted experiments. In college Lightman chose to pursue science over literature, aware that while scientists do become writers, writers almost never become scientists. He studied at Princeton and Caltech, became a theoretical physicist (a highly imaginative pursuit), taught at MIT, and wrote science books, including *Ancient Light* and *Time for the Stars.* Then he fulfilled his dream and became a novelist, one with a unique perspective given his immersion in the highly rarefied realm of physics.

The nature of time fascinates Lightman, as does our relationship with technology and the power of stories, phenomena that inspire his intelligent, elegant, and affecting novels, including *Einstein's Dreams, The Diagnosis,* a fiction finalist for the National Book Award, and *Reunion.* Lightman is also a consummate essayist deeply intrigued with the workings of scientific creativity, so it's no wonder that he is struck by this observation of Einstein's: "The most beautiful experience we can have is the mysterious. It is the fundamental emotion which stands at the cradle of true art and true science." In his provocative fiction and vivid essays, Lightman explores the links between art and science, and between memory, the imagination, our habit of interpretation, and life itself.

Alan Lightman appeared on *Open Books* in 2003.

DONNA SEAMAN: You were writing poetry while you were studying science, and you've continued in your distinguished career as a writer and educator to move between art and science, realms that are usually viewed as separate and very different. What impels you to bridge this gap?

ALAN LIGHTMAN: I'm not sure I am bridging the gap. I feel compelled to work both as an artist and as a scientist. From a young age, I've had these two passions, and it really hasn't been a choice. I had to write and I had to do science, but as I've grown older and had more experience with these two different worlds, I can see similarities and differences. I can see ways that they complement each other, so I guess in a sense that's bridging the gap, in that I see the world of science and the world of the arts as being complementary rather than antagonistic to each other. C. P. Snow, who was also a physicist and a novelist, and author of a now-famous essay "The Two Cultures," had a pessimistic view of the distance between these cultures. I have a more optimistic view and see them as sympathetic and in resonance with each other.

DS: Speaking as someone who doesn't "do" science, but who wants to understand what it's all about, I find scientifically informed and inspired literature—whether it's fiction, poetry, or the sort of creative nonfiction that John McPhee or Diane Ackerman writes—is crucial to scientific literacy.

LIGHTMAN: Yes, and today we do have a lot of wonderful writers who are writing about science and making it alive and interesting.

DS: I also think that in our lifetime science has become urgent. Science and technology shape our lives in so many ways, and there's so much most of us do not understand.

LIGHTMAN: Science is one of few subjects where we're willing to admire someone without understanding what they do. You can't imagine someone saying that they admire Louis Armstrong without wanting to listen to Armstrong play, or saying that they admire

Hemingway without wanting to read one of his novels, but we all say we admire Einstein without knowing what he did.

DS: Was that on your mind when you wrote *Einstein's Dreams*?

LIGHTMAN: No, it wasn't at all in my mind. I just wanted to write something beautiful.

DS: When we think of Einstein's work, we think of formulas and brain-bending concepts, but you slip inside his dreaming mind and discover a set of visions, fables, and reveries full of magic and wonder.

LIGHTMAN: I had a lot of fun with that book, and I never thought of it as either a book about science or a book about Einstein. I thought of it as a book about exploring human psychology and trying to do it in an interesting way. Of course, what a writer says that he or she thought a book was about is irrelevant. All that matters is what the reader thinks, and every reader thinks something different, which is one of the great things about fiction.

DS: There is a great deal of imaginative thinking about time, space, and perception in *Einstein's Dreams,* as well as a conjuring of a subconscious at work. Fiction illuminates the psyche more precisely than any other art or science.

LIGHTMAN: Yes, it does. I think the ideal experience for me when I'm reading other people's novels is that I participate in the creative experience. The writer invites me into the world and then gives me enough freedom to create it. I think that's a big difference between a novel and film. A film is one specific realization of the many possibilities of a novel. And I think that's why you can go from a novel to a movie, but not in the reverse direction: Once you've had a very specific realization of the character in a situation, you can't then generalize it in the way a novel allows many possibilities in the reader's mind. You've already nailed down the one particular realization.

DS: Your fiction voice is exceptionally lucid, almost spare. I wonder if this prose style grew out of your having to write with scientific precision in your nonliterary works.

LIGHTMAN: It probably came out of whatever part of my brain allows me to think like a scientist, and sometimes I wonder how the different parts of the brain influence each other. But I do think the clarity of my writing may be a result of that.

DS: It keeps the reader alert. The reader doesn't luxuriate in your prose as one does in other sorts of fiction. The reader remains sharp and attentive.

LIGHTMAN: There are other writers who are much sharper than I am. I'm thinking of Raymond Carver, who makes me look like a gadfly. He's marvelous.

DS: I thought of Italo Calvino when I read *Einstein's Dreams,* and you mention him in *Reunion.*

LIGHTMAN: He's one of my heroes. I love all of his writing. I think he's one of the most imaginative fiction writers that we've had. It's too bad that he died early.

DS: Calvino tells us the most incredible things, and we believe them because of his directness, his crispness, his surety. *Einstein's Dreams* reminds me of *Invisible Cities* in its use of very short narratives that conjure up astonishingly complicated worlds. But you eschew such compression and concentration in *The Diagnosis,* a novel that captures the frenzy of our days and nights. The first seventy pages or so are just crackling with frantic energy and the panic of sensory overload.

LIGHTMAN: That book came out of many years of suffering and concern about the way that our society is going with the increasing premium on speed and information and money and materialism. It grew out of that, and I think of it as a social critique more than my other books. In that book, I was very influenced by Franz Kafka, who also wrote social critiques involving very bizarre situations. He also begins and ends with an idea. He's an idea writer, and I think in general that even in *Reunion,* which is my most romantic book, I am more on the idea end of the spectrum of writers. Ideas are important to me. That's not necessarily a good thing; that's just the kind of writer that I am. I envy writers who can create a marvelous character in a few lines and have spectacular dialogue, and wonderful storytellers like Annie Proulx. I think my strengths are more in the idea department, although you have to have at least minimally good characters to emotionally involve the reader.

DS: At its best, "idea" fiction tricks us into thinking about tough questions and thorny social conflicts and issues. If you say to someone, "Okay, here's a nonfiction book about technology and how it's ruining your life," most people are going to say, "No, thank you. I don't want to read something depressing." But if you say, "Here's a really exciting novel about a workaholic who loses his memory," then they'll think, "Oh, that sounds pretty good."

LIGHTMAN: Yes, fiction does trick us. I guess one of the arts of the novelist is to pull that trick off—not to get didactic or pedagogical, but to let the ideas seep in through the edges.

DS: That sort of synergy is exciting, and indicative of rapid change in the world and artists' insightful responses; fiction and nonfiction writers are often in sync.

LIGHTMAN: And these ideas should be discussed in every medium: fiction, nonfiction, theatre, music. Important ideas should be everywhere.

DS: It's true—ideas and responses to changes in the texture in life, such as those you elucidate in *The Diagnosis,* namely technology's invasion of every aspect of our lives, including our thoughts. I was struck, too, by how you portrayed people's alienation from nature, how they are utterly surrounded by things human-made.

LIGHTMAN: Yes, the fabricated world. I don't think we realize the price that we paid for this environment that we've created, the epitome of which, for me, is the mall. Nothing is more fake than the mall, but that will be what people remember thousands of years from now when they look back at this point in history.

DS: Yet our fabrications, computers in particular, are a conduit for learning in *The Diagnosis.* The main character's teenaged son takes a course on the Internet and learns all about Socrates. I interpreted this element of the story as an acknowledgment of the tremendous benefits of technology.

LIGHTMAN: I agree. I think technology itself is neutral. It doesn't have values. Values are imposed on it by human beings who use the technology, and we can use it well or we can use it for ill, and it's how we use it that gives it value. What's important is that we think about how we are using technology. I believe that there's too much use of technology that's mindless.

DS: *Reunion* is much more focused, much quieter than *The Diagnosis*, but it is linked to your other novels by virtue of a key theme in your fiction, namely, obsession. In *Reunion*, a man in his early fifties attends his thirtieth college reunion and is taken back to a pivotal time in his life, in a story that involves a dancer obsessed with her art, and other characters obsessed with literature, astronomy, and love. I wonder if these characters came to you on their own, so to speak, or if you were contemplating obsession itself, a force that can be quite destructive.

LIGHTMAN: I think obsession is a positive thing, myself, because if it's an honest obsession it comes from within rather than without. We were talking before about the materialistic world. The commercial world tells us what we should buy, what we need. They almost tell us what our values are. But most of the people I know who are obsessed are creating their own values. They are deciding what's important to them, and by and large, I applaud that. I know obsessions can have darker sides and they can lead to bad consequences, but what I like very much about a person obsessed is that the person has some center. Obsessed people are pulling something out of themselves, and they believe in something that's coming from within and not imposed from the outside.

As you said, many of the characters in *Reunion* are obsessed with different things. The main male character, Charles, is obsessed at a young age with poetry, but he is also terribly confused, as people that age are—which is in contrast to his ballerina girlfriend, Juliana, who doesn't seem to be confused about anything. For me, that was an interesting contrast. I wasn't trying to make any deep point. It was just sort of the way their characters developed as I began listening to them and trying to let them tell me who they were.

DS: I was intrigued by how your characters span the axis between art and science, and between disciplines that are rigorous and cool, if you will, and hot, passionately sensual desires. The story about the German astronomer and the way he links science and seduction is one example.

LIGHTMAN: I think that when a person is passionate about anything they are susceptible to romance. There is something about opening up your pores when you're passionate that makes you receptive to intimacy. I believe that's what happened to Ulrich Schmeken, the German astronomer.

DS: Where did you get that name?

LIGHTMAN: I just pulled that one out of the air. In fact, his whole story is totally made up. I have known a lot of scientists, having been in that world myself, and I think that many scientists are passionate. Sometimes scientists are stereotyped as dispassionate, but I don't think that's true at all. Scientists are passionate, and they are not objective in their work. They're prejudiced; they have points of view. The objectivity in science comes not from the individual scientists, but from the community of scientists who critique each other and find fault with each other's work. That results in something good. I think the best scientists have been the most passionate, and that passion is a good thing because it's what keeps them going, working twenty-four hours a day, working through the night, working under duress, working under hardship, pursuing an idea. Day after day, week after week, you have to be passionate about something to have that kind of dedication and perseverance, so I think passion is really necessary. But it does contradict the common stereotype of scientists.

DS: I was struck by the time frames in *Reunion*. When Charles goes to his college reunion, he runs into Nick, who was in the ROTC in the late 1960s. Charles learns that he stayed in the military and became an officer, which leads to your writing about the Gulf War, our first war in Iraq. You write that it was "a made-for-TV war, a video game, another digitized disembodied nothingness." The story then zooms back to the past, and you're writing about the Vietnam War era, and I thought about the difference between the antiwar protests then, how risky and persistent and wild and outraged they were, so emotional and effective, compared with the 2003 marches, which were impressive in size, but orderly, almost faceless, and completely ignored.

LIGHTMAN: I think part of that is the disembodied way that we communicate now, facilitated by the new communication technologies. But I also think it starts in the mind. The other difference, I believe, between now and the period of the Vietnam War, was that then everything was being questioned. Everybody has said this, but it's true. Everything was being questioned, and questioned in a deep way, and there wasn't yet the disenchantment that there is now. I think the Vietnam War was a major turning point after which we started mistrusting our government. Before that, there was a trust, but that was the beginning of our national disenchantment and mistrust. I think that has contributed to, I don't know quite the right word for it, our being uninvolved, passive—even after the horrible events of September 11th. There is still a passivity that I think is related and partly caused by our disillusionment with our country. We're a country without a center right now.

DS: But things change, and in fact, that's what *Reunion* is about—how one changes over the course of one's life.

LIGHTMAN: Actually, that's the idea that propelled me to write the book. Again, the reasons that an author writes a book are irrelevant in a sense. They are relevant to the author, but they're not relevant to anybody else. But since we're talking about the creation of the book, I have always been fascinated by the idea that every ten years we become a different person. Different things happen to us over a ten-year period, and our mental landscape changes. So how does a person stitch together those decade-long pieces to make one coherent self? Our whole sense of consciousness and self-identity is based on memory of who we were in the past, and that memory is very unreliable. We twist, we add, subtract, in a very complex way, motivated by all kinds of complicated desires. I'm just fascinated by the whole process of how we try to make sense of who we are and who we were in the past and the sort of uncomfortable imperfect union of those various selves. That was something I wanted to explore in the book. The love story that takes up a lot of the book was important to making the book work, but that was not the idea that propelled me to write it.

DS: But it's the love story that hooks us. What's so interesting in *Reunion* are Charles's attempts at telling himself the story of this love affair, a major event in his life. He tests out different versions of certain moments to try to get it right, that is, to try to tell it to himself in a way he can bear. That's what we all do with the story of our lives.

LIGHTMAN: Yes, I think it's very hard to pin down reality. I think reality is actually a myth. You get two people in a room watching the same event, and they have different accounts of it afterwards. We do the same thing within ourselves when we remember our past, especially emotional aspects of our past. There's no way of knowing what really happened; it's all a matter of conjecture. That's one of the fascinating aspects of the human psyche: it's not a computer. The artificial intelligence industry is trying to make computers do what the human mind does, but the human mind is not a computer. It doesn't store data in a reliable way. You can't just go to bit location 735 and extract this little piece of information. There are a lot of storms and chaos going on in there, and the bits are being changed all the time. I find that both a happy and sad thought. It's frightening, but I'm glad that we're not computers.

DS: Are you still writing nonfiction? I've read some of your essays.

LIGHTMAN: I still write nonfiction, and in fact, I'm working on a nonfiction science book about landmark discoveries in science in the twentieth century. What I've done is to identify twenty of the original papers in physics, chemistry, and biology that changed scientific thought, such as Watson and Crick's original paper on DNA and Einstein's original paper on relativity. For each paper, I'm writing a long introductory essay to give the general reader a sense of the history of science leading up to the paper and why the paper changed the thought in its field, and then I give a guided tour through the paper itself. I'm treating each paper not just as a scientific work, but as a literary work that shows the mind of the scientist and the thought processes of the scientist and the language that the scientist uses, which you don't get in any textbook distillation of the discovery. You need the original paper for that. So the book will have the original papers as well as my commentary. Because it will have the twenty great papers, the book will have a biblical quality. My essays will go out of date, but those twenty papers never will.

DS: This is a way to bridge the art-science gap.

LIGHTMAN: That's one way of doing it. I remember when I had finally gotten hold of these twenty papers. I spent about six months talking to colleagues in physics, chemistry, and biology to find out what they considered to be the greatest discoveries in their fields. I whittled the list down from one hundred to fifty to twenty, and then I went to obscure journals and finally got hold of all the papers. When I had them all in my hands for the first time, I burst out into tears. I was overwhelmed to hold what this represented, this achievement of the human mind. I didn't know I was going to react so emotionally; I just lost control.

DS: I understand, and as I'm listening to you I'm thinking that I've never seen those papers. Those treasures. I've only read about them and heard people talk about them.

LIGHTMAN: Even professional scientists don't study the original papers in their fields.

DS: Now there's a serious difference between science and the arts.

LIGHTMAN: That's right; it really is. You can't imagine being a history major and not reading the American Constitution or being a literature major and not reading Shakespeare. I want to restore the importance of the person, of the human side, the human spirit that brings forth the science—and the language that they use and whether they were surprised or not surprised, all of that you can get from the language. Whether they were pompous or humble— you find both kinds of personalities. There is no single scientific personality. You have the full range, and they are exhibited in these papers.

DS: You're in sync with a growing trend in universities, programs that combine the humanities with the sciences. I know for instance that Texas Tech has invited E. O. Wilson and Barry Lopez to collaborate with other scientists and writers to talk about landscape and the ecological perspective.

LIGHTMAN: That's wonderful. Wilson and Lopez are a perfect pairing together. David Quammen would be very good, too, and Terry Tempest Williams.

DS: So you love good science and nature writing. What about science fiction? Have you ever thought about writing it?

LIGHTMAN: People have asked me about that, and I have a lot of respect for the genre, but I have never attempted it myself. If I were to write science fiction, I would go towards the Ursula Le Guin model because she always has very provocative ideas behind her stories. But I haven't yet crossed that threshold.

Barry Lopez

Barry Lopez was born in 1945 in Port Chester, New York, on the Long Island Sound, and grew up in southern California and New York City. Educated in the Jesuit tradition, he considered entering the seminary before he enrolled at the University of Notre Dame, where he planned on majoring in aeronautical engineering, but instead ended up in communication arts. Travel was essential to Lopez's education as he visited nearly every state while earning his B.A. and M.A. at Notre Dame. He then entered the M.F.A. creative writing program at the University of Oregon, where he began studying Native American cultures, a line of inquiry that became a major facet in his work, as did his increasing sensitivity to the spirit of place and the lives of animals. Oregon has remained Lopez's home base.

Desert Notes was Lopez's debut book, the first volume in what became a trilogy of short story collections including *River Notes* and *Field Notes*. The lyrical and often harrowing stories explore the spiritual resonance of landscape, the contrast between traditional indigenous perceptions of nature and scientific methodology, the individual's need to understand, respect, and abide by the ecological imperative, and the possibility of transformation through contemplation of nature.

Lopez's gift for linking natural history with cultural critique, and his love for field work and library research, resulted in the nonfiction *Of Wolves and Men*, winner of the Burroughs Medal. Revolutionary in its in-depth study of a species and synthesis of diverse cultural perspectives, *Of Wolves and Men* launched one of Lopez's key missions as a writer: to reveal and elucidate the nexus between nature and culture. Lopez's work is also driven by his grappling with the paradox of human nature, our capacity for cruelty and perversity versus our gifts for love and creative intelligence.

Lopez began contributing articles to *Harper's, Outside, Orion, Audubon,* and *National Geographic.* Then, having fallen in love with Alaskan landscapes, he also began work on a contemplative natural history of the polar regions, which evolved into *Arctic Dreams,* an epic that won the National Book Award and became a bestseller.

Lopez continued traveling, bringing his unique perspective to bear on a wide range of places, people, traditions, and conflicts. His essays are collected in several volumes, including *About This Life,* and Lopez has received numerous awards, including an American Academy of Arts and Letters Award and fellowships from the Guggenheim, Lannan, and National Science foundations.

While his nonfiction is lavish with detailed descriptions, facts, observations, and interpretation, Lopez's fiction is almost spare. His preferred mode is the concise short story, and his elegantly distilled tales are striking in their psychological intensity and moral questioning, and disarming in their flights of imagination and dismantling of everyday realities. The edgy and provocative short story collection, *Light Action in the Caribbean,* is a watershed in Lopez's oeuvre, followed by *Resistance,* a haunting cycle of stories illustrated with arresting monotypes by artist Alan Magee. Here he imagines a far-flung circle of friends who have sought to live creative lives that benefit others, but who are now under siege from an increasingly oppressive government. Before each expatriate artist, scholar, or activist goes underground, they tell the story of their political, moral, or spiritual awakening, and of the birth of their resistance to their homeland's valuing of wealth over well-being, power over compassion, materialism over community, control over learning, conformity over freedom.

A contributor to, and shaper of, the literature of biological and cultural interconnectivity, Lopez has instigated and overseen a forthcoming, many-voiced reference work, *Home Ground: A Literary Guide to Landscape Terms.* Barry Lopez appeared on *Open Books* in 2000, not long after *Light Action in the Caribbean* was published.

DONNA SEAMAN: Your nonfiction books are often described as nature writing, which I think is too limited a term because you never deny the human presence. You seem to have a great deal of compassion for humanity even when you witness the ways we're interfering with and damaging the wild. Do you find yourself defending one realm more than the other? Drawn artistically more to one or the other?

BARRY LOPEZ: No, what I'm looking for is a synthesis. Most of the men and women who are interesting to me have a foot in two worlds in some way. That can mean that they live in the country and work in the city and are fully resident in both places. They don't disparage the one at the expense of the other. I find that tedious. I spent a lot of my childhood in New York, and I understand how provincial New Yorkers can be about the part of the world I now live in. And in the part of the world I now live in, I encounter people all the time who completely misread the energy and possibility and flights of the imagination that are part and parcel of what goes on in New York every day. What I'm after is trying to put things together in an age that takes them apart. Many people have a common complaint, and that is, they feel fractured. They feel disassociated from themselves and are looking for some way to pull it together, to become whole, or to be able to speak from one strong position, instead of feeling that you are scattered all over the map either by your tasks, or through your ideas. It seems to me that if there is, in the highest and most generalized political sense, a job —or obligation—for writers today, it's to provide trustworthy patterns, to provide stories that people can enter emotionally or intellectually and feel comfortable in. I don't mean that the story reinforces your beliefs about the world, but that the overall emotional impact of the story results in you feeling more coherent when you're finished reading it. It has entered my mind more than once that in a celebrity-driven culture like ours, some writers abandon, or are never acquainted with, this very old obligation of the storyteller to provide a way for people to understand themselves. We often talk about writers as intellects, or writers as people perceptive about social change or individuals who have the ability to capture the essence of a historical moment. All those things are good, but I think most writers' true strength is that they recognize patterns and they make them come alive in language. A real story, no matter what its subject, appeals to a person because of the way it's put together and what it draws up in them emotionally.

DS: The feeling of disassociation and fracturing so many of us experience may be due, in part, to our separation from nature and the old rhythms and cycles that used to order our lives. In your work, you remind readers that in spite of all our technologies, we are still part of a larger sphere and that we're affected by it. I doubt this was deliberate, but I was struck in *Light Action in the Caribbean* by how often you write about characters who work with their hands. There's a gardener and a carpenter. You are quietly celebrating a tactile involvement with the world, that one can love a craft just as one can love a person, land, an animal.

LOPEZ: One of the interesting things about talking to somebody who has read my work is that I realize a lot of what's going on in my writing rises up out of an unknown place, and is true to me. That is, it's not something that I have made up or that I'm trying to use in order to manipulate the reader. I'm digging in places where there's no dissonance between what I am and what I believe. I'm employing techniques to illuminate something in an artistic way, and the art of it is beyond my grasp. I'm not the person who can articulate what it was. But if you said to me, there's a long essay in a collection called *About This Life* about my own hands, and then point out how often characters in my stories are doing something with their hands—they're pruning trees or they're building furniture or they're making gardens, hoeing and weeding, or they're saddling a horse—I realize I don't want to lose contact with all those activities because I fear the maelstrom of ideas. One of the most terrifying pictures to me of modern times is a person who is entirely satisfied to be in front of a computer screen. And what is terrifying to me about it is that there's no evidence of other people.

That's the antithesis of what we mean by community. And yet I know that some people say, "I never felt that I was a member of a community until I sat down in front of a computer and entered chat rooms." To me, the hallmark of a community is the responsibility for what you do and say, and those are both removed when you enter a chat room. You can say you are anybody you want to say you are; you can say things irresponsibly; you can make claims that can't be verified; you can enter a place as a seducer and a charlatan and not be outed—not have anybody really know what you're up to or who you are.

I believe we crave intimacy because we want to be held in some way, literally or figuratively. You want to be embraced. You want to know that your ideas, your voice, your way of life, counts for something in the world. In order to achieve that intimacy, you have to be vulnerable. But we've created a world in which the price for vulnerability is often so high that many adults don't want to risk it anymore. That precludes intimacy with other people, and we end up being something like science fiction automatons gazing at data, but not feeling any sense of satisfaction. An antidote is to enter what I would call the stream of life. You can retrieve an infinite amount of data from a computer, but it's very difficult to put it together in such a way that you feel profound satisfaction. Yet that's exactly what happens in the ten or fifteen or twenty minutes it takes to read a story. You get all these different things: This river flowing through this county; this woman who did this; this car that went there; this price for this kind of wheat. Whatever the components are, they are, in some sense, bits of data, but what's really important is the thing that holds them together, and that's what we call story. It seems to me that we live in a world where people feel that while the availability of information is limitless, the knowledge of what to do with it, or how to put it into the shape of a story that has meaning in your personal life, is out of reach. Therefore, an obligation, a social requirement, a moral responsibility, even, for the writer, is to provide a structure that will hold all this information in such a way that we can make sense of ourselves and our lives.

DS: How have your travels affected you, and your writing?

LOPEZ: I think without intending to do so, I have turned my life into a gaze at human history. I travel back and forth to places that still contain evidence of our aspirations fifteen or twenty thousand years ago, in caves, for example, in northern Spain and in France, where so many of the paintings still look fresh. I've traveled a little with indigenous people in the Arctic and in Australia and in Africa, and when I'm traveling with them, I throw away the rope that ties me to a world that I might perceive as better, as an improvement over the one that I'm in there. I guess I just don't believe in progress. I believe that you can improve the design of a mechanism and make it work better, but I don't think that you can improve people over time. That's one of the lessons of biology. One of the most amazing things, to me, about traditional societies is the facile way in which people step in and out of what we call the modern world, and their emotional and intellectual resistance to our insistence that we have something better. The real questions about human life have to do with being loved and being honored, expressing your love and caring for children, and living with violations of fidelity. Those are the real issues of human beings, rather than career development, or the accumulation of material wealth. So when I travel, I wonder, "If I talk to the most perceptive and most articulate among the people I visit, will I hear an echo of the same voices I seek out in my own culture, which tend to transcend technologies, governments, religions?" I'm very cautious about this, because we have a tendency in the United States to romanticize indigenous people and to project our ideas, our Rousseauian notions about noble savages, onto people.

DS: Your stories are free of references to popular culture, imbuing them instead with a feeling of timelessness, as though they are fables, tales paired down to their essentials.

LOPEZ: When I'm writing, I'm not caught up in pop culture because it's just something passing. And the things we have to face when we look at unalterable facts—global warming, population explosion, the disintegration of all kinds of communities, human and animal—are not going to go away by virtue of a human vote or a piece of technology. Nothing is going to come along to solve it. We have to do that, and we have to do it by dint of will and strength of heart. But one of the things I notice about American culture is that, in many quarters, it's dominated by adolescence, by which I mean a lack of awareness that the history of human endeavor is profound. The focus is always on rights rather than on obligations. The mark of a transition out of the kind of adolescence that all of us and, in my experience, all cultures go through is the desire of young men and women to break away, to leave the family structure and determine the boundaries of the individual self and then come back and become a productive part of society. But we seem to have gotten stuck in just wanting to escape. So all of these ideas are part of a big river that runs underneath my life. When I sit down to write even a simple story—a man looks at some orchards and re-grets the way he condescended to his father years ago and then realizes that through memory he can bring his father back—I draw on the ways in which we assuage our loneliness and regret our mis-takes and see that some other life is possible for us through an act of imagination rather than through buying something, or getting a job. I end up writing about the realization that it's the way we each imagine our lives that is important.

DS: *Light Action in the Caribbean* is a departure for you. Do you know why were you able to write stories so unlike your previous works?

LOPEZ: There's a curious thing about writing: I think any writer would have to admit that it is in some way driven by insecurity. Writing may grow out of an individual artistic vision, but it's a so-cial impulse and the insecurity, or the anxiety that is there, is as-suaged, or even evaporates, in the realm in which you connect with the reader. The way that some writers have dealt with the anxiety of whether or not the story will be liked is to write stories or nov-els until one does very well, and then, in that pivotal place, you can make the fatal decision to try to write that same story again be-cause so much of that insecurity, or loneliness, or feeling of being marginal to life has disappeared. And without realizing it, because we all want to be loved, you end up becoming a caricature of yourself. The hardest thing to do as a writer who is growing older, going through ten or twenty or thirty or fifty years of writing, is to continue to push into places you haven't been before—not as a kind of weightlifting exercise or running more miles this week than last, I don't mean that. I mean that even though you will never solve the problem of insecurity, you have an obligation to keep traveling so that the reader isn't saying to himself or herself, "Every time I read you, I find myself in the same place I was ten or twenty years ago." That's no good for anybody.

DS: The title story in *Light Action in the Caribbean* is a darker tale than any you've written before.

LOPEZ: It's the darkest thing I've ever written. I have no idea where it came from. I wouldn't say that I'm disturbed by it because I know there's something in it that I need to say, and I suspect that in the next few years I'll try to say it again. I just hope that the story ends with a very deep sense of compassion for human beings, because no matter how well we try to lead our lives, we know that when the brakes go out on a car on the interstate, or a kid who is angry because his girlfriend left him brings a gun to school, we're helpless. And I think it's shortsighted to say, "If we just get violence off television, or if we register guns, such tragedies won't happen." No, violence will just turn up in some other way. We have a capacity for cruelty, and the expression of our anger is something every society has struggled with. It's necessary to feel compassion toward people caught up by those strong forces, and that's what's going on in this story, a story that surprised me with its brutality.

DS: Your work is densely layered, rich in both fact and feeling.

LOPEZ: I've had good teachers, and I don't mean solely people I've met in classrooms, but in all the corners of the world where I've been. People were patient with me and with my ignorance about what it is that they do and what I was trying to understand,

and that kindness over many years has created for me a desire to give back. I love dense language. I love language that is working on many different levels simultaneously. But I never could have gotten something like that, or an awareness that such a thing was possible, unless I had been taken to theatrical productions, or had somebody explain to me what happens over the course of Beethoven's Ninth. Or unless somebody took me hunting walrus, and showed me what role spirituality, benediction, and compassion play in the fatal encounter between a human being and an animal for the sake of a human being's food. Many things that I've tried to do in my life as a reporter—traveling with scientists and Eskimos and visiting a lot of out of the way places—have been possible because people were kind to me. And they taught me something crucial: they taught me that something I might object to on the surface, like hunting, was deep and, in the end, holy, and that the history of hunting was not what I came to abhor as a young man watching opening day of deer season in an Eastern state. The people I hunted with as an adult taught me that I had completely misunderstood what was going on. Once they took care of me, I saw that you could tell a story about hunting to a person who hated hunting, and at the end of the story they would say, "Oh, there's more here than I thought."

DS: That can stand as the credo for a serious writer and reader: Remain aware that there's more here than you think. Being a writer means that you're open and receptive and keenly attentive to the world.

LOPEZ: I agree with you. Every writer I know is writing out of a love of humanity, even if you're dealing with ugly stuff. It's out of a sense of compassion for other people, and for yourself.

DS: I believe that's also why we read.

LOPEZ: I do, too. One of the reasons you pick up a work is the hope that when you close the book you'll feel elevated.

Paul West

Paul West has written more than twenty novels, and his list of non-fiction books is nearly as long. A lover of the subtleties and splendor of language, a masterful stylist whether he's writing novels or memoirs, he frolics on the page, giving full reign to his wily sense of humor even as he writes about life at its most dire. Born in Derbyshire, England, in 1930, West was influenced by both his mother's vocation as a piano teacher and his father's memories of World War I, and he pays tribute to his parents in a pair of memoirs, *My Mother's Music* and *My Father's War*. He attended Oxford University, the subject of his insightful and often funny reminiscence *Oxford Days*. West later studied at Columbia University, then moved to the United States permanently in 1961. He has taught literature and creative writing at a number of colleges, including Brown, Pennsylvania State, Cornell, and the University of Arizona. West's fiction workshops are legendary, and he shares his freewheeling yet incisive approach in *Master Class,* a chronicle of his heady sessions with fifteen talented students, and a testimony to his joy in the art of writing and the magic of literature. West is not only an erudite and enthusiastic writer and teacher, he is also a discerning literary critic who believes that criticism merits the same degree of attention and ardor as any other form of literature. His essays and reviews are collected in a three-volume set, *Sheer Fiction,* which provides a remarkable overview of modern and contemporary writing.

West's novels include *Rat Man of Paris,* which is based on a man who lived on the streets of Paris and unnerved passersby with his live rat, and banners portraying Nazi war criminals. This is but one of a stream of novels in which West fictionalizes real-life individuals. There's *The Women of Whitechapel and Jack the Ripper* and

Sporting with Amaryllis, an earthy and surreal portrait of young John Milton. *The Dry Danube* purports to be Hitler's memoir. *A Fifth of November* re-imagines the life of Guy Fawkes and the circumstances that led to the English Gunpowder Plot of 1605. In *Cheops,* West portrays the Egyptian pharaoh, the Greek historian Herodotus, the English composer Frederick Delius, and for good measure, the god Osiris. On more personal terrain, West presents a paean to his wife, Diane Ackerman, and close friend Carl Sagan in *Life with Swan.* West is also dramatizes the psychological impact of war and terrorism: In *Love's Mansion,* a son attempts to understand his parents' suffering during and after World War I. *Tent of Orange Mist* concerns the young daughter of a distinguished Chinese scholar forced to recreate herself in order to survive the brutal Japanese occupation of Nanking.

In *The Place in Flowers Where Pollen Rests,* West captures the interplay of old and new, mythic and sleazy in the American West. An extraterrestrial narrates *Terrestrials,* a many-layered tale about two American military pilots shot down over Africa and the inexorable process by which the heroic is reduced to the mundane. One of literature's most intrepid and adept prospectors of the collective psyche under the duress of war and cataclysmic change, West offers an atomizing rumination on the tragedies of 9/11 in *The Immensity of the Here and Now.*

West is renowned for his originality, rhapsodic innovations, and appreciation for the absurdities, sorrows, and glory of life. He has received a Lannan Prize for Fiction, the Literature Prize of the American Academy, and the Art-of-Fact Prize awarded by the State University of New York. He has been designated Chevalier of Arts and Letters by the French government. Paul West appeared on *Open Books* in the winter of 2002.

DONNA SEAMAN: In *Master Class,* an account of the last of your celebrated fiction workshops, you refute the old saw "Truth is stranger than fiction," when you write "Nothing is stranger than fiction because fiction involves the whole imagination."

PAUL WEST: I was in academia when I wrote that, and I guess I spoke to more conventional minds because they always seemed to say, "You know, truth is stranger than fiction, and you must always aim for truth. Whereas fiction is far-fetched. Fiction is some kind of deliberate product intended to stupefy." I never felt that. I think that fiction, as it should be, is tangled up with the imagination. Then if you're any good, you're home free, and you can imagine all manner of things. There is absolutely no limit. The only limit being that ultimately you have to come back to actual life. It's very hard to imagine something that's not derivative. There is nothing you can write that is not derivative, but doing this is an absolute joy.

DS: Your novels contain a great deal of history, and you often write about historical figures.

WEST: I think about that sometimes and I ask myself, "What are you doing with these historical abstracts and transplantations and so on?" My view is that they are ready-made. They may not look like it, but they are.

DS: Like John Milton in your novel, *Sporting with Amaryllis.*

WEST: He's very ready-made, in my opinion, very ready indeed—too ready. But you pick them up, and then you use them as certain artists use objects as ready-made, and I have no worry about that. I sometimes do figures like Milton, Jack the Ripper, people like that, and take liberties with them, which alarms a few people. The problem is, if you have an imagination, then imagination, in a sense, is going to rule you, and you can't always control it. I think people who don't have much imagination find that very strange because they are groping around for a magic switch that doesn't go on in their case. My problem is to switch the damn thing off. I was chided in the *New York Times* by some Brit reviewer for imagining how Milton would be if he'd ever been to America. He said, "Doesn't he know that Milton didn't go to America?" Of course, I have degrees in English. I knew that, but I decided to transplant him. This offended some people. The only people who worry about this sort of thing are people who really shouldn't be writing novels or reading novels.

DS: You've also written about Hitler. The historical figures you choose seem to fall into two categories, criminals of various sorts and artists and storytellers.

WEST: Yes, I have a lot of criminals, and I've thought a lot about the storytellers and the artists. They are people for whom I have respect. Their lives are very tough, and they work, many of them, without recognition, and stick to it nonetheless. Whereas criminals probably do the same thing, and they do get recognition. In fact, the criminals get more recognition than the artists do.

DS: You've written many novels, and each is quite different from the others. Yet I discern some patterns that I feel come to great fruition in your novel *Cheops,* in which you write from the point of view of a whole array of interesting characters, including several particularly striking figures: one is Osiris, the Egyptian god of the underworld. Another, brought to us via time travel, is the Greek historian Herodotus, the veritable father of history, and then there's the composer Frederick Delius.

WEST: It was fun to transplant Herodotus, and you don't have to transplant Osiris because he's always everywhere, as gods are, and it was fun to take Delius out of the late-nineteenth-century and stick him in old Egypt. It's a novel that takes a lot of liberties.

DS: History is, after all, a form of storytelling. Even though a historian works with facts, he or she is still interpreting them.

WEST: There's a lot of difference between history and fiction. In a sense, history is over and done with, and when people write history, they tend to write in the past tense. If you use history as I tend to, for ready-mades in fiction, you end up writing in the present tense with a redeveloped sense of imminence that this thing has not quite happened yet: the assassination has not yet taken place, but it may take place in the next twenty minutes. I think that's the sort of thing you get into, which I think is freedom. I don't think there is anything limiting about it.

Thomas Carlyle wrote almost in a Joycean fashion about history and absolutely adored doing so and perhaps wrote history as no else has. There's an enthusiasm in Carlyle that is amazing. He had more fun writing history than he had in his sex life, I'm quite sure. I've always liked Carlyle. Even Jacob Burckhardt was getting an aesthetic thrill from these things, although he's rather more solemn. But if you take the plunge and say, "I'm going to use history," all kinds of doors open up—as long as you don't then end up writing something like Norman Mailer's *Ancient Evenings*, in which history becomes as routine as a textbook. That is a real risk.

DS: In your novel *Life with Swan,* you fictionalize aspects of your own life rather than historical figures'. One character is clearly based on your wife, writer Diane Ackerman, and another is a variation on a close friend, Carl Sagan.

WEST: Yes, and I must say we miss him. He came up with something new every second, and it was Carl who got us interested in astronomy. He sort of pelted us with books and maps. He took us all over the place, to the Jet Propulsion Lab and to various space launches. I thought it was utterly fascinating, although as I promptly reveal in that novel, I began to get the feeling that these scientists were only too willing to explain their mystery, and didn't really appreciate the arts sufficiently. They regarded us as very, very distant competitors, which was very strange. But we did meet lots of charming scientists, and they really were very humble, which I think is not true of artists.

DS: I have the sense that astronomy and space travel have inspired your fiction in interesting and subtle ways.

WEST: I think so. It's indelible. Quite often when I'm writing about history, I get a sort of space-scientist perspective on it and regard history as malleable. I think, "It could have been different, and so I'm going to make it different just for the hell of it, just to see what happens." I guess this is a curious kind of science fiction. Although I don't like the term, it is certainly speculative.

DS: *Terrestrials* is a huge novel. It would have taken most writers years to come up with a novel like that, but for you, it's one of many, many books. It seems as though you write a book every few months.

WEST: Not really. It may seem like that, but I'm kind of slow in some aspects of it. I revise very, very slowly. I may write fairly swiftly, but the revision is a slow process, and I think that's appropriate. But you're right, *Terrestrials* is very, very long. I thought it would be six hundred pages, but they compressed it to some degree, which was a pity. It is a writer's book. All the writers enjoyed it and they said so, and I was very pleased about that. It had been brewing in my skull for a dozen years, because a lot of it is based on local traffic and local personalities and very good friends. They find their place in the book rather warming, I think.

DS: Your work is considered somewhat cerebral because of the richness of your language, the wordplay, the elliptical style, the many ideas. But what I sense when I read you is this incredible affection for humankind, a real tenderness.

WEST: That's all I aspire to. I don't know about cerebral, but they're probably right. If you're cerebral, your writing is going to be cerebral, but I think there's a fair amount of counterpoint. There is a relish for humanity even at its most loathsome. I was writing the other day about an uncle of mine, a rather nice man whose forte in life was to invite people in to watch him comb his hair. My father used to say, "Let's go watch Uncle Henry," and there he would be with his comb and his brush and God knows what else, and he would elaborately arrange his hair and then brush the front back and up, and it was one of those primeval moments. And I think that is always there in me, the small boy observing life.

DS: There is a remarkable physicality in your writing. A fascination with the oddities of the body and with the conflict between the body and the mind.

WEST: Yes, although I have a conflict with both the mind and the body. I have trouble with both, and I think actually the mind is easier to discipline than the body. The body always ends up betraying you. I'm not sure the mind does. Actually, the mind is a very resilient thing until a certain point, then you really have to watch yourself and put bicycle bells on it.

DS: In reading your memoirs, *My Mother's Music* and *Oxford Days,* I'm amazed at how fresh and vivid your childhood and college memories are.

WEST: I'm told I have a good memory. If there is any credit due it's to my parents. My father has a terrific memory, and my mother had one even better, and she lived longer. At ninety-four, she had almost perfect memory of her childhood and her adolescence and God knows what. She never lost it. They both, actually, filled me in to a tremendous, almost pristine, degree with all that they recalled. Most people resign themselves to losing early memories, but they never did. They had it all along and would refer to it as something very familiar and easily spoken of.

DS: My guess is that there's quite a bit of family history in your novel *Love's Mansion.*

WEST: That is all family history, and not much mutilated by the author.

DS: It's a very powerful war novel. You write often of war.

WEST: I've just finished a short book about my father [*My Father's War*], and how as a little boy I would get the full brunt of his wartime experiences, and how they were totally terrifying. We would go out during the blitz, each with a brisket sandwich, and watch the Nazi bombers come over and the search lights go after them. He told me a lot. My mother wouldn't listen to this. She really couldn't take it. I think anybody who's been through that either blocks it out completely or can't forget it.

DS: Your father gave you great insight into war. Did your pianist mother give you a gift for music?

WEST: I can't read music, and this was always a bit of a problem. She had prophesied me as a pianist, and I never learned. I just couldn't face entering the conga line of pupils that sat on that music stool and learned from my mother. So it worked out, actually, because suddenly she got it and said, "You play on your keys, which are a typewriter, and I'll play on mine. And you really do appreciate music." And I do. I listen to music all the time.

DS: Do you listen to music while you write?

WEST: Yes, all the time. I listen to Bach and Ravel and Debussy and so on. I gained from her a real passion for music, and I used to listen to her play the piano. She was very good. I believe I have memories of being in the womb and hearing her play music. This is a very strange zone to get into because you can't document it, but there is something going on. There is no doubt. When I'm writing and listening to music, it's a very "uterine" experience.

DS: We touched briefly on your use of storytellers as characters in your novels. These figures intrigue me because they serve as stand-ins for all of us who are trying to make sense of life, who are trying to remember what happens to us and what happens to others, and how we feel, and to imagine lives before and after our own.

WEST: You know, the whole educational system gears us for trying to make sense of life. I find this a bit worrying because it doesn't prepare people for the fundamental absurdity of things. Life is not geared for human consumption. It's a very awkward proposition. I sometimes worry about this, that people are more or less told, "If you take your M.F.A. here or your Ph.D. in writing there, you will be better prepared for understanding the workings of the universe." I think a degree in astronomy would be a lot more useful.

DS: And much more difficult! It's interesting that you say this about our trying to fathom life; it reminds me of a point in *Cheops* when the god Osiris is reflecting on his life. He feels that he hasn't done all that well. He muses, "Are the gods lazy, crazy, or red in tooth and claw? Have they suffered too much and can manage only spasmodic gestures toward the subspecies *in extremis*?" The subspecies being us. I find this a very moving moment.

WEST: It's meant to be a moving moment. If you can't understand what's happening to you, then at least you might take some comfort from the elegance with which you formulate that problem. It ain't much to hang onto, but what else? That's why we have symphonies and wonderful books and paintings. People are trying to reach the surface and trying to see what's in the light, and they rarely can do it. But the music they make in various dimensions is what comes out of it. There's a tremendous amount of yearning in all the arts. I think this is what our old friends the scientists don't really heed. There is so much of it. The universe is full of it. The libraries are full of it. The bookstores are sometimes full of it. You need to have this—I don't know what you would call it—this cushion. Otherwise, life is a very bleak thing indeed.

DS: In *Oxford Days*, you write about your discovery of the solace of literature.

WEST: I guess that obsession began there and has stayed with me. What is all this for? To read, say, a lot of Eugene O'Neill is going to depress the hell out of you. So why do it? The reason is that he will confront you with something that's insoluble and then offer you a tentative way out. All kinds of people, Goethe, Wordsworth, Beckett, offer you something, as do composers. I think music is the ideal response to the idiocy of things.

I was thinking of *Oxford Days* and *Cheops:* reading them is like going to two separate universities. *Oxford Days* is the university of life, where all possible chances are brimming over. *Cheops* is the university of death, which is ancient Egypt where they were grooming you for death from the very beginning.

DS: This perspective is in keeping with the element of myth you always seem to reach. You used the word "insoluble," which is what myths are; that's why they last. And we do keep re-imagining archetypal figures that we all respond to. You bring them to us in new disguises in each of your books.

WEST: I'm delighted to hear that. It's not a conscious attempt. You know, this brings us to something else, another obsession I guess. There is a strange persuasion afoot that has it that writers know exactly what they are going to do, that they always have a design or plan written down. They say, "Oh yes, I'm doing that today," and then they type away. Not my experience at all. I think a great deal of this is involuntary, a matter of phrases that leap onto the page from absolutely nowhere. Of course, it's not nowhere, but I think a lot of my writing comes about when I sit at the typewriter without the faintest idea what's going to happen next. This must be like composing music. A phrase will come into mind, and I'll think, "My god, what's that?" And I type it and look at it and decide if it could be useful or not. That scandalizes people who believe in the deliberate view of creativity.

DS: That intuition and openness to an inner voice is the difference between writing literature and expository writing.

WEST: I think it is, and I'm always amazed by editors who don't acknowledge this. Even certain writers will say, "You mean you don't have a plan?" I don't have a plan. *Terrestrials*, for example, was not planned in any shape or form; it just came. And I was glad to leave it like ectoplasm crucified where it landed, splattering the walls.

DS: There's a tremendous difference in the literary fiction writing that comes from whatever that wellspring is, as opposed to deliberately crafted pop novels and genre fiction. When you read, you can feel the difference between works that stem from the unconscious and formulaic works.

WEST: And there are writers whose work evinces it. Proust has it, and Beckett and Nabokov. Malcolm Lowry has something of it, and Faulkner certainly has it. These are the people I read and re-read. If you don't have this leaning or this inclination, then it's very hard to get. This was a problem in teaching people how to write fiction, because if they didn't have that mythic inclination, they could never find it. They were groping for it, and nobody could give it to them. So it's a given, and if you've got it, you should go through life very grateful.

There are many, though, who don't like it, and want something very prosaic. I ran into this a lot in New York. The one thing that editors nowadays don't like is what they call "interiority." They don't want interiority at any price. I actually heard people saying, "Is there much interiority in this book, because we don't like interiority." I said, "You can't say that." The whole of human performance is based on interiority. This is why we're talking to one another. This is why we're writing things down. This is all interior before it becomes exterior.

Colson Whitehead

Born in New York City in 1969, Colson Whitehead began writing short stories while studying English and comparative literature at Harvard University—where he couldn't get accepted into a creative writing class. After graduating and finding work as an editorial assistant at the *Village Voice,* he decided to become a pop-culture critic, and wrote reviews of books, music, and TV shows, eventually writing a regular TV column. Whitehead's essays and journalism have also appeared in the *New York Times Magazine, Vibe, Spin,* and *Newsday.* Having fulfilled his mission to write pop criticism, he returned to fiction and wrote a novel about a Gary Coleman-like child star, but sentenced the manuscript to life in a drawer. Realizing that he needed to keep his fiction free of pop culture, Whitehead began another novel, which became his first book, *The Intuitionist.*

An original and disarming work that toys with allegory and science fiction, and that has inspired comparisons with Orwell, Ellison, Vonnegut, and Pynchon, *The Intuitionist* takes place in an unnamed metropolis and tells the tale of Lila Mae Watson, the first black female elevator inspector. This position has far-reaching significance in the world Whitehead constructs, because elevators are mystical vehicles and the inspectors are a priestly lot. But all is not unified in the cult of verticality: There is a war on between the Empiricists, who work purely on the physical plane, and the Intuitionists, Lila Mae's sect, who sense, or intuit the state of an elevator's condition through visualization. As the story unfolds, the concept of verticality, of rising and falling, becomes a metaphor for the politics of race, while the sects' philosophies embody the eternal conflict between the material and the spiritual, and the status quo and the need for change. *The Intuitionist* was met with resounding critical acclaim: Whitehead won a 2000 Whiting Writers' Award. He was hailed by the *Voice Literary Supplement* as a "Writer on the Verge" and *Utne Reader* as one of the ten "novelists who are changing the way we see the world." *The Intuitionist* was a Book of the Month/QPB selection and a winner of the QPB New Voices Award; a Barnes & Noble Discover New Writers selection; a *New York Times* Notable Book; a *San Francisco Chronicle* and *Boston Globe* Best Book of the Year; and one of *GQ*'s Top Twenty Books of the Millenium.

John Henry Days, Whitehead's second novel, is a two-track tale spanning two centuries. On one track is the folk hero John Henry. A "steel-driving man" who, as legend has it, won a race with a newfangled innovation, the steam-driven drill, in a contest of man against machine, only to die at the finish line, thus presaging the crushing impact of the Industrial Revolution. The second track sketches the absurdities of the Information Age as it follows J. Sutter, a freeloading freelance journalist who is staging a contest of his own by going for a record of back-to-back junkets that finally land him at the unveiling of a stamp commemorating John Henry. Mythic and satirical, Whitehead's novel considers the dualities of nature and civilization, dream and fact, black and white, integrity and subterfuge, altruism and greed. One of the *New York Times* "Best 5 Books of the Year," it was also designated a "best book" by the *Los Angeles Times,* the *Voice Literary Supplement, Newsweek, USA Today, Salon, Time Out,* the *Washington Post,* and the *San Francisco Chronicle. John Henry Days* was a finalist for the Pulitzer Prize, a finalist for the National Book Critics Circle Award, and winner of the Anisfield-Wolf Prize, which honors books that expose racism and/or explore diversity.

In 2002 Colson Whitehead was awarded a MacArthur Fellowship, and in 2003 his first book of nonfiction was published. *The Colossus of New York* is a cycle of imaginative and evocative meditations and vignettes that pay homage to his beloved hometown. Piquant in his observations, sensuous in his details, playful in his images, and metaphysical in his perception, Whitehead makes the city and its boundless capacity for metamorphosis come to life.

Whitehead is at work on a new novel tentatively titled "Apex Hides the Hurts," which is about, of all things, Band-Aids. He appeared on *Open Books* in late October 2003.

DONNA SEAMAN: There's so much energy in your writing. Everything is in motion; even the inanimate world comes to life. You convey the sense that objects, buildings, vehicles, sidewalks are not only alive but have attitude. This strikes me as anthropomorphic, a cartoonish or even childlike perception. Are you aware of doing this?

COLSON WHITEHEAD: I'm definitely aware of it in *Colossus*. I personify a lot of buildings and streets. I'm definitely more conscious of it in that book, and I think that's because the city does feel for its citizens. We look up to it, and it looks after us, so that approach seemed appropriate.

DS: I think it started in *The Intuitionist*. You invest elevators and skyscrapers with a sort of sentience, a host of philosophical and metaphysical aspects. When I was reading it, I thought, "Yeah, that's true. Elevators can be pretty spooky."

WHITEHEAD: If you're going to go off on a strange philosophical bender about elevators, naturally they are going to start taking on various attributes. When I first started *The Intuitionist*, it began as a fake detective novel, and the more it became focused on elevators and this made-up culture of elevator inspectors, the more life it adopted. I had to make up fake philosophies—Does the elevator have emotion? How do we feel about elevators, and what do they mean in a large scheme? It proceeded along sort of naturally.

DS: It does have the feel of a detective story, and it is noirish. It's also vaguely science fiction-like. In each of your books, you bring things to life that ordinarily we're oblivious to.

WHITEHEAD: I wrote a novel a couple of years ago that no one particularly likes, and I had to figure out what exactly was wrong with it. Then, with *The Intuitionist,* I was very concerned that people would just think it was ridiculous. And, you know, in some ways it is. You have to make people jump that hurdle and come along with you. So I was very conscious of trying to make things believable; I had to make up a whole culture and its slang, and make sure that I wasn't going over the top in a Tom Clancy kind of way.

DS: When I was reading *The Intuitionist,* I couldn't help but think of novels by H.G. Wells and George Orwell. I found it very serious and very funny at the same time, which is a hard feat to accomplish.

WHITEHEAD: These books take so long to write that I end up putting a lot of jokes into them, just to keep me amused. So it's always funny when the book comes out and people finally laugh at the joke you made three years before. I think people talk about the science fiction dimension of *The Intuitionist* because I was using the world-building rules of science fiction. Sam Delaney has a great essay about how we adapt to the new situation present in each story by a science fiction writer. He would cite a sentence like, "The door dilates," which makes no sense, but over time you realize that in this world the doors do dilate—that's the way they open and close. So I was very conscious of making these bizarre, ridiculous elevator rules presentable and understandable.

DS: It works on so many different levels. And as you stay with it you start seeing it in terms of the strata of society, and the whole idea of verticality, of how people are up or down depending on where they fall in the American class system and racial hierarchy. But it's very subtlety done, hence a covert way to get at complicated and crucial matters.

WHITEHEAD: Just the word "elevator" itself—the more I thought about it the more meanings I could tease out of it, so pretty quickly

"Uplift the race" became the subtext. The problem is, how do you say that without saying it so boldly, or say it in a cool way that people will like? I think if you write a book about a chair you're going to keep thinking about chairs and why are some chairs squat and what is the design aesthetic of different chairs. So I think if you concentrate on anything, like a very strange person, you are going to keep coming up with new combinations of meanings.

DS: This makes me think about how an artist will make numerous drawings and paintings about the same object or scene, a chair, vase, or haystack, and just keep exploring it, seeing it anew. This is a type of improvisation; you take a simple theme and go nuts with it.

WHITEHEAD: With *John Henry Days*, that became a big part of the book because the characters have their own ideas of who John Henry is: Did he actually exist, or is he just a folktale hero? Each person has his own sort of machine he is fighting with or his own sort of meaning he brings to the John Henry story. So I definitely expanded on that kind of technique.

DS: It's also a poet's technique. I noticed it in *The Colossus of New York*. But in each of your books I thought, "This is how a poet uses language and images," you know, really digging into metaphor in such a deep way that you break through to a fresh understanding.

WHITEHEAD: It was so liberating to work on *Colossus* because I didn't have to follow any novel-writing rules. I wasn't always thinking, "Is the plot progressing? Is this character being developed?" I was freed from the business of having to use closed quotations—the she said, he said form—which you do a thousand times in a novel, which over time can be a little irritating. So the form of the essays in *The Colossus of New York* was really fun to work with. I spent a lot of time trying to figure out where each sentence should go, and sometimes there was a linear thought that led into another natural thought. Or sometimes the narrative thread is created by puns or rhythms, stuff like that. It is a very different way of getting at something.

DS: I would say each of your books is distinctive. Is it important to you that each work be different?

WHITEHEAD: Oh yes. In my first book, I followed Lila Mae Watson. She's a very good, repressed character and hangs out in a lot of small rooms. I really wanted *John Henry Days* to have more characters and maybe some characters that would crack a joke once in a while. It's set out in the country, so people can roam around as opposed to being caught in the high-rises or basements as in *The Intuitionist*. After *John Henry Days*, which is a big book, I wanted to do something shorter. The novel I started immediately after that, which I'm still working on, is short and in the first person. It's one unified voice instead of a cavalcade of stars as in *John Henry*. It was a lot more fun, and I hadn't done a pure first-person voice since my first crappy novel, so it was nice to actually do it when I knew more about what I was doing. Books do take a long time, so how do you keep them fresh for yourself? How do you keep readers following you from book to book? How do you keep it fresh for them, and new? I like to challenge myself. When I finished *The Intuitionist*, *John Henry Days* seemed like a very daunting task, but it also seemed appropriate somehow. Then when I started *Colossus*, a switch to nonfiction with a unique structure, I was a bit afraid of making it a full-time project. But eventually the sheer difficulty of it made me want to do it because that sort of keeps you on your toes. You're not coasting.

DS: What led you to John Henry initially? Is he a hero figure to you, a mythological figure?

WHITEHEAD: I first heard the story when I was a kid. I attended elementary school in the multi-culti 1970s, so we had a hippy teacher who brought diverse cultures into the classroom, and a cartoon about John Henry. I was six or seven, and he was the first black superhero I'd ever seen. At that time there was John Henry and Muhammad Ali. Also I was an avid science fiction fan and TV watcher. It was a time when there was a lot of anxiety about technology, about nuclear war and computers running amuck, and I absorbed this pervasive anxiety about technology. So when I started thinking about the book, I started thinking about how the information age and more complex machines can have a profound effect on our lives.

DS: You do make profound use of the fact that the story of John Henry—that is, of a man who races a steam-powered drill, wins, but then dies—is a fable of the arrival of the Industrial Revolution. And then in J. Sutter, you create a reincarnation of Henry for the information age.

WHITEHEAD: I was trying to update this industrial age parable for the information age, but then what do you do? There are no John Henry figures anymore. J. Sutter is a hack journalist, a counterpoint to the heroic, muscled, and energetic Henry. Sutter just sits on his butt all day.

DS: You make us think about how the electronic revolution has diminished the presence of, and respect for, a heroic person like John Henry, someone who works with their hands. So many of us are desk jockeys now, and few of us really understand how the tools we use work. Your novel also makes me think about the railroad as the beginning of our world; it was the first web, along with the telegraph. Between those two technologies, our world shrank and became a minute-by-minute place.

WHITEHEAD: I guess two things came together when I was thinking about the book. One is that I had been writing journalism, basically bad music reviews. I'd outgrown the music, but I needed the money so I was writing about bands I didn't care about for the *Village Voice* and *Spin*. I really wanted to work on my fiction, but I had no money, so you do what you have to do. It's a classic artist's dilemma. Somehow I finished *The Intuitionist;* then I moved to San Francisco. It was the height of the Internet boom, so I got off the plane and I had a job in a week. They were virtually trolling the docks for able bodies. I had gone from writing long articles to writing short web blurbs for a would-be Yahoo service. It was my job to write up weekly web chats, so if I was writing up a Pets.com 8:00 Wednesday chat it would be like "Cuckoo for Your Cockatoo," or "Crazy for your Chihuahua. Come to Pets.com every week at eight." I felt so debased and reduced. And when I started researching railroads, you're right, I realized that there is a direct link between the railroads and the web. Instead of information, it's products on the rails, but it's a form of communication, and it really brought the country together in the same way the web brings all of our homes into one little web, if you will. Making those kind of parallels and counterpoints became fruitful.

DS: And let's not forget your brilliant precursors, Frank Norris and *The Octopus* and Henry Miller and *Tropic of Capricorn,* which conjures up the Cosmodemonic Telegraph Company. They were also attuned to the incalculable impact of new technologies. Now you reveal a great deal about our love-hate relationship with technology.

WHITEHEAD: Once I started researching and once I outlined a plot, I saw that John Henry's contest with a machine was applicable, or universal, in different time periods. In fact, there are lots of machines in the novel. There's a songwriter in the early twentieth century who is trying to get his songs on sheet music to get them into drawing rooms, and he is confronting a technologic pop cultural advance. Twenty years later there is a blues singer who is trying to get his songs on wax, and that's a hurdle that he has to face or else become obsolete like John Henry. But I think there are more mundane struggles. J. Sutter is not a hero, and we're not heroic in the sense of John Henry, but I think there's a way that we can view our daily contests as being great and important, such as raising five kids and getting them educated and keeping a roof over your head. We all have our different contests, and it's important even though we don't live in the larger-than-life performance days of John Henry. These things are important to us and keep us going and feed us.

DS: How do you know when to write fiction and when to write nonfiction?

WHITEHEAD: The form of *The Colossus of New York* is so strange. It's definitely nonfiction, but not traditional nonfiction. I am using a novelist's hand to shape experience and to create narrative flow.

DS: There seem to be a couple of characters, a he and a she.

WHITEHEAD: Yes, but most of the he's and she's appear once and then disappear. There are two chapters, the Broadway chapter and the Brooklyn Bridge chapter, where I do follow one character, and that was to vary the form. It's also because those two chapters reflect my own experience, and my feeling that there is something heroic about confronting Broadway and something heroic about crossing the Brooklyn Bridge and leaving your past behind, a transformation I always feel when I cross the bridge. I wanted to have a continuous character who experienced those things. It would have been a lie to call it fiction, yet it is a bit of a stretch to call it nonfiction.

DS: How did this slender book come about?

WHITEHEAD: It's very slender, yes. I think that's because the previous book, *John Henry Days,* was so long. *Colossus* was a nice breather, and it came out of a section in *John Henry* in which I'm describing the country fair in Talcott, West Virginia, and I'm trying to link it to all fairs. What happens in New York is that you go to the Columbus Avenue Fair or the Sixth Avenue Fair and it's always the exact same fair; there is always the Vinny behind the sausage stand. Every fair becomes all fairs because it's just the same stands and folks. So in a broader way I wanted to capture the things that are universal to all fairs, the texture of the raffle tickets, how come cotton candy sticks to the side of your mouth and your teeth? Then when I finished the novel, I was still creatively on, which doesn't really happen that much these days, so I wanted to keep going. I started writing and using that country-fair voice to talk about places in New York City.

I was doing this on the side. As I said before, this is a strange form for me, so I figured I should also start a novel, which is what I knew would keep everybody happy, especially my agent. He was very psyched about me starting a novel, but I kept writing about New York on the side, figuring one day these pieces might add up to a book or something, years down the line. I was halfway through the new novel when 9/11 happened, and I started writing straightforward nonfiction about the city for the *New York Times.* The stuff I was writing was so painful and so hard to write, and I was so spent after it, whatever this other stuff about the city was, it just seemed like what I should be doing. It was really a hard thing to do, to commit to working on the New York book full-time and not worry about who's going to buy what, what's going to sell, is it a novel? I didn't know what I was doing, so I just kept going forward. The nonfiction work also helped because, when I tried to work on the novel during the months after 9/11, I was totally stuck in a rather pretentious frame of mind, asking myself, "What's the rule of fiction now that this terrible thing has happened?" and telling myself, an artist can't do anything.

DS: In reading *The Colossus of New York* I keep thinking about how much you love the city. I think everyone felt an aching tenderness towards New York after 9/11, and I'm seeing mention of 9/11 in all kinds of new books. It's a watershed, a landmark tragedy. Yet you don't write about it.

WHITEHEAD: The towers were always literally in the background in the city, and I think they are still in the background whenever you think about New York now, so I didn't feel that there was any reason for me to mention them. The book did change after 9/11, and a melancholy tenor started to creep into most of the essays, but I think that's only appropriate. My view of how I live has changed so much, and how I view the city has changed. So part of what I really liked about the form of the essays is I can go from granting someone a momentary glimpse of happiness, and take it away from someone else in the next sentence when the city decides to be a little cruel for a moment or two. I think all those things exist on a street corner or a subway car. There are people having great days, people having terrible days, people who just arrived and are still sort of full of hope, and people on their last legs. What I'm trying to get at in these dense paragraphs is that density of emotion and spectrum of human endeavor that exists on every street corner, elevator, and bus.

DS: I think there are many funny moments in *The Colossus of New York*. In fact, I'd say there were quite a few monologues in there, a series of stand-up routines.

WHITEHEAD: I think it's a hit-and-run kind of narrative style, unlike a novel where you have to set things up, build the bottom step on the stairs before you can move up, and before the payoff. With this style, I can make a comment, or an aside, and then go on to the next thought or impression.

DS: I found that humor adds to the poignancy of the essays, that humor is the coping mechanism. Many comedians base their routines on how difficult and absurd the most mundane and routine aspects of our daily lives can become. You do this, too.

WHITEHEAD: It does seem that if you really think about the things you do—all the unspoken strategies for getting a seat on the subway, wrestling with take-out coffee lids, picking out clothes for the big interview—what's true for you really is true for most people. These things are mundane, and you're not going to spend more than four seconds thinking about them, but you do think about them a lot over a course of a lifetime, and they become real and they start to have a life. So I think that, if I can tap into what I can trust a lot of people have the same sensations or thoughts about, I can reveal where we're more or less all the same.

DS: *Colossus* is rich in wordplay. Your language is poetic and painterly, but you often juggle it and jumble it. Sometimes it sounds like pop song lyrics, other times like theater, sometimes there's a toughness to it. I wonder if your wordplay serves as a counterpoint to more tender feelings and if it reflects how the city makes us adopt a gruff and teasing way of talking to conceal our emotions.

WHITEHEAD: I think they go hand in hand. The toughest talking gangster in Brooklyn likes to sit on a park bench every once in awhile. In terms of wordplay and the organization of paragraphs, I would gather various impressions, leave a sentence standing alone in the one chapter, and then a year and a half later suddenly fill out the page in a flurry of activity. I was just taking notes and figuring out what would go here and what would go there, but I would have 90 percent done and still feel really, really dissatisfied. Then I would be like, "Maybe this is the lesson in this paragraph." There was so much tinkering. There always is no matter what you're writing, but with this I felt it more because it didn't have the kind of clues a linear narrative has—like, he has to get to the door, he has to get to the city, so you describe him walking, you describe an airplane ride. With this book, I didn't have that kind of map. I didn't have the sort of signposts that show exactly where each paragraph should go, so I ended up moving pieces around until finally the last one fit.

DS: I'm curious about what literature you've read that helps you orient your writing in this way.

WHITEHEAD: I'm not sure. I think with *Colossus* the direct influence was the camera-eye voice in John Dos Passos. I read *Manhattan Transfer* when I was a very impressionable college sophomore, and I just loved the way he jumped around in people's heads and how the city was depicted in a very impressionistic style so that it becomes an oppressive beast, or it's a place of refuge in a scatter-shot sort of way. I don't think he gives you many clues to what's going on, so I was trying to be conscious of how that draws the reader along. And for some strange reason, Allen Ginsberg's "Howl" keeps coming to me. Where else are you going to find someone yelling "Molok"? But Molok on Times Square. I think Ginsberg's fractured, disintegrating narrator in that particular poem fits in with what I was trying to do.

DS: I thought I detected a bit of Borges.

WHITEHEAD: Yes, Borges is definitely an influence.

DS: I wondered if you'd thought of Henry Miller's *The Colossus of Marissa*?

WHITEHEAD: I haven't read it. I heard about it because people want to know where the title of my book comes from, and it's from the 1950s science fiction movie about a Nobel Prize winner who is in a car accident, after which his father, who is also a scientist, transplants his brain into a robot body. I hadn't seen it until recently. But I did have a book of science fiction and horror when I was kid, and there was a picture of the robot and a kid standing next to it. I didn't know what the word "colossus" meant. I just knew it was bigger than you and kind of scary if you knocked it around. When I was thinking about the title, it just seemed to fit. I rented the movie, and it is so bad—and it's not even shot in New York. There were maybe three location shots of the U.N. and the Colossus walking out of the East River and that's it. He comes to the city like five times, and each time it's the exact same stock footage, so hopefully this is a little more big budget.

DS: Speaking of influences, race certainly plays a role in both your novels, and I was wondering if you feel that you are participating in a dialogue with other African American writers?

WHITEHEAD: I guess I will always go back to people I read in college, when I first started reading literature outside the Victorian hit parade. Reading Ishmael Reed at an important time was really crucial for me, and Jean Toomer, too. He wasn't obsessed with linearity. There is a linear progression in *Cane*, but it's more through symbol and characters echoing each other in situations, and a method of creating meaning over time—techniques I found essential in writing *John Henry Days*. I have also taken things from Pynchon and Borges, so, looking back, I don't see it as a dialogue. It's just that you align yourself with people who have the same concerns as you and who teach you ways of doing it.

DS: Is music an inspiration?

WHITEHEAD: I do play music when I work. I used to drink a lot of coffee and play music really loud. I definitely was in my own little bubble. I grew up in a household where the TV was on twenty-four hours a day, so you had to either learn to deal with it or go insane, so I think maybe that actually helped me as a writer because I just focus on what I'm doing. There can be any sort of chaos going on, and people running around, and I can still concentrate on what I'm trying to accomplish.

DS: Do you see yourself writing for the rest of your days? Is this your dream life?

WHITEHEAD: Pretty much. I'm digging it. I hope I keep coming up with things to write about. I think as long as I can keep trying new things it'll work. There's a play I want to write when I can clear my schedule, and there may be a lot more nonfiction I can work on. I think as long as I can keep doing it in a novel way so that I'm not bored and people don't get sick of me I will be happy. Last year I spent a lot of time teaching at different places, and that was just great to get out of the house for one thing—but also to have to think about literature in a different way and to think about my process. To be forced to articulate what writing is to me, and how I get it done and how I think other people should be doing it was really useful. And it was a nice break from working. I couldn't write when I was doing it, and that was fine. It was good to use my brain in a different way.

DS: That seems really important. One can get into all kinds of ruts. The writing practice isn't simply a matter of habit and hard work. The imagination has to be nurtured.

WHITEHEAD: Between books I really veg hard for months, and then one day I snap into the work mode. But I think those times when you're not thinking about work are important. And you get the chance to read stuff that a year from now you are going to use in your fiction. I think all the things you do, the music you love, the movies you love, the books you love, all these things feed you in ways you don't know about until years later. Like seeing that John Henry cartoon as a boy. I didn't know I was going to write a novel about John Henry, yet that was really a key moment in my life, even though I was just sitting around watching a cartoon.

PART THREE: The Art and Intent of Creative Nonfiction

I didn't know that I was reading creative nonfiction (or narrative nonfiction or literary nonfiction), when I found my way to Rachel Carson, Edward Abbey, John McPhee, and Annie Dillard. I just knew that I was reading lyrical and philosophical works that appealed to my aesthetics and my imagination. Creative nonfiction combines the techniques of fiction with the rigorous observations and research of science and serious journalism. This genre embraces essays, memoirs, medical misadventures, travel writing, tales of exploration, and spiritual reflections. But to my mind, the most vital form of creative nonfiction is nature writing because of the elegance of the prose, the sophistication of the perceptions of the authors, and the overarching significance of the subject matter. Although the beauty and marvels of nature have always inspired writers, as have environmental conundrums—Thoreau worried about over-development—such concerns are more pressing now. All that we hold dear is dependent on the sustained viability of the living earth, on the existence of potable water, clean air, fertile soil, teeming seas, healthy forests, and intact polar ice caps, and all are imperiled by our escalating population and polluting technologies. Fortunately, complex and controversial environmental subjects attract some of today's most artistic and thought-provoking writers, who write in the hope that the stories they tell, the facts they present, the places they describe, and the people they profile will help raise environmental awareness.

My life as a reviewer, critic, and literary journalist has coincided with the rise of creative nonfiction—a genre much debated, misunderstood, and maligned, yet unquestionably thriving. It has been a great pleasure to witness its growth, and to speak with some of its foremost practitioners. I read Diane Ackerman's groundbreaking *A Natural History of the Senses* with a sense of excitement. That excitement has stayed with me as Ackerman has continued to push creative nonfiction to new heights over the years. Wade Davis is a literary scientist with a global perspective and compassionate point of view. His work is exhilarating. As a teacher, editor, publisher, lecturer, and practitioner, Lee Gutkind has been a tireless champion of creative nonfiction. Alex Kotlowitz embodies the best of immersion reporting, the union of social consciousness and art. Phillip Lopate has worked hard to establish a place for essayists in the contemporary literary scene. In his own writing he combines autobiography with natural history and social and cultural critiques. Sy Montgomery brings a sense of adventure and an ecological sensibility to her writing about the animal realm. Terry Tempest Williams writes with knowledge, passion, and courage about the glories of the land and the need for our species to learn to live on Earth without destroying ourselves and the very elements our lives depend on.

Diane Ackerman

Poet and naturalist Diane Ackerman describes her literary awakening in the introduction to *The Moon by Whale Light,* a book in which she celebrates the peculiarities and wonders of bats, penguins, crocodilians, and whales. Born in Waukegan, Illinois, in 1948, she grew up near a plum orchard, which was supposed to be off-limits. One morning when she and three fellow first-graders were late for school, they cut through the forbidden orchard where "the trees were thick with dark plums huddled like bats." Struck by this vision, which she now describes with bemusement as "the sight of my first metaphor," Ackerman stood and stared. An impatient classmate asked her what she was looking at. When Ackerman told her, her young companion was horrified, initiating Ackerman into the pleasure and pain of creativity.

Readers find this lively mix of inventiveness, humor, and reflection throughout Ackerman's work. She offers clear scientific explanations, candid self-disclosures, and descriptions that bring nature's grand panorama into sharp focus. During her undergraduate years, Ackerman attended Boston University and Pennsylvania State University, then earned an M.F.A. in creative writing at Cornell University, where she also received her doctorate. She has taught at the University of Pittsburgh and Washington University. Poetry was her first love, and her first published books were poetry collections, including *The Planets: A Cosmic Pastoral, Wife of Light,* and *Jaguar of Sweet Laughter: New and Selected Poems,* which embody her ambidextrous command of the sensuous and the philosophical, the human and the wild, the earthly and the cosmic.

In *A Natural History of the Senses,* the book that made Ackerman famous, she broke new ground with her appealing subject matter, unique approach, dynamic synthesis of research, observation, and interpretation, and narrative voice that ranges from rhapsodic to insouciant. Here Ackerman puts forth her signature theme: that human beings are as integral a part of nature as any other animal species and that we must recognize and embrace our animal-ness, and our innate connections to other animals.

A staff writer for the *New Yorker* for a spell (after writing a book about learning to fly and one about her stint on a New Mexico cattle ranch), Ackerman traveled all around the world and risked life and limb to enter the realm of whales, sea birds, and alligators while working side-by-side with wildlife biologists, extraordinary experiences that crop up in many of her books, including *The Rarest of the Rare*. For all the joy Ackerman finds in immersing herself in the great carnival of nature, she is every bit as attuned to the wildness of the human psyche. In *A Slender Thread*, she chronicles her work with a suicide hotline; in *Origami Bridges: Poems of Psychoanalysis and Fire*, she explores the dynamics of the analyst-patient relationship. In *Cultivating Delight*, Ackerman chronicles a year in the life of her lush two-acre garden, the ideal place for Ackerman to ponder the complex interaction between the wild and the cultivated. In *An Alchemy of Mind: The Marvel and Mystery of the Brain*, Ackerman has written an erudite and dazzling analysis of "how the brain becomes the mind."

Ackerman's essays appear in the *New York Times, National Geographic,* and *Parade*. She has written books for children, received a Guggenheim Fellowship and the John Burroughs Nature Award, and had a molecule, dianeackerone, named in her honor. Currently she is at work on yet another surprising work of nonfiction and a book of poems. We spoke twice, once when *Cultivating Delight* was released in June 2001, and again in August 2004 when *An Alchemy of Mind* was published.

⌒

DONNA SEAMAN: *Cultivating Delight* is a year's chronicle of an extraordinary garden, a place rampant with roses, daffodils, lilies, deer, squirrel, and hummingbirds. You've been a world traveler and explorer. What inspired you to create such a grand and ambitious garden?

DIANE ACKERMAN: Oh, how could I resist creating my own cosmos? I've always been growing something, and now I have a garden of about two acres. But one geranium is garden enough if you approach it in the right mood of affectionate curiosity, and you're happy to see it each day and see how it's changed. The garden isn't just however many plants you have. For me, it's the whole landscape, including your mood. So my garden contains the plants, the animals, the constellations, the weather, the visitors, all of the different life forms and processes that are changing and that have been growing over the years. It started small; now it's become rampant, which I think is about right. At this point I have 120 rose bushes. At the moment I'm just considering it a kind of passion that's gotten out of hand. The whole front yard is essentially a deer buffet. This year I put a deer fence up around the backyard, but I'm conflicted about the deer, as the psychoanalysts say, so I've left a buffer of about twenty feet of woods and a creek because the deer have to live, too.

DS: The book is bursting with observations of many kinds of plants and animals, and you marvel over every one.

ACKERMAN: I think if you look at any facet of nature in enough detail, you find it fascinating. How could you not? The universe is so full of marvels. Here's an example: rain—the shape of rain. I was minding my own business, working on my book, looking out the window, and it was raining and I was noticing that the raindrops were falling in that classic round-looking way, and I thought, "I wonder if raindrops really are round?" So I started researching it a little, and I discovered that raindrops change shape three hundred times a second. Yes, three hundred times a second and at various stages as they are falling, they assume opposite shapes. I thought, "How like the human personality this is." You see somebody that you've known, and you think that they are continuous. You think they are one whole thing, but the truth is that they are a great swarm of processes holding themselves in equilibrium, and at various times in their lives, they may assume ideas, positions, that are the opposite of what they thought before, but they are still the same person. They change while remaining the same, and that's true of the whole garden, but it's also like the shape of rain, so there is always something interesting.

DS: I believe that the core revelation in all of your books is the fact that human beings are nature as much as a tree is nature, a whale, a penguin, a worm, a jaguar. And, furthermore, that everything we do is natural.

ACKERMAN: We are nature, yes, and people have a difficult time seeing this. I have imaginary visitors in the garden in *Cultivating Delight;* one is John Muir, and I think he and I would have disagreed on this. I think Muir felt that culture is what people invent when they've lost nature, whereas I feel that, just as a termite's mound is natural, our cities are natural. How could it be otherwise? We are animals who create different kinds of dwellings and tools, but chimpanzees also use tools; birds use tools and build homes. But we're conditioned to think of ourselves as beyond animal. Animal is something that embarrasses us. It's something that is beneath us, or behind us. And when we think that, we divorce ourselves from our heritage, from something that we have evolved to require in order to feel whole. That's the source, I think, of the loneliness at the heart of the society we live in. This passion to exile ourselves from the rest of nature becomes an us-against-them contest, but it also bankrupts a lot of what is most satisfying, comforting, and fascinating about us as people.

My interest in the senses really fits into this, too. When *A Natural History of the Senses* came out in 1990, I couldn't figure out at first why people were responding to it. Then I began to see that essentially I had given them a sense of permission, that it was okay to enjoy their senses. Our puritanical ways tell us that you can't be seen to be enjoying your senses in public; that's naughty, naughty,

naughty. The truth is, all the other animals do, and we evolved to be the same way. I think we injure our mental and physical health when we inhibit ourselves from doing that very thing.

DS: You move from meticulously describing the sensuous aspects of the garden to cultivating the garden of literature as you write about works that have deeply affected you, writings by John Muir, Gertrude Jekyll, and Thomas Jefferson. How are you able to synthesize all of this?

ACKERMAN: My muse is very miscellaneous. I've never understood why exactly, but I'll start to think about one thing and it will remind me of something else and then there will be other relevant things that will feed into it, then the whole journey, to use a rather new-age word, will go forward while magnetizing things to it. That's pretty much what happens. Most often when people write books, they are encouraged to do things in a more streamlined way—to have, for example, a beginning, a middle, and an end in that order even though life isn't always like that.

DS: Certainly the mind is never like that.

ACKERMAN: The mind is never like that. Or when you write for newspaper and magazine editors, they like you to put everything about a certain subject, whatever the subject is, together. They like to collect things up, even though, as we've said, the mind doesn't work like that. You think of something; you go on for awhile; something else bolsters it or opens it out in some other way; then you go on with a slightly enlarged knowledge, and something else comes in. That's really more the way the mind works.

I write about Thomas Jefferson as a gardener because he was president only in his spare time. He was mainly a gardener. He sent Lewis and Clark on their expedition to find more seeds. He was a vegetarian, and he needed more variety in his diet. And Gertrude Jekyll, the famous British gardener, she was a trip. She's probably *the* most famous gardener or landscape architect, however you want to think of her, and she was a real bossy boots. I think her attitude was that everyone was entitled to her opinion. Her friends called her Bumps, or Aunt Bumps. She wrote very beautifully. There is a section in one of her notebooks where she obviously just stood and watched the light change on the feathers of a goose for most of the afternoon. I love to read stuff like that. It takes a certain kind of sensibility to stand there and observe that, and she created extraordinary gardens and really taught people to think of the garden as a metaphor.

DS: You've described yourself as an earth ecstatic.

ACKERMAN: Yes, and this is a very small denomination I must admit, and the creed is simple. I believe in the sanctity of life, and I believe in the perfectibility of people. I think we can improve ourselves and act better towards each other, and I think all life is sacred, whether it is on this planet or any other place we may find it. Yes, I'm an earth ecstatic. And I think there might be some minor orders to this. Our Sisters of Perpetual Motion could be one. Seven Day Opportunists could be another. I think John Muir was an earth ecstatic. On at least on one occasion, he climbed up a very tall tree during a thunderstorm to be ravaged by it. Now that's serious ecstasy there. There was an openness to holy conversion, and a kind of religiosity about him that was, I think, erotic as much as anything else in nature, very sensual as well as intellectual—a very interesting man.

DS: You're an involved, hands-on sort of writer.

ACKERMAN: I am, only to the extent that I feel uncomfortable standing back and taking notes. There is something elitist or holier-than-thou about that, that I don't care for. If I'm going to be writing about an endangered animal, I want to physically help it survive. That means if the other field biologists are doing doctoring, tagging, raising baby penguins in quarantine, whatever is happening, I'm doing exactly what they are doing. I'm not doing it any differently than they are, and I'm not just standing back and taking notes. This has a great advantage. It means that I can learn a lot of intimate details about the sensory systems of the animals, and I like that.

DS: This must have something to do with why you have a molecule named after you.

ACKERMAN: Oh yes, dianeackerone. It's a sex pheromone in crocodilians. As I've mentioned, I work with endangered animals sometimes, and one group I worked with was crocodilians, that's crocodiles, alligators, and their kin. I signed on to a research team, which meant that I worked with other scientists, doing whatever they were doing. We needed to conduct a hormone study on alligators, which meant we had to sex the alligators, and because you cannot tell from the outside, you have to get the gator out of the water. Step one, capture your gator: Leap upon the gator and hold its eyes down because alligators have pop-up eyes like bobble-head dogs, you know in the back of cars. And if you hold the eyes down, the gator gets disoriented—which is how gator wrestling is done. Then somebody lifts up the tail, and you do an internal, and you know immediately if it's a "mister" gator. Then the really hard part starts, which is climbing off the alligator, because at that point the eyes are up, and if it swings its snout around and hits you, you've been clobbered with what feels like a baseball bat made of bone, although you do end up with very attractive bruises that you can talk about to people. The pair of chemists who found this molecule, the pheromone, thought it would be sporting to honor me with it, and I love it. I think it's fun.

DS: From alligators to gray squirrels.

ACKERMAN: Yes, I did a National Geographic gray squirrel study; no one had done one before. We're surrounded by plants and animals that are so familiar we take them for granted. There are discoveries just lying in the roadway waiting for us—lying on the lips of lobsters. There was a discovery a couple of years ago about a creature that only lives on the lips of lobsters. You're thinking lobsters don't have lips, aren't you? But there are things right in the back yard that we don't know about, and squirrels was one of them.

I thought, "Great, I'll just capture all the squirrels." So I got the Cornell vet to help me. He brought over a complete intensive care lab. We caught the squirrels. We anesthetized the squirrels. Now they were out cold, and we could look at their paws, their hands, how very unusually soft, at the teeth, at the eyes. I could look very carefully at them, which was great. But as I mentioned to the five or six other people who were working with me on this team, how like an alien abduction story this was. Isn't this exactly how it's described? Aliens pick up humans, and they poke and prod and look them over, and the humans can't move. They don't know what's going on, and then they are returned to their normal life. Biologists do this all the time.

Normally biologists would mark animals with Lady Clairol. They bleach numbers into the fur. But I didn't like that idea, so I dressed all the squirrels up in necklaces. The boys got blue, the girls got pink. They each got earrings.

DS: Your neighbors must have loved this.

ACKERMAN: The neighbors said they would see squirrels standing up at their windows like tiny Masai warriors with their beads, and of course they heard me singing to the squirrels in the morning, calling them in my Snow White voice, you know, "Squirrels, squirrels," at which point fifty squirrels would come running. Beads have been used before, and we put beads on in a way that the squirrels could remove them if they felt they were conferring status, or if they didn't like the color, or anything else. And in time they all did, but they left them on long enough.

DS: And from gray squirrels to roses.

ACKERMAN: There is something really special about roses. They are sanctuaries. They're sumptuous. Their feel is wonderful, and their scent, the colors. They conjure up so many things because they are named after so many different people. The Colette rose, for example, is large, bosomy, blousy, puts forth a lot of delicately scented flowers, and is constantly growing, but also it has some of the thickest and largest thorns I've ever seen—very attractive, very seductive, huge thorns. I think Colette herself would have approved. Roses are named after nineteenth-century industrialists or characters in Chaucer and in Shakespeare, who I'm sure would be flabbergasted to have roses named after his characters. I love the variety of color, and I have so many roses at this point that most summers I don't cut and bring in anything but roses. I make lots of arrangements, and I collect vases. You can never have enough, especially of the small ones that will just accommodate one little flower and show it off to you. I love doing it, and it's a very calm time for me, bright and early in the morning where I'm just choosing the flowers and arranging them before the day has really started, playing with them, feeling the pedals, smelling them. I love those moments. They are very precious. You weren't going to say, "Stop to smell the roses" were you? That expression evolved because it is an extraordinary thing to do.

DS: Is there an evolutionary reason behind our profound response to the beauty of the natural world? And do we pay enough attention to the radiance all around us?

ACKERMAN: I think we don't appreciate it enough, although as long as there have been human beings, there has been a sense of being in the presence of forces that are larger and older than we are. I say that so certainly because if you look at Indo-European, the presumptive original language from which most of our languages came, you find words for awe, for holy. There's a verb for speaking with the deity, so we've always had that sense of wonder. Is it life-preserving to have that sense of wonder? I don't know, it must be. We must think of it as adaptive, if we're going to be good Darwinians. But whatever it is, it's been with us.

DS: You're a poet and you write about science. Your work bridges the two realms of art and science, which leads me to ask: Does science need art? Does art need science?

ACKERMAN: For me, there is no Checkpoint Charlie, on one side of which we have art and on the other side of which we have science; or on one side of which we have nature and on the other side of which we have science. It's all part of the same continuum. I think it's unfortunate that in America you have to choose when you go to college between the arts and the sciences, as if nature and the world were knowable from only one perspective. It really doesn't make any sense at all because we live in a constant bustle and stir of things from every conceivable subject and angle. We are constantly bombarded with things that are scientific, humanistic, artistic, intuitive, all merging together in what may come out the other end as a thought, an insight, a response, a phobia. Whatever it is, it isn't so simplistic as just being a scientific matter or just being an artistic matter. I can say that now because I understand that people think of these things as being separated into different cultures, but that separation was never anything I felt. It always seemed to me to be one mosaic.

When I was in college, I was taking courses like "Physics for Poets." I couldn't do math. Now I think I understand that it was really arithmetic I couldn't do, and really it's a question of how you go about learning something. It may well be that one child doesn't have a special gift in what we call math or arithmetic or whatever. But that doesn't mean that the revelations and wonders of science should be kept from that person, or indeed that that child might not be able to make extraordinary discoveries anyway in those very fields if they go at it from a different angle. And maybe because the child is forced to go at it from a different angle and not take for granted everything that's been done, they see things others miss. I'm fascinated by the revelations of science, but I don't want to be a scientist, so I'm much more of an old-fashioned naturalist. I just love to observe things, think about them, see what they can teach me. Humans are my favorite animal, so I'm always looking to see what nature and human nature can reveal about each other.

DS: In your poetry collection, *Origami Bridges,* the first section is titled, "An Alchemy of Mind." While you were writing those poems, had you already thought about writing a book about the brain?

ACKERMAN: I had already thought about the brain book and about how alchemical the brain is, how you start with what is essentially base metal, and it gets transmuted to gold. I'm calling it "mind gold," and I think of mind as a comforting mirage created by the physical brain.

DS: You draw on many sources, some quite surprising, to help us understand how, as you say, "the brain becomes the mind." I don't suppose most brain books have a chapter dedicated to Shakespeare.

ACKERMAN: As I said earlier, I have so many miscellaneous curiosities going on at the same time, and they very often intersect. I happened to be watching a biography of Shakespeare on PBS and thinking, "Boy we really don't know much about him." I adore his work, so I started reading more about him, and because I had the brain on the mind, I naturally began thinking about his brain—that it must have been different than most and that I bet we would have some intriguing insights now. I don't know that we'd have any answers to the question of how he was able to do what he did, but we might have some very interesting suggestions.

DS: Would we even know about a similiarly brilliant person now? There are so many more people on the planet. Surely there are individuals alive now who are equally amazing but we'll never know.

ACKERMAN: I agree, there are bound to be lots of them, and we won't ever know for sure. There are, indeed, a whole lot of people, which raises the question, have we taken over the role of evolution? And are we changing our own evolution with the things we have created? This question raises many which need to be talked about as part of what is called neuroethics, a field that is going to become extremely important. For example, how valid would it be to take MRI pictures into a courtroom in which a murderer is being tried? Could his defense be that he had an injured brain? That it was not a willful act? Or could a potential father-in-law require that a potential son-in-law get a brain scan?

Then there are larger, societal questions. I rented *Straw Dogs* the other day, and I was shocked to discover how mildly violent that film seems now, compared to what we see. When it came out in 1971, we were absolutely horrified. But we've become so inured to violence on the screen that we're changing our attention span, our sensory response, our startle response. We're changing the way our brains work thanks to our technologies.

DS: You write about how the brain doesn't distinguish carefully between image—a movie for instance—and real life. So we are profoundly affected by all the violence we watch as children on television and in the movies. I also wonder if the continual cascade of commercials that we absorb has an impact on us.

ACKERMAN: So many studies show that watching a lot of violence on TV really does influence kids to be more accepting of violence, and to think of violence as a way to solve problems. And violence is commercialized. The way to get people revved up, excited, to get their adrenalin going so that when you hit them with the commercials they'll be more interested, is of course to provide this arm's-length violence rather than something soothing and comforting. And yes, TV is all about selling, and selling to very young children. There is a lot more subliminal advertising going on than ever before. I think this will undoubtedly make changes in the brains of future generations. Mind you, we've been making changes all along throughout history. Agriculture, there's a big one. Cities. So this is just one more, one more curiosity in the saga of human life on Earth.

DS: Some of the most arresting sections in *An Alchemy of Mind* pertain to the nature of language and the roles language plays in our lives.

ACKERMAN: Don't you think that's *the* miracle? We invent language, and then we are able to use it as a tool, a kind of Swiss Army knife, to do all kinds of other things.

DS: You write with particular insight and panache about metaphor.

ACKERMAN: Out of all my research and all my contemplation, I think maybe that was one of the big surprises, that the brain requires a metaphorical way of looking at life. But we just take this for granted. We don't realize that we use metaphors to protect ourselves from the harshness of life, metaphor as cushion. Life would be intolerable otherwise. There are all sorts of metaphorical ways of existing that are subconscious or unconscious, so we don't know about them, but it seems to be a preferred way for the brain to function.

DS: This is such a rich book, brimming with science, poetry, and passages of memoir. What inspired you to share memories and stories from your life?

ACKERMAN: I just thought it would be helpful. There are so many formal brain books out there in which the point of view is so distanced, I thought it would be helpful to personalize certain experiences. I understood how the brain worked in these various situations so well, and if I let people see through the lens of my sensibility and through my memory, maybe they will, too.

DS: One distinguishing characteristic of all your work is just this sort of generosity. The reader has the distinct impression that you really want to help us to understand ourselves and our world and to live more fully.

ACKERMAN: We're all trying to understand ourselves in the universe, and the mysteries of life. Maybe it's because I'm a child of the sixties. The good part of the sixties tradition was a belief in nurturing, in doing things for others as well as for yourself.

DS: You remind us not only that we share the planet with many other beings, but also that our consciousness is but one of myriad forms of consciousness.

ACKERMAN: I think it's so important that we remember that we are animals, too, and that having an antagonistic view towards other animals—and pretending that they are inferior to us, so that we can then attribute everything we hate about ourselves to them —really isn't very healthy for us in the long run. Being animal has magnificent features to it. The lushness of our senses, all of our passions are animal; our emotions are animal. And there are some animals who are pretty darn clever. If you described some of the antics and the deceit of an orangutan without saying what animal you were talking about, your listeners would assume that it was human.

DS: In reading your work, one feels both your pleasure and delight in the research, the observations, the writing, but there is also an aura of pain, a sense that you're working through things on the page. You've volunteered for a suicide hotline, and *Origami Bridges* chronicles sessions with a psychotherapist. I wonder if you have an affinity for people in the healing professions?

ACKERMAN: I do, but I feel affinity with almost all professions because the only way we can know the world is through the brain. In one way, that imprisons us, but in another way it frees everyone. It allows everyone to extend their bodies and ideas through time and space, and it enables us to identify with everyone else. I feel that, particularly in a time of political upheaval, we tend to feel terribly different from people in other cultures. We think we have very little in common with them, and yet we're intimately related and have essential things in common with everyone who has ever lived on the planet, and probably with everyone who ever will. Because we all have the same brain.

Writing is the way I inquire about the world. It's my form of celebration and prayer, among other things. And I've become more willing to write about the deeper dimensions, about the emotional side of things because, ultimately, I would like to leave a record, as impossible as it sounds, of what it felt like to have once been alive on this particular planet—what it felt like in the senses and passions and contemplations, and what it hurt like, and thrilled like. Deep down I know that would take from birth to death and include all of consciousness, and it isn't doable anyway. And I should probably find that quest overwhelming and fraught with guilt and failure. But I don't think of it that way. I think of it as a mystery trip. As the world reveals itself and human nature reveals itself, it's all seductive and startling enough always to have my attention. The more I learn about life, the more life there seems to be to learn about. The more risks I take, the more risks I feel able to take.

DS: This evolution in your work, this honing of awareness and an artistic and humanist mission, can be traced from book to book, and your effort is risky. People don't always appreciate the baring of a writer's soul, the acknowledgment of our deepest connection with each other and all of life on earth.

ACKERMAN: I think it's in Italo Calvino's *Invisible Cities*, towards the end, when Marco Polo says that his real quest in life was to discover who and what in the midst of inferno is not inferno and make sure it prevails. I think that is my quest. Even though there's a lot of information and so-called science—I just think of it as nature—in my work, that's always secondary to my passion to learn about the human condition, which I don't think we can see whole from any one perspective, or vantage, in the arch of the sciences. I still think of myself as a nature writer. But what I mean by nature is the full sum of creation, and more and more that includes the subjective human experience and the power of the emotions and the mind.

Wade Davis

Wade Davis was born in 1953 and grew up in Pointe Claire, a small suburb of Montreal in which the French and English communities kept strictly apart. This was all the world he knew until he turned fourteen and traveled to Colombia with his Spanish class. This excursion was a revelation and set the course for a life of cross-cultural adventures. As Davis writes, "I learned that summer to have but one operative word in my vocabulary, and that was 'yes' to any experience, any encounter, anything new." This openness to life, matched by an insatiable curiosity and an acute sensitivity to the connection between people and place, inspired him to become an anthropologist and ethnobotanist, a writer and a photographer, a traveler and an educator. Along the way Davis worked as a guide, park ranger, and forestry engineer. He earned degrees in anthropology and biology, and then a Ph.D. in ethnobotany from Harvard University. Davis spent three years during the course of his studies in the Amazon and Andes as a plant explorer, collecting more than six thousand botanical specimens, and living among fifteen indigenous groups in eight Latin American countries. Davis also conducted fieldwork in Haiti, where he investigated the creation of zombies, which was the subject of *The Serpent and the Rainbow*, an international bestseller that was made into a movie directed by Wes Craven and released in 1988.

Davis's ethnographic inquiries also led him to northern Canada and the high Arctic, East Africa, Borneo, Tibet, the Orinoco delta of Venezuela, the deserts of Mali and Burkina Faso, and the forests of Benin and Togo. He has published 130 scientific and popular articles on such subjects as Haitian Vodoun, Amazonian shamanism, the traditional use of psychotropic drugs, and the global biodiversity crisis for a spectrum of publications, including *National*

Geographic, Newsweek, Harper's, and *Outside.* The power of Davis's work rests in his ability to respond to places and people not only as a scientist, but also as an artist. Like Rachel Carson and E. O. Wilson, he has a poetic feel for language, an innate sense of story, and a gift for crafting metaphors that illuminate the workings of both nature and the human mind. Davis is also a writer of conscience with a strong grasp of history, and he has made it his mission to document the predicaments of indigenous peoples, whose lands and traditions are under siege.

Davis's magnum opus, *One River,* is an engrossing history of plant exploration in the Amazon in which he interweaves the history of conquering Spaniards and missionaries; Richard Evans Schultes's pioneering expeditions into the world of hallucinogenic plants; and his own adventures among Indian tribes along with his plant-hunter colleague, Timothy Plowman. In the essay collection, *Shadows in the Sun,* Davis reports on his sojourns with indigenous peoples in Haiti, Tibet, the Arctic, and the Sahara as well as the Andes of Peru and the Amazonian rainforests.

Davis is also a superb photographer. Both his literary finesse and artistic acumen are found on the pages of *Light at the Edge of the World,* a book in which he documents the daily lives and cosmologies of such distinct indigenous groups as the Gitxsan of northwestern British Columbia; the Andean community of Cuper in Chinchero, Peru; the Winikina-Warao of Venezuela; Vodoun acolytes in Haiti; the Penan of Borneo; the Ariaal of Kenya; and the native people of Tibet.

The recipient of numerous awards, including the Explorers Club Lowell Thomas Award and a Lannan Foundation prize for literary nonfiction, Davis is an explorer-in-residence at the National Geographic Society, and lectures all over the world. He is the host and co-writer for *Earthguide,* a thirteen-part Discovery Channel series on the environment, and he has contributed to the award-winning documentaries *Spirit of the Mask, Cry of the Forgotten People,* and *Forests Forever.* He is currently working on a four-part series, *Living at the Edge of the World,* which will air on the National Geographic Channel. Davis's current book is *Lost*

Amazon, a collection of Richard Evans Schultes's photographs of his Amazonian explorations.

Wade Davis showed slides of his photographs and spoke about his work to a standing-room only audience at the Field Museum in Chicago in 2001, just after he appeared on *Open Books.*

~~

DONNA SEAMAN: In *Light at the Edge of the World,* you write: "The key revelation of anthropology is the idea that distinct cultures represent unique visions of life itself, morally inspired and inherently right." That's a remarkable statement and one that leads you to write about a concept you call the "ethnosphere." Would you please explain what the ethnosphere is, and why we should treasure it?

WADE DAVIS: The revelation of anthropology is really the idea that the world in which any one particular culture lives does not exist in an absolute sense, but is just one model of reality, the consequence of one particular set of adaptive choices that our lineage has made, albeit successfully, many generations ago. The great lesson of anthropology is that there are other ways of being, whether it's the Penan of the forests of Borneo or a Voudon acolyte in Haiti or a Buddhist monk on a mountain in the Himalayas. All these people teach us that there are other possibilities. And together, myriad cultures of the world make up a web of life, a web of spiritual and cultural and social life that envelopes the planet and is as important to the well-being of the planet as the biological web of life that we know as the biosphere. And you might coin the term ethnosphere, at least I have coined the term ethnosphere, for this web of social life.

One definition of the ethnosphere would be the sum total of all thoughts and ideas and myths and inspiration—intuitions brought into being by the human imagination—since the dawn of consciousness. The ethnosphere is really humanity's greatest legacy. It's a product of our dreams, the embodiment of all of our hopes, and the symbol of all that we are and all that we have created as a wildly inquisitive and astonishingly adaptive species. And just as the biosphere is being severely eroded, so too is the ethnosphere and, if anything, at a far greater rate. The most apocalyptic scenario in the realm of biological diversity scarcely approaches what we know to be the most optimistic scenario in the realm of cultural diversity. The great indicator of that is language loss.

When each of us was born, there were roughly six thousand languages spoken on Earth. Language isn't just a body of vocabulary or a set of grammatical rules. It's a flash of the human spirit; it's a vehicle through which the soul of each particular culture comes into the material world. Every language is an old-growth forest of the mind, a kind of watershed of thought, an ecosystem of possibilities. Of those six thousand languages, fully half today, as we sit here, are not being whispered into the ears of babies and not being taught to schoolchildren, which means that effectively, unless something changes, they're already dead. We're living through a period where in a single generation or two virtually half of humanity's legacy is being lost. This is what we're talking about at the National Geographic; we're trying to draw people's attention to the loss of our own legacy, the erosion of the ethnosphere.

The reason I coined the term ethnosphere is that sometimes words take on power. Thirty years ago the term biosphere was familiar only to earth scientists, and now it's part of the vernacular of schoolchildren. In a way, it's become an organizing principle for us to begin to think about the fragile blue planet that we live on. By the same token we're hoping that the use of the term ethnosphere will become an organizing principle that will change the way people think about culture and the human legacy.

DS: The term ethnosphere is a magnet for thought and a tool for understanding why all cultures are of value, just as all plants and animals are intrinsic to life. I'm particularly intrigued with, and concerned about, the preservation of the knowledge of hunters and gatherers, the few remaining nomads.

DAVIS: Adaptation makes for profoundly different human beings. For most of our human history, we were nomads, wanderers on a pristine planet. And it was only ten thousand years ago, at the time of the Neolithic, that we all succumbed to the cult of the seed and, as Joseph Campbell once said, the poetry of the shaman was displaced by the prose of the organized priesthood. That was a huge shift in the affairs of human beings, and it's one of the reasons that in *Light at the Edge of the World* I try to bring the reader, both through image and text, to a range of cultures that I've been able to visit and live with on my own limited journeys through the ethnosphere—whether in the high Arctic of Canada or the mountains of Tibet or the forests of the Amazon and Borneo or the mountains of the high Andes—always with the idea of trying to celebrate these points of wonder, cultural adaptations that are so dazzling that they will wake anyone to the wonder of who we are as a species. I think this is really, really important, because all cultures are ethnocentric, fiercely loyal to their own interpretations of reality, and it's not unreasonable for us in the modern world to think of ourselves as the paragon of human potential. Many cultures see themselves that way. The actual names of many societies translate as "the people," the implication being that all other people are somehow marginal, barbarians at the gate of culture.

Because of that, there's a tendency for us to view the modern industrial world as the cutting edge of history, and therefore to view other diverse cultures as perhaps quaint and colorful but somehow failed attempts at modernity—arcane societies destined to fade away as if by some magical law. Nothing could be further from the truth. All of these cultures are fully capable of the dynamic dance of life. In other words, it's not change per se that threatens the integrity of the ethnosphere. All cultures and all peoples through all times are constantly adapting to new possibilities. Nor does technology threaten the integrity of culture. People are always adapting to technical innovation. A Sioux Indian did not stop being a Sioux Indian when he gave up the bow and arrow anymore than an American farmer stopped being an American when he gave up the horse and buggy. So it's neither change nor technology that threatens the integrity of culture. It's power, the cruel face of domination.

Wherever you look in the world, these are not archaic societies that are slowly fading from the human record. In every case, these are dynamic, vibrant, living peoples being driven out of existence by identifiable forces beyond their capacity to cope. For example, the diseases that are sweeping into the homeland of the Yanomami in the Upper Orinoco in the wake of the discovery of gold and the invasion of that land by gold miners. Or at the mouth of the Niger River in Nigeria, the Ogoni can no longer farm their once-fertile soil because they have been poisoned by the effluence from the petroleum industry. Or in the forests of Borneo, the nomadic Penan can no longer find a way to be in that forest because their subsistence base has been violated by egregious forest practices. Wherever you go, you see that there's an identifiable conflict, and this is both a discouraging observation and an encouraging one because although human beings are the agents of cultural destruction, we can also be the facilitators of cultural survival.

DS: You pay tribute to your mentors, including David Maybury-Lewis, who made the distinction between genocide, the physical extermination of people, a horror everyone condemns, and ethnocide, which is what you're describing, acts that destroy people's way of living.

DAVIS: The curious thing is that genocide, as you suggest, is universally condemned but ethnocide is not only not condemned throughout the world; in many instances it's promoted as appropriate development policy. I mentioned certain obvious sources of conflict evident around the world, and sometimes the clash is indeed exclusively political, for example the invasion of Tibet by the Chinese. But often the impact is caused by development initiatives that have the characteristic of bringing together good intentions with bad ideas to create chaos.

The perfect example of that is in northern Kenya, where I write about the pastoral people, the Rendille and the Ariaal, the Samburu and the Gabbra, people who have moved across the desert with their vast herds of camels and cattle for several thousand years. During the late 1960s, when people began to notice that the Sahara was moving south, long before we appreciated climate change and other phenomena, there had to be an explanation for the desertification of the sub-Sahara belt and the development community settled on the notion that became known as the "tragedy of the commons," the idea being that somehow the nomads themselves were culpable because, after all, since they did not own land, they had no incentive to protect it. The diagnosis was to encourage them to sell off some of their herds, settle down, and begin to practice some form of range management that would be more appropriate to Montana than the desert, and the consequence was a disaster. Not only is drought not some kind of cruel anomaly in that particular area of the world, it's a regular feature of climate, and surviving drought is a key imperative that has made the people who they are and allowed them to live lightly on that land for thousands of years. In order to survive drought, the key mechanism is to have enough animals so that at least some percentage of the herd will survive a period of extreme desiccation. When the animals were sold off, suddenly the people were not able to overcome the periods of want, and they ended up drifting toward settlements which became oases of dependency. Then their young children are taken into schools where they learn a modicum of literacy, perhaps, but they also learn to have contempt for who they had been. And they were spat out into an economy that had a 50 percent unemployment rate for those with a high-school education. So having been torn from their past, they were propelled into an uncertain future, and they found themselves on the bottom rung of an economic ladder that went nowhere, and they drifted into the slums of Nairobi.

DS: How familiar this is. It parallels the treatment accorded Native Americans.

DAVIS: I think it's really important to understand the genesis both of our own relationship to landscape and that of indigenous people. Going back to this idea that all cultures are fiercely loyal to their interpretations of reality, if a Martian landed on Earth and looked through an anthropological lens at various cultures, including our own in the West, the Western modern paradigm, the Martian "anthropologist" would see many things. If, for example, the measure of success was technological wizardry, we'd certainly come out on top. But if the measure of success shifted to other criteria, we would perhaps not come out on top. Clearly, they would look at our social structure and ask some basic questions, such as: these people say they revere marriage, and yet half their marriages end in divorce. And they say that they embrace their elders, yet only six percent of them are prepared to have grandparents living amongst their grandchildren. They say they love children, yet they embrace an obscene slogan like 24/7, implying the abdication of all family responsibility in favor of the workplace. Then they wonder why the average American father and mother spend so few hours a day with their children. When you add to that the propensity of our worldview empirically to compromise the very biological life-support system of the planet, you suddenly realize that we're many wondrous things, but the paragon of humanity's potential we most assuredly are not.

One of the obvious places in which our society has come up rather short is in our relationship to landscape. So when we turn our hungry eyes to indigenous people and try to understand what it is that they do that we don't do, or what is the essence of their relationship to the land, we often make two critical mistakes. We either invoke Rousseau and imply that somehow indigenous people are genetically closer to the earth than we can possibly be—which is an idea that is not only silly but almost racist in its simplicity, the noble savage canard—or we invoke Henry David Thoreau and imply that indigenous people must be, through their traditions, more self-consciously aware of their place on the planet then we are. Again, that's an idea that's flawed in the sense that it persists in examining the question through the Western lens.

Indigenous people are neither weakened by nostalgia, nor are they sentimental. There's not a lot of place for sentimentality or nostalgia in the fierce winds of Tibet or in the chilly ice of the high Arctic or the swamps of the Asmat. Indigenous people have nevertheless forged through time and ritual a traditional mystique of the earth that is based not on a self-conscious idea of being a part of it, and therefore close to it, but on a far more subtle intuition: the idea that the earth itself only exists because it is breathed into being by human consciousness. Now what do I mean by that, and what is the consequence?

A young kid in the mountains of Peru, for example, raised to believe that a mountain is the abode of an Apu spirit that will direct his or her destiny, will be a profoundly different human being than an American kid raised to believe that a mountain is a pile of rock ready to be mined. Now, is a mountain a pile of rock? Or is it the abode of a spirit? Who is to say? What is critical is how the belief system mediates the relationship of the human being to the natural resource. This is the key to understanding how different cultures interact.

Here's another way to look at cultural differences. I've brought several Penan to North America as part of an effort to raise awareness of their plight in the forests of Borneo, and it's been fascinating to take individuals who have virtually never been outside of the forest, drop them into a place like San Francisco, and see that nothing impresses them except the homeless people in the street. We, of course, are raised to think that a homeless person is either an individual who is lazy, or, alternatively, an unfortunate consequence of our economic system. But the Penan are raised to believe that a poor man shames us all, and they found it astonishing that in the midst of such bounty, we could indulge such poverty.

DS: In reading your work, and listening to you talk, my knee-jerk reaction is to think that land-based cultures are more humane, sane, and healthier than ours has become, which I know is inaccurate, even romantic and absurd. But one can't help but notice that out of all the diverse interpretations of our place in the grand web of life, our approach, our materialism, our obsession with technology, has led to dire ecosystem damage.

DAVIS: In no way am I flogging the West, my own tradition, but I think about what the anthropologist Margaret Mead said: As we drifted from a polychromatic world of diversity into a monochromatic world of monotony, as we drifted toward a blandly amorphous generic world culture, her greatest fear was not only that the overall imagination of the human species would be increasingly restricted to a single modality of thought, but that we would awake one day as from a dream, having forgotten that there were ever other possibilities. One of the things I try so hard to do in the book both in the photographs and the text is to celebrate these points of wonder. I find it all incredibly interesting.

When we hear that the last lion has been vanquished from the plains of the Serengeti, or there is no longer a giraffe, or there's no longer a mountain gorilla, we'll feel a loss. By the same token, how sad it is for all of humanity and for all of the earth itself to know that a belief system such as that of the Kogi of the Andes, so baroque in its eloquence and yet so passionate in its implications and so moving in its resonance, will be lost through a process of acculturation and assimilation.

What we're witnessing and experiencing to an increasing degree is the clash between the haves and the have-nots. We must understand that the worlds of the haves and the have-nots are going to keep coming together in the next century. That's why September 11 will rank as one of the seminal moments of this new era. If I had to name the key event of the twentieth-century, it would be the assassination of the Archduke Ferdinand in Sarajevo in 1914 because it precipitated the Great War, which killed the sense of optimism and progress that were the hallmarks of the Victorian age, and brought in the idea of the nihilism and the alienation and the existential angst of the twentieth century. Of course, it was followed by the Depression and Hitler and Mao and Stalin and the Second World War and the Cold War and so on. September 11 really ranks not only as the most successful act of asymmetrical warfare since the Trojan horse, but I think it will also be seen as the seminal moment when these two worlds came together. No longer can we live in isolation. CNN and the global media carries the disconnection between our affluence and the rank poverty of the majority of humanity to every corner of the world. The ultimate lesson is that there has to be a new global declaration of interdependence where we recognize that no longer can we live in our bounty isolated, immune from the forces of revenge, envy, and desire that will inevitably come at us from those who do not share in this bounty. We have to find a way to live in a pluralistic, multicultural world where the bounty of the planet is more equitably shared.

DS: You draw the big picture, going beyond politics and corporate greed to the very basics of human nature. Modernity went wrong partly out of materialism, and partly out of a detachment from nature, which is the first and best manifestation of diversity, of pluralism. An equalizer in so many ways.

DAVIS: The exciting thing is that I'm not suggesting in any way that indigenous people be frozen in the past, as some sort of zoological specimen. On the contrary, it's completely possible that all societies in all corners of the earth can benefit from the proper advances of the technological age, whether it's medical care or the Internet, without our having to imply the end of ethnicity—although one of the problems I have with the development model is that it never measures the quality of life itself. The earnings of a man in Lahore, Pakistan, who was once a farmer living a cash-free existence on land that had been in his family for generations, may go up, but what he spends that cash on may offer far less in terms of what he lost.

DS: It's an innate human urge to try to make things simple, to say this is good, this is bad, but of course life isn't like that. The model for this realization is nature, in which nothing is good or bad, but all is intricately connected.

DAVIS: Yes, and going back to the model of nature, diversity is not simply the foundation of stability as the ecologists have learned, but it is also in a deeper sense an article of faith, a fundamental indication of the way things were meant to be. Cultures, of course, have come and gone through time, just as species have come and gone, but in general, over the course of human affairs and over the course of the earth, both biological and cultural life have flourished and diversity has been the norm. Right now we're living through a time of an unprecedented collapse of biodiversity and clearly an unprecedented collapse of cultural diversity. What could be more lonely than to be the last of your people to speak your language? to have no way of passing along the wisdom of your elders? to have no child to listen to the knowledge you've achieved through life? Yet that dreadful fate is the fate of someone every two weeks, because every two weeks somewhere on the planet an elder carries a language to the grave. I think this is a profoundly disturbing trend in the affairs of human beings and something we really have to address. I'm not sure ultimately what we will do about it. I like to think that there are a great number of things we can do about it, but I also remember the adage of the writer Peter Matthiessen, who said anyone who thinks that he can change the world is both wrong and dangerous. At some level, the first step is simply to bear witness to the phenomenon and to try to explain, through books and films and all the various ways we try to communicate in the world, what is taking place.

I believe that politics never change anything, and that polemics are never persuasive, but that storytelling changes the world. What I'm trying to do is share these stories of the ethnosphere so that people will realize that this is really humanity's greatest legacy and something that we really must embrace and celebrate.

DS: You've been traveling the world and exploring the ethnosphere for over two decades. The drastic and negative changes you've seen are clearly delineated. Have you seen positive changes?

DAVIS: I tend to be extremely optimistic. We're always impatient with the pace of social change and would like it to move faster, but it is actually moving at a breakneck speed if you think about it in historical terms. Thirty years ago, getting people to stop throwing garbage out of the car window was considered a great victory. No one thought of the ozone layer and climate change. Or look at the attitude toward women and the different opportunities that were possible for your mother, for you, and for a girl growing up now. It's a sea change in attitude, as is our attitude toward homosexuality. It's amazing how fast human perspective and priorities shift. We've entered a whole new realm in the last forty years in terms of what is important and what challenges need to be addressed. This leaves me remarkably optimistic that we will come to terms with the wonder of who we are and find a way to live in a pluralistic world. 9/11 demands it. My fervent hope is that it will not be forgotten. There is a challenge before all of us, particularly for Americans, as wealthy and influential and powerful as we are, to really begin to address the fundamental inequities that have created these seas of humiliation and fountains of hatred.

DS: I appreciate your positive view. Knowledge of other ways of being, of other visions of reality, enables us to imagine and admire different lives and empathize with others. To alter our perception of reality is the work of artists and scientists.

DAVIS: On that note I'd like to remind us of another seminal moment: the vision of the first astronauts who traveled around the dark side of the moon and saw for the first time over the surface of the moon not a sunrise or a moonrise, but an earthrise. Suddenly you realized that instead of seeing the products of human ingenuity or the limitless horizon you see from Earth, you see this blue planet floating in the velvet void of space and there's the stunning realization of the interconnectedness of life, the isolation of this lonely planet. I think that moment will radiate through history as the time in which we really began to lift up our heads to look around and chart a new course for humanity.

Lee Gutkind

Lee Gutkind is the author of eleven exemplary works of creative nonfiction, including *Many Sleepless Nights: The World of Organ Transplantation, Stuck in Time: The Tragedy of Childhood Mental Illness, An Unspoken Art: Profiles of the Veterinary Life,* and the book under discussion here, a collection of personal essays titled *Forever Fat.* A tireless and innovative advocate for a genre that remains somewhat ill-defined and even controversial, Gutkind has written two books about the art of creative nonfiction and edited a number of innovative essay anthologies, among them *Surviving Crisis* and *The Essayist at Work.* A Pittsburgh native born in 1945 and a professor of English at the University of Pittsburgh, he created the first M.F.A. writing program for creative nonfiction and established the Mid-Atlantic Creative Nonfiction Summer Writers' Conference at Goucher College, which he directs. In addition to all the aforementioned endeavors, Gutkind founded and edits the pioneering literary journal *Creative Nonfiction,* which celebrates its tenth anniversary in a collection titled *In Fact: The Best of Creative Nonfiction.*

Gutkind has been both lauded and criticized for his zeal. James Wolcott anointed him the "Godfather" of creative nonfiction in a *Vanity Fair* article in which Wolcott attacked the legitimacy of the creative nonfiction genre, especially the memoir. Others have followed suit, but Gutkind, like a good martial arts practitioner, has turned his opponents' assaults back against them, arguing eloquently and steadfastly for the genre's validity and supporting the writers who give it increasingly vibrant, diverse, and lasting life. Gutkind travels around the world to talk about creative nonfiction. When he attended the annual Association of Writers and Writing Programs conference in Chicago in March 2004, Gutkind took time out to appear on *Open Books.*

DONNA SEAMAN: You're dedicated to a literary form called creative nonfiction. How do you define this genre?

LEE GUTKIND: Wherever I go, and I have been visiting many places because of my new book, that's the first question: What is creative nonfiction? I'll give you an answer, but let me say that I'm answering in protest because you wouldn't talk to a poet and say, "What's poetry?" Or ask a novelist, "What's fiction?" So why is it that wherever I go the first thing I have to do is tell you what it is I do? Art defines itself, it would seem to me.

DS: Yet readers, and writers, can't seem to get comfortable with the concept of creative nonfiction. Is that because it's a newer form than poetry and fiction?

GUTKIND: Creative nonfiction is in many respects new, although we can talk about *Walden* as a piece of creative nonfiction. We can talk about George Orwell's work as creative nonfiction, or James Baldwin's work in the 1940s and 1950s. What is new is the special spin on it. It is something we are beginning to focus on and to think about more than ever before. Here comes the definition: Creative nonfiction allows the nonfiction writer to use literary techniques usually used only by fiction writers, such as scene-setting, description, dialogue, action, suspense, plot. All those things that make terrific short stories and novels allow the nonfiction writer to tell true stories in the most cinematic and dramatic way possible. That's creative nonfiction. Because we are so involved in television, because real-life coverage is exploding all around us, creative nonfiction is becoming very popular—because it's hard to write a novel anymore that is as interesting as real life. The other reason is that we are more candid and honest with one another than ever before. Our secrets aren't just in the bedroom or in the psychiatrist's office. We're pretty open about how we feel, and that's part of the creative nonfiction movement, too—to say who you are and what you feel and who your enemies are right out loud in as subjective, and sometimes as nasty, a way as possible.

DS: Creative nonfiction comes in many forms, but the one that gets the most attention, the one people criticize the most vociferously, is the memoir. It has been condemned for being too personal, too whiny, too self-obsessed. It was the rise of the memoir that prompted the critic James Wolcott to dub you the Godfather of creative nonfiction.

GUTKIND: Wolcott says it's naval gazing. I'm not exactly sure what that means, but it is supposed to be bad. For Wolcott and for many others, it's bad that we're looking inside of ourselves.

DS: Others would say that it is healthy and that by writing about traumatic experiences, as many memoirists do, they are helping others. They are refusing to suffer in silence and shame. Do you feel that in writing about one's painful past, as you do in your book, *Forever Fat,* you're refusing to accept pain as something that should be kept secret? Does that motivate you to write about yourself and your family?

GUTKIND: I'm not exactly certain what the motivation was, because it's all so complicated. What people like to talk about are the victims of memoir. In this case, you might want to say that my father and mother and family are victims. Not that I've said terrible things about my parents, but in a very small way, growing up the way I did was painful to me. Now I have a son, and I've done a lot. I've published, I don't know, ten books or whatever it is. I have traveled around the country on my motorcycle, and I've been all over the world. So I have a life, and I feel very confident, and I'm not afraid to talk to anyone or do anything. I feel pretty brave and pretty confident. Yet why is it that the scars that were inflicted on me when I was seven and eight and twelve and thirteen are still torturing me? This isn't something you're shocked by, of course, because so many of us carry these things around for so long. You might examine it and say, "Oh well, my father was angry at me from time to time, and he would lock me in the basement as punishment." That wasn't a terrific thing. I didn't love it, but, okay, get over it. We're fine. My father and I speak. He's a fine grandfather to my son, Sam, but I still think about those days sitting in the dark and being all alone, and if it haunts me now, then that's something significant to discuss and to figure out. I think we all share this. What you want to be able to share with your readers is the way in which you survived, and the strengths that you have gained by confronting what haunts you and dealing with it so that it doesn't affect your entire life. And that's the incredible challenge of writing memoir, and the goal. It isn't just telling the sad story of neglect and abuse or whatever it is that happened to you. The real challenge is finding clarity in what happened to you and capturing and communicating the clarity to a larger audience.

DS: It's true that many of us carry scars from our childhoods, and it is interesting that we dwell on these traumas. I suspect that it has something to do with survival instincts. You were made to feel weak at some point, which is exactly what you don't want, so you're always trying to compensate for that, and learn from it in the hope of preventing its happening again. And you keep testing the wound, so to speak, to make sure that it's healing.

I also suspect that having gone through such pain can make you a more compassionate person, that is, if you're willing to look deeply into yourself and the people you've had to deal with to try to understand them and yourself. This can be an act of love, and this willingness to examine difficult matters opens both writer and reader to the life stories of others. When I read your essay about a young man, Daniel, who's suffering from mental illness, I think, "Gutkind suffered a tough boyhood, so he can look at a struggling kid like Daniel and feel empathy for him." Is giving voice to people like Daniel part of your mission as a writer?

GUTKIND: My mission as a human being with Daniel, and some other kids that I spent some time with, was to try to provide strength to them when they needed it, and a mature and cool head to help guide them through tough situations. I never had that kind of guidance. You wake up one morning and decide that doing what you're doing is fine, whatever your profession, but that you want to take it one step forward. You want to try to make sure that what you do makes an impact on other people. I think this is really important as a writer, and I think most writers must think about it. That's why we become writers, to affect other people and, in just the smallest but best way, change the world. We want to change something in the world that we think is wrong. We want to try to make it better or make it right—especially creative nonfiction writers, because we are men and women who believe in involvement. The spirit of creative nonfiction is immersing yourself in your life or in somebody else's life. Not necessarily taking part in that life, but to be involved deeply enough so that you can understand it in a three-dimensional way and, if the opportunity does arise, make your own special action-oriented impact.

It wasn't enough that I was just writing about the things that concerned me. Did I want to come into Daniel's life? Daniel was a kid who was sexually and physically abused by his parents and eventually taken away from his parents and put in a state psychiatric institution. He was eventually released to a shelter, which is where I met him. I looked for a kid who needed help and who I thought had some sort of a future, and now, twelve years later, I'm going to be the best man in Daniel's wedding. Everybody would have told you when Daniel was twelve and self-destructive and alone that he would never, ever survive to be twenty-one and get married. I wrote about Daniel twice. I wrote about him in *Stuck in Time*, and then I wrote about him in *Forever Fat*. If you want to say I used his life, you can say that. On the other hand, I became part of his life, and I think I've helped him. So this is the glory to me, the triumph of creative nonfiction—that you're a writer who lives it, not just writes about it. You become a more sensitive person, and you become more able to capture in words the excitement, the exhilaration, the challenge, and the tragedy of life.

DS: The reader becomes more sensitive and empathic, too, more open to worlds he or she might otherwise never engage with. Yet for all the revelations in memoir, clearly much is held back. In *Forever Fat*, for instance, I had the sense on every page that decisions had been made about what was said and unsaid. So I wonder, did you write in a great torrent, expressing everything on your mind, and then go back and edit and revise?

GUTKIND: Yes and no. That book took six years to write, and some of it was, in fact, written in great torment and with explosive emotions, and some of it came out very slowly, deliberately, and carefully. And I have to say that almost all of the prose that exploded onto the page has been removed and saved for the sequel.

DS: But I bet it felt really good to write it.

GUTKIND: Absolutely. When you're screaming and yelling and throwing things, literally, figuratively, or symbolically, you're incredibly emotional and you don't make a lot of sense, but it brings sense. It's like sitting and talking to a shrink. You talk to your shrink for three years, and you babble. Once a week for three years, you babble along, and you're not making any sense at all, and then one day clarity is exposed. That's all part of the wonderful writing experience. What did Hemingway say? You only see the absolute tip of the iceberg; down below is 90 percent of what he wrote. He said he wrote the last chapter of *Farewell to Arms* thirty-nine times. So that's what happened to me. I wrote lots and lots and lots of words, some of which I discarded, some of which I knew needed more clarity and more depth, so I did put it aside for another book. Writers do this; we save up.

DS: You used the word "clarity," and the word "clear," and those qualities are essential to all writing, but particularly to the essay. Essays are concentrates, and there's an incredible amount of energy packed into each page. That's the difference between writing in your journal and writing a memoir: the craft, the revision, the distillation. Personally, I find that part of the writing process to be the really exciting part. Writing the first draft can be so difficult, or so wildly out of control, you get lost. Once it's there, on the page, however, you can work with it, you can start creating patterns and order. You gain the necessary distance.

GUTKIND: I tell this to my students, and they shake their heads. But good writing is good thinking, and that's the challenge of being a writer. Writing is easy; it's the craft of writing that's difficult. That's why it took Joseph Heller twelve years to write *Catch-22*. It wasn't because he was a slow typist; it was because he had a lot to think about. Edmund Morris spent seventeen years on his biography of Theodore Roosevelt, which won the Pulitzer Prize.

The challenge in creative nonfiction is how deeply and clearly you think, and how you can communicate that thinking in your action-oriented words. And you need to always remember—and this is such a danger in memoir—to be as universal as possible. Your story, as fascinating at it may well be, will only be of interest to your neighbors, your friends, and your relatives, unless you can take that story and infuse in it a quality of universality that will connect to readers all across the United States and perhaps the world.

DS: And it takes real patience and discipline and dedication. In *Forever Fat*, you talk about when you were in the Coast Guard and how the military changed your life, how it infused in you a great belief in discipline and habit and routine. It makes me wonder if you feel that to be a good writer one has to be driven?

GUTKIND: I think to be a writer you don't have to be driven, or obsessed. But to be a really good writer, to be a good anything, you must have the drive and the obsession. I don't know why, but recently I began rereading things that I have written about people who impress me. I wrote a book about baseball umpires called *Best Seat in Baseball, But You Have to Stand,* which is back in print just recently, and I was really attracted to the obsession of these umpires to get the calls right. I also wrote a book about the motorcycle subculture, and those people who rode motorcycles all the time, especially the outlaws, the Hells Angels type, who were obsessed by the bike. I also wrote about the most amazing man I ever met, Thomas Starzl. He was both the hero and the villain of my book about organ transplants, *Many Sleepless Nights.* When everyone told him in 1972 that organ transplantation would never work, he didn't listen to them for a second. He was absolutely obsessed with doing it no matter how many people died under his knife, no matter how many families he hurt. He knew he could make it happen. And for better or for worse, thirty years later, it's happened. Peoples' lives are being saved and extended through organ transplantation because of his absolute obsession. Now I'm writing about robotics, and I've met some people in that world who refuse to listen to the word "no."

I tell my students about getting up, as I do, at 4:30 or 4:45 every single morning and addressing my keyboard and writing whether I like it or not, whether I was up to 2 A.M. the night before or not. I'm not promising you clarity at that moment, but I'm promising you regularity and the need to do this work. I mean, you do the work. That's what writers do, and they are obsessed by it. You do the work everyday; you do the work all the time; you do the work again and again until the work you do is the right work. And that's the writing life whether you like it or not. That's the serious writing life.

DS: And it's a good one. To be committed to something is both anchoring and liberating. It both simplifies and complicates your life. Speaking of which, I wanted to talk about the reactions of the people you write about to what you write about them, particularly family. Has your father read your essays about him?

GUTKIND: Yes, he has. You know, I was inspired by Czeslaw Milosz, who said—and I'm paraphrasing—that when a writer is born into a family, that family is finished. So let's begin there and move on.

DS: You know, I think you need to write a handbook, or a survival guide, for the families of writers.

GUTKIND: That is a fascinating idea. That's a riot. We'll have to talk about this.

DS: But we were talking about how, when a writer is born into a family, the family is doomed.

GUTKIND: My father, who's in his nineties, said a number of things to me after he read the book. He said, "Well, you have your story and I have mine." And that's so true. We do see the world quite differently. He was not affected at all, and that was good. And he didn't want to talk about it either, which I really was happy about. I didn't want to have to discuss what happened twenty-five years ago or fifty years ago. But I did hear from a lot of people whose lives I touched in one way or another, many of whom were very supportive, but many were also focusing on factual details. It's like, "Oh I got you. Back in 1912 this really didn't happen." As memoirists, you have to rely on your memory, and of course, we know memory isn't so reliable, but you have to have confidence in yourself. You don't make things up. This is not what a memoirist does. A memoirist tries to recreate from life the things he or she remembers as vividly as possible, to be as true as possible to the memory and to the experience.

I tell a story in *Forever Fat* about this suit I was wearing during my bar mitzvah and how I was punished by the rabbi for sweating all over the Torah. I tried to explain in this essay that it was because of this brown wool hothouse of a suit that my mother made me wear. I weighed almost 230 pounds, so my size was a 44 husky, and the suit was wool, and it was like a big tent over my whole body. I'm standing there on the podium with the cantor and the synagogue elders and the rabbi, and I'm leaning over the Torah, the sacred Torah, and I'm supposed to read, and the Rabbi is grabbing me. First he puts his hand on my shoulder as a friend, but then slowly but surely, he starts to squeeze my shoulder and my neck. It took me a long time to figure out what was going on. He kept staring at me until I realized that the sweat was coming down off my forehead and dropping onto the sacred parchment of the Torah. It was terrible. I realized, also, that I was fatter and bigger than anyone else on that little podium. They were four times my age, and I was double their size, and I couldn't move. It was a very traumatic experience. It sounds funny, but it wasn't at the time.

My mother read this essay, and she said, "You have a very fertile imagination. I would have never bought that brown wool suit for you. What kind of mother do you think I am? I would have never done that." And my father said, "She's right, Lee, we would never buy you that suit." Then I started getting e-mails from people saying that other details were wrong. A guy that I went to high school with, for instance, wrote to say that the rabbi didn't yet have a beard at my bar mitzvah.

So I was feeling bad that details in my memoir were wrong. Then I'm walking up the street and there walking down the street, out of the blue, is this guy named Allen Levy. I hadn't seen Allen Levy in thirty-five years. My grandparents were so poor that they had to share a two-bedroom apartment with the Levy family. My grandparents lived on the first floor, and in order for the Levys to get into their house, they had to walk through my grandparents' bedroom. The Levys lived on the second floor. In order for us, when we visited, to go to the bathroom, we had to go upstairs into the Levy apartment to go to the bathroom. Allen Levy saw me, and he said, "I just read your book, and I have something to tell you about that brown wool suit." And I thought, "Oh no, he's going to tell me how wrong this whole story was, the key story in the book." We sit down and we have a cup of coffee, and he said, "My parents were so poor, if you remember, that we had to share this apartment with your grandparents, and they couldn't afford to buy a suit for me for my bar mitzvah. So they went to your grandparents and asked if they could lend them some money for a suit for me. They said, "We don't have any money either, but guess what? We have Lee's old bar mitzvah suit. So I wore your bar mitzvah suit." And I said, "Allen, tell me, was it a brown wool hothouse of a suit?" He said, "Why are you asking? Of course it was." So I was right. I was absolutely right. Of course, I went back to my mom, and I said, "I just saw Allen Levy. Remember him? He wore my suit, and it was a brown wool suit." You know what she said? "He's crazy."

DS: What a great story. Memories are so subjective, although I suspect writers possess, or develop, a unique type of working memory.

GUTKIND: Great creative nonfiction and journalistically oriented people like Gay Talese, who has been my hero for years and years, certainly do train their minds. Gay Talese doesn't use tape recorders. He doesn't like to take notes in public because he feels the notes are going to intimidate the people he's hanging around with. So he keeps it all in his head, or if he has to take a quick note, he literally goes to the bathroom or turns his back. Then he relies on his memory when he goes back home or to his hotel or to his rental car, wherever he is, and puts it all down. So even the best of the best journalists, and there is nobody in the world as far as I'm concerned better than Gay Talese, don't have to take those notes every second. They remember. They rely on their memory, and usually it's right.

DS: This loops back to our conversation about clear thinking. A good memory is vital to that practice. This is another aspect of writing that I think is invaluable. It sharpens one's attention; it heightens one's awareness. The best creative nonfiction evinces an avid passion for detail. People sometimes criticize creative nonfiction as an accretion of littleness, too much detailed description, but I love that. That's the nature of life, and the attempt to capture that in writing makes storytelling vivid and compelling.

GUTKIND: Yes, a term I like to use is "intimate details"; that's what makes your prose real. It's the little things in life that you remember most vividly.

DS: Intimate is a good word. It takes a lot of chutzpah to write memoir. You reveal yourself, and you make yourself vulnerable.

GUTKIND: This is true. I had my attorney read part of this book. None of us want to be sued, and litigation is everywhere. So he read it, and he said there was probably nothing there that was going to get me in trouble with the law. But he said that he wouldn't be surprised if I was walking down the street one day and someone I wrote about would come up behind me ready to smash me on my skull. But so far I have been safe, and most everyone has been incredibly supportive. This is the thing that's been very surprising to me. This was my first really personal book, and I've been very surprised by how responsive my readers have been, even if they want to tell me that I got a fact wrong. There are so many readers who are thanking me for the honesty I shared, and that's a really great feeling. Not only are you writing well, but you're making a connection with real people.

DS: You've been such an advocate for the creative nonfiction form. You founded the first M.F.A. creative nonfiction writing program at the University of Pittsburgh, and you created the creative nonfiction conference held each year at Goucher College, and you founded and continue to edit the literary journal *Creative Nonfiction*. You've created a community around this genre. It's quite remarkable.

GUTKIND: Everyday I say I have to stop, but I evidently need to do all these things as well as write every day. *Creative Nonfiction*, which I not only started, but had to go out and raise money for because the university, which is a fine place, would not support it, is celebrating its tenth year. We're publishing a best-of collection titled *In Fact: The Best of Creative Nonfiction*. And there are now eighteen creative nonfiction programs that we know of in the United States, and creative nonfiction is exploding in Europe. I just came back from giving readings and talks about creative nonfiction in Switzerland and England and Ireland. In Australia two years ago I helped launch the creative nonfiction movement there, and now in two different places in Australia you can get a Ph.D. in creative nonfiction. And I know that a program is now starting in Israel. Creative nonfiction is becoming a worldwide language and community.

Alex Kotlowitz

Alex Kotlowitz was born in 1955 and grew up in New York City in a house full of books. He had no intention of following either his writer/editor father's footsteps or those of his social worker mother when he attended Wesleyan University in Connecticut, but he could not escape his love of literature or interest in other people's lives—especially individuals maligned and marginalized by society. So Kotlowitz became a journalist with a passion for urban affairs and volatile social conundrums. As a freelance writer, he wrote for *The MacNeil Lehrer NewsHour*, National Public Radio's *All Things Considered* and *Morning Edition*, and various magazines, until he became a staff writer at the *Wall Street Journal*, a position he held from 1984 to 1993.

Kotlowitz explains that he moved to Chicago in the mid-1980s "because as a journalist I thought it would be a good perch from which to peer into America's heart, but I didn't expect to find a home here. I expected to stay a year, maybe two. It's been twenty, and counting," and he has pursued his self-assigned mission to amplify the voices of Chicagoans who are not easily heard. This calling has led him to the Henry Horner Homes, a public housing complex, and Lafeyette and Pharoah Rivers and their mother, La-Joe, the subjects of his first book, *There Are No Children Here.* This probing and unforgettable portrait of a family, and inquiry into the consequences of poverty and racism became a bestseller and received numerous awards, including the Helen B. Bernstein Award for Excellence in Journalism, the Carl Sandburg Award, and a Christopher Award. *There Are No Children Here* was selected as one of the 150 most important books of the century by the New York Public Library, and in 1993 it was adapted for television as an ABC Movie-of-the-Week starring Oprah Winfrey.

Kotlowitz's second book, *The Other Side of the River,* is a chronicle of the conflict between two racially segregated Michigan towns, Benton Harbor and St. Joseph, and how it was exacerbated by the unexplained death of a black teenager in 1991. Once again, Kotlowitz performed the feat of immersion journalism, becoming a part of people's lives to try to understand the dynamics of race, the power of place, and the subjectivity of perceptions. *The Other Side of the River* received the *Chicago Tribune* Heartland Prize for Nonfiction and the Great Lakes Booksellers Award.

Kotlowitz's articles appear in the *New York Times Magazine,* the *New Yorker,* and the *Atlantic Monthly.* He contributes to National Public Radio's *This American Life* and to *Chicago Matters,* an annual series on Chicago Public Radio that consists of personal narratives on such subjects as home, love, and money. Kotlowitz is a writer-in-residence at Northwestern University and a visiting professor of American Studies at the University of Notre Dame. His journalism honors include the George Foster Peabody Award, the Robert F. Kennedy Journalism Award, the George Polk Award, and the Thurgood Marshall Award.

After such arduous efforts—Kotlowitz's first two books took over his life—it was time for a less harrowing and consuming project, and it's obvious from the first page of *Never a City So Real: A Walk in Chicago* that Kotlowitz is having fun. Yet he continues to tell the stories of people who have made their own way in a world that undervalues them. These slice-of-life essays not only portray Chicago but also shine a light on American society as a whole. Critically acclaimed and selected as one of the best books of the year by the *Chicago Tribune, Never a City So Real* brought Alex Kotlowitz to *Open Books* during the summer of 2004.

DONNA SEAMAN: *Never a City So Real* is basically a set of profiles of Chicagoans, including a man named Ed Sadlowski. I was quite amazed to read that you first ran into this steelworker from South Chicago at a union meeting in Connecticut in 1976. How did this come about?

ALEX KOTLOWITZ: I was a student at Wesleyan University, a small liberal arts college in Middletown, Connecticut, and I had gotten to know the head of the local machinists' union, a guy who probably taught me as much as some of my professors did, and got me very interested in labor. Ed Sadlowski was running for president of the International Steelworkers Union and touring the country. He was a real firebrand and a maverick, a smart, intellectual, working-class hero in a country that doesn't even believe it has classes. I heard he was going to be in Bridgeport, Connecticut, at a steelworkers' local. So myself and a few of my friends, all with our long hair, went down to the steelworkers' union hall and snuck into the back to hear this outspoken steelworker try to get the votes of the locals, and the incident has really stayed with me.

DS: At the time, had you already thought about being a journalist?

KOTLOWITZ: No, actually I had gone to school thinking that I was going to be a biologist. It was my love at the time. I wanted to be a zoologist, in fact, and had gone to this school because they had a fairly good biology department. Then two things happened. I took organic chemistry and realized I was not cut out for this, and I realized that I couldn't imagine spending the rest of my life in a laboratory. So I actually dropped out of school for a while and, this was fortuitous, ended up working at a settlement house on the south side of Atlanta, which at the time was the second poorest census tract in the country. I worked primarily with kids, and it was an experience that forever formed me.

DS: Were you a serious reader?

KOTLOWITZ: I was a great reader. My father is a writer. He is a novelist, and he was also an editor, and was managing *Harper's* back in the late 1960s under Willie Morris. So I grew up in a very literary household, and my mother was a social worker and anti-war activist. She used to drag my brother and me off to the anti-war rallies, so I think I got the best of both parents. And every wall in our house was just lined with books, and still is. My father still lives in the same house of books.

DS: When did it occur to you that you could tell other people's stories?

KOTLOWITZ: When I was at Wesleyan, myself and a group of friends and some people from town ended up starting a small community newspaper. I think we put out maybe three issues if we were lucky. But I was amazed at the kind of response we got. It was a pretty small, amateurish newspaper, but it made me realize the power of the printed word. In fact, I remember we were also threatened with a lawsuit. I mean, who were we? Why would anyone care what we had written? Then after I graduated from college, I went off to work at a cattle ranch for a year, which was kind of a boyhood dream.

DS: New Yorker heads west.

KOTLOWITZ: Right, urban cowboy. I loved it out there. I'd love to get out there again at some point. But after the cattle had been rounded up, I needed to find a job, and there was a classified in *Mother Jones* magazine for an associate editor at a small alternative newsweekly in Lansing, Michigan. I applied and flew out there and ended up taking a job at this paper. It was there that I realized that this was what I wanted to do with the rest of my life. I just loved it. I'm a fairly private person, so one of the things I loved about it was how it really pushed me out into the world in a way that I probably wouldn't go otherwise. And I love the artistry of putting together a story.

DS: Did you realize, too, that you were attracted to certain types of stories? Your work goes so far beyond what we think of as regular reporting; your involvement is so much deeper.

KOTLOWITZ: I don't think that was necessarily conscious. I think it's just where my own soul takes me. But one thing is, I tend to avoid crowds. I avoid where others are going, so in some ways, by the nature of that tendency, I find myself in communities and with people that other journalists probably are not spending a lot of time with.

DS: Like the projects in Chicago.

KOTLOWITZ: Right. I love the exhilaration of finding stories that haven't been publicly told before. There is nothing more difficult for me as a writer than telling stories that have already been told. For me the thrill of it is finding stories that have laid dormant for years, decades, sometimes longer.

DS: Your first book, *There Are No Children Here*, started out as a newspaper article, and you became very close to the family you wrote about, LaJoe Rivers and her children. Did that make you feel that there was more to say and that you needed to spend more time with them?

KOTLOWITZ: It did and it didn't. As you point out, I was working as a correspondent for the *Wall Street Journal* here in Chicago, and I spent a summer with Lafeyette, the elder of the two brothers, to write about the violence in his life. This was 1987, and it was written in diary form, and the story got more attention than anything else I had ever written, certainly as much attention as anything else the *Journal* had printed. I remember even the *New York Times* wrote an editorial about it, and Bill Bradley, then a senator, came out to visit the neighborhood. The response was pretty overwhelming. I was actually convinced that I had said all that needed to be said. I had an agent call me from New York, David Black, who has been my agent ever since. He insisted there was more to tell. We went back and forth. He finally convinced me that there was more to be told about this story and that having it in a book would give it a life that it wouldn't find otherwise, and he was right. He was absolutely right, so I ended up spending the next two years with the family.

DS: That's an intense way to work. This seems to exemplify the term "immersion journalism."

KOTLOWITZ: It was an intense experience. I was with that family and those boys just about every day over the course of a year and a half to two years. It took a lot out of me. I was single at the time. I have a family now, and to be honest I don't know that I could do something of quite that intensity again. You spend so much time with people in such an intimate way, unless you're inhuman, you build up relationships with them. It's inevitable. For me it's part of the thrill of what I do. People say, "That must really affect your objectivity. It must get in the way." First of all, I don't believe there is any such notion as objectivity. We all have our preconceptions. We come to the world from our specific places, and we have our own set of experiences, and I think the best we can ask of ourselves in my profession is to be willing to challenge ourselves at every bend and question those preconceptions. That was certainly the case working on *There Are No Children Here,* and I did build up very real relationships working on that book.

DS: I'm glad to hear you say that about objectivity. What makes the book so powerful is your personal commitment, your genuine engagement.

KOTLOWITZ: Yet I should point out that I'm not in the book. I'm in the introduction, but I made a very conscious decision not to include myself in that book, and the reason is I knew the minute I appeared in the narrative, it was going to become a story about my relationship with Lafeyette and Pharoah Rivers, and that's not what I wanted to write about. But you're right, I think there are probably other people who could have gone down to that neighborhood, and seen what I saw and heard what I heard, and come away with very different impressions.

DS: Your writing style is beautifully detailed, your observations both sensuous—you're terrific with body language—and keenly psychological. At times you vividly recount scenes that you yourself did not witness, and you tell us what your subjects are thinking.

KOTLOWITZ: I'm a big reader of fiction. I probably read more fiction than I do nonfiction, and of course, the best of fiction is filled with character. And it's filled with wonderful detail, so that you get to know people in a very intimate way. In good fiction, it's not all put in your face. Personalities begin to reveal themselves gradually over time, and I think a good work of nonfiction should do the same. And you do that with detail. You do that not by telling, but by showing.

DS: You also develop our vocabulary of place by bringing this public housing project, this hellish high-rise, to vivid life.

KOTLOWITZ: I think sense of place is so important, and I don't think enough writers pay attention to it. In all my books, especially my last, it's a given.

DS: Place becomes a character, too. You enable us to see how people are shaped by their environments, and how they feel about that. Naturally, that's key to your book about Chicago, *Never a City So Real*. To extend our discussion of your relationship with the people you write about, I was struck by something one of the Chicagoans you profile said. Robert Guinan—an artist whose inspiration, you write, "comes from the street, from the people who are seen but not heard," a painter whose gritty portraits are not appreciated in his hometown—tells you that he is completely dependent on the goodwill of his subjects and that he worries about taking advantage of them. When I read that, I thought, "This describes Alex Kotlowitz's situation, too."

KOTLOWITZ: I remember when Bob was talking about that. I thought, "Well, Bob, that describes exactly what I wrestle with all the time, that we're really servants to the goodwill of others." In fact, and Bob feels this very much, it's a privilege to be allowed into these people's lives. He goes in there for a day or two, maybe a little longer. Sometimes I go in for weeks, months, maybe even years. But Bob's work is extraordinary. He has for twenty-some-odd years now painted people in the taverns around Chicago, people who otherwise we would never see or hear from. They're beautiful oils. They are just exquisite. And Bob's work is adored in France. He's been exhibited in museums there. Mitterand owns one of his works. And yet he's virtually ignored in Chicago, his hometown and the city that gives him the material and the inspiration from which to paint. But I don't think Bob Guinan is a bitter man. In fact, when you talk to him, he will tell you he feels pretty fortunate that somebody likes his artwork regardless of the fact that they may be two thousand miles away.

DS: I hate to say this, but by being unknown here, Guinan does have a useful sort of privacy. He can work inconspicuously.

KOTLOWITZ: You're right, and he does like the anonymity here, the fact that he goes places to paint and people don't recognize him. But I hope that maybe as a result of this book he will get some attention. He's going on seventy, and he's a wonderful man. I just had a great time with him. It was one of the good things about working on this book, getting to know some of the people that I wrote about and being able to hang out with them.

DS: You wrote about another artist, Milton Reed, whom you call the Diego Rivera of the projects.

KOTLOWITZ: Milton Reed is a wonderful character. I met him a number of years ago when I was working on an article about the razing of public housing. I was touring a high-rise in the Stateway Gardens complex, and I went in to talk to a woman in one of the apartments, and there was this gentleman in his late forties painting a black panther, a gold-trimmed black panther, on the wall and drinking a bottle of beer. I was really intrigued by it, and I took his name and number and just kind of filed it away, and maybe two years later I tracked Milton down. It turns out that for the last ten to fifteen years Milton has been painting murals in public housing apartments. People pay him. And what's nice about it is he talks about the kinds of things that people request. Some of it mirrors the realities of public housing. He's had to paint gravestones of people who have been shot, portraits of people who have been killed. But the thing I love about his work is that he's also painted the imaginings of people. It turns out a lot of people have asked him to paint landscapes. So he's painted beautiful landscapes on people's walls. He's painted pictures of Jesus Christ.

My favorite story he tells in the book is about a woman who lived on the tenth floor of a high-rise. If you looked out the window of her living room, you could see the John Hancock building, the Sears Tower. You could see downtown. She asked him to paint downtown, the Loop, all lit up at night. He spent a week painting, so that when you walked into the apartment it looked as if there was no wall there, as if you were looking right through the wall. He asks how she likes it, and she says, "I got one more request," and he says, "Well, what's that?" And she asks him to paint a picture of her with her arm out the window, almost as if she were dancing. So he did. And then she said, "I just have one more request. I want you to paint my boyfriend upside-down with his feet up in the air." And he knew her boyfriend, so he painted her boyfriend and stood back and realized he had painted a picture of this woman pushing her boyfriend out the window. And as he says, he probably kept her from killing him.

DS: Talk about a cathartic image—. I was very touched by the need for beauty that induces other clients to ask Milton Reed to paint idyllic landscapes. You write that they would then have their pictures taken next to the mural, as though they had gone to that place.

KOTLOWITZ: He said to me at one point, "I'm giving people what they couldn't get otherwise." It was as simple as that. It was their respite to be able to walk into their living rooms and see a beautiful place.

DS: In another profile, you write about two women I recognized from *There Are No Children Here,* Mildred Wortham and Brenda Stephenson.

KOTLOWITZ: I met Millie and Brenda when I was working on my original piece for the *Wall Street Journal.* They lived at Rockwell Gardens, which was a neighboring housing complex just as tough and violent as the Henry Horner Homes. Actually, it was worse. It was one of the most, if not the most, violent neighborhood in the city. For years Brenda and Millie have worked at West Side Future, an organization that assists young mothers. They are basically professional busybodies. They go around and make sure everybody is okay and hand out toothbrushes. When I had my first child they loaded me down with gear. Every couple of months Brenda and Millie and I have lunch and gossip or, if one of us is having some dilemma, some problem we need help with, just to get together. We go to small restaurants on the West Side. So there is a chapter in the book about my friendship with Brenda and Millie, and about the different restaurants that we go to and the stories behind some of these restaurants. They are just terrific, terrific women.

DS: Each essay in the book is so rich, you cover so much history, so many traditions, such subtle aspects of a neighborhood. Each piece is an incredible distillation. It has to be difficult to achieve that fullness.

KOTLOWITZ: The hardest part about it was finding my way. This book is part of a travel series, Crown Journeys, and when Crown Publishing asked me if I was interested in participating, my eyes kind of lit up. I love to canoe up in the north woods and I thought maybe I could go up to the Upper Peninsula of Michigan and write about the U.P. But my agent said, "I think they want you to write about Chicago."

DS: No vacation for you.

KOTLOWITZ: No vacation. And as I was telling friends what I was working on, everybody would say, "You can't write about Chicago and not write about the city council. You can't write about the city and not write about the board of trade. So I spent a whole summer compiling a list of all the people and places that I felt obligated to include, and I realized there was no way I could do that. Then I came across a wonderful piece by Richard Wright, a beautiful essay about Chicago that he wrote in the 1940s, in which he talks about Chicago as the known city. This goes back some sixty years ago, and the city has been studied and considered over and over again. It made me realize that whatever I was going to write about Chicago, it was going to have to be the Chicago that I know, the Chicago that I love. So I ended up writing about people who I either have known in my twenty years here, or people like Eddie Sadlowski, who I wanted to meet, or Bob Guinan, and this was my excuse to spend time with them and to kind of look at the city from the ground up.

DS: Your book is wonderfully idiosyncratic; you use the word "skewed." And it's no chamber of commerce piece.

KOTLOWITZ: And it's probably not a Chicago that a lot of people know.

DS: That's what makes it a book of discovery for the reader. You also tap into Chicago literature. You've mentioned Richard Wright. I couldn't help but think about Studs Terkel.

KOTLOWITZ: I've known Studs for years, and I'm a big fan of his work, which has had a huge influence on me. I remember reading *Working* back in the early 1970s, and it stayed with me. His books have really taught me how to listen. Listening doesn't come easily. It doesn't come easily to me. It doesn't come easily to most of us, and his books really taught me that. At one point in an interview, he talks about how the lingo of everyday people can often be quite

ALEX KOTLOWITZ **403**

poetic and quite extraordinary, and he's absolutely right. So this is in some ways very much in the tradition of what Studs has done. I acknowledge him. I acknowledge his work and his friendship because it's had an enormous impact on me.

DS: You write in the book about how you grew up in New York and never intended to stay so long in Chicago.

KOTLOWITZ: I've stayed, right. The wonderful thing about New York is its vital literary scene, which you don't quite find here in Chicago. But having said that, I couldn't live in New York City. I know I would be looking over my shoulder every minute to see what everybody else was working on. Here I feel a kind of freshness in what I do, or at least I hope that there is a kind of freshness to it. What was nice for me about this book is that it made me fall back in love with the city.

DS: And it had to be a little more fun than your other two books.

KOTLOWITZ: It was a lot of fun. I hope it's equally fun to read, because I had a great time working on this.

DS: You really put yourself on the line, because you're writing about living people.

KOTLOWITZ: In the end when it's all said and done, I do worry what the critics are going to say. I worry about it finding readers. But what I worry about first and foremost is what the people I have written about will think about what I've written. So the first thing I do with a book like this is send it out to all the people I've written about, and then I anxiously await those phone calls.

DS: What changes have you seen in Chicago since you first started writing about public housing fifteen years ago? And what changes have you seen in terms of what is written about the city, and about race and affordable housing?

KOTLOWITZ: I think one thing has changed: There is much more exceptional journalism about our poor, about those pushed along the margins. There has been more of an effort by both newspaper and book writers to spend time with these individuals in their communities. Having said that, I think many of these communities are not dramatically different than they were fifteen years ago. If you were to go into Englewood, for example, you'd find very little has changed. What is changing in Chicago is a massive transformation of public housing. They are tearing down all eighty-three family high-rises in the city. I think that will forever change the landscape, not just here but across the country, as we're re-thinking how we take care of our poor. I'm not convinced yet that it's necessarily going to turn out for the best. So I do worry about that, and now—with all our attention rightfully geared towards the Middle East and towards our own public safety—there is even less time, effort, and money for these communities.

I still think journalists have a long way to go in covering these communities and covering them in any real, complete way. We're not there yet by any means. I was reminded of my second book, *The Other Side of the River,* which is about two towns in Michigan, the black community desperately poor. I write about an incident that happened in 1991, and last year, twelve years after that incident, there were riots in that community having everything to do with what I was writing about twelve years earlier.

DS: Investigative reporting and writing such as yours is urgently important, and not practiced courageously enough, although we're now experiencing an explosion of books that vehemently criticize the Bush presidency.

KOTLOWITZ: There is a lot of shouting going on at the moment, and I'm not big on shouting. There is a lot of political theatre going on, but I hope that the best political theater has the power to change minds. Ultimately, what has the power to change minds is story in which there's no apparent ideology. It's not that I don't have very strong politics, very strong feelings, obviously, about

what's going on and what's wrong. But for me, what's most important is to try to find readers who don't necessarily agree with me
and get them to read my stories.

DS: That's such a crucial point. To reach people who don't share
your perspective, you have to offer more than polemics; you have
to make art. You have to write stories that dig deeper, that reach to
feeling and universal understanding. This is awfully hard to accomplish when someone is on deadline. It takes time.

KOTLOWITZ: Right, and I have the time to do it. I'm an incredibly compulsive, obsessive writer, and I couldn't do what I do on
deadline. That's why I don't work at a newspaper anymore. The
other joy about writing books is that there's a life to them: they are
going to be around, they are not going anywhere, you hope. I've
been pretty fortunate in that regard. What's hard for me, especially
in these times, is to realize the urgency of what's taking place and
to so much want to find a way to contribute. That's why I write for
magazines and do some public radio work, because I do want to
find a way between the books to be able to contribute to that public discourse.

DS: You've worked on a radio documentary series called *Chicago
Matters.*

KOTLOWITZ: I've done two series, and I'm about to do a third
for Chicago Public Radio. It's an avocation. I've had such a good
time doing it, and I do it between my writing. They are very short
personal narratives, personal stories. The first year they were about
home, the second year about love, and this year they will be about
money. I work with a young producer, Amy Dorn, who is absolutely terrific. We go out and interview people, sometimes two or
three times, and then we piece together the story. Then I do the introduction. There are limitations to that, but I just love to hear the
wonderful stories, and all the varied voices. It takes time; the hardest thing is finding the stories. But in the end, once I've gotten
them all collected, it feels as though they have somehow captured

the heart and soul of this country. And they all take place in Chicago.

DS: They are very powerful, and you really seem to choose well, finding people who can express themselves compellingly.

KOTLOWITZ: Part of that is pushing them. Part of it is what Studs is so good at, which is listening.

DS: And you edit the conversations you've had?

KOTLOWITZ: Right. Sometimes the conversations are four or five hours long, and they get distilled into ten minutes.

DS: That parallels what happens in a book. I don't know if most readers realize that a book is the tip of the iceberg, the concentrated tip of a huge amount of research. You do a great deal of research, as well as your immersion work. You even include bibliographies in your books.

KOTLOWITZ: Right. Even for *Never a City So Real*, there are probably two or three stories that I had reported fully that didn't find their way into the book. I didn't feel in the end that they had a place. One story in particular I felt was too dark. Another story I felt had already been told. I may someday find a place for those stories. People, particularly young writers, don't realize how painstaking the actual writing is: it's from draft to draft to draft. I find it exhilarating at times, but you can be sweating blood as well. It takes a long time. Then, what I often will do even before I send it off to my publisher, is have a couple of friends read it to make sure I've really distilled the essence of what's there, so that there's no extra baggage.

DS: You also teach writing.

KOTLOWITZ: I'm a writer-in-residence at Northwestern University, so I'm there every quarter teaching writing, and I'm also a visiting professor at Notre Dame, where I teach a course on narrative nonfiction. I love my students, and one of the things I love about teaching is I've been doing it long enough to see many of them go on to write professionally.

DS: Reading and writing are so important for kids like Lafeyette and Pharoah, and that's why it distresses me that schools are as poor as they are. It is really important that kids be able to read and write and express themselves.

KOTLOWITZ: In the end, storytelling is one of the most potent agents for change. Good storytelling does two things: it can offer more experiences and makes us feel less alone, and it brings us into places and introduces us to people we might not otherwise meet—which is the cheapest way to travel. I think literacy is vital for both those reasons, for the ability to hear other people's stories as well as to tell your own.

DS: Do you feel then that you've helped the people you worked with in your books, that you've given them a voice, that you have, in a public way, validated their experiences?

KOTLOWITZ: Yes. One of the most rewarding things about writing about people who otherwise would not be in the public eye is that it gives some affirmation to who they are and to their experiences, a sense that they are not alone, a sense that their lives have been worth something. And I think it gives them a sense of recognition for what they've accomplished in their lives.

DS: In *The Other Side of the River*, you write with great sensitivity about the elusiveness of facts and truth, of the distortion of memory.

KOTLOWITZ: As a nonfiction writer you want everything to be factually accurate. John McPhee refers to it as "the literature of fact," and that's exactly what it is. It's literature based on fact. But the truth itself can also be elusive. People can perceive things differently. We know from our criminal justice system how much eye-witness accounts can vary. My second book deals with that notion about myth and reality. We can come to the world with such a different set of personal and collective experiences. As a result, we see things differently, and because mine is a book about race, it's about how blacks and whites come to the world with very different perceptions of reality.

We all have myths. We not only have myths about each other, but we also have myths we build up about ourselves. So a part of what you're doing when you're telling stories is trying to decon-struct those myths and demystify them, if you will, and in some way get to the truth because it's not all relative. There are facts out there. There are things that are impenetrable in their truth, so we have to recognize and acknowledge that.

Phillip Lopate

Phillip Lopate was born in 1943 in Brooklyn, which continues to be his home base. Lopate earned his undergraduate degree at Columbia University and his doctorate from Union Graduate School. His twelve years' work with children as a writer-in-the-schools was the subject of the memoir, *Begin With Children,* and he has taught creative writing and literature at Fordham University, Cooper Union, University of Houston, and New York University. Currently, Lopate holds the John Cranford Adams Chair at Hofstra University and teaches in the M.F.A. graduate programs at Columbia, the New School, and Bennington. Lopate is the author of two novels and two poetry collections. He also writes architectural and movie criticism, the latter collected in *Totally Tenderly Tragically.* He is best known as an essayist. His frank and nervy autobiographical essays charting his life from boyhood to the present run the gamut from confessional to hilarious to elegiac to piquant to curmudgeonly, and he is a master at combining personal reflections with cultural observations and artistic and literary critiques. Over the years, Lopate's vivid essays have been gathered into various collections, including *Bachelorhood, Against Joie de Vivre, Portrait of My Body,* and a Phillip Lopate reader, *Getting Personal: Selected Writings.*

Lopate is also an inspired and expert anthologist. He established himself as an authoritative advocate for the essay in what has become a standard in literary collections, *The Art of the Personal Essay: An Anthology from the Classical Era to the Present.* He evinced his love for the city he knows so well and for its writers in the acclaimed *Writing New York: A Literary Anthology.* Lopate then combined his knowledge of New York culture, architecture, and literature with the more visceral understandings he has acquired as an avid walker and city explorer in *Waterfront: A Journey Around Manhattan.* Here his intrepid ramblings along Manhattan's waterfront serve as a conduit to a rich and thought-provoking history of the once bustling world-class port, now shabby and neglected. Witty and penetrating, as concerned with social, political, and environmental issues as with aesthetics, *Waterfront* is a dynamic synthesis, and a vital work of creative nonfiction.

Lopate continued his inquiry into the history of maritime New York in *Seaport: New York's Vanished Waterfront,* a collection of historical photographs, most taken by Edwin Levick between 1900 and 1929. Lopate then embarked on another journey through the annals of the city and deepened his study of the romance between photographers and New York in a stunning monograph on the life and work of Rudy Burckhardt, whose velvet-rich black-and-white street photographs stand as elegant icons of mid-twentieth century New York.

Lopate has been awarded a Guggenheim Fellowship, a New York Public Library Center for Scholars and Writers Fellowship, and grants from the National Endowment for the Arts and the New York Foundation for the Arts. His essays, fiction, poetry, and film and architectural criticism have appeared in the *New York Times, Harper's,* and *Esquire.* Phillip Lopate appeared on *Open Books* in March 2004.

DONNA SEAMAN: When I recently reread the introduction to *The Art of the Personal Essay,* I was struck by your observation that the hallmark of the personal essay is intimacy and that "the struggle for honesty is central to the ethos of the personal essay." I like the word "struggle," because it's tough to be honest and accurate when writing about memories, isn't it?

PHILLIP LOPATE: Yes, and I think you shouldn't claim you've gotten to the truth. You should try to get to levels of honesty, but as soon as you begin to write about yourself, for instance, or your memories, your work is ripe for defensiveness, rationalization, subjectivity, and all those inevitable blind spots. So rather than say, I'm going to avoid all that, I like the game of rationalization, then piercing that and trying to get to a deeper truth.

DS: What is the appeal of personal essays and memoirs? Why should readers care, for instance, about a writer's childhood?

LOPATE: To read a personal essay is to be in a conversation with somebody whose mind and feelings you've come to care about, so that when you fall in love with a personal essayist's work it doesn't matter if they are writing an essay about toothpaste or about the decimation of the planet. Either way, you're going to want to engage with them sentence by sentence. The French essayist Montaigne, who started the essay form, is my god. With some writers, you don't want to follow their stream of consciousness, but Montaigne has such a well-stocked mind that you're happy to be in his company. So the question isn't "Why do I want to hear about a writer's childhood?" but rather "What is he or she going to make of their past? What are they going to make of their other experiences?" There's what happened, and then there's what the writer makes of it.

DS: In thinking a bit more about your use of the word struggle, I feel that in the best essays writers haven't figured out beforehand what they will make of their experiences or observations.

LOPATE: Exactly. And the writing is going to surprise the writer as much as anybody else. It's wonderful when you get to a passage where the writer is discovering something for the first time, because the rhythm changes and the prose takes off in a way—so it's not about being self-convinced. That's why doubt is so important to the personal essay, because doubt and self-doubt allow you to explore some question to which you don't have the answers, so you just take it as far as you can; you surround it in a way.

DS: That's what makes it exciting to read, and that's the source of the intimacy you speak of.

LOPATE: It's exciting because of the intimacy. The tone I always look for in other writers is one that makes me feel as though the writer was almost whispering in my ear, talking in that three-o'clock-in-the-morning way. Not delivering a speech, not on a high horse, but, instead, leveling with me—in the way, let's say, that when you have a conversation with one of your best friends, you don't get to the good stuff immediately. You have to work through the built-up patina of defensiveness, or armor, that you need to get through the day until eventually you tell it like it is.

DS: Wit is also an invaluable element in essays.

LOPATE: I certainly feel that when I write something it needs to amuse me on some level. After you write something, you have to read and reread it over and over again, so if it's solemn I quickly get bored. But if it can bring a smile to my face once, it will probably bring a smile to my face on the tenth time or the twentieth time. One of the reasons that I'm drawn to being mischievous on the page is because that entails wit, humor, a contradictory, contrarian sense of doing not what the reader expects. The reader is expecting piety, and I'm giving them something else. This is the humor that W. C. Fields perfected with his remarks about children and dogs and Philadelphia. When I write, I try to look at whatever I'm writing about from a fresh point of view and not necessarily go into what's expected. Humor and wit are very important to me. I love the idea of the epigram as being the dessert of prose, when you finally make a succinct formulation of what you think. But you can't do it every sentence because then it would be too whip-creamy, and too rich.

DS: The interesting thing about writing about your life, writing memoirs and personal essays, is that really you are writing about other people. You write about relationships. Do you have qualms about that? Do you worry about betraying privacy? Do you edit yourself very carefully in some way to preserve relationships?

LOPATE: To protect the guilty? This is a much-vexed subject, and I can't be a lawgiver. I can only say it's different for each writer, and in my case I do feel that the materials of my life belong to me, and inevitably some of that's going to involve other people. I try to write with enough detachment or attempted objectivity so that I'm not writing with an ax to grind. I'm trying to be at least minimally fair. I'm not writing for revenge. But having said that, when you write about another person in order to bring that person alive you have to balance positives and negatives. You can't just write a gushy eulogy, because people aren't perfect. It seems to me, I'm paying people a great compliment by trying to look at them and see how their strengths and their weakness are intertwined. I feel the same about myself. I have certainly annoyed some people by writing about them, and I think my recommendation is that, if you want to be a personal essayist or memoirist, get a lot of friends because you're going to lose some along the way. The problem is with family members: you can't keep multiplying your family members.

DS: It makes it very stressful, yes, but it really is your life. It's your story, and this is your version of your life and your story.

LOPATE: And they're entitled to write their versions. Ultimately, what I'm trying to do is to create a successful piece of writing, something that will work on the page. There's a certain point when the piece itself takes on an independent existence and you're trying to serve it, to shape it, so that it will be dramatically or emotionally most interesting. You're never going to get the exact report even of your own mind because at every moment at least three thoughts are going through your head. You're thinking you're hungry and when are you going to eat next, and you're thinking about this highly intellectual thing because you're having a conversation with somebody who you respect, and then your nose itches, or your eyebrow or something, so you're always editing things out.

DS: I think that you bring balance to your work in the way you write about yourself, because you're critical of yourself, and you're amused with yourself.

LOPATE: I think that's so important because, as a teacher of these forms, I can see that a lot of talented student writers get stopped because they are not amused by themselves. They're very down on themselves; they don't approve of themselves. It's like the old joke, "'I'm a nobody.' 'Who are you to think you're a nobody?'" So, who are you to think that you should be perfect? I have a slightly detached view towards myself, and I sometimes think of it the way Charlie Chaplin or Buster Keaton created the Little Tramp or Buster. These personae are clearly connected to them, but not exactly themselves. So it isn't that the Phillip Lopate I write about is not me; it's that it's not entirely me. When people criticize me or things that I've done, I'm almost never shocked. I never think, "Oh, you're wrong. I would never do that." It's, "Yeah, that's me too." We're all filled with subterranean urges, as our therapists tell us. So who knows? At moments, an odd hostility may leak out or clumsiness or maladroitness or the wrong words will come out of your mouth. I think if you know yourself well enough you'll come to accept that as part of you.

DS: That's what we want to read about, that quirkiness, the obdurate mystery of our own selves, which makes it so difficult to understand anyone else.

LOPATE: Frank O'Hara referred to it as a catastrophe of one's own personality. We each have our own personal catastrophe, the way we are put together. And to return to Montaigne, he really wanted people to become more accepting of themselves. That was ultimately the conclusion he came to. He didn't like zealots who expected perfection or sainthood; he wanted people to become friends with their minds and friends with themselves.

DS: That wisdom is part of Buddhism, too, the precept to love one's self, a teaching people often misinterpret as somehow selfish.

LOPATE: It's not narcissism; it's the opposite of narcissism, because in order to begin to look at yourself you already have to have some detachment. Narcissism is a kind of myopia where there's a blur around you so that you can't see other people because you're in your own fog. And narcissism isn't the same thing as vanity. There are people who are very vain, but also very objective. They know which colors flatter them, they know which is their right side and their wrong side if they are going to be photographed, they want to present themselves well, but that doesn't mean that they are in a blur.

DS: You really can't be a writer without being curious about yourself, and how your mind works, which, in turn, makes you curious about other people and how their minds work.

LOPATE: I really feel that I'm at least as interested in, if not more interested in, other people than in myself. When I write, I use the Phillip Lopate character to go out and fetch back the world. He's like a dog that I send to bring back my slippers. He goes out there, and he interfaces with the world, and because of his own set of bumbling characteristics he draws people to him. It's not too different from the way Joan Didion used her shyness as an attribute in her early essays in *Slouching Towards Bethlehem.* So in writing *Waterfront: A Journey Around Manhattan,* I wasn't entirely abandoning the personal essay. I was still making myself into a character who walks, but I was also engaging with a much larger world. For me, the proportions change, and *Waterfront* is more about the world than it is about myself.

DS: *Waterfront* is personal, in part, because anyone who has read your essays knows that you're a New Yorker who loves the city. Also because the connection between walking and writing is wonderfully organic, and has engendered an intimate tradition that you call "walking around literature," in which the self interacts with place.

LOPATE: Absolutely. The essay is a kind of walk, and a meditation. You're walking around in your mind, not sure what you're looking for, but your eyes are open. And there is actually another kind of connection between the physiological act of walking and writing. Apollinaire, the French poet, used to walk around, and look around, with a tune in his head, and then he would write his poems to that tune, so there's the rhythm of your feet, and there is something in the back of your mind that's trying to put words to it. Gertrude Stein described writing the long sentences in *The Making of Americans* as walking down the steps from the Sacré-Coeur in Paris. By the time she got to the end of the steps she had a sentence. So yes, in the middle of *Waterfront* I take a breather and talk about this tradition of the aesthetics of walking around, which is a kind of meta-perception—asking what is it that's going on here. In a way, I'm asking the reader to be more self-conscious about what this animal is.

DS: Contrary to the impression that every square inch of Manhattan is claimed and developed, your walk along the island's waterfront reveals that it's neglected and shabby.

LOPATE: It's very patchy. Some parts are developed, some parts are completely neglected, and some parts are just wild. They are like a jungle with high weeds. There are historical reasons for this. A lot of the waterfront was given to maritime and industrial functions, so they built the piers there, and they put factories and power plants there. As a result, the waterfront gained a reputation of being seedy, malodorous, and raffish, filled with taverns and brothels. It was a kind of city within a city for transients, you might say. It wasn't that it slipped the minds of New Yorkers and they forgot to develop the waterfront; it was that something else was there and that "something else" was the enormous economic engine that was driving the whole area, the Port of New York. When containerization came in the 1960s and 1970s, the port was moved to New Jersey, and suddenly there was a kind of empty-harbor syndrome, which fascinates me.

DS: Was writing *Waterfront* an idea that came to you, or was it suggested to you?

LOPATE: I had wanted to write a big New York book for a long time, and I couldn't figure out the angle or the premise or the theory. Then an editor came to me and said, "Why don't you write a little book about walking around the edge of Manhattan?" We didn't even think about it then as the waterfront. We just thought it was one way to get around Manhattan. As I started walking, I saw that there was this strange phenomenon of the patchwork, the erratic; everything that the city didn't want to deal with was shoved to the edges. The strange combination of presence and absence was haunting. It wasn't like Broadway, where everybody is rushing by you. Chicago has it's wonderful Burnham Plan for the lakefront, so a lot of the destiny of Chicago is tied up with that plan just as a lot of the destiny of New York is tied up with the grid plan—and Central Park. When Central Park was built, all the swells and all the people from the high social class gravitated to the middle of the island, not to the edges. They left the edges alone. Another very important thing that people don't always think about, is that there tends to be no mass transit out to the edges of the waterfront. Mass transit is so important to New York. If you don't have trains or buses going to the edges, then in order to go there you have to make a very intentional move. You have to say, "I'm going to explore that." It tended to be the more lonely, geeky sorts seeking solitude who walked there, people who are running away from the law, or poets.

DS: So when you starting walking, you realized that this would not be a "little," impressionistic book.

LOPATE: Right, I started walking and I realized that I needed to know things. If I had been in my twenties, I could just have had the kind of lyrical gush that possesses young poets, and written tons of stuff. But I had already written a lot of poems, stories, and essays which came out of that sort of impulse. Here I really needed to learn things and to figure out what was there, what could have been there, and what is going to be there, and I hit the books. I did a ton of research, and there's a part of me that's a wanna-be scholar who wants to really be buried in research. I think it's a natural movement for the personal essayist, or the memoirist, to enrich his material by moving outward. You can still keep the autobiographical persona, but you have to expand somewhere. You can't keep going over and over how your mother didn't love you enough, or your mother loved you too much. You have to connect to something larger.

DS: I'm an avid reader of what's called, for lack of a better term, creative nonfiction because it's driven by a writer's curiosity, whatever its topic or its genesis. The scholarship in *Waterfront* is phenomenal, as is your engagement with a vast amount of material covering matters social, political, economic, criminal, literary, and environmental. We read about Walt Whitman and the shipworms that are devouring the wooden piers.

LOPATE: Yes, the science, ecology and marine biology—I spent a month researching shipworms. They became a kind of metaphor, I suppose, but they really did fascinate me. When the rivers were cleaned up around New York, the shipworms came back and started eating away at all the understructure. They did billions of dollars worth of damage. I wrote a chapter about them that is a little bit tongue-in-cheek, mock-learned, you might say, slightly parodying the tone of the science writer and the scholar. This book allowed me to create lots of different tones. In effect, what I did was to write a kind of one-man anthology of essay writing that would have different techniques. So there are pieces that are highly journalistic in which I do a lot of interviewing, and there are pieces that are like lyrical meditations, and there are rants, and there are mock-learned passages, and there are autobiographical vignettes, and there's some literary criticism. I have a whole chapter in which I analyze Joseph Mitchell. Walt Whitman and Melville and some more obscure writers get into it. It really gave me the opportunity to try a lot of different essay modes and essay techniques. This kept me engaged on the technical level when I was trying to figure out how in the heck was I going to work with this material, because the biggest obstacle I faced was that I had all of this factual material I had to assimilate and boil down for the reader, and I had to impose a sense of literary style on it. I would read a sentence like "To build the Brooklyn Bridge they sunk shafts that went down 1,243 feet," and my eyes would glaze over, and I would think, "How can I make this interesting?" There were lots of sentences like that. I ended up learning a bit about engineering and actually coming to admire engineers much, much more. But I had to do things to the sentences to tweak them, to give them little ironic spins so that the reader could feel my presence, to enliven the prose somewhat.

DS: Your ecological point of view is important, reminding us that nature isn't only found in wilderness. Nature is present in the city. You mention a book by Anne Matthews, who is one of a handful of people writing about urban nature. You've now joined the group. You also reveal how much there is to discover in a city, even one you've explored your whole life.

LOPATE: A big city really is infinite. It doesn't matter if you live in it all your life, there are always going to be parts that you don't know about, that you haven't explored. That was a great challenge and excitement for me.

DS: Your excitement is palpable. And what adventures you have: you go inside the Brooklyn Bridge.

LOPATE: Yes, I crawled inside the Manhattan side, the anchorage, which I didn't even know you could get into. I kind of belly flopped into it, and it was very dark at first. It had been intended as a site for workshops and a place to store things, and it had been rented out until about the 1960s, after which it was forgotten. I love the idea of urban archeology and finding the layers of what was there before. I think that prose is something like that. You have the assertion, and then you have, syntactically, the counter-assertion, which is a way of breathing life, or breathing a kind of syncopation, into the prose. That's what I'm always trying to do, and I'm not always successful by any means. But there are moments, passages, where I'm able to get a sense of something which is both serious and ironic at the same time. A friend of mine, and a wonderful poet, Vijay Seshadri, was the first reader of the book, and I think he understood it very well. He said, "Phillip, this book is about your consciousness." And it is about my consciousness, even though it's not a memoir or autobiography per se. Of course, there is a narcissistic element, which is that I identify very strongly with New York City. But let me also say this: I am a lover of cities. I don't just love New York; I love Chicago, Los Angeles, Pittsburgh. Some of my favorite cities are Buenos Aires and Istanbul. Whenever possible I would take a look at other cities, and I realized that the dilemmas New York was facing in terms of what to do with its waterfront, with how to remake its waterfront, were being faced all around the world because ports were being detached from cities, and the age-old connection between city and port was breaking down. All around the world, the same kinds of solutions were being proposed, the same sterile and boring solutions. Talk about globalization.

DS: Did you surprise yourself by becoming so interested in civic affairs, and urban design issues? New York politics and policies?

LOPATE: It's scary, because one of the things that I could trust as a personal essayist was that I could say, "I understand my own experience even if I don't understand these other things." But this was my first political book, if you will, the first book in which I was taking sides, and stating opinions, and it was frightening. The odd thing is that the writers of my generation, the generation of the 1960s who got all involved in anti-war protests and civil rights protests, didn't become public intellectuals. Instead, most shrank into a more private discourse. It's as though when we were in our early twenties we were so saturated with shrill discourse that we mistrusted it, and so we mistrusted taking stands on things that we didn't entirely understand. I particularly felt mistrustful of the tendency to give people marching orders, to tell people what to think.

So in this book, I examine what I actually thought about certain things, not what my peer group was telling me to think about them, and not what a good liberal New Yorker was supposed to think.

I came to the conclusion, for instance, that I'm not as anti-development as I thought I was. I realized, what is any great city except a development? How can you say "no more"? The question is "Can we do the right kind of development?" Not the statement, "We must not build anymore." What fascinated me is the question of how we can continue to make cities. How can we add urban texture that's vital and that has a good feeling on the street?

DS: Jane Jacobs has written seminal books on this very question.

LOPATE: I consider myself a child of Jane Jacobs, one of her followers. But I've had to rethink my position toward Jane Jacobs because I realized that, while her aesthetic of city life is right-on, her hostility to city planning means that we can never look at the problems regionally, and some problems can only be solved in a regional manner. Not everything that's good for the city is good for the neighborhood. Sometimes you have to do things that are for a larger good. Even large projects like Central Park or the Brooklyn Bridge or the water delivery system required a consensus on the part of many groups and governing bodies. New York has become a place where it's far easier to shoot down something than to let something happen. I felt that one of the bad influences of Jane Jacobs is that she analyzed the defects of planning, but she didn't propose anything in its place that could deal with things that were larger than the street.

DS: You have a clearly articulated ecological view of city life, which is crucial, and has been lacking in both traditional nature writing and in urban writing.

LOPATE: One of the conclusions I came to is I like density. I think density makes good ecological sense. There used to be a prejudice that cities were too dense and we need to decentralize them as much as possible. In fact, people's response against density is usually against a density of poor people. Park Avenue, which is a very expensive neighborhood, is one of the densest places on earth, but nobody says it's too dense. I think what we really need to have happen is for the urbanists and the ecological people to make common cause and promote greater density in the cities and fight against suburban sprawl, which takes over all acres of woods and farmland and which pollutes the water table thanks to chemical run-off. Cities can be ecologically sound, and I'm much more for that kind of solution.

DS: The percentage of people living in cities around the world is now enormous. We are an urban species, but here in America we still like to picture ourselves out on the frontier.

LOPATE: Yes, our national ethos is so rural, so tied to the ranch idea. Americans have never been at ease with the notion of city life.

DS: The attitude seems to be that cities are dirty and dangerous: foreigners and people of color live there.

LOPATE: The immigrants and people of color, and the sense that somehow the native white Anglo stock was being watered down. My grandparents were some of those immigrants, yet I walked down the hall of my family's apartment wearing David Crockett chaps. We wanted to be cowboys and cowgirls, but ultimately it wasn't going to work. I think it's interesting that there's no cabinet post for urban affairs. There's no real urban policy, and I don't just blame the Republicans. Bill Clinton, when he was trying to get elected, never used the word "cities" in any speeches because it was considered a turnoff. There has to be some way of addressing the needs of cities on the federal level.

DS: Cities are so complex, they lend themselves more to the discerning eyes and ears of novelists, poets, and essayists, lovers of ambiguity and lushness, than to political folks dedicated to simplifying life into yes-or-no issues.

LOPATE: When I came to the conclusion that I did not have a large theory, I realized that maybe a mosaic approach was necessary. I had to write this book incrementally, and oddly enough I came to the realization that the genius of New York's development was incremental. That is, it happened with one building after another instead of the construction of large zones like Park City. So my method was essentially one foot after the other. And I can tell you that when I wrote this book there were moments of great fear and trembling when I really did not know whether this stuff was going to hold together. I mean, what was holding it together? I tried to will it together by my personality and the sentences, but I didn't know if that would be enough. So I thought, "What is this thing? I'm putting everything into this book." Everything but the kitchen sink, and then I put the kitchen sink in. To me, it became a maximalist book like *Tristram Shandy* or something where people stick in a lot of stuff.

DS: What better way to approach a city? It is a maximal experience, itself, made up of countless people and all the things people do.

LOPATE: I kept writing and writing, and the first draft had a hundred pages more than the final version.

DS: As a finished book, *Waterfront* is exceptionally well made and beautiful.

LOPATE: That means a lot to me. Books are beautiful physical objects, and that's why I think they are never going to be replaced by the Internet. You want to be able to hold a book in your hand, not just cuddle with a laptop.

Sy Montgomery

Nature writer Sy Montgomery has traveled to wilderness regions all around the world, roaming far from her childhood terrain in Brooklyn and New Jersey. Born in 1958, Montgomery attended Syracuse University, where she pursued a triple major in magazine journalism, psychology, and French language and literature. She has written about nature and conservation in "Nature's Journal," her popular column for the *Boston Globe,* and her essays have been collected in several books, including *The Wild Out Your Window.* Montgomery is heard frequently on National Public Radio as a guest on *Living on Earth,* and her work is featured in a number of anthologies.

Described as "part Indiana Jones and part Emily Dickinson" by the *Boston Globe,* Montgomery truly has gone on hair-raising adventures in her quest to learn about elusive, even mythic animals. She has been stalked by a tiger in India, bitten by a vampire bat in Costa Rica, chased by a silverback gorilla in Zaire, and undressed by an orangutan in Borneo. She writes with the lyricism and insight of a poet, as well as the knowledge and reasoning of a scientist.

In *Spell of the Tiger,* she chronicles her journey to Sundarbans in Bengal, India, the world's largest tidal delta and mangrove swamp, a mysterious, amphibious realm where tigers hunt humans. As Montgomery ponders the mix of fear and reverence the people feel for their predators, she realizes that there is no revelation more basic than what the tigers of Sundarbans teach: that we, like every other animal, are meat. She investigates another profound connection between animals and people in *Journey of the Pink Dolphins,* an account of her often baffling attempts to study the freshwater pink dolphin, also known as the botos. Long the subject of myth and nearly unknown to science, the botos are believed by the people of the Amazon to be shape-shifters who fall in love with and seduce humans. As Montgomery unravels a mesh of myth, history, and biology, she arrives at a startling explanation for the botos' intriguing reputation.

The next major quest Montgomery undertook carried her to Southeast Asia. As the book's title, *Search for the Golden Moon Bear,* explains, she and her traveling partner, evolutionary biologist Gary Galbreath, set out to look for the rarely seen golden moon bear to determine if it is, in fact, a new species or subspecies. Rather than traverse pristine wilderness, however, the searchers found themselves visiting captive bears and confronting the horrors of the illegal wildlife trade and the grave suffering of endangered hill tribes. Montgomery's reportage, scientific explanations, spiritual interpretations, cultural analysis, and humor combine to form a tale of adventure, discovery, and compassion. *Search for the Golden Moon Bear* was one of *Booklist's* Top Ten Science Books and a *Booklist* Editors' Choice title for 2002.

Montgomery's commitment to raising awareness about science, nature, endangered animals, and conservation has inspired her to write books for children, which have been received with delight and acclaim. *The Snake Scientist* won a number of awards, including the International Reading Association Prize. *The Man-Eating Tigers of Sundarbans* was a *Booklist* Editors' Choice title and was featured on the *Today Show. Encantado: Pink Dolphin of the Amazon* was selected for outstanding book lists by the National Science Teachers Association and the Children's Book Council, as was the children's version of *Search for the Golden Moon Bear. The Tarantula Scientist* was a *School Library Journal* Best Book of the Year for 2004.

Montgomery's future plans include a trip to the cloud forest of Papua, New Guinea, to visit orange and yellow tree-dwelling kangaroos for a kids' book, and a journey to a remote New Zealand island to study a species of giant, flightless parrot. Montgomery is also working on a memoir, "The Good, Good Pig," about her life with Christopher Hogwood, her much-loved 750-pound pig companion, who recently died at age fourteen.

Sy Montgomery appeared on *Open Books* in October 2002, with Dr. Gary J. Galbreath, her partner in the search for the golden moon bear, and a professor of evolutionary biology at Northwestern University and research associate at the Field Museum.

DONNA SEAMAN: What inspired you to become a nature writer, one who risks life and limb to visit and write about rare and endangered animals?

SY MONTGOMERY: I've always been drawn to animals. I think a lot of us, as children, have a natural affinity for animals—particularly small animals because we're small and we're down on the ground where they are. We also don't have the idea implanted in our brains yet that there's a great divide between us and the rest of creation, which I think is false. To a child, there's the spider and then there's your mother, and there's your teacher and then there's a robin and there's a worm, and they are all experiencing the world in their own way. That has always fascinated me, the fact that animals are experiencing the world in a different way. I always yearned to know what my dog knew with her incredible hearing. As I began to understand that other animals are gifted with extensions of the senses that we don't have, such as being able to see infrared light or being able to hear ultrasound or infrasound, these things drew me even deeper into the world of animals.

DS: So, were you a tomboy? Did you play outside a lot?

MONTGOMERY: I don't know if I'd say "a lot," but my closest friends were not human. My closest friends were animals. I had a whole series of lizards and turtles and a parakeet, and then another parakeet and then another parakeet, and a Scottish terrier. When I was in first through fourth grade, I lived on an Army base in Brooklyn, New York, and this is not exactly in the middle of the deepest, darkest nature. When we moved to New Jersey, I thought, "Wow, this is the wilderness. It has granite curbing, not cement." But I do remember discovering with a friend of mine, who later grew up to be a veterinarian, a place called The Creek, where you could go and be almost guaranteed to find a box turtle—which to me was an incredible gift.

DS: I suspect you also read a lot

MONTGOMERY: Oh, yes, it was my favorite thing to do. I was always at the library looking up animals and keeping notes on them. I was a young naturalist.

DS: You started early. I think that often holds true for scientists. E. O. Wilson has written a memoir about his nature-bedazzled boyhood.

MONTGOMERY: He's my hero.

DS: Mine, too. Dr. Galbreath, were you animal-struck as a child, too?

GARY GALBREATH: Oh, yes, and I had the advantage of living in semirural Kentucky, so there was more possibility to wander through woods and pastureland and quarries because I was as interested in fossils as I was in looking at living animals. By the time I was in the sixth or the seventh grade, I had already decided that I had to be either a zoologist or a paleontologist. I couldn't decide for sure which, but that's pretty specific for a kid.

DS: You two met in Peru, while Sy was researching the pink dolphins.

MONTGOMERY: That's right. We met five years ago at the Tamshiyacu-Tahuayo Community Reserve, and that's what gave birth to this book. It was one of those times when one thing arises out of another. While everyone else was talking about family or photography or something, I knew that if I could be with Gary we would talk about evolution. So we would go out together in a canoe at night, and he would tell me about evolution. He would tell me about animals. He would tell me the most incredible stories, and they were all true. He was the one who told me that the dolphins I was researching arose from animals that had lived on the land and had not only legs but also hooves, which paleontologists just recently found. It was there in the Amazon that he told me about this mysterious golden bear that he had seen a decade before in Yunnan, China, and that he had remembered all that time and always wondered about but had never been able to find out more. That was really the genesis of this book.

I remembered what he told me about a bear that had been living like a mascot in a little town. I remembered it for a year, until I was at a birthday party in my hometown of Hancock, New Hampshire, population fifteen hundred, when, of all things, there appeared the deputy director for the Wildlife Protection Office of Cambodia. Because I knew that they had the jet black moon bear and the jet black sun bear, I asked him, "You haven't happened to hear of a bear in your part of the world that isn't black?" He dropped his jaw and said, "My gosh, I just got word of this incredible golden animal, the captive of a wealthy palm plantation owner. No one knows what it is." I raced home and called Gary and said, "We've got to get together with this guy." So we met with Sun Hean. The men whipped out their pictures taken eleven years apart, and a thousand kilometers apart, and they are both the same kind of animal. That's when we knew that Gary's original animal was not Joe Mutant Bear who just happened to have this strange coat color, but that this was a new creature, that it was undescribed and that there were more out there. That's when we started to plan the expedition.

DS: You go to Cambodia to try and find out if the golden moon bear is simply a rare color variation of a known bear or a species new to humankind. But you quickly discover that Cambodia is a terrifically dangerous place, and this becomes as much a theme in the book as the golden moon bear. Not only do you have to worry about millions of land mines, you are also forced to confront the horrors of the illegal wildlife trade, a criminal world few outsiders know much about.

MONTGOMERY: We were just astonished. When we arrived in the capital of Cambodia, Phnom Penh, Sun Hean took us on a tour of bears illegally in residence throughout the city. People have them as pets or as attractions, you know, "Come to our restaurant because we have some poor bear in a tiny cage." There he also took us into illegal pharmacies, where animal parts of all kinds were on sale, and everything about it was creepy. They had sheets of totally illegal python skins hanging there like curtains. They had elephant tails. They had tiger skins. They had bear skulls. They had the organs of animals which are used in medicine. And they knew Sun Hean. They knew that he was in charge of enforcing the laws, but they also knew about a loophole in the law that prevented him from enforcing it.

Seeing all this was so hard. It tore your heart out. On the one hand, it was incredible to be on a voyage of discovery with a fantastic scientist. I loved traveling with Gary. I respect his work so much, and he's a joy to be around. You're in this beautiful country full of culture and learning. Monks in saffron robes everywhere remind you of the effort to find serenity and to sculpt a path of compassion for humanity. On the other hand, here's this horrible trade in animal parts, the knowledge that there are still four to eight million land mines in this place, and inevitably, many encounters with people who have lost limbs, eyes, and family members. The horror and the sorrow—the juxtaposition was almost too much to process.

DS: It's maddening to read about how bears are mistreated to secure bodily substances and body parts for allegedly medical purposes.

GALBREATH: Most of which are nonexistent. I think it's safe to say that most of the supposed medical advantages of bear parts are wholly nebulous. Only the gallbladder, as far as we know, has real medical properties, and those same properties are found in the gall of other organisms. We all have the same substance in our gall. As

Sy explains in her book, that substance is now commercially available for pennies. But because there is a belief that it only works if it's torn out of a living animal, there is still an intense trade in bear body parts. Some bears are actually exported overseas to other countries so that the person who wants the gallbladder can watch as the bear is killed. They then immediately buy the substance, which is really pretty appalling.

DS: Let's talk a bit about the science behind this. Here's a really beautiful animal that few people know about, a small golden bear with large ears. You want to figure out if this is a distinct species, in light of the fact that there are not many species of bears on the planet.

GALBREATH: Currently eight are recognized, and these are small bears if you compare them to, say, a grizzly. But they are probably larger on average than an American black bear. Some of the animals we saw were absolutely enormous. One bear was so large, weighing 235 kilograms, we had to anesthetize it to pluck hairs from it. In terms of deciding if it's a new species, we needed to look at the mitochondrial DNA of the animal and compare it with that of ordinary black bears from approximately the same place. If we had found differences, let's say, from a blonde moon bear and a black moon bear in another place, it wouldn't necessarily have told us very much because the difference might have been due to being in different populations, geographically separated. We had to sample both color types in the same place, which wasn't all that easy. Then we became interested in genetic variation in the entire species across Southeast Asia, which is what I'm continuing to study.

DS: Not only did you have to try to see the bears, you also had to secure samples of their fur.

GALBREATH: Yes, and the first bear we went to see belonged to a gentleman named Mong Reththy, who had an oil palm plantation and who actually owns a lot of things in Cambodia. You see

Mong Reththy computer stores and Mong Reththy supermarkets. Businessmen of his stature in Cambodia have things American businessmen don't have, such as an armed militia, so it's a curious situation. It was tricky to get in to see his bear; you have to get by guys with AK-47s. Then you have to try to explain why you need to pluck hairs from the bear. The explanation is that we wanted the DNA in the hair bulbs.

DS: So you have to yank hairs out of the bear's hide.

GALBREATH: Which Sy proved very adept at. I am not particularly adept at this; I'm not a person with quick reflexes, which you need because you have to get your hand in there and get the hair and then you need to get your hand out of the cage.

DS: While we're on the subject of fur, why are they called moon bears?

GALBREATH: All of these animals have a relatively light, even white, marking on their chest, very often in the shape of a V or a U, a crescent shape that has reminded people of a half moon. Each animal has a genus and a species name. The original genus name was *Selenarctos,* after Selene, the Greek goddess of the moon. The moon bear is now included in the genus *Ursus,* which includes grizzlies and black bears and sun bears, so it's now *Ursus thibetanus.* It has the species name because in the old days Tibet referred to a larger region, and the earliest described specimens came from the borders of the Himalayas, and, I believe, what is now Bangladesh. This animal has a huge distribution, stretching from the borders of Iran and Pakistan all the way east to the Vladivostok area in Russia, and throughout much of China and much of southeastern Asia. It's in danger now almost everywhere, but the distribution itself is very large. Happily it turns out that there are some moon bears in Tibet proper, which wasn't properly understood by any of us until quite recently. That means that the species name is reasonably descriptive after all.

The first blond bear we saw was captured in a forest that is very close to being a real rain forest and quite far south. People think of these bears as being temperate animals—they have long shaggy coats, and in many areas they have an undercoat of wool under their long shaggy hair. So they look like animals basically constructed for the temperate, yet they do make it into the tropics, and one imagines that these big shaggy moon bears have a problem with overheating. The sun bears that live alongside of them in the tropics have short coats and they are sleek. They really look like animals adapted to the tropics.

MONTGOMERY: That's one of the things that Gary's work has shown. It gives us a way to travel back in time and see how is it that these great shaggy beasts, that look like they should live in frigid mountain areas, live in steamy jungles in places like Cambodia and Laos.

GALBREATH: By looking at that DNA variation, we're attempting to, in effect, plot migration during the Pleistocene, during the last half-million years or so, of these animals crossing southern Asia. We're not talking about one-way migrations either, because as the climate has fluctuated the bears have undoubtedly moved in and out of different geographic regions. We're getting excellent data along those lines, and we can compare our data with that gathered by people in Japan and southern China. But no one has any idea where most of the moon bears in zoos around the world originally came from, or where their parents came from, so that's frustrating. If you know the "Mitochondrial Eve" story, the "out of Africa" story for human beings, you'll understand that we're trying to do the same thing with moon bears. That's why we need to get hair from them and why we need to have a pretty good idea where they were captured, because we have to link the DNA variance with geography. That's the hard part.

DS: What you had to contend with on your quest is amazing. You made discoveries in cities and in wildlife sanctuaries. You met all sorts of people. You had to deal with guns and other potential dangers, the legacies of the Pol Pot regime. But there's an ironic aspect to that history. You make the point that, during the Khmer Rouge years, wildlife and natural habitats were relatively safe in Cambodia because people were busy killing each other. Today, the forests are being destroyed at an alarming rate. Are the moon bears now endangered?

MONTGOMERY: As you say, ironically enough, war protected them, and peace and prosperity now threaten them. That was one reason for writing this book: Southeast Asia is now facing a fabulous opportunity because it can avoid the mistakes that we've made. This area has been like a little hidden and protected Eden for all this time, and it could be saved.

DS: Over and over again, you make the point that everything is connected, that everything people do affects every aspect of life. You are so attuned to why we need animals, to what their role is in the grand scheme of things. But you also write so tenderly about the hill tribes who are being dispossessed as soon as they come into contact with the wider world. It's painfully reminiscent of what happened to the indigenous peoples of North America.

MONTGOMERY: Yes, who would think that a scientific quest like this would lead us into that? You never know where the animal is going to take you. Very few scientists think outside of the box, but Gary Galbreath is one who does. The way he does science has now got a name: the total-evidence approach. He doesn't just do test-tube science, he also consults with local people to see what their wisdom has to show us, and he looks at historical accounts. We got to journey into the cultures of people who are seldom consulted, but the new species that were found in the Annamites—since 1992, no fewer than six new kinds of animals have been discovered in the Annamite Mountains of that region, including a two-hundred-pound antelope, and a zebra-striped rabbit—were largely found because they were known to the local people.

GALBREATH: Of course, you don't necessarily accept the information you get from old accounts or from local people as being scientifically correct, but I think it's reasonable to treat it as data just as you treat DNA data as data, or observations on skulls or pelts. Mistakes occur in data of those kinds of information, too. I think it's reasonable to take verbal accounts and old written accounts of explorers in the same vein. You don't necessarily assume that everything is correct, especially since many of these things are second- or third- or tenth-hand accounts of knowledge. But to assume that it's all false or useless is silly. Some people in the late nineteenth and early twentieth centuries were writing about animals that they saw all the time but that are now lost or very rare, so we must rely on past accounts of extinct species and on museum specimens.

MONTGOMERY: People can tell you things that are true in a different sense than science may see it, so as a writer, I found myself in very rich territory indeed. People can tell you something that is true in a metaphorical way. When I was researching *Spell of the Tiger,* people would tell me, "Oh, yes, the tiger flies through the air and it becomes invisible." They were telling the truth, because the tiger can leap for a dozen feet easily in a single bound, and that's flying, and become invisible because of its stripes and coloration. So it stretches your mind to visit these cultures. As a scientist, Gary is also able to look at the context within which such stories are true. He made the very good observation when we went to talk to hill tribes in northern Thailand that these people were telling us truths that had been handed down from their ancestors, who may have come from China and may have even remembered panda bears. He perceived the fact that their words were coming down across time and through layers and layers of meaning and layers of migration. He was able to tease that apart almost like you tease apart the genetic code embedded in the little tiny bits of flesh at the base of the hair.

DS: You introduce us to an array of Southeast Asian landscapes and cultures, and then your research brings you to Skokie, Illinois, where you speak with members of a Hmong family about moon bears.

GALBREATH: After the war in Vietnam and Laos, a large number of Hmong ended up in the Midwest, many in the Chicago area, particularly in Skokie. The Hmong are renowned hunters, and I was able to speak with one man who had been a bear hunter in Laos. It can be very difficult to know whether people are talking about what you're talking about, but he had a great knowledge of bears, and he may very well have seen one of our golden bears. It was a very informative session, and it gave us a lot of neat ideas about how to proceed.

DS: Another fascinating person you spoke with is Gary van Zuylen, whose life story is full of surprises.

MONTGOMERY: Yes, two Garys. That made it rough. And yes, that was one of the great things about this book: although it is full of horrid sorrows, it is also full of heroes, and he's one of them. He had been a very successful building engineer, had tons of money, got sick of it, and decided, "I think I'll get a journalism degree in London." On the way, he stopped off in Bangkok and helped a girl with her luggage and ended up running a Thai charity for the protection of Thai wildlife. He wasn't even one of these people who has a great affinity for animals. Yet he was essentially running a refugee center for bears that had been rescued from the illegal wildlife trade, and he was doing it in conjunction with the Thai Forestry Service, which had never been in the business of finding decent homes for these individuals. Their facility, Banglamung, was mainly for breeding endangered deer. The next thing you know, they have fifty to sixty moon bears living there. He basically created a Club Med for bears. We drove through this area, and you look out your window and there is a bear lounging in a pool, and then over there is a bear in a tree, and then here comes the truck bringing the hot food right to the bears. It was great, and it was there that Dr. Galbreath took the picture of Stripe that's on the cover of the book. It's a gorgeous picture of a bear moments before he tried to put his head through the window of the jeep.

GALBREATH: It really is an amazing place. It's the size of a very small golf course, and there are areas of tall grass, and there are shade trees, and there are at least a couple of pools for the bears to swim and lounge in. And those bears are not in bad condition at all. In fact, if suddenly dumped in the wild, a lot of the bears would probably think, "Oh my God. Take me back home." Almost all of the bears we deal with came into captivity as cubs, so their experience of life is largely in captive circumstances. These bears have nice captive circumstances. Here are these huge shaggy bears with no restraints, and they're chewing on the wheel wells of your jeep.

MONTGOMERY: We went in twice on foot among those bears. The second time was when we darted over to get a hair out of this particularly large individual. We thought he might have a unique lineage, so we really wanted him. The other time, I went in when they were feeding them. It's fantastic to be among these animals in a semiwild situation in which you're in their element and surroundings. You're so close you can smell their breath. It's incredible to feel their power and to know you're at their mercy, and trusting them not to take your face off.

GALBREATH: Individualism matters here. There are bears who are very charming individuals, even though they are so powerful you have to be very careful, because they could hurt you without meaning to and have been known to do this to people. We've gotten to know some bears pretty well. There are other individuals that are very skittish and very likely had bad experiences in their lives with people before they ever reached Banglamung. One would always want to take a great deal of care with them. In that sense they are certainly like people.

DS: What sort of future do you see for the moon and sun bears of Southeast Asia?

MONTGOMERY: That was the hard thing about this book. Traveling in areas with land mines and unexploded ordnance is one thing, but thinking about the future of this place really tears your heart out. This was the hardest book I've ever done. I've done nine books, and this one was just murder because of all the suffering that we saw, human and animal, and because you know how strong that siren song of greed is now that Western money and Western-style development is coming to this area. It was important, though, to feel some hope, and I do. The heroes that we introduce in this book, Dr. Galbreath, Gary van Zuylen, and Sun Hean—who is really putting his life on the line every single day for the survival of the incredible wildlife treasures of Cambodia—give me a great deal of hope.

Another wonderful source of hope is what can be done with the data that we collected. An unexpected blessing was that the black moon bears yielded DNA data that allows us, as Dr. Galbreath explained, to create a mitochondrial map of where these bears came from. Now there's actually a move afoot to have that happen. There's good scientific data on other species that shows that your chances of survival are greatly enhanced if you are put back in the place where your DNA best suits you to be. If this comes off, it would be the first project ever for replacing known captive animals—not just trans-locating one wild animal from one place to another, but taking an animal who was once wild and is now in captivity and putting it back where it belongs. So that gives me a lot of hope, too. And at the end of the book, I drew a lot of hope from looking at the incredible history of Cambodia, an area now considered impoverished and crippled, but once the site of a great empire. These are the people who built the incredible splendor of Angkor Wat, the largest religious edifice in the world. No one believed when it was first found in the jungle centuries ago that the Cambodians had built this, and that gives me hope.

GALBREATH: I think that, in each of the countries involved, the questions are a little different and the answers are a little different. In Cambodia, there are large areas of intact forest with relatively intact wildlife. Best of all, although in some cases for truly horrific historical reasons, there are hardly any people living in most of these areas. So you don't have the problem of potential conflicts between the needs of indigenous people and the wildlife. The potential is there to set a lot of that land aside as the equivalent, or the actuality, of the biosphere reserves that the U.N. has been setting up. In Laos there is a lot of forest left, but a lot of the forests are empty because hunting has been the greater problem there. I do sense, though, that a number of people in the Laos government are sincere about trying to conserve their wildlife. In Thailand, most of the forest is gone, but the government is now serious about protecting what is left. I think in Thailand we are just about at the point where one can seriously talk about the reintroduction of animals where they've been wiped out. If that happens with bears, it will be with the use of our genetic data and possibly with some advice from us along the way. To some extent Southeast Asian governments are especially eager to do the right thing with regard to wildlife in wild areas because doing so is being tied to foreign aid. And we're not talking about huge amounts of money. A tiny amount of the money in the Enron scandal, for instance, could probably provide all the money that is necessary to conserve wildlife in Southeast Asia for the next fifty years.

DS: Much of the power of *Search for the Golden Moon Bear* resides in its mix of the scientific and the cultural, the biological and the spiritual, the tangible and the emotional. You not only describe your journey and your interactions with people and bears, you also chronicle your nightmares. And you write about your visit to a shaman to participate in a soul-binding ceremony.

MONTGOMERY: I still carry with me evidence of that soul-binding ceremony. I still have the string that was emblematic of what I was experiencing and what many others experience. Soul loss is a big problem in those cultures. The shaman bound our souls to our bodies with string at our wrists—they read your future not in the creases in the palm of your hand but in the veins of the wrist. And

according to him, I have marvelous wrists. He said, "This is a wonderful wrist. You will always be happy." I was feeling miserable because we just had seen an elephant who had a leg blown off while
illegally logging in Burma, and we had seen all of these horrors in
the marketplace, and I was feeling very unlucky indeed. But I realized he was right. It was my great good fortune to be there with
Gary Galbreath at a time in history that is so crucial. And it was my
luck to be able to record all of this, and hopefully contribute to
helping Southeast Asia reclaim this Eden.

Terry Tempest Williams

Terry Tempest Williams is a sixth-generation Mormon and a native of Utah's redrock desert, a realm of dramatic, almost otherworldly beauty and fierce conflicts over land use. Born in 1955, Williams has been shaped by her love for her home ground and by her struggles to reconcile her belief in the sanctity of the land with the Mormon tradition. Hailed as a lyrical naturalist, a provocative voice of the New West, an environmentalist, a feminist, and a writer of erotica, Williams is also a spiritual writer and a social critic.

Williams's first mentor was her grandmother Kathryn Blackett Tempest, who took her bird watching and presented her at age five with Roger Tory Peterson's *Field Guide to Western Birds*. Under her grandmother's influence, Williams began writing about her observations of the wild and about her dreams. Williams majored in English and minored in biology at the University of Utah and pursued a master's degree there in environmental education. She taught Navajo children in Montezuma Creek, Utah, and in 1979 she became curator of education at the Utah Museum of Natural History and wrote two science books for children.

By temperament an investigator and a questioner of assumptions, Williams worked toward expressing both a "poetics of place" and a "politics of place." In *Pieces of White Shell: A Journey to Navajoland*, she compares and contrasts the stories and traditions of the Navajo with the voices and practices of her Mormon ancestors, two cultures occupying the same redrock land. *Coyote's Canyon* is a collection of tales that blend essay with myth to bring the history of the desert to life. Williams's attunement to, and exploration of, the link between the body and the landscape, and between women and nature, took a tragic turn in 1983 when her mother, then fifty-one and a twelve-year survivor of breast cancer, was diagnosed with ovarian cancer. At the same time, Great Salt Lake was rising beyond its customary levels, threatening the Bear River Migratory Bird Refuge where Williams had spent many idyllic days with her grandmother. Between 1983 and 1990, Williams's mother and two grandmothers died, even as waters flooded and closed the bird sanctuary. She filled twenty-two journals in an effort to cope with and chronicle these devastating losses. From those pages came *Refuge: An Unnatural History of Family and Place*, which concludes with a shocking revelation about the connection between the cancer that has afflicted her family and the radioactive poisons seeded in the desert by the testing of atomic bombs. Widely read and discussed, *Refuge* helped launch inquiries into the fate of so-called "downwinders" and opened new vistas for writers of memoirs and environmental literature. As a result of her work, Williams received a Lannan Foundation Fellowship.

In *An Unspoken Hunger*, Williams trains her naturalist's eye on the Serengeti Plain of Africa and the wetlands of New York, and reflects further on the unique bond between women and nature. In *Desert Quartet: An Erotic Landscape*, Williams collaborates with painter Mary Frank to pursue her meditation on the dynamic between the sensuous and the spiritual. In *Leap*, she radically alters her focus and immerses herself in a world born of the imagination, the triptych known as *The Garden of Earthly Delights* by the fifteenth-century Flemish painter Hieronymus Bosch. A deep study of the three paintings leads Williams to aver that we need both art and wilderness for our spiritual well-being, and that we should accord Earth the same reverence and care we bring to art.

An activist as well as a writer, Williams has been arrested while participating in an antinuclear demonstration at the Nevada Test Site and in a protest against the Iraq war in Washington, D.C. Williams explains her belief that love of place requires participation in public debate over land use and the fate of what little wilderness remains in *Red: Passion and Patience in the Desert*. A collection of works new and selected, including her eloquent testimony before the Senate Subcommittee on Forest & Public Land Management in 1995, *Red* was released on September 11, 2001, while Williams was in Washington, D.C. Williams pursued her vision of a politics of participation during the presidential campaign of 2004, writing a trilogy of essays that were published in a volume titled *The Open Space of Democracy* and illustrated with paintings by Mary Frank.

As an undergraduate, Williams longed for a curriculum that addressed both literature and the environment. She is now involved in creating a new "environmental humanities" program as the University of Utah's first Annie Clark Tanner Fellow in Environmental Studies. Williams appeared on *Open Books* in June 2003, after she had spoken at Chicago's Printers Row Book Fair.

DONNA SEAMAN: Which came first for you, a love of reading and writing or a love of the outdoors?

TERRY TEMPEST WILLIAMS: It's hard to separate them. We grew up with a wonderful confluence of language and landscape. Our parents and our grandparents read us stories about nature, and we spent our entire lives out in nature since I grew up in Utah during the 1950s, when there weren't so many people and our family's construction business was putting in natural gas lines in rural parts of the state. While my father was doing construction work, we were playing in the rivers and streams and deserts. So there was a strange convergence of word and place and family.

DS: In *Red,* you use a term that I love, "revolutionary patience."

WILLIAMS: Think about how many years, decades, eons—the thousands upon thousands of years of evolutionary persistence and adaptation that has taken place. I look at the desert tortoise and how he or she is trying to live in the midst of fierce development in St. George, Utah, one of the fastest growing towns in America right now. And the desert tortoise is being pushed to the absolute periphery. And there's so much deceit. The developers signed a pact with government agencies, saying that they will honor and protect the desert tortoise preserves, but the preserves have all been sold under the table, and the desert tortoise is on the fringes, struggling. And yet I do believe, and maybe this is just my own denial, that the desert tortoise will survive. But it's so very difficult, and revolutionary patience is exactly what is required. Writing does require patience, and I think it does require revolutionary patience to be able to maintain some semblance of faith and hope as we face heartbreaking betrayals in terms of democracy.

DS: Your work has always been exquisitely personal, yet you push yourself to address issues as well as states of being. Clearly, there's pleasure in writing about the desert, birds, the night sky—in paying a sort of high attentiveness to your surroundings and the natural world. I wonder if you feel that we also need to apply that attentiveness and awareness to social and political realms?

WILLIAMS: You use the phrases, "state of being," and "a heightened state of attentiveness," and I would add, "participation." We're so quick to separate, to compartmentalize. This is what we do as writers, this is what we do as citizens, this is what we do on Sunday in pews, and I think what we really need to concentrate on is how do we live a whole life? How do we live a life of greater attention and intention so that there aren't these kinds of manufactured separations? So that the attentiveness we take to the desert or to the shores of Lake Michigan is the same kind of heightened state of awareness and attentiveness and participation we bring to civic life, whether it's voting, whether it's letters to the editor, whether it's letters of outrage to our elected representatives. It's a resolve that we will not be complacent or complicit.

DS: It's a hard choice for writers and artists. The creative process is a powerful one, but it is also fragile. To enter into the public arena is, to some extent, a sacrifice. But if you're going to write about the wild, if you're going to write about nature, you are compelled to become an advocate for it. If something you love is under siege, don't you have to speak out?

WILLIAMS: It just doesn't seem honest any other way. I used to struggle with the question, am I an artist or am I an activist? But

I'm a human being, and how can we not respond? I think of Emily Dickinson in the letter to her friend when she wrote, "Life is a spell so exquisite that everything conspires to break it." If we're writing about the natural world, if we're writing about wildness both from a philosophical point of view as well as a very practical and real on-the-ground point of view, to not talk about what we're seeing "off-frame," so to speak, is irresponsible. Yes, I can write a beautiful piece about the redrock desert, but if I don't talk about the fact that if you just switch your eyes a little bit to the left you'll see the results of oil and gas leases with forty thousand-pound thumper trunks roaring through, somehow that doesn't quite seem honest. And one hundred years from now, I don't want someone to say, "Where was she? Why didn't she tell us the truth?" I think the challenge is, how do we speak a language that opens the heart and doesn't close it? How do we stay true to the creative process and a sense of discovery so that our work doesn't turn into polemics?

DS: I believe that, if you're writing with integrity, beauty asserts itself.

WILLIAMS: I love that you said that beauty asserts itself. It reminds me of Rilke when he says that beauty is the beginning of terror.

I was seven years old in 1962, and I remember my grandmother (who gave me a copy of *Peterson's Field Guide to Western Birds* when I was five) having a copy of *Silent Spring* on her desk, and she picked up the book and said to me, "Can you imagine a world without birdsong?" I couldn't. Now it doesn't seem so far away, and in fact, there are places where there really is that unsettling silence. We really are seeing the degradation of so much that we have taken for granted.

DS: My seventh year was pivotal for me, too. That's the age at which you're able to start reading on your own, and I was shocked at what I discovered. I'll never forget the fury I felt when I learned about the atomic bomb and pollution.

WILLIAMS: I feel so schizophrenic because on one hand, I think, "Are we just going the route of our elders, saying, 'Oh, life used to be so much better'?" Good things have happened. Polluted places have been cleaned up. Practices have improved. In 1992, George Bush I, under pressure from Bill Clinton, his opponent in the presidential race, was forced to put a moratorium on nuclear testing. But Bush II takes office and immediately starts trying to undo that and reinitiate nuclear testing in the desert. Gains and losses. What scares me most is that as a society we are losing those points of engagement. We are losing a frame of reference to the natural world, even though it's all around us. But some things are clear. For instance, our public lands are still our public commons, and I still think there's reason to fight for them.

DS: Some people believe that our standards for wilderness have become too high, and that environmentalists are too nostalgic, not adaptive enough, and out of touch with most people's concerns. Part of the conundrum is that people really haven't been given a choice about what happens to the land and its water, forests, animals, and plants. I believe that more stories need to be told about who gets to decide how land is used and why. This is where writers come in, to help us track the changes we bring to the earth, to help us weigh the benefits and the dangers of our ways.

WILLIAMS: And what is our ethic of place and how do we respond?

DS: And what are we giving wilderness up for? What are we getting?

WILLIAMS: I think that's really important. The creative process ignites our imagination, and I believe that that same imagination is what will propel us forward with issues of social change. I do think we have to acknowledge that we are a very capitalistic and consumptive country, and talk about conservation or environmentalism is never going to be popular with the dominant culture because it means a checks and balances on money and an economy that is reserved only for the dollar, rather than an economy that talks about spiritual resources and the right of all life to participate on the planet, not just our own species. I like to think that we are engaged in our own reformation, an ecological reformation where we're learning to extend, as Aldo Leopold suggested, our notion of community to include plants, animals, rocks, and rivers as well as human beings.

DS: One of literature's gifts to readers is to bring the past into the present. You often write about Navaho stories, and you remind us of a previous generation of nature writers, including Mary Austin and Henry David Thoreau. One of the startling realizations one has when reading Thoreau is that he's complaining about overdevelopment in New England in the 1830s.

WILLIAMS: I was reading some journals of Leonardo da Vinci's, and there's a passage written in 1510 about greed and arrogance and separation from the land that you would think was written today. I read it, and I just burst into tears. I thought, "This was in 1510, during the Renaissance. What is it in us that has no restraint? What is this insatiable hunger?"

DS: It's interesting that you use the word "hunger." You often put yourself in your work in such a way as to remind us that we're animals, that we have bodies, and that it is through our senses that we know things about the world. You touch trees and pick up feathers. You sit on sun-warmed rock; you swim naked. Many of your readers love this aspect of your work, but I know that others cringe. They can't take it.

WILLIAMS: Many. One woman said, "This is so embarrassing. I can't believe you would put this on paper." A critic at a very prestigious American university said that this was just an incredible example of auto-eroticism and self-indulgence. I had to look up auto-eroticism, and when I found that it means masturbation, I thought,

"Well, this is lovely." But I just want to say, "Are we not animals? Do we not feel the sensuality?"

DS: What are we afraid of?

WILLIAMS: That is always the question. Can we not take the language back? When we hear the word "erotic," we associate it with pornography. My definition of pornography is "separation from." To me the real definition of Eros and erotic is "in relationship to," participatory, again that word "engagement." As you said, what are we afraid of? If we surrender to those impulses, to those instincts, how would our lives be different?

DS: And wouldn't we know to value nature more?

WILLIAMS: Again, no separation. Our land and our body are the same. I think we are terrified right now of "other" in all of its manifestations. And I keep thinking there are many forms of terrorism. Environmental degradation is one of them. We have to take a warrior's stance, and it requires both reflection and engagement. Eyes looking out; eyes looking in—both are required. I don't believe that this is a time to be comfortable. I think we really have to voice our concerns over what we see. I really believe democracy is being thwarted right now.

DS: This is how art and activism become one. People feel that they don't have a voice; they feel isolated, but stories break down barriers. They give us common language and common ground.

WILLIAMS: And it's not art as escape, but art as engagement—art that ignites our highest selves, our human selves, our humanity. Art allows us to go back into the river.

DS: More books are being published than ever before. Maybe more people are writing. Are more people reading? Does literature have an impact?

WILLIAMS: I think people will always read because stories save our lives. We are storied animals, we are storied beings, and story bypasses rhetoric and pierces the heart. It's the connective tissue that holds us in place. Story becomes the conscience of the community and we remember who we are and who we are not and what we are tied to.

I was so hopeful today, the audience was incredible, and what was so thrilling to me were all the questions that were asked about Utah wilderness, about public lands, about the government's stealth attack on wilderness protection. I found it unbelievably inspiring that people in our urban landscapes know what wildlands mean to the soul of this country, that our public lands are in fact our public commons and belong to all Americans.

DS: Yes. Speaking for myself, I want wilderness to exist whether I ever go there or not. I don't need to travel to wilderness for it do something for me psychologically and spiritually. And I suspect a lot of people living in cities feel that way. They just need to know that unspoiled lands exist, and they want the wild to be protected. Literature has brought Utah to life in my imagination, and I treasure it without ever having set foot there.

WILLIAMS: You've just given a beautiful definition of empathy, and if we lose our empathy, I think we will lose our souls.

This interview previously appeared in a slightly altered form in Ruminator Review, *Winter 2003–2004.*

PART FOUR: **Related Readings**

I was the sort of book-struck girl who kept lists of all the books she read, and who gave herself various reading assignments. Drawn by the title, I read Dostoyevsky's *The Idiot* and then set out to read every Russian novel I could get my hands on. A story by Eudora Welty launched a Southern-writers binge. These habits of mind propelled me to *Booklist*, where, wonder of wonders, we are paid to read books, write about books, and create thematic lists of books. So when I began to assemble lists of books that I felt were in sync in some way with the books written by the authors who appear in *Writers on the Air,* I drew on a lifetime of reading and making connections. Yet I cannot deny that these lists are idiosyncratic. The way I think about a fiction writer's work, the way I perceive his or her place in the constellation of fiction, may or may not line up with the perceptions of other readers. I might emphasize a novelist's interest in coastal life, for instance, while another reader will talk about how he orchestrates familial relationships. In attempting to answer variations on the question, "If I enjoy reading this particular author, who else might I like to read?" I sought answers in books that share themes, style, perspective, and atmosphere. Wherever possible, I also wanted to broaden the definition of related readings by not being too literal, allowing myself instead to indulge in a bit of literary impressionism.

The lists that follow, therefore, reflect my taste in literature and my interest in certain topics, places, and points of view. I see these lists as an opportunity to recommend my favorite writers (too many of whom are too little known or, in my opinion, underrated), and to set up some stimulating comparisons and contrasts. I've tried to cover as many aspects of each writer's oeuvre as possible, or, in the case of very prolific writers, I've sought to list works that revolve around the writer's bedrock concerns and obsessions. These are by no means comprehensive lists. Indeed, I hope they will inspire readers to create associations and connections of their own.

My far-roaming, perhaps eccentric, most likely unruly, and always enthusiastic suggestions are meant to be useful, inspiring, provocative, and fun.

PART ONE: FICTION

SECTION ONE: FIRST-TIME NOVELISTS

Dennis Bock: Novels about the Atomic Bomb
Martin Booth, *Hiroshima Joe*
Jay Cantor, *Krazy Kat*
James Conrad, *Making Love to the Minor Poets of Chicago*
Don DeLillo, *Underworld*
Rick DeMarinis, *Apocalypse Then*
Marguerite Duras, *Hiroshima Mon Amour*
John Hockenberry, *A River Out of Eden*
Helga Königsdorf, *Fisson*
Lydia Millet, *Oh Pure and Radiant Heart*
Bradford Morrow, *Trinity Fields*; *Ariel's Crossing*
Craig Nova, *Trombone*
Brenda Peterson, *Duck and Cover*
Carter Scholz, *Radiance*
Nevil Shute, *On the Beach*
James Thackara, *America's Children*
Gerald Vizenor, *Hiroshima Bugi: Atomu 57*
Kurt Vonnegut, *Cat's Cradle*
Kate Wenner, *Dancing with Einstein*

Julia Glass
John Casey, *Half-Life of Happiness*
Michael Cunningham, *Flesh and Blood*

Mary Gordon, *Spending*
Jane Hamilton, *A Short History of a Prince*
Jim Harrison, *The Road Home*
Julie Hecht, *The Unprofessionals*
David Leavitt, *The Body of Jonah Boyd*
Lorrie Moore, *Who Will Run the Frog Hospital*
Antonya Nelson, *Nobody's Girl*
Paul Russell, *War Against the Animals*
Richard Russo, *Empire Falls*

Edward P. Jones
Barbara Chase-Riboud, *Sally Hemmings*; *Hottentot Venus*
J. California Cooper, *In Search of Satisfaction*; *The Wake of the Wind*; *Some People*; *Some Other Place*
Toni Morrison, *Song of Solomon*; *Beloved*; *Paradise*
Suzan-Lori Parks, *Getting Mother's Body*
Jewell Parker Rhodes, *Douglass' Women*
Alice Randall, *The Wind Done Gone*
Lalita Tademy, *Cane River*
John Edgar Wideman, *Twelve Stories*; *Sent for You Yesterday*; *The Cattle Killing*; *God's Gym*

SECTION TWO: FICTIONAL LICENSE: NOVELS ABOUT REAL PEOPLE

Here are two lists of fictionalized lives that range from impressionistic to historically precise, lyrical to sardonic in their interpretation of the lives of artists, eccentrics, and leaders. If you like the work of Madison Smartt Bell, Peter Carey, Anchee Min, and Kate Moses, you may like these books.

Novels about Writers and Artists

Julia Alvarez, *In the Name of Salome* (Poet and activist Salomé Ureña de Henríquez)

Kate Braverman, *The Incantation of Frida K* (Frida Kahlo)

Francisco Goldman, *The Divine Husband* (Cuban poet Jose Martí)

Katherine Govier, *Creation* (John James Audubon)

Joseph Heller, *Picture This* (Rembrandt)

John May, *Poe & Fanny* (Edgar Allen Poe and Frances S. Osgood)

Bárbara Mujica, *Frida* (Frida Kahlo)

°Joyce Carol Oates, *Blonde* (Marilyn Monroe)

Jay Parini, *Benjamin's Crossing* (Walter Benjamin)

Elena Poniatowska, *Tinisima* (Photographer Tina Modotti)

Rudy Rucker, *As Above, So Below* (Peter Bruegel)

Miranda Seymour, *The Summer of '39* (Robert Graves and Laura Riding)

Susan Sontag, *In America* (Polish actress Helena Modrzejewska)

Emma Tennant, *Sylvia and Ted* (Sylvia Plath and Ted Hughes)

Colm Tóibín, *The Master* (Henry James)

Evelyn Toynton, *Modern Art* (Jack Pollock and Lee Krasner)

William T. Vollman, *Empire Central* (Dmitri Shostakovich)

Susan Vreeland, *The Passion of Artemisia* (Italian painter Artemisia Gentileschi); *The Forest Lover* (Canadian painter Emily Carr); *Life Studies* (Stories about Cezanne, van Gogh, Renoir, Berthe Morisot, Edouard Manet)

Novels about the Inspired, the Eccentric, and the Powerful

°T. C. Boyle, *The Road to Wellville* (John Harvey Kellogg); *Riven Rock* (Stanley McCormick); *Inner Circle* (Alfred Kinsey)

Kathryn Davis, *Versailles* (Marie Antoinette)

E. L. Doctorow, *Ragtime* (Harry Houdini, J. P. Morgan, Henry Ford, and Emma Goldman)

Margaret Drabble, *The Red Queen* (Lady Hyegyong of Korea)

Gore Vidal, *Burr*; *Lincoln*

William T. Vollman, *Argall* (John Smith and Pocahontas)

°Names of authors who appear in *Writers on the Air* are marked with an asterisk.

SECTION THREE: WORLDS IN TRANSITION

Margaret Atwood

Paul Auster, *In the Country of Last Things*; *Leviathan*

Ray Bradbury, *Fahrenheit 451*

Bryher, *Visa to Avalon*

Anthony Burgess, *A Clockwork Orange*

Kathryn Davis, *The Walking Tour*

Joseph Heller, *Catch-22*

Russell Hoban, *Riddley Walker*

Eva Hoffman, *The Secret*

Aldous Huxley, *Brave New World*

Ursula Le Guin, *Always Coming Home*

Jonathan Lethem, *Amnesia Moon*

Haruki Murakami, *Hard-Boiled Wonderland and the End of the World*

Craig Nova, *Wetware*

Michael Ondaatje, *The English Patient*

George Orwell, *1984*

Richard Powers, *Galatea 2.2*; *Plowing in the Dark*

Thomas Pynchon, *Gravity's Rainbow*; *Vineland*

Sheri S. Tepper, *Beauty*

Kurt Vonnegut, *Piano Player*; *Slaughterhouse-Five*; *Galápagos*

Marina Warner, *The Leto Bundle*

Jeanette Winterson, *The PowerBook*

T. C. Boyle: An Ecofiction List

These novels dramatize our perception of nature and the connection between nature and culture.

Edward Abbey, *The Monkey Wrench Gang*; *Hayduke Lives!*

Andrea Barrett, *Servants of the Map*

Russell Banks, *The Darling*

Rick Bass, *Where the Sea Used to Be*; *The Sky, the Stars, the Wilderness*; *The Hermit's Story*

Wendell Berry, *A Place on Earth*; *Jayber Crow*; *Hannah Coulter*

A. S. Byatt, *The Biographer's Tale*

Louise Erdrich, *Tracks*; *The Master Butchers Singing Club*

Molly Gloss, *Wild Life*

Linda Hogan, *Mean Spirit*; *Solar Storms*; *Power*

Seth Kantner, *Ordinary Wolves*

Barbara Kingsolver, *Poisonwood Bible*; *Prodigal Summer*

°Barry Lopez, *Light Action in the Caribbean*; *Resistance*; The trilogy: *Desert Notes*, *River Notes*, and *Field Notes*

Peter Matthiessen, *Far Tortuga*; *On the River Styx and Other Stories*

Kent Meyers, *Light in the Crossing*; *The Work of Wolves*

N. Scott Momaday, *House Made of Dawn*; *The Ancient Child*

John Nichols, *The Milagro Bean-field War*

Simon Ortiz, *Men on the Moon*

Ruth Ozeki, *My Year of Meats*; *All Over Creation*

Brenda Peterson, *Animal Heart*

Annie Proulx, *Close Range*; *That Old Ace in the Hole*

Eden Robinson, *Monkey Beach*

Marilynne Robinson, *Housekeeping*; *Gilead*

Leslie Marmon Silko, *Ceremony*; *Almanac of the Dead*; *Garden of the Dunes*

Wallace Stegner, *Angle of Repose*; *The Spectator Bird*

John Steinbeck, *The Grapes of Wrath*; *Cannery Row*

Paul Theroux, *The Mosquito Coast*

James Welch, *Fools Crow*

Alex Shakar: Novels of Commercial and Corporate Madness

Jonathan Dee, *St. Famous*; *Palladio*
Don DeLillo, *White Noise*; *Mao II*; *The Body Artist*; *Cosmopolis*
Jennifer Egan, *Look at Me*

Stanley Elkin, *The Franchiser*
Jonathan Franzen, *Strong Motion*; *The Corrections*
William Gaddis, *JR*
°Alan Lightman, *The Diagnosis*
Jay McInerney, *Story of My Life*
Richard Powers, *Gain*

SECTION FOUR: BETWEEN WORLDS

Sandra Cisneros

Ana Castillo, *So Far from God*; *Loverboys*; *Peel My Love like an Onion*
Oscar Casares, *Brownsville*
Denise Chavez, *Loving Pedro Infante*
Judith Ortiz Cofer, *The Meaning of Consuelo*
Dagoberto Gilb, *Woodcuts of Women*
Nina Marie Martinez, *¡Caramba!*
Elena Poniatowska, *Here's to You, Jesusa!*; *The Skin of the Sky*
Mercè Rodoreda, *Camellia Street*
Susan Straight, *Highwire Moon*

Chitra Divakaruni

Amit Chaudhuri, *Freedom Song*; *A New World*; *Real Time*
Vikram Chandra, *Red Earth and Pouring Rain*
Anita Desai, *Diamond Dust*; *Fasting, Feasting*; *The Zigzag Way*
Amitav Ghosh, *The Glass Palace*
Alice Hoffman, *Blackbird House*; *The Probable Future*
Jhumpa Lahiri, *Interpreter of Maladies*; *The Namesake*
Rohan Mistry, *Family Matters*
Bharati Mukherjee, *The Middle Man and Other Stories*; *Desirable Daughters*; *The Tree Bride*

Aleksandar Hemon

David Bezmozgis, *Natasha and Other Stories*
Courtney Angela Brkic, *Stillness*
Boris Fishman (ed.),*Wild East: Stories from the Last Frontier*
Josip Novakovich, *Salvation and Other Disasters*; *April Fool's Day*
Vladimir Nabokov, *Bend Sinister*; *The Gift*; *Invitation to a Beheading*
Imad Rahman, *I Dream of Microwaves*
Katherine Shonk, *The Red Passport*
Gary Shteyngart, *The Russian Debutante's Handbook*
Lara Vapnyar, *There Are Jews in My House*

Jamaica Kincaid: Caribbean Fiction

Here are books by writers from Cuba, Dominica, Guyana, Haiti, Puerto Rico, Santa Domingo, Trinidad, and the West Indies.

Julia Alvarez, *How the Garcia Girls Lost Their Accents*; *In the Time of the Butterflies*
Robert Antoni, *Blessed is the Fruit*; *My Grandmother's Erotic Folktales*, *Carnival*
Maryse Condé; *Tree of Life, Desirada*; *Windward Heights*

Edwidge Danticat, *The Farming of the Bones*; *The Dew Breaker*
Junot Diaz, *Drown*
Cristina Garcia, *Dreaming in Cuba*; *The Aguero Sisters*; *Monkey Hunting*
Oscar Hijuelos, *The Mambo Kings Play Songs of Love*; *The Fourteen Sisters of Emilio Montez O'Brien*, *Empress of the Splendid Season*
Oonya Kempadoo, *Buxton Spice*; *Tide Running*
Earl Lovelace, *Salt*; *The Dragon Can't Dance*
Paule Marshall, *Daughters*
Pauline Melville, *The Ventriloquist's Tale*
Mayra Montero, *In the Palm of Darkness*; *The Red of His Shadow*; *Deep Purple*
V. S. Naipaul, *Away in the World*
Achy Obejas, *We Came All the Way from Cuba So You Could Dress Like This?*; *Days of Awe*
Caryl Phillips, *Cambridge*
Jean Rhys, *Wide Sargasso Sea*

Chang-rae Lee
Ann Beattie, *Falling in Place*; *My Life*; *Starring Dara Falcon*
John Cheever, *The Wapshot Chronicle*; *Bullet Park*; *The Stories of John Cheever*
Richard Ford, *The Sportswriter*; *Independence Day*
Ha Jin, *The Crazed*; *War Trash*
Kazuo Ishiguro, *The Remains of the Day*
Gish Jen, *The Typical American*; *Mona in the Promised Land*; *The Love Wife*
Walker Percy, *The Moviegoer*
John Updike, *Rabbit, Run*; *Rabbit Redux*; *Rabbit Is Rich*
Richard Yates, *Revolutionary Road*

SECTION FIVE: WORLDS WITHIN WORLDS

Stuart Dybek
James Agee, *The Morning Watch*; *A Death in the Family*
Sherwood Anderson, *Winesburg, Ohio*
Max Apple, *Free Agents*
Isaac Babel, *The Complete Works of Isaac Babel*
Nina Berberova, *The Tattered Cloak and Other Stories*
Italo Calvino, *Difficult Loves*
William Faulkner, *The Sound and the Fury*
Ernest Hemingway, *In Our Time: Stories*
James Joyce, *Dubliners*; *Portrait of the Artist as a Young Man*
Osip Mandelstam, *Selected Poems*; *The Noise of Time: Selected Prose*
Gabriel Garcia Marquez, *One Hundred Years of Solitude*
William Maxwell, *Time Will Darken It*; *So Long, See You Tomorrow*
Howard Norman, *The Museum Guard*
Yannis Ritsos, *Selected Poems, 1938–1988*
George Saunders, *Pastoralia*

Chicago Fiction
Nelson Algren, *The Neon Wilderness*; *The Man with the Golden Arm*

Carol Anshaw, *Lucky in the Corner*
Saul Bellow, *Dangling Man*; *Humboldt's Gift*
Ana Castillo, *Peel My Love like an Onion*
Maxine Chernoff, *Signs of Devotion*; *American Heaven*
°Sandra Cisneros, *House on Mango Street*; *Caramelo*
Elizabeth Crane, *When the Messenger is Hot*
Don De Grazio, *American Skin*
Theodore Dreiser, *Sister Carrie*
°Stuart Dybek, *The Coast of Chicago*; *I Sailed with Magellan*
James Farrell, *Studs Lonigan: A Trilogy*; *Chicago Stories*
Leon Forrest, *Divine Days*; *Meteor in the Madhouse*
°Aleksandar Hemon, *Nowhere Man*
°Ward Just, *An Unfinished Season*
Adam Langer, *Crossing California*
John McNally, *The Book of Ralph*
Joe Meno, *Hairstyles of the Damned*
Audrey Niffenegger, *The Time Traveler's Wife*
Achy Obejas, *Memory Mambo*; *Days of Awe*
Sara Paretsky, *Total Recall*; *Blacklist*; *Fire Sale*
Harry Mark Petrakis, *Twilight of the Ice*; *Orchards of Ithaca*
April Sinclair, *Coffee Will Make You Black*; *I Left My Back Door Open*
Sharon Solwitz, *Blood and Milk*; *Bloody Mary*
Richard Stern, *Father's Words*; *From Almonds to Zhoof*
Jean Thompson, *City Boy*
Richard Wright, *Native Son*

Ward Just

Robert Olen Butler, *On Distant Ground*; *The Deep Green Sea*

Joan Didion, *Democracy*; *The Last Thing He Wanted*
Leslie Epstein, *San Remo Drive*
Samatha Gillison, *The Undiscovered Country*; *The King of America*
Neil Gordon, *The Gun Runner's Daughter*
Graham Greene, *The Quiet American*
Jessica Hagedorn, *Dream Jungle*
Patricia Henley, *The Hummingbird House*; *In the River Sweet*
Maureen Howard, *The Silver Screen*
Penelope Lively, *Cleopatra's Sister*
William Maxwell, *The Chateau*
Susan Minot, *Folly*
Cees Nooteboom, *All Souls Day*
Craig Nova, *Cruisers*
Tim O'Brien, *Going After Cacciato*; *In the Lake of the Woods*
John O'Hara, *Appointment in Samarra*
Gore Vidal, *Empire*

Alice McDermott

F. Scott Fitzgerald, *The Great Gatsby*
Mary Gordon, *The Other Side*
Thomas Hardy, *Tess of the d'Urbervilles*
Susan Minot, *Monkeys*; *Evening*
Alice Munro, *Hateship, Friendship, Courtship, Loveship, Marriage*; *Runaway*
Vladimir Nabokov, *Lolita*
Edna O'Brien, *Time and Tide*; *Wild December*; *In the Forest*
Muriel Spark, *Loitering with Intent*
William Trevor, *Death in the Summer*; *The Story of Lucy Gault*
Edith Wharton, *Summer*; *Age of Innocence*

Joyce Carol Oates

Emily Brontë, *Wuthering Heights*
Mary Gordon, *Final Payments; The Company of Women*
Nathaniel Hawthorne, *The House of Seven Gables; The Blithedale Romance*
Mary McCarthy, *The Group; Cannibals and Missionaries*
John O'Hara, *Butterfield 8; A Rage to Live*

Marge Piercy, *The Third Child*
Katherine Ann Porter, *Pale Horse, Pale Rider; The Collected Stories*
John Steinbeck, *East of Eden*
Robert Stone, *Children of Light, Outerbridge Reach*
Anne Tyler, *Dinner at the Homesick Restaurant, The Amateur Marriage*

PART TWO: GENRE CROSSERS

Lynda Barry: Fiction in the Spirit of *Cruddy*

Bonnie Jo Campbell, *Woman and Other Animals; Q Road*
Ian Chorao, *Bruiser*
Katherine Dunn, *Geek Love; Truck*
James Ellroy, *Killer on the Road*
Kinky Friedman, *Elvis, Jesus and Coco-Cola; Roadkill*
Cris Mazza, *Homeland*
Lydia Millet, *My Happy Life; Everyone's Pretty*
Howard Norman, *The Northern Lights; The Bird Artist*
°Joyce Carol Oates, *Foxfire*
Tom Robbins, *Another Roadside Attraction*
Sam Shepard, *Cruising Paradise*
Brooke Stevens, *Tattoo Girl*
Hunter S. Thompson, *Fear and Loathing in Las Vegas*
Jim Thompson, *The Grifters*
Joy Williams, *The Quick and the Dead*

Edward Hirsch: Poetic Criticism

John Ashbery, *Reported Sightings*
Gaston Bachelard, *The Poetics of Space; The Poetics of Reverie*
Walter Benjamin, *Illuminations; Reflections*

Isaiah Berlin, *Vico and Herder*
Harold Bloom, *How to Read and Why; Where Should Wisdom Be Found?*
Joseph Brodsky, *Less Than One; On Grief and Reason*
Martin Buber, *I and Thou*
Denis Donoghue, *Ferocious Alphabets*
Ralph Waldo Emerson, *Essays: First and Second Series*
William Gass, *Finding a Form; Tests of Time*
Martha Graham, *Blood Memory*
Jane Hirshfield, *Nine Gate: Entering the Mind of Poetry*
Richard Howard, *Paper Trail*
Alfred Kazin, *God and the American Writer; Alfred Kazin's America*
Federico García Lorca, *Poet in New York; In Search of Duende*
Czeslaw Milosz, *To Begin Where I Am*
Eugenio Montale, *The Second Life of Art*
Octavio Paz, *The Labyrinth of Solitude*
Susan Sontag, *Where the Stress Falls; Regarding the Pain of Others*

Wallace Stevens, *The Necessary Angel*

Susan Stewart, *Poetry and the Fate of the Senses; The Open Studio*

Lionel Trilling, *The Moral Obligation to be Intelligent*

Marina Tsvetaeva, *Art in the Light of Conscience*

Peter Turchi, *Maps of the Imagination*

Derek Walcott, *What the Twilight Says*

Alan Lightman: Fiction: Metaphysics and Quantum Theory

Nick Arvin, *In the Electric Eden*

Paul Auster, *The Music of Chance; Oracle Night*

Jorges Luis Borges, *Ficcones; Labyrinths*

Italo Calvino, *Invisible Cities; If on a Winter's Night a Traveler*

Jim Crace, *Being Dead*

Matthew Derby, *Super Flat Times*

Carol Muske Dukes, *Saving St. Germ*

Rebecca Goldstein, *Strange Attractors; Properties of Light*

Siri Hustvedt, *What I Loved*

Franz Kafka, *The Trial; The Castle*

Penelope Lively, *Heat Wave*

Steven Millhauser, *Little Kingdoms*

Amos Oz, *The Same Sea*

Cynthia Ozick, *Heir to a Glimmering World*

Carter Scholz, *The Amount to Carry*

Jeanette Winterson, *GUT Symmetries*

Barry Lopez: Nature-Oriented Writers Who Write Both Non-fiction and Fiction

Edward Abbey, *Desert Solitaire; The Monkey Wrench Gang*

Rick Bass, *Caribou Rising; The Diezmo*

Wendell Berry, *Citizenship Papers; Hannah Coulter*

Annie Dillard, *Teaching a Stone to Talk; The Living*

Linda Hogan, *Dwellings; Power*

Barbara Kingsolver, *Animal Dreams; Small Wonder*

Peter Matthiessen, *At Play in the Fields of the Lord; End of the Earth*

Chris Offutt, *Out of the Woods; The Same River Twice*

Wallace Stegner, *The Big Rock Candy Mountain; Where the Bluebird Sings to the Lemonade Springs*

Joy Williams, *Ill Nature; Honored Guest*

Paul West

John Barth, *The Sot-Weed Factor*

Walter de la Mare, *Memoirs of a Midget*

William Gass, *Cartesian Sonata*

Henry Green, *Caught*

Harry Mathews, *The Sinking of the Odradek Stadium*

Georges Perec, *Life: A User's Manual*

Thomas Pynchon, *Mason & Dixon*

Raymond Queneau, *Zazie in the Metro; The Blue Flowers*

Alain Robbe-Grillet, *Repetition*

Susan Sontag, *The Volcano Lover*

Curtis White, *Memories of My Father Watching TV; Requiem*

Jeanette Winterson, *Oranges Are not the Only Fruit; Sexing the Cherry*

Virginia Woolf, *Orlando; The Waves*

Marguerite Yourcenar, *Memoirs of Hadrian*

Colson Whitehead

Colette Brooks, *In the City: Random Acts of Awareness*

Michael Chabon, *The Amazing Adventures of Kavalier & Clay*

E. L. Doctorow, *City of God*

John Dos Passos, *Manhattan Transfer*

Percival Evertt, *Glyph*; *American Desert*

Jeffrey Eugenides, *Middlesex*

Jonathan Franzen, *The Twenty-Seventh City*

William Gaddis, *The Recognitions*; *Agape Agape*

Stanley Elkin, *The MacGuffin*

Ralph Ellison, *The Invisible Man*

Toni Morrison, *Song of Solomon*; *Paradise*

Jim Shepard, *Love and Hydrogen*

David Foster Wallace, *Infinite Jest*; *Oblivion*

John Edgar Wideman, *Philadelphia Fire*; *Two Cities*; *Hoop Roots*

PART THREE: THE ART AND INTENT OF CREATIVE NONFICTION

Diane Ackerman

David Abram, *The Spell of the Sensuous*

Douglas Adams, *Last Chance to See*

John Burroughs, *Birds and Poets*; *Riverby*

Noam Chomsky, *On Nature and Language*

Antonio Damasio, *The Feeling of What Happens*; *Descartes' Error*; *Looking for Spinoza*

Loren Eiseley, *The Immense Journey*

Sue Hubbell, *A Country Year*

Gertrude Jekyll, *The Gardener's Essential Gertrude Jekyll*

°Jamaica Kincaid, *My Garden [Book]*; *My Favorite Plant*

Maxine Kumin, *In Deep*; *Women, Animals, and Vegetables*

John Muir, *The Mountains of California*

Michael Pollan, *Second Nature*; *The Botany of Desire*

Lewis Thomas, *The Lives of the Cell*; *The Medusa and the Snail*

Stephen Wise, *Drawing the Line*

Wade Davis

Rose Arvigo with Nadine Epstein, *Sastun: My Apprenticeship with a Maya Healer*

Gregory Bateson, *Mind and Nature*; *Steps to an Ecology of Mind*

William Burroughs and Allen Ginsberg, *The Yage Letters*

Joseph Campbell, *The Hero with a Thousand Faces*

Bruce Chatwin, *The Songlines*

Maya Deren, *Divine Horseman*

Isak Dinesen, *Out of Africa*

Mircea Eliade, *Shamanism*

Brian Fagan, *Clash of Cultures*

Eduardo Galeano, *Memory of Fire*

Robin Hemley, *Invented Eden*

Carl Jung, *Archetypes and the Collective Unconscious*

Claude Lévi-Strauss, *The Savage Mind*; *Myth and Meaning*

David Maybury-Lewis, *Millennium*; *Peoples of the World*

Terrence McKenna, *Food of the Gods*

Mark J. Plotkin, *Tales of a Shaman's Apprentice*

Thomas J. Riedlinger (ed.), *The Sacred Mushroom Seeker*
María Sabina, *Selections*
Richard Evans Schultes, *The Healing Forest; Plants of the Gods* (with Albert Hofmann); *Ethnobotany; Vine of the Soul*
R. Gordon Wasson, *Maria Sabina and Her Mazatec Mushroom Velada*

Lee Gutkind: Memoirs

A. Manette Ansay, *Limbo*
Kim Barnes, *Into the Wilderness*
Judy Blunt, *Breaking Clean*
Annie Dillard, *An American Childhood*
Andre Dubus, *Meditations from a Movable Chair*
Vivian Gornick, *Fierce Attachments*
Lucy Grealy, *Autobiography of a Face*
Patricia Hampl, *I Could Tell You Stories*
Katharine Butler Hathaway, *The Little Locksmith*
bell hooks, *Bone Black; Wounds of Passion*
Mary Karr, *The Liar's Club; Cherry*
Joyce Johnson, *Minor Characters; Missing Men*
Maxine Hong Kingston, *The Warrior Woman*
Lisa Knopp, *The Nature of Home*
Ved Mehta, *Continents of Exile*
Ann Patchett, *Truth and Beauty*
Richard Rodriguez, *Hunger of Memory*
Oliver Sacks, *The Man Who Mistook His Wife for a Hat; Uncle Tungsten*
Alix Kates Shulman, *Drinking the Rain; A Good Enough Daughter*
Charles Siebert, *A Man After His Own Heart*

Floyd Skloot, *In the Shadow of Memory*
Mark Spragg, *Where Rivers Change Direction*
Gay Talese, *Unto the Sons*
John Edgar Wideman, *Brothers and Keepers*
Tobias Wolff, *This Boy's Life*

Alex Kotlowitz

Nelson Algren, *Chicago*
Charles Bowden, *Blood Orchid; Blues for Cannibals; Down by the River*
Robert Coles, *The Moral Intelligence of Children; The Secular Mind; Lives of Moral Leadership*
Joan Didion, *After Henry*
Tracy Kidder, *Among Schoolchildren; Home Town; Mountains Beyond Mountains*
Jonathan Kozol, *Amazing Grace; Ordinary Resurrections*
Adrian Nicole LeBlanc, *Random Family*
Studs Terkel, *Division Street; Working; Hope Dies Last*

Phillip Lopate

Edward Abbey, *Slumgullion Stew: An Edward Abbey Reader*
Paul Auster, *Collected Prose*
James Baldwin, *Notes of a Native Son*
Joan Didion, *Slouching Toward Bethlehem; The White Album*
M. F. K. Fisher, *The Art of Eating*
Carlos Fuentes, *This I Believe: An A to Z of a Life*
Edward Hoagland, *Compass Points: How I Lived*
Jane Jacobs, *The Death and the Life of Great American Cities; Dark Age Ahead*
Alfred Kazin, *A Walker in the City*

Anne Matthews, *Wild Nights*
Joseph Mitchell, *Up in the Old Hotel and Other Stories*
Michel de Montaigne, *Essays*
Cynthia Ozick, *Quarrel & Quandary*
Grace Paley, *Just As I Thought*
Ted Solotaroff, *Truth Comes in Blows*; *First Loves*
Gerald Stern, *What I Can't Bear Losing*
Rebecca Solnit, *Wanderlust*
John Tallmadge, *The Cincinnati Arch*
John Updike, *Self-Consciousness*
E. B. White, *Here is New York*
Virginia Woolf, *The Common Reader*; *The Death of the Moth and Other Essays*; *Moments of Being*
Gore Vidal, *United States: Essays 1952–1992*

Sy Montgomery

Marc Bekoff and Jane Goodall, *Minding Animals*
Osha Gray Davidson, *Fire in the Turtle House*
Richard Ellis, *Tiger Bone and Rhino Horn.*
Birute N. F. Galdikas, *Orangutan Odyssey*
Dian Fossey, *Gorillas in the Mist*; *No One Loved Gorillas More: Dian Fossey's Letters from the Mist* (With text by Camilla de la Bédoyère)
Jane Goodall, *My Life with Chimpanzees*; *In the Shadow of Man*; *Through a Window*, *Reason for Hope* (With Phillip Berman)
Nancy Lord, *Beluga Days*
Peter Matthiessen, *The Tree Where Man Was Born*; *African Silences*
Farley Mowat, *Never Cry Wolf*; *A Whale for the Killing*
Katy Payne, *Silent Thunder*

Doug Peacock, *The Grizzly Years*
Joyce Poole, *Coming of Age with Elephants*
David Quammen, *The Song of the Dodo*; *Wild Thoughts from Wild Places*; *Monster of God*
Rachel Smolker, *To Touch a Wild Dolphin*
Alan Tennant, *On the Wing*
David Rains Wallace, *The Klamath Knot*; *Beasts of Eden*

Terry Tempest Williams

Edward Abbey, *The Journey Home*
Susanne Antonetta, *Body Toxic*
Mary Austin, *The Land of Little Rain*
Leonard Bird, *Folding Paper Cranes*
Helen Caldicott, *The New Nuclear Danger*
Annie Dillard, *Pilgrim at Tinker Creek*
Gretel Ehrlich, *The Solace of Open Spaces*; *A Match to the Heart*; *The Future of Ice*
Susan Griffin, *A Chorus of Stones*; *The Eros of Everyday Life*
Linda Hogan, *The Woman Who Watches Over the World*
Candida Lawrence, *Fear Itself*
Aldo Leopold, *A Sand County Almanac*
Wangari Maathai, *The Green Belt Movement*
Peter Matthiessen, *The Snow Leopard*; *The Birds of Heaven*
Ellen Meloy, *The Anthropology of Turquoise*
Kathleen Norris, *Dakota: A Spiritual Geography*
Arundhati Roy, *War Talk*
Rebecca Solnit, *As Eve Said to the Serpent*; *Hope in the Dark*; *A Field Guide to Getting Lost*
Wallace Stegner, *The Sound of Mountain Water*

More Essential Eco-Writers

Jane Brox, *Five Thousand Days Like This One*; *Clearing the Land*

Rachel Carson, *The Edge of the Sea*; *Silent Spring*

Alison Hawthorne Deming, *Temporary Homelands*

Annie Dillard, *Pilgrim at Tinker Creek*; *For the Time Being*

Richard Ellis, *Deep Atlantic*; *The Empty Ocean*

John Elder, *Reading the Mountains of Home*; *The Frog Run*

Sue Halpern, *Four Wings and a Prayer*

William Kittredge, *On Owning It All*; *The Nature of Generosity*

William Least Heat-Moon, *Prairy-Erth (a deep map)*

Bill McKibben, *The End of Nature*; *Enough: Staying Human in an Engineered Age*

John McPhee, *Coming into the Country*; *The Control of Nature*; *Annals of a Former World*

John Hanson Mitchell, *Living at the End of Time*; *The Wildest Place on Earth*

Gary Paul Nabhan, *Cultures of Habitat*; *Coming Home to Eat*; *Cross-Pollinations*

Janisse Ray, *Ecology of a Cracker Childhood*; *Wild Card Quilt*

Sharman Apt Russell, *Anatomy of a Rose*; *An Obsession with Butterflies*; *Hunger*

Carl Safina, *Song for the Blue Ocean*; *Eye of the Albatross*

Scott Russell Sanders, *Writing from the Center*; *The Force of Spirit*

Gary Snyder, *The Practice of the Wild*

E. O. Wilson, *Naturalist*; *Consilience*; *The Future of Life*

Acknowledgments

Literature is a grand conversation, and I'm grateful to everyone who has made it possible for me to participate. I would like to thank all of my colleagues and friends at *Booklist,* a reader's sanctuary if ever there was one, with special appreciation to Bill Ott and Brad Hooper. I want to express deep gratitude to all the other editors I've been so fortunate to work with, especially Elizabeth Taylor, Bart Schneider, Todd Maitland, Susan Hahn, Laurie Muchnik, and Teresa Weaver. No matter how many times I've listened to and read the *Open Books* interviews, I'm still amazed at my good fortune in speaking with such creative and soulful writers. I will be forever grateful to each and every *Open Books* guest, not only the writers who are present in *Writers on the Air,* but also the writers I had hoped to include in the book but could not, due to the fact that when it comes to publishing, size does matter. I also want to thank the writers who have appeared on *Open Books* after *Writers on the Air* was put together. I appreciate the assistance of everyone in the publishing world who has helped bring authors to our studio, including Sheryl Johnston and Bill Young. I send out a big thank you to everyone who works for and contributes to WLUW, a community station that gives genuine meaning to the term alternative radio, and everyone at our nurturing sister station, WBEZ, Chicago's National Public Radio station. I am so very grateful to the Illinois Arts Council, a state agency, for its continued support of *Open Books* in particular and the arts in general during a time in which the powers-that-be often fail to recognize how crucial the arts are to our well-being. And I thank my dear friends, especially Mary Mills and Angela Bonavoglia, and my wonderful and inspiring parents, Elayne and Hal, and my cherished and sustaining husband, David, with love.